CAN-AM CHALLENGER

CAN-AM CHALLENGER
THE COCKNEY F1 MECHANIC WHO DESIGNED AND BUILT AMERICA'S BEST CAN-AM CARS

PETER BRYANT / FOREWORD BY JACKIE OLIVER

DESIGN BY TOM MORGAN

DAVID BULL PUBLISHING

DEDICATIONS - This book is respectfully dedicated to Reg Parnell, who made me into a racer; Mickey Thompson, who gave me an opportunity of a lifetime when he brought me to America; and Ernest Kanzler Jr., who unhesitatingly gave me my start in race-car design and sponsored my first Can-Am car.

Copyright © 2007 by Peter Bryant and David Bull Publishing. All rights reserved. No part of this book may be used or reproduced in any manner whatsoever without written permission from the Publisher except in the case of brief quotations embodied in critical articles and reviews.

We recognize that some words, model names, and designations mentioned in this book are the property of the trademark holder. We use them only for identification purposes.

Library of Congress Control Number: 2007928806

ISBN-13: 978 1 893618 86 2

ISBN-10: 1 893618 86 2

David Bull Publishing, logo, and colophon are trademarks of David Bull Publishing, Inc.

Book and cover design: Tom Morgan, Blue Design, Portland, Maine

Printed in the United States

10 9 8 7 6 5 4 3 2 1

David Bull Publishing
4250 East Camelback Road
Suite K150
Phoenix, AZ 85018

602-852-9500
602-852-9503 (fax)

www.bullpublishing.com

PAGE 2: The Mk 3 leads "the best of the rest" at Road Atlanta in July 1972. (Shadow Publicity)
RIGHT: In a Bowmaker publicity shot, Neil Robson (right) and I observe a kneeling Eric Broadley at work. In the background, John and Tug Wilson check over John's Lola F1. (Lola Heritage)
PAGE 6: I drive the Lola away from the gas pump and back to our pits in Australia. For me, driving an F1 car whenever possible was the rule! (Peter Bryant)
PAGES 8-9: A dramatic perspective on the Shadow Mk 2 at Mosport in 1971. (Pete Lyons)

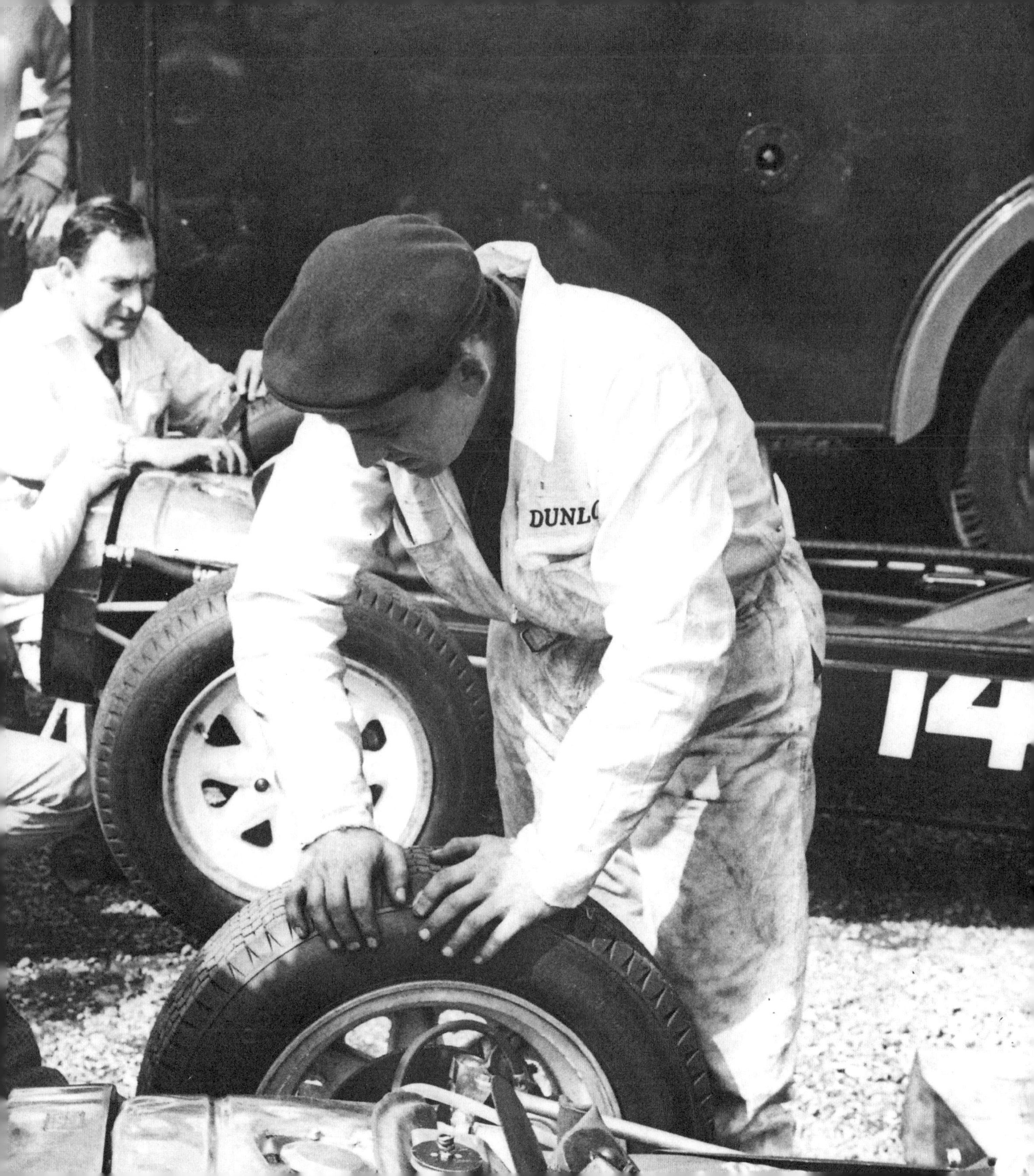
DUNLO
14

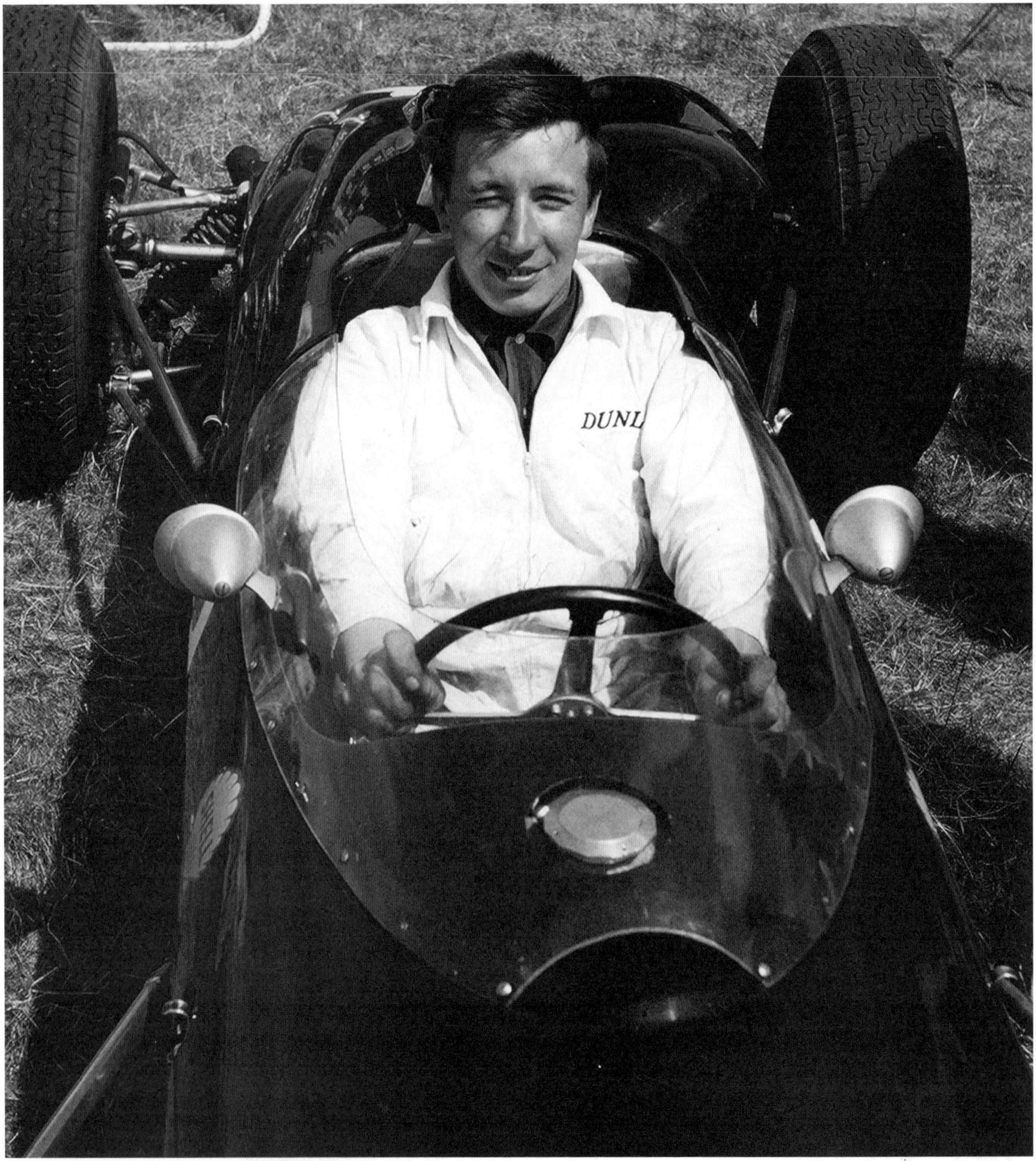
DUNL

CONTENTS

ACKNOWLEDGMENTS 10

FOREWORD 13

INTRODUCTION 17

PROLOGUE 19

CHAPTER 1 / Catching the Bug 21

CHAPTER 2 / The Lotus Space Program 26

CHAPTER 3 / Blokes and Chaps 31

CHAPTER 4 / Moving Up in the World 41

CHAPTER 5 / Venturing into Formula One 47

CHAPTER 6 / Fire and Cold Drinks at the 'Ring 53

CHAPTER 7 / My First Jackie 65

CHAPTER 8 / An Interlude Down Under 77

CHAPTER 9 / My First Full F1 Season 85

CHAPTER 10 / A Long Season with Lola 95

CHAPTER 11 / An Epic Tasman Trip 111

CHAPTER 12 / Farewell to Formula One 125

CHAPTER 13 / Wowed in America 137

CHAPTER 14 / The Road to Indianapolis 145

CHAPTER 15 / Portents of Disaster 155

CHAPTER 16 / Carnival and Calamity 167

CHAPTER 17 / A Circuitous Route to Can-Am 175

CHAPTER 18 / Can-Am Reality Check 183

CHAPTER 19 / On the Learning Curve 189

CHAPTER 20 / Two Little Words 196

CHAPTER 21 / Understanding the Problem 201

CHAPTER 22 / From Concept to Reality 211

CHAPTER 23 / On Track with the Ti22 221

CHAPTER 24 / On the Pace at Riverside! 233

CHAPTER 25 / College Football Wins in Texas 242

CHAPTER 26 / Teppanyaki and Pole, Please 249

CHAPTER 27 / Testing Times 257

CHAPTER 28 / Head to Head with McLaren 265

CHAPTER 29 / Strong Stuff, Titanium 273

CHAPTER 30 / Ti22 Mk 2 Delivers 281

CHAPTER 31 / In and Out of a Bomb Hole 294

CHAPTER 32 / Decisions, Decisions 299

CHAPTER 33 / A Fragile Piece 307

CHAPTER 34 / Trouble with Rubber 320

CHAPTER 35 / Peter Bryant, B.I.S.I.A. 329

CHAPTER 36 / Mixed Emotions 333

CHAPTER 37 / Aero Advances 341

CHAPTER 38 / Porsche Spoils the Party 347

CHAPTER 39 / A Job on the Line 355

CHAPTER 40 / The End Game 363

EPILOGUE 374

INDEX 376

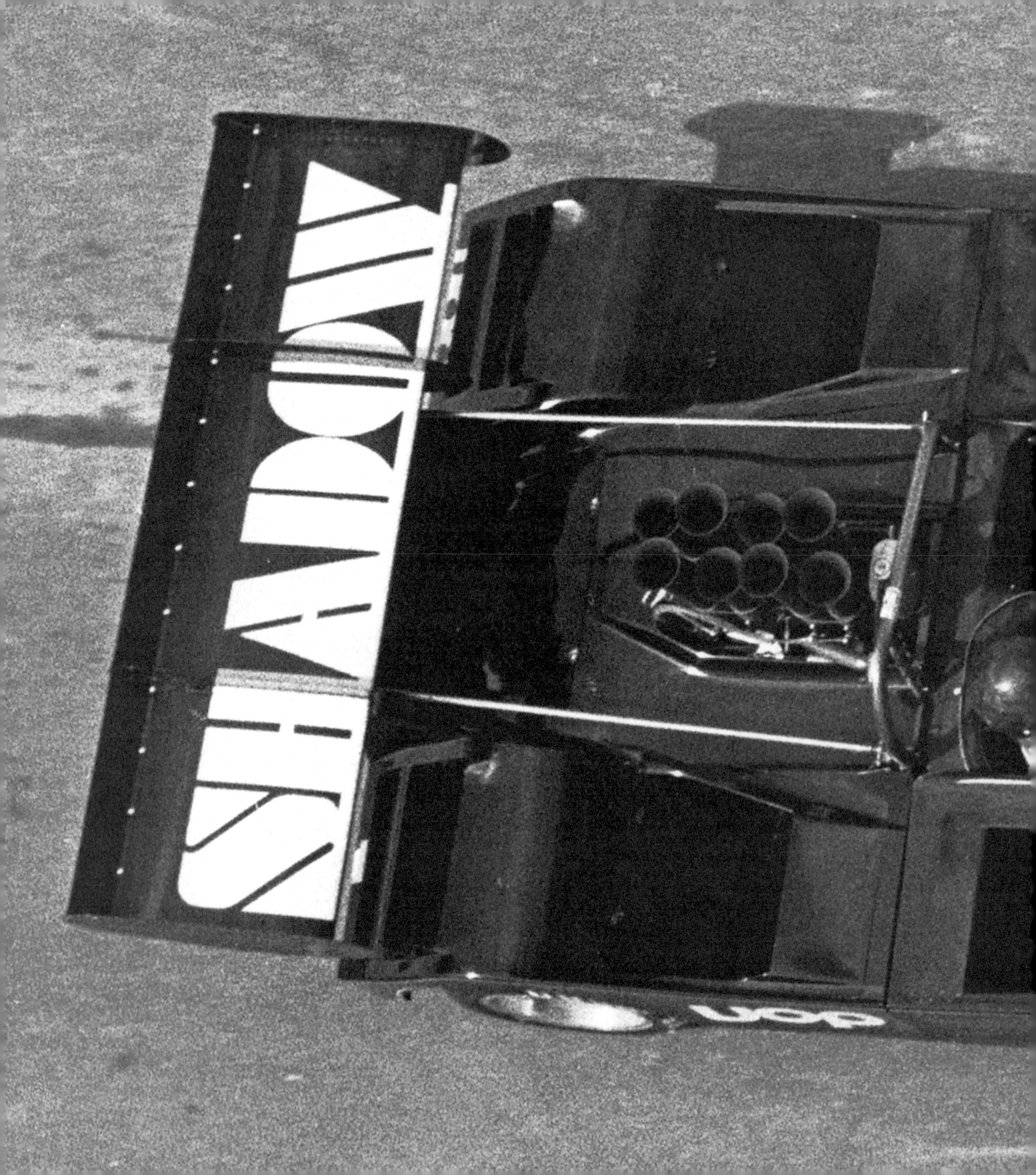
SHADOW
uop

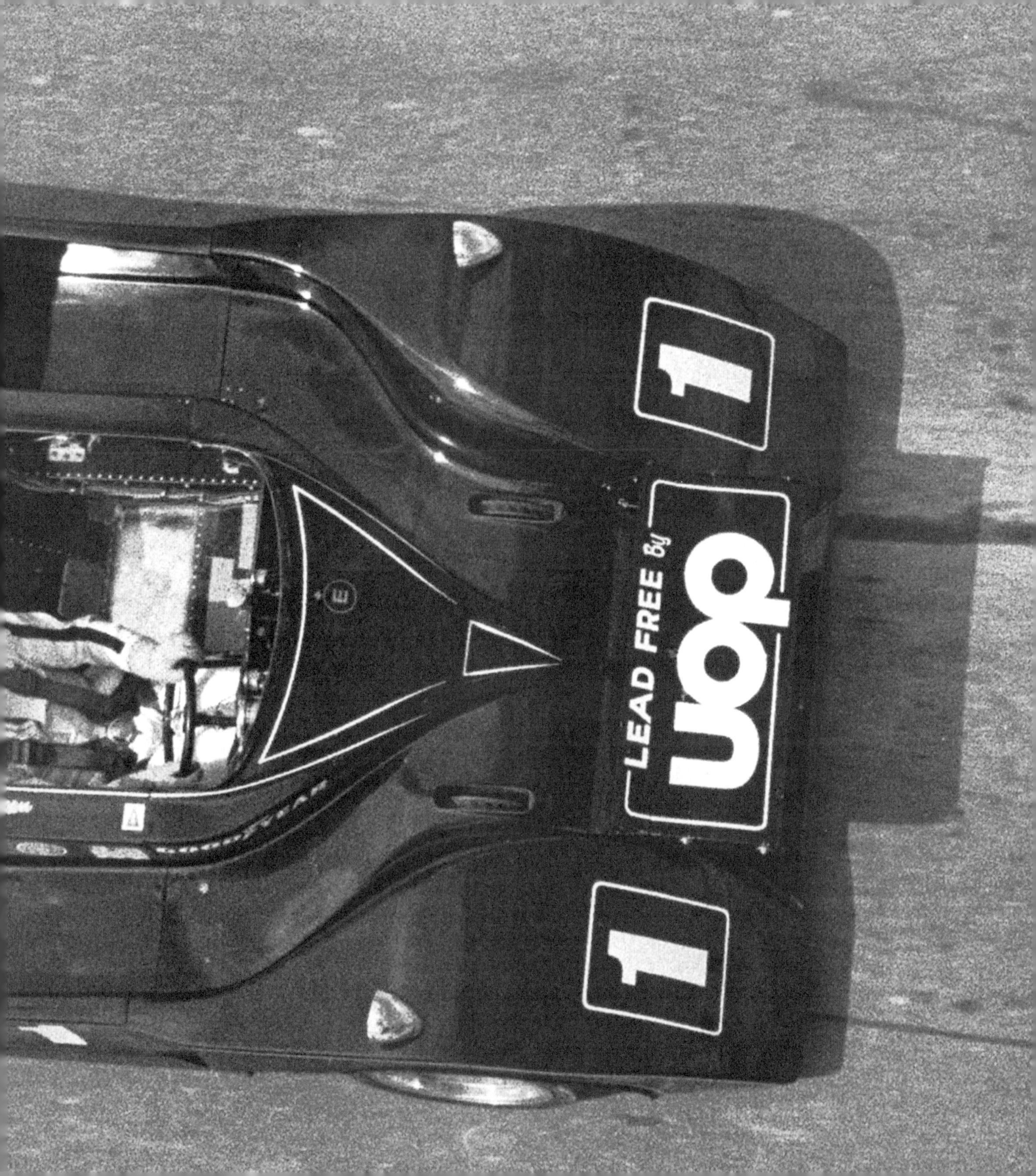
1
LEAD FREE By
UOP
1

Acknowledgments

I will always be grateful to Reg Parnell for starting me out in my career as a Formula One mechanic. I will also be eternally thankful that Mickey Thompson brought me to America to work on his Indycar in 1964, thus opening a door for me that changed my life for the better. I will always be thankful that Masten Gregory introduced me to Mickey and suggested he give me a job.

Thanks to Ernie Kanzler Jr. for allowing me the opportunity to design and build the Ti22 cars. I guess it would be remiss of me not to thank Don Nichols for the Shadow job—it was a pity it ended in rancor.

Special thanks to Pete Lyons just for being there—and recording the whole Can-Am story in his wonderful books *Can-Am* and *Can-Am Photo History*. Without those incredible books to stir old memories, I could never have written this book.

I had a lot of enthusiastic help with research and acquiring the pictures for the book, and I really appreciate the patience and generosity of all the people who helped me, and the great photographers whose pictures you see here. Special thanks are due to Tom Schultz, the photographer and historian at Road America.

Thanks also to Bruce McLaren's former personal secretary, Eoin Young, whose encouragement and help were priceless. And to Jesse Alexander, Doug Stokes of Autobooks/Aerobooks of Burbank, Dr. Bob Norton, Jerry Entin, Bob Tronolone, Pete Biro, Bill Warner, Alex Greaves, Ike Smith, Gil Munz, Mike and Pat Smith, Dale Von Trebra, Jim Shaw, David Friedman, Ben Williams, Deke and Olga Houlgate, Hal Crocker, Doug Bane, and Ed Moody and Bill Colson.

Thanks to Ann Adam of PAM Racing, Ben Jamieson of the Tasman Series web page, Bruce Sergent for the Tasman race data and pictures (www.sergent.com.au/nzmr.html), and my pen pal in Tasmania, Anthony Robe, for his great encouragement. Thanks to Maurice "Mo"

Levy, who raced with me in the early days, for his help in getting some old facts sorted out. Thanks a million to Jennifer Revson (Peter's sister) for her help. Thanks to Alan Lis in the United Kingdom for his enthusiasm and help.

Thanks a bunch to Donald Davidson, the historian at the Indianapolis Motor Speedway, and thanks to the great IMS photo staff. Thanks to the BARC and their great staff for helping clear the fog about the good old days at Goodwood. Thanks to the International Motor Racing Research Center at Watkins Glen and its curator, Mark Steigerwald. Thanks to the Canadian Motorsport Hall of fame and its director, John Waldie. Thanks so much to Glynn Jones and Gerald Swan at Lola Heritage. Thanks to Dan Davis and Pam Shawtraw at *Victory Lane* magazine, and my friends at *Vintage Racing*. Thanks to Chris Economaki for being such a neat guy.

Thanks beyond words to John Surtees, Roy Salvadori, Jo Bonnier, Innes Ireland, Mike Taylor, Jack Brabham, Mike Hailwood, Chris Amon, Tony Maggs, John Cannon, Peter Revson, Mike Goth, Carlos Pace, Chuck Parsons, Skip Scott, Bob Bondurant, Ken Miles, David Hobbs, Charlie Hayes, Ed Hamill—and above all Jackie Oliver. These were the drivers whose skills made all the hard work on the cars so worthwhile. Thanks especially to the late Bruce McLaren and Denny Hulme for all the encouragement and friendship that made it all such a wonderful and memorable experience. Thanks to Jim Hall for setting such a high mark. You gave us all so much.

Finally, from the bottom of my heart, thanks so much to David Bull and his editorial staff for their help in publishing my scribble, and to Quentin Spurring for the great job he did editing it.

BELOW: The car was so new that I hadn't yet installed the driver's mirrors. Jackie Oliver supervises from the cockpit. (Dave Friedman)

Foreword

As an up-and-coming professional race driver, 1969 was a pivotal year for me. I had spent the previous three years with Colin Chapman at Lotus, first as an apprentice driver and later as teammate to Graham Hill on the 1968 Lotus Grand Prix team. With Lotus taking both the drivers and constructors titles that year, in 1969 both my phone and my cash register were ringing. I received lucrative offers to drive with the BRM F1 team and John Wyer's Ford GT40 world sports-car championship–winning team, among others.

When the phone rang again later that year, I had my first contact with Peter Bryant. "Come to California and participate in the last rounds of the Canadian-American Challenge," he said. His proposal had a pleasant ring to it, and my time in the United States turned out to be a fantastic journey—not only for Peter, but for myself as well, as we joined forces to contest the iconic series known as the Can-Am.

As I stepped into the California sunshine to meet Peter for the first time, I saw him as an exercise in fortitude. Here was an Englishman who, in coming to America (and losing his London accent), had brought with him a huge amount of practical and technical knowledge about road racing in Europe. Now he was putting that knowledge to good use in the design and production of his innovative Ti22 Can-Am racer. I liked him and his car immediately, and along with lashings of his tremendous sense of humor, our association could only flourish.

Peter's Autocoast team was a bright-burning light that burst onto the Can-Am scene in the late sixties. With a little more luck and better funding, it could have become one of the established American marques of the seventies. To design, produce, and finance a major entry in the Can-Am was a bold step, and it was a tremendous credit to Peter. Although the sixties was a fertile period for new racing marques, most of the ones involved in road racing were established in Europe and the United Kingdom, where they were greatly helped by a growing number of local support industries that specialized in manufacturing various components. McLaren and Lola were two good examples, and both were already competing successfully in the Can-Am series. Although Peter had contacts in that world from his earlier experiences, he chose to design and produce a car in America essentially on his own, and to challenge the established marques in the series. His success in this endeavor testifies to his considerable talent as an American race-car designer.

Peter tells the story of his journey from cockney mechanic to Can-Am challenger with fascinating insights on racing and technology, and plenty of amusing tales. It was a pleasure and privilege for me to have been a small part of it, and I'm truly grateful to Peter for giving me the chance.

Jackie Oliver

OPPOSITE: The Ti22 starts its second race on the second row at Riverside, alongside Chris Amon's Ferrari and behind the two McLarens. (Pete Lyons)

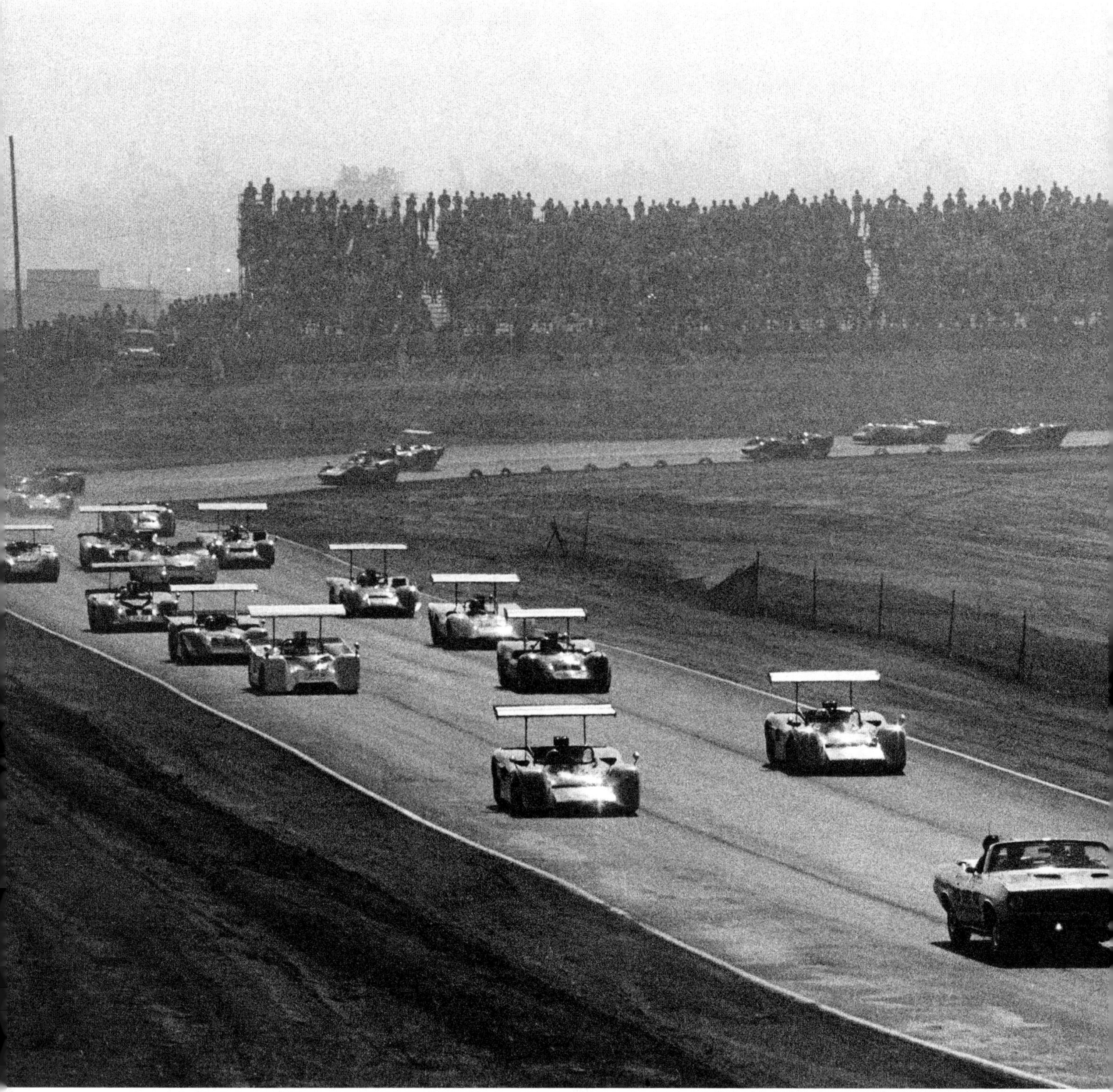

BELOW: An isometric drawing of the new Ti22 chassis, which used the engine as a stressed member. (Peter Bryant)

Introduction

This is the story of Peter Bryant's auto racing journey, from toiling as a lowly fabricator at Lotus Cars in London to becoming a Formula One mechanic to designing and building a competitive American Can-Am car that took on the best in the world.

Most of the story is set in the 1960s. Computer technology was just in its infancy. Any enthusiastic automobile owner could tune his own engine easily, and there were no smog regulations for cars. It was the age of the muscle car and the pony car, and Ford's rival manufacturers were trying to catch up with the success of the Mustang. Auto racing was the second-largest-paid spectator sport next to pari-mutuel horse racing. Riverside Raceway in California would draw 80,000 people to see the annual *Los Angeles Times* Grand Prix sports-car race. The movie Winning, starring Paul Newman, was instrumental in publicizing the excitement of powerful sports cars racing against each other.

ABOVE: Ray Brimble applies the decals to the Shadow Mk 3 bodywork. Note the NACA ducts on top of the fenders for feeding air into the radiators. (Tom Schultz)

The timing was perfect for the Can-Am Challenge Cup. The Sports Car Club of America started this major auto-racing championship in 1966 with an exciting series of races in Canada and America for unlimited sports-racing cars, with no engine restrictions. They were technically known as FIA Group 7 sports cars. Everywhere they went that also held a Formula One race, the Can-Am cars were faster.

The Can-Am prize money was better than Formula One and everyone was after some of it. The series attracted some of Europe's best teams and drivers in addition to the fastest cars and drivers from the United States Road Racing Championship, which finished each season just before the Can-Am began. Factory team cars from Lola, Ferrari, McLaren, and Porsche were driven by F1 drivers and sports-car specialists from all over the world.

The series became dominated by the intense efforts and expertise of the McLaren team. With Grand Prix aces Bruce McLaren, Denny Hulme, Dan Gurney, Peter Revson, and Peter Gethin driving, McLaren produced a display of such dominance that the media began to call the Can-Am "The Bruce & Denny Show." Many tried to beat McLaren, and all failed. But then Porsche produced the most powerful car it had ever built—the turbocharged, 1000-horsepower 917/10.

For Americans, the real Can-Am challenge was to create a car that could beat the Europeans. And this was the challenge taken up by Peter Bryant.

LEFT: Jackie Oliver stands up in the Shadow Mk 2 to talk to me while testing at Jim Hall's Rattlesnake raceway in 1971. Behind him is mechanic Mike Lowman; his knees are level with the top of the car's body, which shows how low it was. A bearded Don Nichols is on the right. The small, white vacuum cleaners were used to blow cool air onto the inboard front brakes. (Peter Bryant)

Prologue

It was just after 2:00 p.m. on October 10, 1969, when we drove over the track bridge into the infield at Laguna Seca, California, for the ninth round of the Can-Am Challenge Cup. The traffic suddenly stopped. Just at that moment, Bruce McLaren and Denny Hulme in their orange McLarens, followed closely by Chris Amon in his bright red Ferrari, came around the fast first turn and went under the bridge. They looked like they were doing 300 miles an hour. A lump came up in my throat and I thought to myself, "Shit— what am I doing here in this truck, carrying a homemade race car with all these virtually untested ideas? How could I ever have believed it could beat those cars?"

My mind went back to the last time I had been at Laguna Seca, the year before, and my words to Charlie Parsons, the Carl Haas Lola team driver.

We were at a small party at his house at the end of the Can-Am season. For several seasons, Charlie had driven a Lola to good purpose for Carl Haas. The wine was flowing freely and none of us was feeling any pain. As always, Charlie's wife, Sherrie, had put on a great spread. I found out during the party from Colin Riley, who was Charlie's chief mechanic, that Carl Haas was not planning to run two cars in 1969. That meant that Charlie's teammate Skip Scott, whose car I had prepared in 1968, was now out of a drive. And it meant that I was now out of a job.

I asked Charlie if it was true, and he confirmed it. I hated to hear that. I reacted by saying things that I later thought were a bit strong: "So I'm fired, huh? I've worked my ass off for Skip Scott and Carl Haas. I've tried damn hard to make Skip's car go as fast as your car with all the latest factory tweaks from Lola. Well, Charlie, I'm going to find a way to design my own car, race it in the Can-Am, and beat the pants off your damn Lola, with you in it!"

Charlie laughed and said, "I'll remind you of those words one day, Peter!"

Was this going to be the day? As the traffic started moving again and we went into the racing paddock to unload the cars, I was thinking about how it had all begun.

BELOW: Juan Manuel Fangio's race lasted just 11 laps in the fabulous-but-fragile Raymond Mays–designed supercharged BRM. (LAT Photographic)

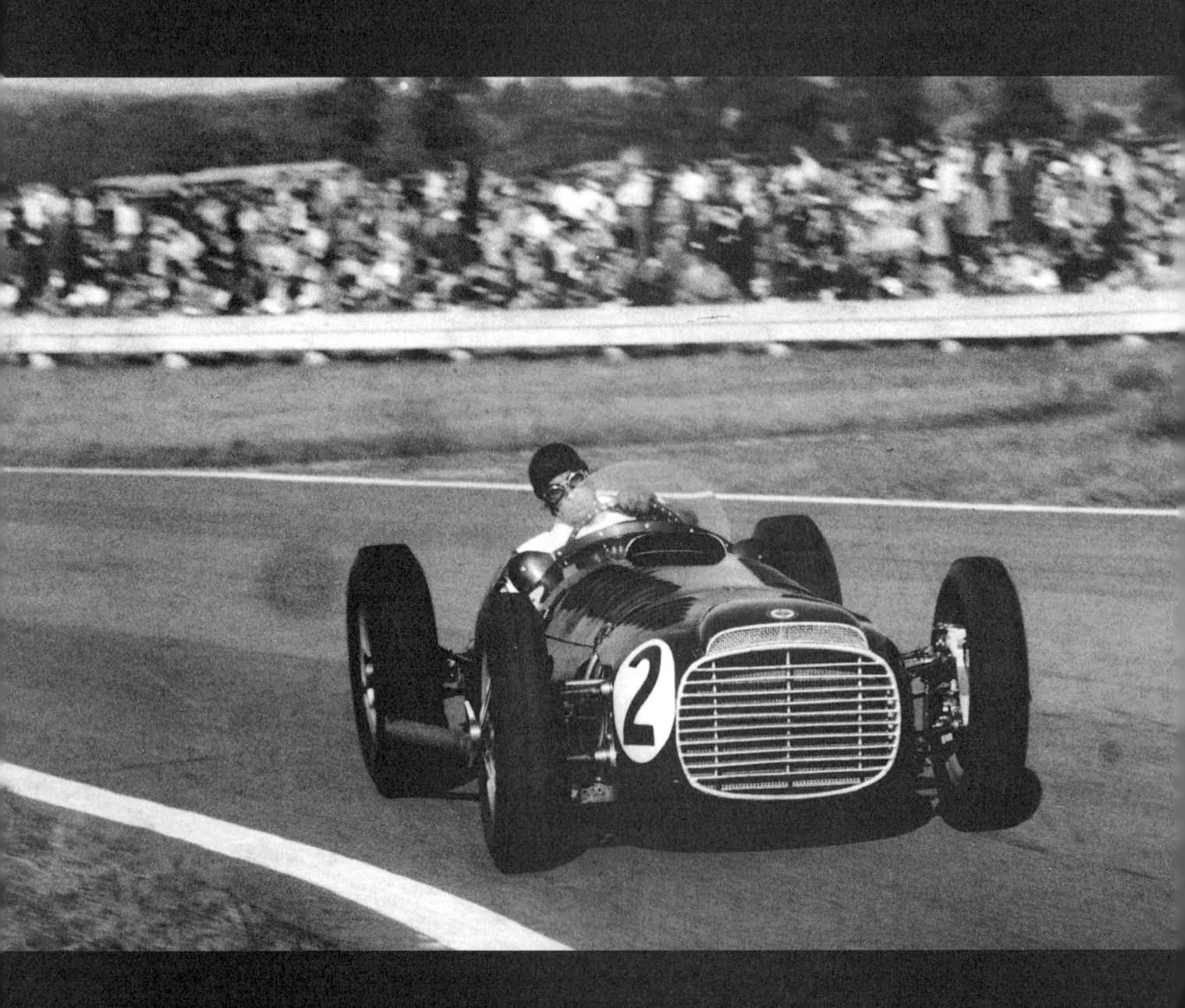

CHAPTER 1

Catching the Bug

The day I caught the auto-racing bug was Saturday, September 26, 1953. It was cool and overcast in southern England, and I desperately hoped it wouldn't rain. I was a passenger in an open sports car built by Donald Healey and I was being driven to Goodwood, a former wartime airfield that had been partially converted to a motor-racing circuit and was managed by the BARC—British Automobile Racing Club. David, a friend of my father who was driving the Healey, owned a small local garage in Islington, London, where I lived. I worked for him on weekends if he needed me, and that was where I earned my extra spending money.

At that time, I was working full-time at the Gladwell & Kell repair garage in Clerkenwell, London. I was 16 years old, one of five children, with a twin sister, Eunice, two older brothers, Allan and John, and a younger brother, David. I was one year out of the Quintin Hogg Grammar School in Regent Street, central London. Following my early matriculation from school, my father had decided that I'd had enough education and needed to start paying for my keep. He had indentured me at 15 years old as an apprentice automobile mechanic so that I could learn a trade and support myself. I was paid nine pence three farthings an hour for a 44-hour working week. I took home one pound fifteen shillings and nine pence, after taxes. That's the equivalent of about $4 at 1953 exchange rates. I actually made more money getting the tea for the other mechanics in the tea breaks.

I gave my mother one pound a week towards my keep, and I had the rest to buy my own clothes and so forth. I had been an avid motor-racing fan since the first time I heard it on the radio, and I occasionally saw it on a TV set through the window of the local TV shop—my parents didn't own a set.

I loved cars. I was very easily hooked on racing. I often helped David to get his Healey tuned and ready for his BARC races, but this was the first time I'd ever been to a race meeting.

As we neared Goodwood, I was excited about the prospect of seeing some of my heroes, like Mike Hawthorn, Stirling Moss, and Roy Salvadori, driving in the BARC's Goodwood Trophy race. Reg Parnell, another of my favorites, was rumored to be driving Raymond Mays's V16 BRM again. He'd broken the Goodwood lap record the previous September in the car. I really admired him mostly because he'd won the 1951 International Trophy at Silverstone in torrential rain, beating the likes of Juan Manuel Fangio by over a minute in Tony Vandervell's 4.5-liter V12 "Thinwall Special" Ferrari. This was the car Hawthorn would drive at Goodwood.

Having never seen the cars close-up before, this was going to be a really big thrill. David was not going to be racing that day, so he was my tour guide. We stopped at the members' gate, and David kindly paid for my guest pass while I invested two shillings in a souvenir program.

The grandstands were reserved for BARC members, such as David, but there were plenty of good viewing spots for nonmember "peasants." My favorite was near the chicane. I was totally surprised to see that horse-racing bookmakers were taking bets near the paddock. I didn't even know that motor racing was a betting sport.

OPPOSITE: Totally devoid of safety belts, Mike Hawthorn takes the modified Ferrari-engined V12 Thinwall Special through the chicane en route to victory at Goodwood in 1953. (LAT Photographic)

David provided a paddock pass for me so that I could see the cars and drivers close-up, and that was where we headed first. I had a million questions to ask the competitors, but there wasn't much time for drivers and car mechanics to chitchat because of the hectic schedule. The races were close together, and some cars did more than one race, plus there was a morning practice session. So we just kept a respectful distance and watched it all happen.

In those days, it was easy to foul a sparkplug with oil during an engine warm-up. I watched in wonder as the mechanics changed the "hot" start-up plugs for the harder "cold" racing plugs when the engines had been run for a while. The BRM mechanics had a tough job because they had 16 spark plugs to change, instead of the average 6. I noticed that they used a T-handle socket wrench and were easily able to twirl out the tiny, 10-millimeter spark plugs once they were loose. I thought it was pretty good that they did it so fast.

I watched as the Formula One and Formula 2 cars were push-started. I wondered why they didn't equip them with self-starters, like road cars had. David pointed out that the starter motors weighed about 35 lbs. and the battery that could crank over these high-compression engines would weigh 50 lbs. or 60 lbs., so that was a lot of weight to lug around to use only once. I noted that the sports cars had to have them, and he laughed and said that it would be tough to have a Le Mans–type start (where the drivers ran across the track and jumped into the cars) without starter motors. He told me the extra weight in the sports cars was not as critical as in the formula cars, and all the formula cars had magneto ignitions, anyway, so they didn't really need a heavy old battery.

There were seven races scheduled and the fifth, the 15-lap Goodwood Trophy, was the featured race. The entry list for that race looked like a Who's Who in racing at that time in its history. It was a Formule Libre event, meaning that it was open to all racing cars. A few were Formula One cars but most of them were Formula 2 cars. In those days, the

Formula 2 engine displacement was 2000cc and Formula One was 4500cc (or 1500cc supercharged).

There were two supercharged V16 BRMs for Juan Fangio and Ken Wharton to drive. Can you imagine a V16 engine of just 1500cc displacement? The pistons were only about two inches in diameter, the stroke of the crankshaft was only about two inches, and the engine could rev to about 11,000. The exhaust pipes literally screamed as the drivers ran through the gears. Stirling Moss was in the works F2 Cooper-Alta (with famous racing mechanic Alf Francis at the spanners). Roy Salvadori was in one of the latest Connaughts that he had used to win the first race of the day for F2 cars. Tony Rolt was in a similar car entered by Rob Walker, of Scotch whisky fame. Two other drivers, Jason Henry and Len Marr, drove similar cars. Paul Emery was in his own F2 Emeryson and there were three old ERA cars with Ron Flockhart and Gordon Whitehead in two of them. Lance Macklin drove a lone F2 HWM. There were also four Cooper-Bristol F2 cars, to be driven by Duncan Hamilton, Harry Gould, Bob Gerard, and James Hall. In those days, many of the cars entered didn't make it into the race because they blew up or broke in practice. In the races, attrition was really high.

Much to my delight, Hawthorn won the historic Goodwood Trophy in the Thinwall Special after a spirited duel with Wharton's V16 BRM, while Gerard finished third in his 2-liter Cooper-Bristol. Unfortunately Fangio dropped out after 11 laps with mechanical problems of some kind in the other BRM. There were many mechanical woes in those days, and it was unfortunate Fangio had been the victim of one of them. But just seeing the legend driving was a big enough thrill for me.

One of Hawthorn's mechanics was a man named Britt Pierce. He looked a lot like Adolf Hitler, with a small moustache under his nose. He was obviously very close to Hawthorn, and I saw them talking to each other a lot. During one of his cigarette breaks, I asked him if he could spare a moment. He asked what I wanted, and I told him about my ambition to get into racing. He was kind enough to answer some of my questions and talk to me about being a race mechanic.

He told me that if I was going to be a decent mechanic, I should learn to weld. And he was dead right! It would be as a welder that I landed my first job at Lotus in 1957. Amazingly, Britt Pierce and I were destined to work together for a private Lotus Formula One team owned by Michael Taylor in 1958–59. Although it didn't seem important at the time, that small conversation we had at Goodwood helped me get the F1 job.

I loved the sounds of the engines being warmed up and the smell of Castrol R oil burning in the exhausts. In those days, the technology of piston design had not advanced much, and the engines had to be gradually warmed up after they had been started to give the pistons time to expand and close the gap between them and the cylinder bores. Otherwise the pistons would scuff and seize up. As the pistons expanded, the engines stopped burning as much oil, and the smell almost went away.

Hawthorn, wearing his famous bow tie and coveralls, had a very successful day. Earlier he had also won the Woodcote Cup race for F1 cars, beating Fangio and Wharton in the BRMs. Many of the drivers drove in more than one race; among them was Roy Salvadori, who won the seven-lap Formula 2 event in a Connaught ahead of Stirling Moss in the Cooper-Alta. Salvadori also drove a Maserati in the sports-car race. There was some exciting stuff in that race, and watching Duncan Hamilton's Jaguar XK120 dicing with the Aston Martin DB3 of Gordon Whitehead was incredible.

The prizes were not that big in those days. You had to be reasonably wealthy to race. Hawthorn, whose dad owned a garage, received a Goodwood Trophy replica and 50 guineas for winning the feature race. The other races paid the winners 20 guineas or a trophy—they could choose. A guinea was equal to £1.05.

Naturally, being England, it rained from time to time, but nothing could have dampened my ardor for motor racing that day. As we drove home from the track that evening, with the sound of those 16-cylinder BRM engines still ringing in my ears, I became totally committed to the goal of becoming a race-car driver—and if I couldn't do that, I was determined that I was going to be the best damn racing mechanic anyone had ever seen!

In retrospect, I consider myself extremely lucky to have been around in those early days, when the cars were not as sophisticated as they are now and a driver's skill showed clearly. I also marvel at the fantastic advances that have taken place in the last 50 years in racing. The tires of old were crap compared with today's, but the drivers all had the same. In those days, the drivers didn't wear restraint belts and were all very visible. You could see their heads, shoulders, arms, and elbows working away. It was a unique, beautiful time to be growing up and getting involved in auto racing.

CHAPTER 2

The Lotus Space Program

I had a tough time breaking into racing. It was a catch-22 situation: You couldn't get a job in racing without experience, and you couldn't get experience unless you had a job in racing. So how do you start?

I thought about Britt Pierce's advice about learning to weld. I signed up for classes at the Paddington Technical College in London. Then I applied for a job at Lotus Cars—and got it.

I started working for Lotus as a "prototype fabricator" in the small factory that they first occupied in the borough of Hornsey, in north London. The sign over the door outside read "MAC Fisheries." A national fish distributor had previously occupied the building, and no one had bothered to take it down. I worked for the production shop manager, Derek "Nobby" Clark. With benches around the walls, the 1500 square-foot production shop held a total of about six cars and two chassis fixtures. Parts storage was in a loft upstairs.

Most of the fabrication welding was done using simple oxygen/acetylene equipment. We used gas welding to make A-arms and weld up tubular chassis for the Lotus 7 and Lotus 11 cars that we had in production. They had arc-welding equipment in the plant, but it was used only for making the Lotus De Dion rear axle tubes. All machining was farmed out. We had a band saw, a small cut-off lathe, a mill, and some sheet metal fabricating equipment.

There was a separate, two-story building, which was split into sections. One section was used for engine and gearbox preparation, and Keith Duckworth worked in there. Mike Costin and his assistant built prototype cars in the middle section. Downstairs was the receptionist/secretary, and upstairs there were two offices—the drafting office, where Len Terry worked, and Colin Chapman's "inner sanctum."

After welding up A-arms and frames and pedals for a while, I was assigned to help Mike Costin. It was very hard work, and we put in a lot of overtime as it got near time for the annual Le Mans race. One time I had just got home at 11:00 p.m., and the telephone rang. The engine for Frenchman Gérard Crombac's 1958 750cc Lotus 11 Le Mans car had just arrived and it was equipped with Weber carburetors. On that little 4-cylinder overhead camshaft engine, the intake and exhaust ports were on the same side of the cylinder head. I had previously made an exhaust system for a mock-up engine with SU carburetors. The exhaust system had to be completely redone, and the car had to leave the next day. It was Colin Chapman on the phone. Could he send his car over to pick me up so that I could work all night on the exhaust system? He would pay me double time if I went. Who could refuse an offer like that?

I ended up falling asleep in the cockpit of that Lotus at about 8:00 a.m., while trying to sew and fit a cockpit tonneau cover. They had to get the car to the ferry at Dover, and the tonneau had to be finished. So they loaded the car with me asleep in it. It went right up onto the top of the double-deck transporter to leave for the docks. Luckily I woke up, or they would have taken me to Dover—still in the car. I jumped out just in time and I got my double pay!

All 15 of the Lotus workshop staff were pranksters at heart. One day, one of them took an empty matchbox and filled it with the gas mixture we used for welding. It was easy to light the torch, kink the tubes to extinguish the flame, let the tubes go, and insert the tip of the torch into the matchbox. Once he had the matchbox full of gas, he relit the torch and pointed it at the matchbox. The amount of gas was tiny but the explosion was deafening. It was a great weapon if you wanted to make someone jump.

Next someone decided to blow up the aluminum teapot that Nobby Clark had in his office. We waited until Nobby went out. It didn't shatter as we thought it would. Instead, it flew up and made a very neat, teapot-shaped hole in the thin corrugated tin roof about 20 feet over our heads. Naturally the explosion was even bigger than the matchboxes made, and everyone in the shop cheered. Nobody rushed in to investigate except Len Terry, who came down from the loft office in the building next door to see what had happened. We kept quiet, and he went back upstairs mystified.

We worked long hours in those days, and a little comic relief was always good for morale. We did receive one other perk for working overtime, and that was dinner. Colin Chapman's father owned the pub next door, and if you worked after 6:30 p.m., you were given a chit to have a free dinner and a pint there.

The Lotus Mk 1 rocket magically appeared about a week after the teapot went through the roof. Made out of the 1.5-inch aluminum tube we used for engine water pipes, and nicely pointed at one end, Mk 1 had no guidance fins but was about 10 inches long. A base that the rocket could slide over was made out of a short piece of steel tube welded to a flat square plate. A small hole was drilled to permit rocket fueling.

The "rocket design and fabrication staff" selected a time for the launch that hopefully wouldn't cause any interruption—9:00 p.m.—and countdown started. At 9:00 p.m. minus five seconds, it was fueled; and a volunteer, wearing his welding helmet, eagerly lit the mixture. The rocket was on top of a pile of empty pallets that had been used to deliver rear axles, and as it shot into the air, the pile collapsed. The rocket exploded and went about 60 feet up. We never recovered it because it came down on the electric train tracks over the backyard wall. But it spurred us on to attempt greater things. Our rockets gradually got longer and bigger until Mk 4 arrived.

Mk 4 was going to reach outer space without a doubt. It was made out of the 4-inch diameter aluminum tube we used for water header tanks. Pointed nicely for minimum air resistance, it was three feet long with guidance fins. On its customized launch pad, it looked like a miniature V2 rocket from World War II. It was painted Lotus racing green with white stripes and fins.

Britain had not had a space program before, but it had one now. The only question was: Who would volunteer (that is, be stupid enough) to set it off? The explosion could be so violent that it might kill the launcher and deafen or blind the rest of us. Discussions on how to do it took several sessions to resolve, and it finally came down to this: We would nail together a pile of the axle pallets and run a tube from the rocket to the bottom of the pile. The welding torches used to fill the rocket and light it would be placed inside the doorway of the gearbox assembly shop, and the tube would run to there. That way, the launcher could be protected from the explosion by a wall and some distance to the actual missile. Everything would work with military precision—we thought!

It was decided that this would be a daylight launch so that we could all witness it, and the afternoon tea break was chosen as the time. The only condition that could delay the launch would be the presence of "Chunky" Chapman (as we fondly called him behind his back), so we chose the first day the Formula One team went testing. All the biggies, like Chunky, Costin, and Duckworth, would be at the track, looking after the Team Lotus F1 driver, Cliff Allison. None of the race-team mechanics was in on this, so security was OK. Meanwhile Mk 4 was kept hidden from view.

Launch day dawned bright and clear. Everyone eagerly helped Willy Griffith, the chief mechanic of the race team, and Jim Endruit, team mechanic, to load the transporter before they headed off to Silverstone to test the new Lotus 16, the front-engined, Vanwall-shaped F1 car. We watched as the team took off. Incidentally Jim Endruit later became the chief mechanic for Jimmy Clark on the Lotus 25.

At launch time minus one minute, we all stood at the curb near the entry gate to get both the best view and an escape route. Following a brief countdown, the volunteer lit the pipe. The explosion was so loud it was heard for many miles around. The rocket took off into the sky. But it was a disappointing flight—it only went 150 feet or so before it fell back onto the roof of the office building. Meanwhile the pallet launching pad rocked once and fell over sideways. Everyone laughed except the volunteer launcher, who was shaking his head as if to clear water from his ears and crying, "I'm deaf! I'm deaf!"

The local police were there within a few minutes with the fire brigade, bells a-clanging. "What blew up?" asked a policeman. "Is everyone OK?"

Just then Len Terry appeared with the remains of Mk 4 in his hands. "Who made this?" he yelled at us. "It scared the hell out of me! It came through the skylight and just missed me!"

Nobody confessed. One of us said, "It looks like a rocket. Do you think the Army launched it from somewhere?" The police questioned everybody and left the crime scene with this warning: "We know one of you did this, but don't even think about doing it again!"

It was over: no more space program. When Chunky found out about it, he threatened to fire someone if it happened again. So it was back to the grindstone for all of us. But I will never forget it because the Lotus Space Program was a highlight of working there. The low pay and long working hours certainly were not. But how else was a bloke supposed to get a start in racing?

BELOW: Here we are testing at Snetterton in my new position as racing mechanic for John Ewer's new Lister Corvette. I am second from the right. (Peter Bryant)

CHAPTER 3

Blokes and Chaps

"The most powerful sports car in England!" That was how BBC commentator John Bolster described the Lister Corvette when he saw it racing for the first time in 1959 in a race at Aintree, near Liverpool. There were two of the Lister Corvettes in the featured sports-car race, but I was at home, listening on the radio. The Corvette was still fairly new in America and Lance Reventlow was using the engine in his now famous Scarab sports cars. They were cleaning up in the States, and Brian Lister, of Lister Jaguar fame, had decided that if he put a modified 5-liter Corvette V8 into his car instead of the 3.8-liter Jaguar straight-six, theoretically it should go like a bat out of hell. He also commissioned Mike Costin's brother, Frank, to redesign the aerodynamics of the Lister body.

At that time, I was building the prototype Lotus 15 sports cars, and my boss was Mike Costin, who would later co-found Cosworth Engineering with Keith Duckworth. Frank Costin worked for De Havilland, the British aircraft manufacturer, and did some aerodynamic consulting for Lotus in his spare time. The new Lister car was very slippery and looked classically beautiful, and still does today. But in those days the distance between America and England made owning and maintaining a Chevrolet Corvette engine in England a bit tough parts-wise, to say the least. I would find out how tough real soon.

About a week after the Aintree race, I saw an advertisement in *Autosport* magazine.

ABOVE: I go under the Lister to check the axle temperature; John Ewer is alongside me. (Peter Bryant)

It read: "Racing mechanic wanted for a Lister-Corvette car. Must be experienced in racing and capable of tuning and rebuilding engines."

I figured that if I stayed at Lotus, I would be a fabricator for the rest of my time there and I seriously wanted to go racing. I had helped to build the factory and customer cars for Le Mans, but I had only been taken to one race by Lotus—the 1958 British Grand Prix at Silverstone, where I had helped Alan Stacey win the 1100cc class in the sports-car race with his works Lotus 11. Stacey and Cliff Allison were the works Formula One drivers, and Graham Hill sometimes drove if there was an opening. In those days, he worked in the factory, like me, in his spare time.

I answered the advert and, to my surprise, got the job. It was working for a privateer racer named John Ewer. He owned a fleet of tour coaches called Grey Green Coaches and had one of the very first Lister-Corvettes. It was red with gold pin-stripes and looked fantastic. The front-engined sports-racing car was powered by a special Corvette engine that had been built in the United States by a short-track racer named Bill "Stroker" McGurk.

The engine had been built for drag racing. The crankshaft had been welded up on the journals and remachined so that the stroke was half an inch longer. It had a high-lift camshaft and Hilborn fuel-injection and should have been run on methanol instead of gasoline. It was designed for dirt car sprint racing and it was not really suitable for sports-car racing, because it had no driveability. When you opened the throttle and the fuel was injected into the intake ports, the air-fuel mixture ratio did not reach the required 14:1 until it got up to near maximum revs, at which point the power came on in one big lump, and the car went like a rocket. This may have been OK for a dragster, but it was not very good for a sports car that needed handily metered power, much as you would get from a carburetor or a decent fuel-injection. The car would actually have been better off with the stock Corvette fuel-injected engine.

John showed me the car and told me that, for the first order of business, he needed to somehow cool the rear axle housing. In his last race, it had overheated and boiled the axle grease. So I made some copper fins, took the back cover off the differential and put some grooves in it, and silver-soldered the fins into the grooves. I put the car back together and made a duct that would get much-needed cooling air to the fins. The next weekend, we went to a club race at Snetterton and tested them.

They worked fine, but the engine still acted up and started to burn oil. John finished the 10-lap race but the engine had started to run very rough. After the race, at the local pub where all the racers stopped for dinner, John asked me if I could do anything with the engine. I told him that I'd read all the stuff in the American racing magazines about the Scarab cars and that they used a similar engine with carburetors on it and the stock Chevrolet camshaft. He told me to tear the engine down as soon as I got back to the shop.

The next day, I took the engine apart and found that not only were the high-compression pistons cracked but the crankshaft was too. John said he could buy a stock Corvette cam and even a crankshaft, but could not get high-compression pistons to fit the enlarged cylinder bore. Normally the cylinder bore was smaller, but Stroker had opened it up. I went to the only Chevrolet service place in London and bought all the engine gaskets and spare parts that they had for a Corvette—an easy task because they didn't have many.

After much searching, I found a custom piston maker in a small town just outside London, and he agreed over the telephone to make aluminum pistons to our own design. The following week, I set out in the converted coach, which was our race-car transporter, to the piston maker's shop in Oxfordshire.

The converted motor coach carried the race car behind the driver and passenger seats on some ramps built into the rear floor area. There were two rear doors that had originally allowed baggage to be loaded under the floor behind the rear axle. The car was loaded through those doors. You could barely shut them when the race car was in the coach, and when you drove, you could reach back and touch the nose of the car with your hand from your seat. Because a ramp had been built into the floor, there was room under the car for tools, spare wheels, and fuel cans.

The coach was too small to put in any kind of front lounge, but there was a plywood shelf above the driver's compartment that was big enough for someone to sleep on. When we went to the races, the driver stayed in a hotel—as befitted his rank, of course—and the mechanic (now me) was relegated to sleep in a sleeping bag on some foam rubber on the shelf. I would wash up in the usually convenient men's room at the track and eat at the ever-present mobile catering service.

John had put the words "Lister Corvette" on the side of the coach near the roof and the words "John Ewer" on the door. He now added, in fine print, "P. Bryant, Mec." I loved it. I was officially a racing mechanic now.

There was a permanent smell of gasoline and oil inside the coach, and I constantly got the feeling that if I struck a match, the whole thing would explode. I smoked in those days, but decided I had better not in that "transporter."

BELOW: One of the first tuning assignments I identified for myself was improving the piston design of the high-strung Chevrolet Corvette engine. Here, the man who executed my Scarab-inspired design, Mr. Showalter, poses by the transporter with the new piston. (Peter Bryant)

I took the engine in pieces to the piston maker, a Mr. Showalter, and he was very cooperative. I had taken one of the old pistons and made a wedge-shaped dome on top of it out of modeling clay so, instead of having a flat top, it looked just like the Scarab piston in the magazine pictures. I was careful to ensure that the overhead exhaust valve wouldn't hit the dome when the camshaft pushed it full open. That was the critical clearance to watch out for because if the engine was over-revved, the exhaust valve would open faster than the piston went down. If they collided, it would be a disaster that usually ended up with bent and broken valves that would smash the pistons into pieces.

The incredible Mr. Showalter, without much in the way of drawings to go by and only a few critical measurements, machined eight pistons out of some blank castings he had in stock for a tractor engine. It took him only two days to do everything. We even weighed each piston and balanced their weights by grinding out the metal under the piston skirts. I stayed in the "Hotel Shelf" (as I called it) each night above the driver's seat in the bus. When it was all done, I took Mr. Showalter's photograph standing by the bus, holding our creation.

The next race was to be at Silverstone in about a week, and I hurried to get the engine together and back in the car. John told me he wanted to test the car before we got to the track. At my urging, he had ordered a Scintilla Vertex magneto from Bosch, and we were going to pick it up on the way. It would be good to get rid of the unreliable "trick" American ignition system that had come with the engine. John had booked himself into the local pub/hotel at Towcester, near Silverstone, for the following Friday and Saturday nights. I would be staying again in the fabulous Hotel Shelf in the parking lot of the pub.

Early the next Friday morning, with John driving the coach, we went around the North Circular road of London to Bosch and picked up the magneto, which had been modified to fit the standard Corvette engine. We drove out toward Silverstone, and when we got near the village of Towcester we stopped at a big lay-by on the main road near a lorry drivers' café (or truck stop, as we say in the States). We unloaded the car in the lay-by, and I installed and timed the new magneto in place of the distributor. The cylinder firing order of the big V8 was 1-5-4-8-6-3-7-2—for some dumb reason, I have never forgotten it. All that was left to do was to connect the magneto to a grounding switch so that the engine could be shut off. I had disconnected the battery power to the ignition switch and used that as the grounding switch. All the time I was working, a strange-looking man was intently watching everything I did, and I was starting to get a bit annoyed by his constant questions.

"What kind of car is it? How fast does it go? How much did it cost?"

When all was done, John Ewer put on his crash helmet and got behind the wheel of the Lister. "Go ahead, John, start it up," I said. He cranked the engine, but it didn't start. He tried again—no good. I opened the hood and looked at the magneto. I could see nothing wrong and pulled a plug wire to short-out and see if there was any spark coming from the magneto. "Try again," I said. But the engine still refused to start. Just then, the stranger said to me in a whisper, "It won't start if that wire from the magneto is grounded."

I quickly disconnected the wire going to the magneto and replaced the disconnected plug wire. The engine started straight away. The wire had needed to go through the switch so that when the switch was in the "on" position, the wire was disconnected. When the magneto was grounded to the chassis, it shut off. I had wired it the other way around. I smiled at the stranger and said, "Thanks a lot, mate, you've saved my bacon!" I told him lunch was on me and slipped him five shillings.

John never knew that the bum had solved the problem for me. He said, "Grab a couple of tools and lock up the transporter. Let's take it for a spin." I locked up, put some tools in my pocket, and jumped in the car. John had registered the car for the highway, and it had the license plate number on the front. We drove off.

There was no passenger seat, so I sat on the floor and held on to the dash mounting frame tubes. I was in heaven. I had never ridden in a race car before, and this one was doing over 100 mph with me in it. As soon as the car had accelerated from standstill, all vibrations stopped, and it seemed to be flying on the ground. I soon got used to the speed. We did about 25 miles and came back to the coach. John said, "The engine seems to be fine, so let's load up and go to the pub."

There was another Lister Corvette entered in our race, owned and driven by Ron Brightman. He had a converted bus as a transporter, too, but his was long enough to create a front lounge that made up into a nice sleeping area. Ron owned a business making slipcovers for car seats, so the interior décor was, as John Ewer used to say, "Very high claaaaass."

The two Lister owners were very good friends. Between the racing activities at the track, they would sit in the luxury and splendor of Ron's transporter "salon" and sip drinks of various kinds. Both Ron and John had close friends and racing buddies who drove their own cars to the races, and they were also privileged to be invited into Ron's private salon.

Dave (whose last name I never knew) was Ron's mechanic; he was the first person ever to point out to me the difference between "chaps" and "blokes." The drivers were the chaps, like officers in the British Army, a privileged class because they were often from aristocratic stock. They were in charge, they owned everything, and they had loads of money. Whereas we blokes were like regular soldiers, we owned nothing, we had no power, and we worked our asses off for the glory of the chaps. And, what's more, we loved it!

Very rarely did a bloke become a chap. "Blokes like being blokes," was Dave's opinion. It all sounded like a weird sort of reverse snobbery to me. I told Dave jokingly that I hated the very idea that I may never get to be a chap! I wanted to be a race-car driver, and if it meant becoming a chap, then so be it. I didn't know at that time how close I would come to becoming a chap that very day.

Practice came and went and both cars did fairly well. They were both entered in a 10-lap Formule Libre event, as well as in a 10-lap sports-car race. Our car was on the second row

LEFT: Our lap timer Stan Smith and I guard the Lister in the paddock of the Crystal Palace circuit in London. This was my last race meeting with John Ewer. (Peter Bryant)

of the grid for the first race. With 20 minutes to go, I popped my head into Ron's bus and said, "John, it's 20 minutes to the start of your first race. I've warmed up the car. Do you want me to take it to the grid for you?" He was sipping something from a glass and sort of nodded in my direction. Just as I had done before at Snetterton, I grabbed his helmet, put it in the passenger side of the car, and drove down to the starting grid. I loved any excuse to get behind the wheel. All John had to do then was walk across the paddock to the grid and get in the car. That was what most chaps did in those days. It was only about a two-minute walk.

As I arrived in the pre-grid area, a marshal waved me out and onto our grid slot in front of the pits. I switched off the engine and sat in the car, waiting for John to appear. With five minutes to go before the start, I was getting more than a bit anxious. Where was John? I started the car and began warming it up again. Suddenly a marshal ran over and shouted at me to put my crash helmet on for the start. I was wearing Dunlop racing overalls exactly like John's, albeit a bit dirtier than his. Then the marshal held up the two-minute board and again ran over to me and yelled, "Put your helmet on—what are you waiting for?" So I put the helmet on as I tried to figure out the situation. My heart was racing like a mad clock. What should I do? Here I was, living my biggest dream, sitting in one of the most powerful sports-racing cars in Britain on the grid at Silverstone. I had never done a lap at Silverstone and didn't even have a racing license. If I raced the car, would I be arrested? I definitely would get fired, but what the hell, how often in my life would this happen?

Suddenly the starter's flag was up right in front of me. I decided that I would start the race, do only part of one lap and bring the car into the paddock the back way before entering Woodcote Corner. That way at least I would get to drive the car around Silverstone for one lap. After all, here I was, with nowhere else to go except around the track. My heart raced as I put the car into first gear and the flag dropped.

I slammed down the throttle pedal and released the clutch. The acceleration took me completely by surprise, and I nearly hit the car in front of me up the ass. I almost forgot to change gears, and my heart felt like it would jump out of my chest as we neared the first bend. Then I pulled the car to the inside lane of the track and let everyone go past me. Feeling good about it all, I happily drove around the track as fast as I dared until the back entrance to the paddock came up just before Woodcote Corner.

It had been really exciting, and I had loved it. Driving a real racing car on a real track was an experience that I never thought would ever happen to me. I felt confident that, given the opportunity, I could do as well as these other chaps any time.

I drove the Lister back to our sport in the paddock and found John still sitting in Ron's bus. It turned out he simply had not heard me telling him that I was taking the car to the grid. He was indignant at first but then he saw the funny side and was very good about it.

They both raced in the Formule Libre race, and John finished about seventh with Ron just ahead of him. I decided then and there that if a chance to be a chap ever came again, I would race the car and face the consequences later. Meanwhile, I went back to being a full-time bloke.

At the end of the 1959 club racing season, John Ewer decided that he had wasted enough money trying to race the "most powerful sports car" and sold it to someone in South Africa. My time with the Lister Corvette had been fun and very interesting, because I had learned a lot about being a racing mechanic. We parted ways on amicable terms, and once again, I checked out the "Positions Vacant" ads in *Autosport*.

BELOW: Silverstone pits, 1958: Colin Chapman gets on his haunches with the mechanics to check out the left front tire of the works Lotus 16 as Cliff Allison waits in the cockpit. This was the car Mike Taylor wanted in 1959. (LAT Photographic)

CHAPTER 4

Moving Up in the World

When John Ewer laid me off, I found a temporary job repairing rental cars for Wellbeck Car Hire Company in the West End of London. It was an easy job, maintaining new Ford Consul and Zephyr cars, and I got to take them home for "road tests." The pay was decent, but after only a month I was bored. I started looking in *Autosport* again.

One week there was an ad for a racing mechanic who "must be able to weld." I applied and was interviewed by an up-and-coming driver named Michael Taylor and by Britt Pierce—the same Britt Pierce who had been Mike Hawthorn's mechanic and I had later met several times at Lotus when he was working for Innes Ireland. It had been six years since I had first spoken to him at Goodwood, but he remembered me. I told him I had heeded his advice about learning to weld. I proudly showed him my certificate from Paddington Technical College that proved I had gotten top honors in Welding & Metallurgy. With my Lotus and recent Lister experience, I was the best candidate for the job and I was hired.

ABOVE: Mike Taylor in the Lotus 15. (Bill Colson)

The shop was in a Belgrave Mews garage next door to the repair shop of the Berkeley Motors Mercedes dealership, which was owned by Michael Taylor's father. It was in the heart of Mayfair in downtown London, and a half-hour by Tube train from my apartment. I was thrilled to have got another racing job so quickly.

It was a couple of months before Christmas 1959, and I was now working for the Taylor & Crawley Racing Team, which prepared cars for four or five wealthy individuals. Britt was the chief mechanic. He had just been to the Cooper Car Company in Surbiton, Surrey, to help them build a new Formula Junior car for Jonathan Sieff, one of the team's owner-drivers and a member of the Marks & Spencer chain-store family. At that time, the team already had five or six racing cars in their stable, including two Lotus 15 sports cars, an ex-works Lotus 16 Formula One car, and a Lotus Elite. After I had been hired, there was now a grand total of two mechanics to prepare them all for the various events they wanted to contest in 1960. It promised to be a very busy year.

My first job was to overhaul the 2-liter Coventry Climax engine in Mike Taylor's Lotus 15 and get it ready to race at the Nassau Speed Week in the Bahamas in early December. I explained to Michael that I was unfamiliar with the engine and asked him if I could take it back to the factory for overhaul so that I could learn how to do it myself. He thought that was a great idea. Next day, Michael talked to Harry Spears, the manager at Coventry Climax, and I ended up with a week at the factory, watching and learning as they overhauled the engine.

ABOVE: Mike Taylor with his BARC Trophy from a Goodwood event. Joining Mike's team reunited me with Britt Pierce, who had been Mike Hawthorn's mechanic. (LAT Photographic)

I quickly found out why the team needed someone who could weld. Each of the Lotus 15 cars had a broken space frame, just behind the driveshaft tunnel where the rear axle differential mounted. I had to remove the aluminum seatbacks, cut out the broken tubes and replace them with new ones. When I finally got the chassis repairs finished, I had just about rebuilt the seatback bulkheads completely.

Michael insisted that I test the Nassau car before putting it on the boat for the Bahamas. What a thrill it was to take a Lotus 15 out onto public roads that weekend and just drive it! On Monday, I drove it down to the docks and saw it loaded onto the boat. I was really hoping that I would be sent to Nassau to look after the car, but Britt took that honor for himself. But just in case he changed his mind, I got myself a passport.

Right after one Lotus 15 had left for the Bahamas, I was asked by Mike to get the other one ready for his racing team partner Doug Graham. He wanted to drive it at Brands Hatch during the traditional Boxing Day races. Doug was a bit of a playboy—his father owned the *Manchester Guardian*, a prominent British newspaper. He liked the Boxing Day meeting, and it had become a tradition for him to do it. In my view, going to work at a race in England the day after Christmas was not the greatest thing to do on that special day. In fact, it bewildered me why anyone would want to schedule a race on Boxing Day. I really looked forward to the holidays as a time to relax and enjoy the family or play a little snooker and have a beer or two with my mates.

Then I discovered that, besides getting Doug's engine and car ready for Brands Hatch, it was my responsibility to get the engine done for the Formula Junior Cooper while Britt was in Nassau with Michael. Plus, I had to go to Liverpool when the Nassau car came back and get hold of it before the dock workers had a chance to play with it. It was scheduled to return two weeks before Christmas.

And then more crap happened. Britt called and told me that Doug's engine needed to be taken out and delivered to the Lotus factory as a mock-up for a new 2-liter Lotus Elite that was being built for the next Le Mans 24 Hours. So I should take it out of the car I had just put it in, and get it to Lotus ASAP. For Doug's Boxing Day car, he told me to take the engine out of the car that was not even back from Nassau yet.

Mike won the 2-liter class in the Governor's Trophy sports-car race at Nassau, although he was beaten by Bob Holbert in a 1500cc Porsche 718 RSK. The overall winner was Stirling Moss in a works Aston Martin DBR2. When Britt got back, he went to Coopers with the engine I had built to finish off the new Formula Junior. He said he would take it direct to Brands Hatch on Boxing Day for Jonathan Sieff to drive.

Six days before Christmas, I drove our Borgward station wagon with an empty trailer to Liverpool. I spent the customary two days arguing with the stevedores and customs people until they released the Nassau Lotus 15 to me. When I finally got back to London and could start work on it, it was only two days before Christmas.

What else could go wrong? During the Nassau race, the engine had blown the head gasket and water had got into the cylinders. It needed another overhaul. So I had only two days to remove and overhaul the engine and put it into Doug's car. I would be working at least one all-nighter. I should have told Mike right then that it was impossible to do all that before Christmas. But, being a bit of an egotist, I hated to admit that there was something I could not do. So I just did it.

I told my wife, Sally, that I had to work day and night before Christmas to get the car ready. She said I was mad. "Why did you go back to racing when you had such a nice job with the car hire company? You had good wages and a free car every weekend, but these people treat you like crap and you go back for more! Tell them you're not working Boxing Day. Tell them you have to go to your mother's house for dinner!"

Sally obviously didn't share my enthusiasm for racing, and I understood why. It really made no sense. But I had an obligation to Mike and I couldn't let my reputation as a race mechanic suffer. I told her that it was all great experience and one day, if she could stick it out, we could go anywhere in the world we wanted to live, because good race mechanics were in international demand. I said all I needed was a couple more years to make my way into Formula One. She relented and agreed I should do it. But I had to meet her at my mother's house as soon as I could after the race. "Don't hang around at the track or go to the pub with Britt!" These were my strict instructions, and I hastily agreed.

I worked until about 10:00 p.m. on Christmas Eve in the Belgrave Mews garage. I had just tied the car onto the trailer when the door of the upstairs flat opened and out stepped the tenant. His name was Bobby Howes and he was a famous old Vaudeville performer from the London stage who had become a bit of a racing fan and often popped into the shop. He looked and sounded a little the worse for wear.

"What on earth are you doing here on Christmas Eve, Peter?" he asked. I explained what was happening and told him I was about to leave. "Well, you can't let Christmas Eve go by without at least drinking a toast with me," he said. We went up to his flat, and he opened a bottle of wine. Later I walked over to Mike Taylor's flat to let him know I was taking the car home on a trailer and would leave for Brands Hatch from there on Boxing Day morning. He gave me a bottle of gin as my Christmas gift. I didn't drink gin but I told him I would give it to my mother as consolation for being late for her Boxing Day dinner. When I finally got home, Sally was in bed and asleep. Christmas Eve was a time we liked to party a bit. Before going to bed, I sat alone at the kitchen table and drank a large whisky. It was the least I could do to let my liver know I was still alive!

Christmas Day was better. My mother always gave all five of her children new carpet slippers for Christmas, and this year I had a pair of red slippers with thin leather soles and uppers made from woolly felt. They were as warm as toast. We had Christmas dinner with Sally's mother, who lived alone, and had a nice, relaxed day.

On Boxing Day, at 5:00 a.m., I woke up to the dreaded alarm. I put on my new carpet slippers, washed, shaved, and dressed. Then I went into the kitchen of our little two-room flat and made tea and toast. I took it upstairs to share with Sally and at 6:15 a.m. I left for Brands Hatch with the racing car in tow. It rained all the way, and when I arrived, the grass paddock was just a big, muddy quagmire.

Britt had roped off a piece of it for us. The driver of the Lotus 15, Doug Graham, missed the first practice session because he was late getting up. I was disgusted with him. What was worse, though, was that I realized I was still wearing my red felt slippers!

I contemplated taking them off and working in bare feet all day, but it was too cold.

I was terrified in case my mother caught me ruining my new slippers in the Brands Hatch mud. The races were being televised live on the BBC, and my family would all be watching, hoping to get a glimpse of me! I tried to keep a low profile and stay clear of the cameras.

The Formula Junior Cooper was what did me in. It was a brand new type of racing car, and many people were interested in seeing one, including John Bolster, the BBC commentator. I was changing the plugs when I heard a voice behind me say, "Well, here we are in the paddock and looking at the newest Formula Junior from the winning John Cooper stable." It was Bolster, and he was about to stick his microphone and camera under my nose and ask me a bunch of questions about the car. Nothing got past Bolster. He was one of Britain's most famous racing characters, with his tweed suit and deerstalker hat and big handlebar moustache. He was very knowledgeable about cars and had competed himself. He had a great sense of humor and everyone in racing loved him.

He interviewed me about the Cooper and was just about to leave when he spotted the slippers. Bolster looked at the camera and back to my feet, and the camera followed his gaze. My goose was cooked!

Doug Graham led the sports-car race at first, but he let Alan Rees's Lola past him and then Tom Threlfall's Lotus, finishing third. At the end of the day, our Lotus was a distant second in the sports-car section of the Formule Libre race, behind Gordon Lee's Lister Jaguar. Doug said, "Sorry, Peter, I guess I had too much turkey for Christmas dinner—I just couldn't concentrate today!" He grinned, gave Britt and me £10 each as our Christmas gifts, and left. After all I had been through in the previous weeks, I wanted to tell him to shove his car and his money up his ass!

I told Britt I would rather have been at home for the Christmas holidays and that I didn't like good losers. He said, "That's club racing, Peter. Formula One drivers don't do stuff like that. They do anything to win." He bought me a quick pint at the clubhouse, and I drove back to London in record time.

When I got to the house, my whole family gave me such a razzing about wearing my slippers on TV that my face was red for about an hour. My mother never did let me forget it, but later she bought me another pair to show she still loved me. I gave her the gin and told her where I had got it. "Is that all he gave you for Christmas after all the work you've done for him?" she asked in her cockney accent. "Bloomin' ungrateful little sod." My thoughts, exactly.

BELOW: The front row takes off at the 1960 Glover Trophy race at Goodwood. The number 8 and 9 Cooper cars of the Yeoman Credit team sandwich Stirling Moss in his Lotus 18. The Coopers were two of the cars I worked on in New Zealand when Reg Parnell took over the Yeoman Credit team. (LAT Photographic)

CHAPTER 5

Venturing into Formula One

My first two Formula One experiences came in 1960 with Mike Taylor, but both were both big disappointments because of mechanical problems with the cars.

The first was the older, front-engined Lotus 16, powered by a Coventry Climax engine. Buying a used F1 race car in those days was definitely akin to settling for second best. The development cycle was a lot faster than it is now because there was so much unknown territory yet to be covered in race-car technology. A "last year's car" would never be competitive with a "this year's car." Colin Chapman and the other constructors understood that very well. They wouldn't show the latest car to the press until they had sold the older team cars to private racers just champing at the bit to get one to race. Buying a one-year-old car was a very big risk, especially if it had been a prototype, like this Lotus 16.

On close inspection of the car, I quickly found that it needed lots of chassis welding repairs. Where the tubes came together with any sort of component mounting boss, there were cracked welds and cracked tubes next to the welds. I had to cut out the cracked tubes and replace them with new pieces. I couldn't believe how thin the tube wall was in the space frame (about 40 thousandths of an inch thick in many of them). Many times the expansion of the frame from welding heat had made the tube next to a weld distort and crack. It took me two weeks to get the frame fixed.

Although the Formula One rules permitted 2.5-liter race engines, no English supplier made one. The biggest displacement Coventry Climax made with their famous FPF (fire pump) engine was 2.2 liters at that time. The lack of displacement didn't mean they were unsuccessful—Jack Brabham had already proved that engine size was not the key factor in winning an F1 race. But the key to losing a race was always reliability, and unfortunately the Lotus 16 did not have much going for it in that respect. Mike Taylor bought the car less the engine, so I put one of the team's 2-liter sports-car engines in it. That actually made it fit the Formula 2 regulations, so Mike could race it in F1 or F2 races.

The Lotus 16 was equipped with a Lotus-designed-and-built transaxle (a rear axle with a gearbox inside). That was its Achilles' heel. It was not the first "positive stop" motorcycle-type gearbox to be used in a racing car. The old 500cc Formula 3 cars, with their motorcycle engines and transmissions, were probably the inspiration behind it.

With the engine in the front and the transaxle-type gearbox in the rear, the offset driveshaft ran right under the driver's legs and the seat. I used to wonder what would happen if the universal joint broke on the back of the bell housing. Spinning at 6500 rpm, the driveshaft would probably have chopped off the driver's leg or even his private parts—not a nice thought. I recall taking great pains to ensure that the driveshaft axis did not line up perfectly with the center of the crankshaft. If it did, the needle bearings in the driveshaft universal joint wouldn't rotate and would eventually cause the joint to fail. Nowadays, the Indy-type cars all have this type of gearbox, but they are rear-engined so there is no separate driveshaft from engine to transaxle.

There was no H-pattern gearshift. The driver pulled back on the lever to go up a gear, and pushed it forward to go down. A ratchet and pawl arrangement slid a gear inside the input shaft along to engage one of the gears spinning around so that it was engaged with the output shaft gear connected to the shaft of the pinion gear.

The only problem with this gearbox was the strength of the teeth on the pinion gear. Originally from a standard Volvo rear axle, the pinion couldn't really handle the torque of a race engine during hard acceleration and often sheared off one of the pinion teeth. The broken tooth would then fall into the shifter mechanism and stop it working properly. That was how you could tell the pinion gear was broken.

The thing I always liked about that gearbox, and the one in the Lotus 18, was the fact that the pairs of gears always had a total of 44 teeth between them. Even if you had to change the ratios in a hurry, it was almost impossible to mismatch a gear set. If one gear had 20 teeth, its mate had 24. If one gear had 18 teeth, its mate had 26. I thought whoever had designed that feature was a genius. It meant, of course, that all the teeth had to be the same size, so first gear was as strong as top gear.

When the FIA announced that Formula One maximum engine displacement would change from 2.5 liters to 1.5 liters in 1961, it meant a big reduction in power and torque. That was probably why they used basically the same gearbox design in the Lotus 18. I guess

ABOVE: Mike Taylor driving his Lotus 18 for the first time at the Silverstone International Trophy race. He finished a disappointing seventeenth. (LAT Photographic)

Colin Chapman thought the lower torque of the 1.5-liter engine would allow the pinion to last a race.

In April 1960, Easter Monday, Mike raced the Lotus 16 in the Glover Trophy at Goodwood. There were 13 cars in the race, and Mike had qualified in 13th position—not good omens if you were superstitious. He obviously had an inferior car against the latest F1 machinery, because the teams were using this non-championship race to check out the opposition. The 12 cars ahead of him on the grid included 2 works Lotus 18s for Innes Ireland, who won the race, and Alan Stacey, who broke down after only six laps. Stirling Moss finished second in his Cooper-Climax, and Chris Bristow and Bruce McLaren finished third and fourth in similar cars. The last three to finish the race were Graham Hill, Jo Bonnier, and Tony Brooks, all in BRMs. Roy Salvadori (Cooper-Climax), Harry Schell (Cooper-Climax), new F1 driver Keith Greene (Cooper-Maserati), and Dan Gurney (BRM) all failed to finish. So did Mike. He managed only eight laps before the pinion broke.

The first four cars were rear-engined, and they lapped everyone else. The writing was on the wall. Unless you had a rear-engined car in 1960, you were not going to be competitive. Mike talked about it to his friends Innes Ireland and Stirling Moss. Within a couple of weeks, he had made a deal with Colin Chapman to buy the prototype Lotus 18.

This time it came with the 2.2-liter Climax engine. We got it just in time to race it in the BRDC International Trophy at Silverstone on May 14. There was barely time to go over the car before that race, but luckily Mike had hired a former Team Lotus mechanic, Maurice "Mo" Levy, who had worked on the 18 before. I was glad to see him come onboard. I had been carrying a heavy load with all the sports-car preparation and I was still responsible for the engine rebuilds. Now we had three mechanics and seven cars! When Britt hired a kid fresh out of school as a handyman, we had a staff of four.

The Silverstone race meeting began very badly when Harry Schell was killed. The American driver was thrown out of his Cooper when it hit a retaining wall at Abbey Curve during practice. There were 22 cars in the F1/F2 race, and Ferrari was there with Phil Hill and Cliff Allison. Mike did much better with the rear-engined car and was going well until an elusive short circuit to the magneto forced him to pit several times. He completed only 32 of the 50 laps and ended up in 17th position. He did finish but was not classified in the results. It was a bit disappointing, to say the least.

Again the winner was Innes Ireland with his works Lotus 18, with Jack Brabham (Cooper) and Graham Hill (BRM) second and third. The Ferraris finished fifth and eighth.

Next on our busy agenda was the fourth round of the FIA World Sports Car Championship, one week later at the Nürburgring in Germany. We raced back to the workshop and worked around the clock for three days and nights to get our two Lotus 15 sports cars loaded onto a borrowed coach-type transporter. Oh, and Mo had to rebuild the Lotus 18 for the Monaco Grand Prix. I still had to overhaul the engine in the F1 car. We would all need to hustle.

BELOW: Giorgio Scarlatti's Ferrari Dino 196S goes up in flames in the Nürburgring pits as Britt Pierce and I watch it from the Taylor & Crawley pit stall (encircled). (Jesse Alexander)

CHAPTER 6

Fire and Cold Drinks at the 'Ring

When the time came to set off for the Nürburgring, we picked up the converted tour coach that we had borrowed from Jonathan Sieff and loaded up the cars. The plan was that Mo and I would take the coach to Germany, and Britt would bring the apprentice when he brought the Formula One car over the Channel. I don't remember his name, but I can't forget his nickname: "Mahogany Boots" Malone. We gave him this name when he repaired a hole in the sole of his shoe by cutting and shaping a piece of eighth-inch plywood and using it like an arch support.

The coach was an old single-deck bus with the seats removed and ramps installed to hold the cars. It had a single-seat cab, as most English *charabancs* (tour coaches) did in those days, so one of us had to sit either under the front of a car loaded on the sloping ramp, near the left side entry door, or in a car on the ramp. The coach had been sitting idle for a couple of years and was a slow, smelly, noisy, Leyland diesel thing with six gears. Mo drove us down to the Dover ferry because I didn't have an English Heavy Duty driver's license. After the 1000-kilometer race,

ABOVE: Dan Gurney, who won the 1960 Nürburgring 1000 teamed with Stirling Moss, signed my pit pass armband. (Peter Bryant)

the plan was that Britt and Mo were to go to Monaco to try and get Mike qualified for the F1 race, while Mahogany Boots and I would bring the coach and sports cars back to England. I guess nobody was bothered by the fact that I didn't have a license to drive the thing.

The Nürburgring was a brand new experience for me, and I was very excited. By the time we got to the ferry it was late, so we had to sit in the lounge and sleep if we could. That was easy, because we had been up all the previous night working on the cars. We got off the ferry and had the usual two-hour nonsense with the French customs about our papers.

We finally got away after paying the usual bribes to the automobile club man for helping and the French for doing their job. We still had quite a way to go, and it would take us all day and more to get out of France and Belgium and into Germany via Aachen. We stopped once on the way for fuel and the usual runny French omelette.

It was dark when we got to Adenau, the small German town near the track where we were staying. I stopped the bus outside the Hotel Eifelhof, and Mo told me to back it into an alley by a service station opposite the hotel while he checked us in. That was when the fun started.

I was very proud of the way I maneuvered that big old bus backwards into the narrow alley in the pitch darkness. I turned off the engine and lights, and jumped down from the cab. I couldn't see the ground and landed very nicely with one foot on the road and the other inside a large pan of dirty motor oil from the gas station. Mo reappeared and said, "What are you doing? Don't you want to go to bed tonight?" I showed him my oil-soaked leg and foot and he laughed. "They won't let you into the hotel like that," he said. "You'd mess up all their carpets."

I remembered someone telling me that the Russians used to use gasoline for dry cleaning. I took a churn of racing gasoline out of the bus and removed my trousers, shoe, and sock. I washed off the leg of my pants with the gasoline, soaked my shoe and sock in it, and waited 10 minutes for them to dry. Finally we walked into the hotel. "Hey!" said the doorman, "what's the smell of benzene?"

I hastily explained, "I got a little on my shoe when I was refueling our car." We carried on up to the room. Both Mo and I smoked, and I badly wanted to light up, but I decided it wasn't a good idea at that particular moment. I really didn't want to get burned to death. So I rinsed off my clothes in the bathtub, hung them out the window to dry, and went to sleep listening to Mo still laughing about the oil. Little did I think that being burned to death at the circuit was a very real possibility.

The next day, we went into the Nürburgring, picked up our armband passes, and were assigned a garage in the *fahrerlager* (paddock). We still had a lot of things to do before qualifying, so we started work on the cars straight away. They needed windshield wipers to be race-legal and a lot of other niggly crap had to be done to make them legal before tech inspection.

The weather started out cloudy, but at about 1:30 p.m. it began to get quite warm. A short, stocky German came through the paddock with a tray around his neck full of soft drinks in bottles. "Cold drinks!" he yelled, and kept yelling, in a thick guttural German accent. It was too hard to resist the temptation to play a joke on him. As he came by, we called him into the garage. We bought a couple of drinks and asked him politely if he was selling many drinks. "Not as much as I vood like," he replied. We told him people needed to know that the drinks were very, very cold. He would sell more that way, for sure. We told him that in England, when they sold drinks and wanted to emphasize how cold they were, they yelled out, "Fucking cold drinks!" He thanked us, and said he really appreciated the advice. Every few minutes through the rest of our stay at the Nürburgring, we could hear him loud and clear, "Fucking cold drrrrrinks!"

The word spread around the paddock that some English mechanics had persuaded him to do it, so everyone would buy his drinks and pat him on the back for letting them know how really cold they were. The war didn't feel nearly as remote as it does now, and many of us Brits had been through the Blitz. So we still carried a dislike of the German race as a whole, and any time we could get one of them, we did. And the expressions on the faces of paddock visitors when they heard those words were priceless.

The Taylor & Crawley Lotus 15 Climax cars were in the 2-liter sports category and no Lotus had ever won an international sports-car race, although many had led them. We had four drivers: Doug Graham shared one car with Keith Greene, and Mike Taylor shared the other with Christopher Martyn. There were only four of us mechanics to do the lap timing, the lap chart, the refueling, and the pit work—a very low-budget operation compared with our competitors at Porsche. The organizers provided the refueling rigs, which were 55-gallon fuel drums, placed on the roof of the pits with the hoses hanging down. The teams had to provide their own fire extinguishers.

In those days, the Nürburgring was fourteen and a half bumpy miles long, with about 145 discernible turns—a tough track to learn. Most drivers took private cars or rental cars, paid a fee of a single Deutschmark per lap, and flogged around it for a week or so before the race weekend. A driver new to the Nürburgring could easily improve his lap times by 20 seconds just during a practice session.

There was a loop of track that started at the pit exit, went around the 180-degree South Turn, and allowed you to return to the pits through a "back door" entrance. This enabled you to sort out the car a little without going all the way round the track. When they did go for a timed lap, they went round the loop and then through the back door to go over the start-finish line to start the timing. At the end of the lap, they flew over the finish line to get their time recorded, rounded the loop, and came in the back door. Without the loop, each car would have had to do three very long laps just to record one.

But what we mechanics liked about the Nürburgring was that because it took up to 10 minutes for a car to go round the track, we had enough time to sneak away for a smoke. The drawback of the place was that it could be sunny at the start-finish line and raining like crazy over on the Adenau side of the track, and there was no way to know until the car came into the pits. There was no radio communication with the driver at that time, of course, so you just had to wait it all out—a bit nerve-wracking all around.

Fifty-eight cars practiced, and 55 started the race. Our cars qualified fairly well with Keith Greene leading the way, and we were excited about the possibility of winning the 2-liter class. Britt had insisted on changing the Lotus transaxle because it was so unreliable, and we were using the MG gearbox instead. Nevertheless, we did have a broken gearbox during practice, so we told the drivers not to do any racing downshifts from fourth to third because they were too hard on the gears. This was a weakness of the MG gearbox.

There were so many of my heroes driving that weekend, I felt lucky to see them all in one race and privileged to be playing even a small part in it all. Stirling Moss was fastest in practice with the Camoradi team's "Birdcage" Maserati—and his co-driver Dan Gurney was no slouch, either. Masten Gregory and Gino Munaron were in the team's other Tipo 61 Maserati. Ferrari had entries in both the over and under 2-liter classes. In the big Testa Rossas, Phil Hill was paired with Wolfgang "Taffy" von Trips, and Willy Mairesse was with former Team Lotus driver Cliff Allison. Richie Ginther was sharing a Dino 246S with Ludovico Scarfiotti, and in 2-liter Dino 196S cars were the Rodriguez brothers, Ricardo and Pedro, and Giorgio Scarlatti was with Giulio Cabianca. Other notable entries included young Formula One driver Jim Clark, who was paired with Roy Salvadori in the Border Reivers Aston Martin DBR1, and Lola boss Eric Broadley, who was driving his 1150cc Lola Mk 1 Climax with David McNab. The Porsche team was also at full strength with the manager, Huschke von Hanstein, yelling at the mechanics. The Germans really wanted to win their home race. I actually saw him strike a mechanic, and I remember thinking, "Who would want to work for that maniac?" It seemed that half the cars in the race were Porsches of one type or another.

When the race started, we had no action until the first refueling stop. Our pit was sandwiched between two of Ferrari's, with the Rodriguez car on our right and the Scarlatti car on our left. I was standing at our pit counter waiting for Doug Graham to come in for our first stop, when both the 2-liter Dinos came in to refuel.

BELOW: Doug Graham, one of the four Taylor & Crawley team drivers, in his Lotus 15 at the 'Ring in 1960. (LAT Photographic)

The organizers only permitted two mechanics and one driver over the wall and working on the car. Ferrari's system was to have the driver who was taking over do the refueling while the mechanics checked or changed the tires and topped up the oil and the incoming driver got out. The pit stop to our left began first, and we were watching that. Scarlatti switched off the engine and started to get out, Cabianca grabbed the fuel hose, and the mechanics checked the oil. Before Cabianca pulled out the fill hose, fuel had already spilled down the outside of the body and onto the hot exhaust pipe. I watched helplessly as flame ran up the vapor to the fill gun and suddenly the whole fill neck and hose erupted into flames with a loud *whump*!

Cabianca dropped the hose and turned towards the pit with his hand and arm on fire. Now the car and the hose up to the tank were burning, and so was the vented 55-gallon drum on the roof. A couple of small explosions came from the fire. It seemed like hours before the German firemen trundled up their ancient firefighting trolley. Meanwhile, the Dino was burning to the ground. On our right, I saw Ricardo Rodriguez literally pick up Pedro and throw him into the cockpit of the other Dino. Pedro was gone in a flash.

We were looking out for our car, but we couldn't see because of the black smoke from the burning Ferrari. I remember Britt saying that if the fire spread to all the full fuel drums on the roof, there would be nothing anyone could do and nowhere for us to go. I was really scared.

Suddenly our car appeared in front of our pit. The Ferrari was still burning a little but we jumped down, fueled the car, changed the drivers, and sent it on its way. The organizers should have stopped the race to put out the fires but, for some reason known only to them, they let the Dino burn out.

There was a giant grandstand building opposite the pits, and part of it was the "Sport Hotel"—it was very upper class, far too expensive for mere mortals like us mechanics. The press liked to congregate there because they had a great view of the pits. Jesse Alexander, the great American photographer, was in the grandstand that day and captured the big fire for posterity.

Amid all this chaos, we lost track of our other car and wondered what had happened to it. Keith was faster than Doug and had been in front of him. After about 20 minutes, just as the fire went out and the burnt-out Ferrari was dragged away, Keith finally appeared. The wire had somehow come out of the coil, but he had found the problem and repaired it himself.

That track really beat the crap out of the cars. It was old, the surface needed repairs in places, and there were also places like the Flugplatz, where the cars took off over a bump at high speed. The 1000-kilometer race was a real test of endurance for both the car and the drivers. We had put a small tool kit—pliers, a screwdriver, and some tape—into each car for just this sort of thing. Keith knew what to do, and the car continued in the race.

We didn't win our class but both our cars were there at the end—the first time any Lotus 15 had finished a long-distance sports-car race. Keith and Doug finished 18th, third in the 2-liter class behind two works Porsche 718s, which actually finished second and fourth overall driven by Jo Bonnier/Olivier Gendebien and Hans Herrmann/Maurice Trintignant. Mike and Chris were classified 27th, fourth in class. The race was won overall by Moss and Gurney, and the best Testa Rossa, with Phil Hill co-driving Allison and Mairesse, was third.

What a race it had been! We were totally exhausted by the end. It had had every element of drama of a Hollywood film, including one period of heavy rain. That night we mechanics lifted a few steins to ourselves at the Eifelhof hotel and fell into bed. The drivers were all staying somewhere else—once the race was over, we never saw hide nor hair of them.

The next day we loaded up the cars on the bus, and Britt and Mo took off for Monaco, towing the Lotus F1 car on a trailer. All that was left was for Mahogany Boots and me to get the bus back to England. That turned out to be as much as an adventure as the race had been.

The Nürburgring is in the Eifel Mountains, and you have to go over a couple of them to get to and from it. We said our goodbyes to the doorman at the Eifelhof, and he replied with a hearty, "Gut fahrt!"—meaning "good drive." Any time a German says *gut fahrt* to a Brit is a time for a smile. We smiled, and I drove off.

We didn't make very good speed up the mountain road towards Blankenburg and, as we came down the other side considerably faster, things started to happen. I had the brakes on almost continuously because I needed them to keep the bus under control, even in second gear. My first warning of impending doom was frantic banging on the bulkhead behind my back from Mahogany Boots. The bus was filling up with choking smoke. I looked in the wing mirrors. To my horror, I saw the left rear wheel arch on fire!

We jumped out and I saw a little stream running alongside the road. There seemed to be a sort of well sunk into the ground in front of a small cottage, and the stream was running into it. A closer inspection showed that someone had put a 55-gallon barrel into the ground to act as a catch basin for the water.

Mahogany and I ran back to the bus, grabbed a bucket each, and ran to fill them from the well. I pushed mine under the water, and Mahogany pushed his past mine—and let it sink. I ran back to the bus and threw my water over the fire, expecting Mahogany to be right with me. But he was nowhere in sight. I ran back to the well to refill my bucket.

Just as I got to the well, Mahogany surfaced from beneath the water! It turned out there were three 55-gallon drums with the ends removed to deepen the well. Mahogany had jumped in to retrieve his bucket, and had sunk several feet before he hit the bottom and could push himself up again. I told him not to go swimming while we were working. I laughed all the way back to the bus.

It took several trips by both of us to finally put out the fire. Turned out the outside tire had gone flat and caught fire from the overheated brakes, and that had set fire to the wooden frame of the wheel arch. If the fire had spread, we could have lost three cars and the bus.

After we had calmed down, we put the spare wheel on the bus but noticed that the inner wheel and tire of the dual rear wheels were severely damaged. I counted my money, and Mahogany counted his. Between us, we barely had enough for the fuel we needed to get home. In those days, credit cards were nonexistent. It was going to be a very long trip. I figured we had to stay well below 30 mph to avoid tire problems, and we set out again.

We eventually got to the Jabbeke Highway that ran from Brussels to Ostende on the Belgian coast and were cruising along at about 30 mph when a loud bang woke up Mahogany, and he was banging on the bulkhead again. We had two flat tires on the right rear. We put the bus on jack stands and sawed off both tires with a hacksaw. We took off the outer left rear, put it on the outer right rear, and used the two empty rims as spacers. It took three hours to get rolling again. It was now a four-wheeled bus, and we were down to about 8 mph, maximum.

We crept exhausted into the port of Ostende at about 4:00 a.m. I parked the bus outside an all-night café and went in for some coffee and a large cognac. Mahogany went to sleep in the bus. Some guy decided to see what he could steal from the bus. He sneaked up to the side door and slid it open. Mahogany was 6 feet, 2 inches tall and now looked like a madman, with a dirty face and clothes, dark rings around his eyes, and wild hair. The guy screamed at the sight of him and ran down the road.

When the boat got to Dover, we drove off as slowly as we could, but as we started up the London road at 8 mph, the right front tire blew. It scared the crap out of me because it was just under my ass.

That was it! I could take no more! I was exhausted, both physically and mentally. I found a phone box and called the Mercedes dealership, but only the morning cleaning staff were there. I asked the cleaning lady to take down a message for the senior Mr. Taylor (Mike was in Monaco). My message said, "We've had to park the bus in a lay-by on the side of the Dover-London road about 10 miles from the port. It's all locked up. We have no money, and the bus has a blown right front tire and two blown rear tires. It is standing on three wheels. The keys are hidden on a ledge just in front of the left rear tire well. We're going to hitch a ride home, so please have your people take care of the bus." We hitched a lift the 75 miles to London on a Guinness delivery truck that had been on the ferry with us.

I went to Berkeley Square on Thursday morning to see Mr. Taylor, Sr. He made me wait an hour and then called me into his office. He started to give me a major ass-reaming for leaving the bus with all that valuable stuff in it. He accused me of driving the bus so fast that I blew all the tires. It was obvious this was not going well, and I was getting pretty angry myself. I told him I was not going to listen to any more of his abuse and would take it up with Mike. It was Mike who had hired me, not him. I left and went home.

Mike failed to qualify for the Monaco Grand Prix and came back early. I told him what had happened, and he said he understood what we'd been through. Mike apologized for his father's behavior and asked me to come back to work to help get the F1 car ready for the Belgian Grand Prix. He offered to pay me a bonus and give me a raise after Spa.

I never saw Mahogany Boots Malone again, although he paid just one more surreptitious visit to the workshop at Beaconsfield. When I got to work the following Monday, the only trace of him was a chalk circle around his shoes with the wood inside and a hole right through the wood. It was his way of saying goodbye, I guess. He was a likeable, hardworking kid. I bet he still talks about his time as a racing mechanic at the Nürburgring—and his swim on the way home.

When Britt and Mo returned from Monaco, we got Mike's Lotus 18 ready for the Belgian Grand Prix at Spa, in the Ardennes. That race ranks as one of the most disastrous in Formula One history.

In Friday practice, Stirling Moss crashed, and Mike stopped to see if he could help. Someone told him to get back to the pits and have an ambulance sent out to get Stirling. On his way back, Mike crashed when his steering column sheared at speed and he flew off

LEFT: The Cooper Car Company presents its cars in 1960. From left to right are the Cooper Monaco, the Cooper T47 F2 car, the Formula 500cc race car, and world champion Jack Brabham's F1 car. Note the gas pumps outside. Not many petrol stations built championship-winning Formula One cars. (Cooper Car Company Publicity)

the track and hit a tree. He broke his back when he was thrown out of the car. It turned out that, when Lotus had owned the car, somebody had shortened the steering column. They had cut it into two pieces halfway down, welded it back together, smoothed off the surplus weld bead, and zinc-plated it. The weakened weld failed at Spa.

Britt Pierce never did like Colin Chapman very much, because he said he tended to sacrifice speed for safety and make components that were too light and/or too weak. Britt had previously worked for Innes Ireland, who had several suspension parts and even magnesium wheels fail when he drove his works-supported Lotus 11 sports car. As a result, he had crashed and suffered injury a few times. The sight of Britt chasing Chapman down the pit-lane, brandishing the broken steering column, will live in my memory forever. Luckily for Chapman, Britt wasn't much of an athlete.

The race resulted in a 1-2 for the latest Coopers, driven by Jack Brabham and Bruce McLaren, but sadly that is not why it is remembered. On the 17th lap, British Racing Partnership driver Chris Bristow lost control of his Cooper Climax while dicing for sixth place with Willy Mairesse in a Ferrari. Bristow crashed and was thrown out of the car and killed. A few laps later, my old pal from Team Lotus, Alan Stacey, was killed by a bird when it hit him in the face as he drove through the wooded hillsides. He was also thrown out of the car.

That was just about the end of the Taylor & Crawley racing team. Mike eventually recovered from his injuries but, to my knowledge, never raced again. He sued Colin Chapman over the component failure, and there was an out-of-court settlement for £25,000—a lot of money for those days. It was the first time that an English race-car manufacturer had been sued.

BELOW: When Mike Taylor stopped racing halfway through the 1960 season, I moved to the H & L Motors F2 team. Here is driver Jackie Lewis at speed in his F2 Cooper-Climax at Snetterton. (Peter Bryant)

CHAPTER 7

My First Jackie

"Haven zee zum boxen, bitter?"

I worked with three racing drivers named "Jackie" during my career in auto racing. The first was Jackie Lewis, the second was Jackie Stewart, and the third was Jackie Oliver, who came into my life later on. This story is about my time with Jackie Lewis. The words were those of his father.

After Mike Taylor had so suddenly stopped racing halfway through the 1960 season, I packed my tools and luckily, thanks again to an advertisement in *Autosport*, quickly found an opening in Stroud, Gloucestershire, with the H&L Motors team and its up-and-coming Formula 2 driver, Jackie Lewis. His father, who was the largest Triumph motorcycle dealer in the west of England owned the team, and his race shop was a garage behind his stately looking house in the village. They had "lost" their mechanic for unspoken reasons midway through the Formula 2 season. The job meant being away from home more, but I needed the experience if I was ever to get into a decent Formula One team.

ABOVE: A youthful-looking Jackie Lewis sits in his F2 Cooper at the Pau, France, F2 race in May 1960. (LAT Photographic)

Those strange words were concocted by Mr. Lewis Sr. to use at various shops in Adenau, Germany, near the Nürburgring. Mr. Lewis volunteered to go into town and get some empty boxes for me. He had invented a very simple formula for "speaking' German—just take each word in English and add the letters "E" or "N" on the end. He said it might be wrong, but it worked most of the time. I was about to perform "open-heart surgery" on three four-cylinder, 1.5-liter Coventry Climax Formula 2 racing engines, and I needed the boxes to keep all the parts separated after I had disassembled them.

One engine belonged in our Cooper and another belonged in a Cooper owned by Count Carel Godin de Beaufort. Only a week before, during the Grosser Preis der Solitude, Jackie's engine had run its main bearings when an oil pump failed, and the block was ruined.

I liked "Carel," as Count de Beaufort preferred to be called. He was the son of a genuine Dutch aristocrat and lived in Holland in a real castle, called Maarsbergen. Carel was a very unlikely looking race-car driver because he was about 6 feet, 4 inches tall and rather portly, but he loved racing. He drove a big American Cadillac because it was the only road car he felt comfortable in. All his race cars had to have special seats, but he still had to sit in a very upright position to make room for his legs, so he stuck out the top of the cockpit. At dinner one evening in Adenau, he told me how he had got his parents to pay for his very first race car. He had waited until one evening when they were sitting in the garden with their cocktails. He went up onto the battlements of the castle, climbed out onto a parapet and yelled, "Father, I am so unhappy that I want to throw myself down and kill myself! I want to be a racing driver but you won't let me, so I'm going to end my life!" His father panicked and promised to do anything if only he wouldn't jump. So he bought Carel a Porsche.

Anyway, the Count had graciously arranged for us to borrow a third engine for spare parts, and in return, I was to rebuild his engine and tune it up. This third engine was out of a car that belonged to Wolfgang von Trips, who was entered to drive a works Porsche in this race. It needed a new cylinder head, a new piston, and God knows what else to make it good again, but for now, we only needed the cylinder block from it. We had no other source at such short notice and had agreed to take the engine back to Coventry Climax when we got back to England, and have it overhauled for Trips at Mr. Lewis's expense.

It was a bit doubtful whether all the operations could succeed. There was a serious complication with a warped Climax aluminum cylinder head because, if you tried to resurface the face, the clearance between the gears on the overhead cams and the corresponding block gear could become too small and jam the gears together. The answer I came up with was to make up some fine wire "rings" and lay them in the crease in the head gasket that compresses to seal the head around each cylinder. The idea was that when I tightened the cylinder head nuts, the wire would compress to the shape of the head. The first time I did this, the water leaked out between the head and the block because the paper water-sealing gasket needed to be thicker. So I doubled up on the gasket, and amazingly, it worked. I was chuffed about that! I used the crankcase from the Trips engine to rebuild ours.

Luckily for me, Aussie mechanic Tim Wall was in the Nürburgring garage next to ours, tearing down the engine of a Cooper-Climax for his boss, Jack Brabham. Tim carried lots of engine spares and agreed to loan me some gaskets. I promised to replace them as soon as I got back to England. The Nürburgring garages were part of the permanent *Fahrerlager*, or paddock area, of the famous track but were completely bare when we moved in. Without even a workbench to use, we learned quickly that the name of the game was improvisation. I took the loading ramps out of our single-car transporter and set them up on the spare racing wheels to use as a work surface. We had a vise that clamped onto the side of the transporter.

After a couple of very long days and late nights, the two engines were back in the cars and ready for the practice sessions. That year, the Formula 2 race on the Nürburgring Sudschliefe was given the title Grosser Preis von Deutschland. I reckoned that the Automobile Club von Deutschland, the organizing body, did it so that a German car could be the Grand Prix winner. Porsche hadn't yet entered Formula One because they didn't have a 2.5-liter engine at that time, but they did have a very quick Formula 2 car. It was not unusual for race organizers to stack the deck in favor of their fellow countrymen.

We had some really stiff opposition. Porsche had four of the latest 718 cars with Jo Bonnier, Wolfgang von Trips, Graham Hill, and Edgar Barth driving, and there was a private 718 entered for Hans Herrmann. Cooper Car Company had Jack Brabham and Bruce McLaren, and Team Lotus had Innes Ireland and Jim Clark. Dan Gurney was in Louise Blyden Brown's private Lotus 18. Gurney's mechanic, "Lofty," was a real friendly guy with a hook for one of his hands after he had bailed out of a burning bomber in World War II. He was not familiar with the foibles of the Lotus 18, but I was so I was able to help him out a little. Finally there were several private Coopers, to be driven by men like Maurice Trintignant, Lucien Bianchi, Olivier Gendebien, Jo Schlesser, Masten Gregory, Henry Taylor, Tony Marsh, and George Lawton, the New Zealand champion.

It rained for most of practice, and that was a distinct advantage for the factory Porsche team, which had Continental's new, "high-hysteresis" rain tires. Jackie paddled the H&L Cooper T45 round carefully on the soaked South Circuit on his Dunlops to 11th place on the grid, immediately behind Gurney's Lotus.

At the appointed time on race day, it was still raining when the drivers drove up through the curving tunnel from the *Fahrerlager* to the starting grid. But the start was delayed because there was a river running across the track at one point, and it had to be diverted. The organizers didn't announce how long the delay would be, so we all stood out in the rain and waited—except the Porsche team. They seemed to have a direct line to the officials and covered their cars with tarpaulins while their drivers went and sat in the pits. We turned off our engine, and Jackie sat in the car under an umbrella. After what seemed an eternity, the rain eased up a little, and Porsche pulled off their tarps. Just as the drivers were getting into their cars, they showed the five-minute board.

Everyone hurried to push-start the cars—the preferred method in those days. Unfortunately, Jackie had forgotten to switch off the electric fuel pump, and our engine was absolutely flooded with gasoline. There was no time to change the plugs. It meant pushing his car a long way down the hill towards the start-finish line, then pushing it back up to its grid position. Mr. Lewis and I started to push it, and Jackie tried to "bump" it, but it wouldn't start. Lofty started Gurney's Lotus and then ran over to help me because Mr. Lewis had conked out, totally out of wind. Lofty shouted, "If they drop the flag, don't push it over the start line, you'll be disqualified." The engine fired just as we got to the start line and then—horror of horrors!—the starter dropped his flag with us still pushing. As Jackie took off, there were cars whizzing all around us. It scared the daylights out of both Lofty and me.

I went back to our pit to watch the race. The South Circuit at the Nürburgring was only 3.2 miles long, and pretty soon the cars swept by in a frenzy of spray and noise. As I watched Jackie come past, an official furiously waved a black flag at him.

I looked at Mr. Lewis. His face was bright red. He told me to run up to the starter and see what it was all about. I ran to a little office at the start-finish line where the officials were all gathered. I saw the official with the black flag still in his hand and asked him why our car was black-flagged. He said, "Outside assistance! You pushed your car across the start line after the race had started. It's disqualified!"

After all the work I had put in to get us into this damn race, I was really angry. I demanded to know, "Why did you start the race with mechanics still on the grid? We could have been seriously injured! On top of that, how do you know we crossed the line? The rain was so heavy, you couldn't even see where it was! This is very wrong. We'll protest to the FIA about it. I want your name and everyone's name who took part in this debacle." He pushed me out of the door, saying, "Get out of here! You're disqualified—there's nothing more to say!"

Despondent, I walked back to the pits just as Jackie came in. "What a load of twaddle," said Mr. Lewis. "All I can say is, they had better pay us our starting money!" He helped me push the car back to the entrance of the little tunnel that wound down to the garages. I faced the car down the slope and got in to steer it as it rolled down and round the bend into the garage area. Our garage was the second one from the tunnel. I pushed in the car, came back out, rolled down the door, and started walking back to fetch my tools from the pits. I had gone about 10 yards when I felt a heavy blow on the back of my head, near my neck. I went down in great pain and temporarily blacked out. As I came to, a hand grabbed me by the back of my overalls and pushed me back down the tunnel. It was a security guard. I looked round, and there were two of them, in dark green uniforms with jodhpur-like pants and jackboots. One of them had a gun in his hand. They looked like officers of the German army in World War II. I was shocked and amazed—apparently I had been pistol-whipped.

"What the hell was that for?" I asked one of the police. He pointed to a wet string around my bicep and shouted something at me. I realized what he was saying. We had all been issued cardboard armbands and the rain had all but destroyed all trace of mine. I hadn't even noticed. I was incensed. I yelled in his face, "You fucking stupid Nazi bastard! The rain has washed it away! I'm wearing racing coveralls! I've walked past you 50 times in the last week, and you know who I am! I'm going to have you arrested for attacking me!" I tried to make a mental note of his face and staggered back to the garage to wait for Mr. Lewis. My neck was very painful, and my head was throbbing. I could feel a lump coming up.

ABOVE: Much to everyone's surprise, Jackie Lewis was the fastest qualifier at Pau, but he had engine problems during the race. Here he is seen after being passed by Jack Brabham, Maurice Trintignant, and Olivier Gendebien. (LAT Photographic)

In a few moments, Mr. Lewis and Jackie and his fiancée, Andrea, arrived, carrying the signaling board and watches and so on. I told them what had just happened and Mr. Lewis became very angry. "I'll take care of this," he said, and with Jackie behind him, he took off up the tunnel. He went to the office at the start-finish line and demanded to see Herr Schmidt of the Automobilclub von Deutschland, the man in charge of the race, with whom he had negotiated our starting money. He told him about the attack and insisted that Schmidt go with him immediately to have the guard arrested. Schmidt was very surprised, and they came down to the garage with both the guards and a senior officer. Herr Schmidt asked me for my account of the incident. There was a lot of German spoken and a little English, and then the policemen all left together. Schmidt then apologized to me for the incident and offered to have someone take me to the medical center for treatment. He then said he had to get back to the race, but asked Mr. Lewis to bring me to the prize-giving at the Sport Hotel that evening so we could all discuss this further. In those days, mechanics were rarely invited to those functions. Mr. Lewis agreed, and we all went back to our small hotel.

We changed and had dinner together before going to the Sport Hotel. There was a special table reserved for us near where Schmidt was sitting. We were served champagne and watched the trophies being given out—why Schmidt thought we would enjoy that was beyond my comprehension. The race had been won from pole position by Jo Bonnier ahead of Trips, Brabham, Hill, Herrmann, and Barth—all except Jack in the Porsches with the "trick" tires. The best-placed Lotus drivers, Ireland and Gurney, were lapped. Brabham must have driven his backside off in his Cooper.

OPPOSITE: The 718 Porsche in the *Fahrerlager* garage area at the 1960 GP for F2 cars. In the background are jackbooted policemen like the ones who attacked me. (Jesse Alexander)

Carel de Beaufort drove sensibly and finished in 14th position with the engine I had built for him purring away nicely. He was delighted and thanked me profusely. He said he was very sad to hear about our disqualification and said it had not been fair at all. Clearly the word had spread and a lot of drivers came by our table to commiserate with Jackie and Mr. Lewis, including Wolfgang von Trips.

When it was nearly over, Schmidt came and sat with us "for a chat," as he put it. He gave Mr. Lewis an envelope with our starting money in it and said how regrettable it had all been, but rules were rules and exceptions were never allowed. He hoped I had fully recovered from the "regrettable incident." Then he smiled at Mr. Lewis and said, "We're organizing another race at the Avus circuit in Berlin and we would like to invite your excellent team to come." Mr. Lewis looked straight at me and asked, "What do you think, Peter, shall we go to the Avus?" I looked at Jackie. He smiled and slowly shook his head. So I said straight to Schmidt, "Herr Schmidt, I don't think we have any interest at this time to race in Germany again this year." We loaded up and, after our three-week stay in Germany, left the next morning.

The race the week before on the 7-mile Solitude track, near Stuttgart, had not been without drama, either. It had been a bit of a disaster for Porsche because Trips had won it with a works Ferrari 156 Dino, with Porsches in the next three positions. Luckily for them,

DUNLOP
REIFEN
zu Ihrer Sicherheit
19
Haftung
nicht übernommen.
9

Ferrari didn't show up for the Nürburgring race, although they had entered.

It was also a disaster for us, of course, because our engine had blown after Jackie had qualified in sixth position, solidly among the works Porsches. So the thing I remember most about Solitude was seeing John Surtees come screaming all alone down the hill on the first lap of the motorcycle race, only to lose it at the greasy hairpin bend. He fell off sideways and slid onto the grass. He was so far in front of everyone else that he had time to check himself out, get back on his MV Agusta, restart it, and go on up the hill without losing a place. He then drove a Porsche 718 in the F2 race. I think it was the only time in his life that he raced both a car and a motorcycle on the same day. I was very impressed by his versatility.

The other bit of excitement was after we left the Hotel Koenig in Stuttgart to go to the track on race day. Our Ford transporter had only a cab with a flatbed platform on the back, a flat panel over the top, and canvas curtains that dropped down each side to keep the car clean. It kind of looked like an English milk delivery van, so I called it the milk float. The neat part about it was that the engine had been tweaked, and it could do nearly 100 mph. Mr. and Mrs. Lewis had their car, and Jackie and Andrea had a little Ford van that was used to chase parts. We usually drove to the races in that order on the road. That morning, we tried to slip into the circuit where we had before and just drive around it to the pits. But the circuit was closed, which meant that we had to go back out of Stuttgart and go along the *autobahn* to get to the track—a 25-mile trip, and we were short on time. Mr. Lewis was leading the way, but we were all stuck behind everything creeping along in the slow lane. I figured we would miss the race at that rate, so I pulled to the inside and started up the hard shoulder, blowing the horn to simulate the *parp-parp-parp* of a police car. It worked! Soon we were doing 60 mph on the inside shoulder. When the other motorists saw what we were doing, they quickly got behind Jackie, and soon we had opened a whole new lane on the two-lane *autobahn*. It was great fun. We made it to the paddock with half an hour to spare.

We did a couple more F2 races that year, and our best result was in the Paris Salon race on the historic, banked Montlhéry track. It was raining the whole race, and Jackie won after a great dice with Lucien Bianchi and Jo Schlesser, both in Coopers. Our touring manager was Gérard "Jabby" Crombac, whose Lotus 11 I had worked on at Chapman's behest in 1958. Crombac had arranged our entry and took us all to the famous Lido nightclub for dinner after the race. I had planned to leave for England and the last F2 race of the season at Brands Hatch the next morning, but after dinner, Jabby asked me to stay for a minute.

Jabby invited a friend of his to join us. His name was Jean-Claude Thiery, and he was the speedboat champion of France. There was a six-hour race coming up in two weeks, and his boat had an 1100cc Climax engine. Apparently there was no one in Paris who could tune it. Jean-Claude said that if I would stay and tune his boat engine, he would see I was well taken care of and put me up in his home. Jabby spoke to Mr. Lewis, who agreed, so I moved our rig to Jean-Claude's garage. He lived in a beautiful apartment on the fashionable rue Victor Hugo.

I grabbed my tool box and a set of plugs, and we went down to the river Seine where the boat was moored. It was a small, skiff-type thing. I changed the plugs and adjusted the valves to the correct tappet clearance—they were way off. Then I dismantled the SU carburetors, cleaned them, and set them up to standard specifications. We changed the oil and filter. That left one last chore—to set the correct distributor setting for spark advance. There was only one way to do it properly, and that was the method we used on the dyno at Coventry Climax. You start the engine, bring it up to maximum torque rpm, and "swing" (rotate) it slightly to reach peak torque reading, then lock it down with the retaining clamp. Only one problem: we were on a boat on the river Seine, not in a dynamometer cell.

So we did the next best thing. Jean-Claude untied the boat, I loosened off the distributor clamp a little so that I could just about rotate it, and he steered out onto the river. I was hanging over the back of the engine as he brought it up to about 4600 rpm. The boat was now leaping up and down over the water at high speed. At times, I was a foot in the air and only my grip on the engine was holding me in the boat. I slowly moved the distributor, and he told me when he saw peak rpm. Then I locked the clamp down, and he shut off the throttle. I hadn't been that scared since the Blitz in World War II. I thought we would surely crash and burn.

Actually it was total madness to try that on a crowded river Seine, but Jean-Claude had no fear at all. I found out later that the reason he raced boats was because he had lost an eye in a car crash in an Alfa Romeo and could not pass the physical to drive race cars. I was glad I had not known when I had been hanging for dear life onto the back of his boat.

Jean-Claude was so delighted with the performance of the boat that he gave me a giant bonus that equaled a month's pay. We went back to his place to change clothes, and he took me out to an exclusive French restaurant where we had a delicious *steak chasseur* and champagne. I left the next morning and drove back to Stroud. I later found out that I had eaten horsemeat for dinner that night. My mother used to feed us horsemeat during the food rationing in World War II, but it had never tasted like that.

Two weeks later, Jean-Claude won the famous Paris Six-Hour boat race. I was sorry to have missed it, but I was back in Stroud. Sally and I still lived in our flat in London, but I was staying in boarding houses in Stroud during weekdays when I was not on the road. Mr. Lewis loaned me motorcycles or scooters for transport, but the trips home on free weekends were sometimes a bit hazardous. Once I was riding a BSA, and the gas tank split as I was doing about 50 mph up a country road. I felt something hot on my legs and looked down. The gasoline had caught fire, the whole engine was burning, and so was the crotch of my pants. There was a stream running alongside the road and I had no choice but to run the bike off the road and straight into the bed of the stream and lay it down. I was just in time, and I only had some blisters on my legs.

On another occasion, Mr. Lewis loaned me an Italian Vespa scooter. I was going about 50 mph on the wet Oxford road when it ran out of petrol. When two-stroke engines run out of petrol, they also run out of oil because it's added to the petrol to lubricate the inner workings of the engine. So the engine seized and the rear wheel locked, putting me into a long, wild-assed skid. I was screaming in my helmet as I threw out the clutch and coasted to a stop. After that, I insisted on using the parts van or I said I couldn't work there, and Mr. Lewis agreed.

My last race with H&L Motors was the Stuart Lewis-Evans Trophy race at Brands Hatch, counting towards the *Autocar* Formula 2 championship. If Jackie did well, he could overhaul Jack Brabham, the reigning World Champion, and take the title. We went early to Brands Hatch to do some testing. I was working on the engine afterwards when I noticed that two men were watching me. They looked on intently as I checked the valve clearances, waited politely until I was finished, and then introduced themselves. They were Jimmy Potton and Gerry Svenson, two race mechanics who had just left the 1959 Le Mans–winning Aston Martin sports-car team to work for a new Formula One team being put together by the former Aston Martin team manager, Reg Parnell. They were there to recruit mechanics for the new team, which would be sponsored by Yeoman Credit, a leading financial house associated with the Credit Suisse corporation.

They told me that Harry Spears, the manager at Coventry Climax engines, had suggested they talk to me, because they had no one who could rebuild Coventry Climax engines and they were going to run new Cooper-Climax cars in 1961. Would I be interested in working on the team? I asked who the drivers were going to be, and they said they would tell me in confidence, because the press didn't know yet. They were to be John Surtees and Roy Salvadori.

I was overjoyed by the offer—but the best part was yet to come. They called up Reg Parnell on the telephone and put him on. Parnell had a rasping northern English accent and he said that if I wanted, I could start right after the F2 season was over. He would pay me £1100 a year and, with the other mechanics, I would receive an equal share of 10 percent of any prize money. At that time, Innes Ireland only made £1200 a year as a Team Lotus F1 driver!

I was also to be paid a traveling allowance of £10 a day, and accommodation would be found within that budget by Gillian Harris, who had been Parnell's secretary at Aston Martin. She spoke fluent French and was an amazing woman. She made all the arrangements for everyone and traveled with the team. She could time every car in practice with just two watches and keep an accurate lap chart of every car on every lap. Parnell said I should count on starting no later than November 1, 1960. I readily agreed and, with his phone number in my pocket, went back to work on the car.

Jackie finished second in the race to Tony Marsh's Lotus and clinched the *Autocar* F2 championship for 1960. After the race, Mr. Lewis Sr. said he would like to take my wife and me to dinner in London during the following week and had some new plans to discuss with me. He said I could take some time off after I had returned the car to Stroud. I did go to dinner with them, but I broke the news that I was leaving to go F1 racing with Parnell. Mr. Lewis said he was also going into F1 and was thinking of ordering a new BRM for Jackie to drive. I told him that the only reason I had to leave was because we lived with Sally's invalid mother and living part-time in Stroud didn't work for us. I could get to Reg Parnell's shop in Hounslow by Tube train every day. It was just better all round for me. I sincerely apologized and told him I would have loved to work on a new BRM. He was very nice, and we parted on the best of terms.

I was excited about working for the legendary Reg Parnell, but I was thinking what it would mean to leave a team in which I was my own boss and chief mechanic. But I could not possibly have turned down the best job offer I had ever had. 1961 promised to be exciting.

November 6, 1960. Fellow mechanic Jimmy Potton and I board the Pan Am flight to New York, the first leg of our trip to New Zealand. I was thrilled that Reg Parnell had hired me as part of his Yeoman Credit Formula One team. My experience with Cooper and Lotus cars and the Climax engine had stood me in good stead. (Peter Bryant

CHAPTER 8

An Interlude Down Under

I quickly found out why Reg Parnell needed me to start my new job "as soon as possible."

When Aston Martin quit racing at the end of 1960, some of the mechanics went with Parnell when he created his new Yeoman Credit Formula One team. Although they were very experienced racing mechanics, they had no experience with Cooper or Lotus chassis, nor with Coventry Climax engines. That was where I came in.

Parnell had bought three 2.5-liter Formula One cars that had been owned by the Yeoman Credit team previously run by Ken Gregory's British Racing Partnership. There were two Cooper T51s and a Lotus 18. After the United States Grand Prix at Riverside, California, in the fall of 1960, they were loaded on a ship bound for New Zealand. There Parnell had entered four races, which would later form part of the Tasman Series. One of the Coopers was to be raced by Joachim Bonnier, the former Porsche and BRM driver, and the Lotus by Roy Salvadori. The engine of the Lotus had been removed after the U.S. Grand Prix and sent back to Coventry Climax for a rebuild. The other Cooper was to be loaned to young Denis Hulme, the newly crowned New Zealand champion. The drive was part of his prize, but he would have to run the car himself.

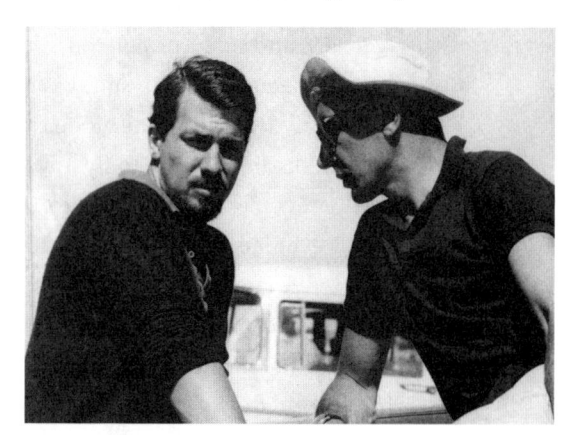

ABOVE: Jo Bonnier (left) would drive one of the Yeoman Credit Coopers, and Roy Salvadori would drive the Lotus. It was exciting to now be working with top-line drivers. (LAT Photographic)

The plan was that Jimmy Potton and I would fly to New Zealand to prepare those cars while the other mechanics began preparing the team's new Cooper T53s for the 1961 World

Championship. John King, who had been the chief mechanic at Aston Martin, was the new team's chief mechanic and he would start preparing some new 1.5-liter, four-cylinder Coventry Climax engines for the new F1 cars.

The FIA had changed the maximum Formula One engine swept volume from 2.5 liters to 1.5 liters for the 1961 season, and it had caused all kinds of repercussions with the teams. They had a fortune tied up in engines that were soon going to be extinct, so they didn't take the FIA's decision lying down. They talked some event promoters into running a new series of races for what they called the Intercontinental Formula, for cars with 2500cc engines. In other words, they kept the old F1 cars active in defiance of the FIA and its new rules. There would be five Intercontinental races, and the new Parnell team was going to race in both classes. It promised to be a busy year.

In 1960, Pan Am World Airways started using the new Boeing 707 jet for flights from the United Kingdom to the United States. McDonnell Douglas then brought out their rival DC8 and sold a bunch to United Airlines. The term "jet-setter" was coined, and I was about to become one myself. I had never flown before and was excited by the prospect of flying halfway around the globe from England to New Zealand. From London's Heathrow Airport, it's impossible to fly any further than the 14,000 miles or so to Christchurch—if you do it, you're only flying back the other way!

In December 1960, shortly before the trip, something happened to cool my enthusiasm. A United Airlines DC8 collided with a TWA Constellation over New York City, killing 134 people. I badly needed to create a diversion to stop Sally from dwelling on this tragedy, so I decided to take her to see a movie on the Saturday before I was scheduled to leave. In the United Kingdom, they showed next week's movie on the banner outside the movie house on Saturday, but the movie showing inside was usually the old one. We thought we were going to see a Doris Day movie but it was one called *The Crowded Sky*—about a military jet fighter crashing into a jetliner. That didn't go down well with Sally at all. It only served to heighten our nervousness about my upcoming flight halfway around the world.

Our Pan Am flight to New York was delayed by fog in Germany, where it originated, and we missed our connecting flight from New York to Los Angeles by four hours. Pan Am found us another flight right away, but we had to run to make it. When we got to the gate, I saw that we had been switched to a United Airlines DC8. Jimmy Potton told me to relax: "When it's your turn to go, there's nothing you can do." I told him he was probably right, but what about when it was the pilot's turn to go? Did that mean it was our turn too?

I was really glad when we arrived safely in L.A. We stayed overnight there and flew on to Honolulu and Fiji on a Pan Am 707. In those days, big jets couldn't land in Auckland, so you had to fly from Fiji on a piston-engined DC6 that took six hours to get to New Zealand. By the time we arrived, we had been airborne about 29 hours and on the ground about 12.

For days afterwards, I felt like the ground was going up and down. It was a really weird sensation. I also soon found out about a new condition I had—it was called jet lag. Being overcome by fatigue just when you should be at the top of your game ruins your concentration and makes working on race cars very tough. We had to be careful to keep our act together.

I had no idea how much work the Tasman races were going to involve. It was a whole lot. First, we had to get the cars from the docks and take them out of the giant wooden crates they had been shipped in. We had three more big crates, one with 75 tires, one with spare parts, and one with tools, plus the Lotus engine that had been flown in from Coventry Climax. We took all this stuff to a Daimler dealership in Auckland called Coutts Garage and stored it there for the first race, which was going to be run nearby, at Ardmore. After each race, we had to pack up everything and have it shipped to the next location. There was only Jimmy and me, so we recruited the son of the dealership manager to help us. His name was David Oxton, and I don't know what we would have done without him. The three of us worked on the cars from the time we got there right through Christmas Day until the first race a week into January.

ABOVE: Steve Oxton, the Coutts garage manager, tries out the Salvadori Lotus 18 for size. Note the total absence of any rollover bar. Jimmy Potton and I had recruited his son David to help us prepare the cars. (David Oxton)

The cars had to be registered at the New Zealand Department of Motor Vehicles, and a license plate had to be issued for each one. This turned out to be a blessing because it meant that we could drive them on public roads to the races. I got a ticket for doing over 140 mph on the way to the Ardmore circuit. The cop laughed when he gave me the ticket and said, "Here's a souvenir for you, son. I don't expect you'll be around to pay it."

I could see why Reg Parnell liked racing in New Zealand. Besides the fantastic weather, the people made you feel so welcome. The day we arrived, we were loaned a car by one of Reg's old friends. It was a 1937 Singer Le Mans, and on Christmas Eve it nearly killed me.

We were staying in the Station Hotel, which was built into a hillside. You could walk in on the ground floor, take the elevator up about eight stories, and walk out onto another ground floor halfway up the hill. That night, when we got home late from the garage, I parked the car on the street about 100 yards above the upper doorway, almost blocking someone's driveway. We dipped into the hotel bar on the top floor to have a quick beer before turning in. In a friendly way, I complained to the bartender about the lack of hotel parking. Half an hour later, the telephone rang in our room and it was the bartender, telling me a parking spot had opened up right outside the door—and if I wanted it, I should take it now. It was a kind gesture, and I couldn't ignore it.

I got dressed and went up to move the Singer, which was facing up the hill. The curb space behind it was now clear so, instead of starting it up, I just released the parking brake to let it coast down to the hotel. I knew the car had cable-actuated brakes, but I didn't know they didn't work very well in reverse! The car gathered speed. When I applied the brakes, there seemed to be no effect. The car just gathered some more speed. By the time I got almost level with the hotel doorway, I was going about 20 mph, backwards. My heart was racing like mad. I was in the middle of the road and looking out the back window when I saw a side street coming up on my right. It was another hill—going upwards. I yanked the wheel over to back the car up the turning. The Singer did a 360-degree spin in the middle of the road, and I yanked the wheel again and it went against the curb—just up the turning. This slowed it down, and I could apply the parking brake and stop it. I started the engine and parked the car in front of the hotel with my heart still pounding in my ears.

I guess my face was as white as a sheet when I walked into the bar, because the bartender asked me what had happened. I told him and he laughed a lot. He offered me a double scotch, on him, because I looked like I could use one. I had the drink and went back to bed. I didn't tell Jimmy about it, but afterwards, every time we went in the bar for a beer, the bartender would ask, "How's it going, Fangio?"

The first race on January 7 was the New Zealand Grand Prix on the two-mile Ardmore circuit, and the F1 fraternity took it pretty seriously. There were works cars from Lotus (John Surtees and Jimmy Clark), Cooper (Jack Brabham and Bruce McLaren), and BRM (Graham Hill and Dan Gurney). There were 38 cars, and the event started with two 15-lap qualifying heats, which determined the grid positions. Stirling Moss won the first heat with Rob Walker's Lotus 18, and Brabham won the second heat with his works Cooper T53. Moss led the 75-lap final but failed to finish due to some transmission failure, so the works Cooper team landed a 1-2 with Brabham ahead of McLaren. Jo Bonnier in our Yeoman Credit Cooper T51 had a clutch failure in his heat and pushed the car over the line to qualify for the final, but there was no time to repair it. Roy Salvadori's Lotus finished fifth in his heat but was forced out of the final with a broken ring gear. But Denny Hulme got fifth place in the Grand Prix—a fantastic effort, all of his own doing.

An interesting thing happened when the Lotus broke a transaxle input shaft in practice. I took the box apart and was looking at the two pieces of the broken input shaft when a man named Arnold Stafford asked me if he could help. He told me that Team Lotus was using the garage at his house and he had a complete machine shop. I showed him the broken shaft. He said, "She'll be right, mate!" He took it with him and, next morning, handed me a brand new one he had made himself. It was better steel than the original and was perfect in every way, down to the splines on it to engage the clutch plates. I was staggered. Arnold refused to take a penny for it. He became a good friend, and a year later when he showed up at our workshop in England, Reg Parnell arranged for some free workshop space for him to use for a Formula One car he was campaigning for another up-and-coming Kiwi driver named Tony Shelly. One more thing about Arnold: years later, his daughter would be married to Carroll Shelby for one day.

Those four races in New Zealand seemed to involve working all the time. Next we went to Levin, a small town on North Island, and our team scored its first victory. Bonnier won from Jim Clark, but Salvadori's Lotus broke its gearbox. Next we were on South Island for the Lady Wigram Trophy race on an airfield near Christchurch, where it rained all race day, and Brabham won from Moss. Bonnier was stopped by a broken suspension wishbone and Salvadori by a gearbox breakage.

Finally, in Invercargill, the southernmost town in New Zealand, we produced a really great 1-2 in the Teretonga International feature race with Bonnier and Salvadori, and Hulme was third. Salvadori then won the last "Flying Farewell" race, but only after a tussle with Bonnier for the lead had resulted in Jo crashing the Cooper. He ended up in a ditch with a small branch sticking through his cheek. They pulled it out and stitched him up, and he was fine. But we had a boxful of wreckage to send home.

Jo and Roy were good friends and must have had the longest-running gin rummy game ever. They played cards before, between, and after all the races. Everywhere we went, they were at it. To this day, I don't know who the big winner was, but I suspect it was Salvadori. He was one smart race driver.

Denny Hulme won the NZ Gold Star award for his efforts in finishing every single race in the top five. I was really impressed by his dedication. He was very quiet for a 24-year-old and didn't like to wear shoes. I remember walking into a garage one day and seeing Denny washing his feet in the engine parts washer. He said, "Well, you can't go in the house with grease all over your feet, can you?"

I had never worked so hard on a race team in my life as we did in New Zealand that year. When I see Formula One races these days, with so many people around the cars, I wonder what the hell they all do.

We had around-the-world air tickets, so we were able to stop over in Hong Kong on the way home, where we bought some "made overnight" clothes. We flew on a De Havilland Comet from there and got back to England in mid-February. Less than 18 months later, the Comets would be taken out of service because of a series of dreadful crashes caused by metal fatigue.

When I got home, Sally broke the news that she was pregnant. It was a happy event at the time, but it was not destined to turn out well. Sadly for us, she had a miscarriage at six months. When I called her doctor at 11:00 p.m. that fateful night, he said it was nothing to worry about, and if she lost the baby, it would just be like a bad menstrual event. We never trusted English doctors again.

BELOW: John Surtees tested the new Cooper F1 car at Goodwood. Parnell had signed the motorcycle champion to his first full season in F1. From left to right are Reg Parnell, Yeoman Credit principal Fabian Samengo Turner, an unnamed mechanic, and Jimmy Potton. (Yeoman Credit Publicity)

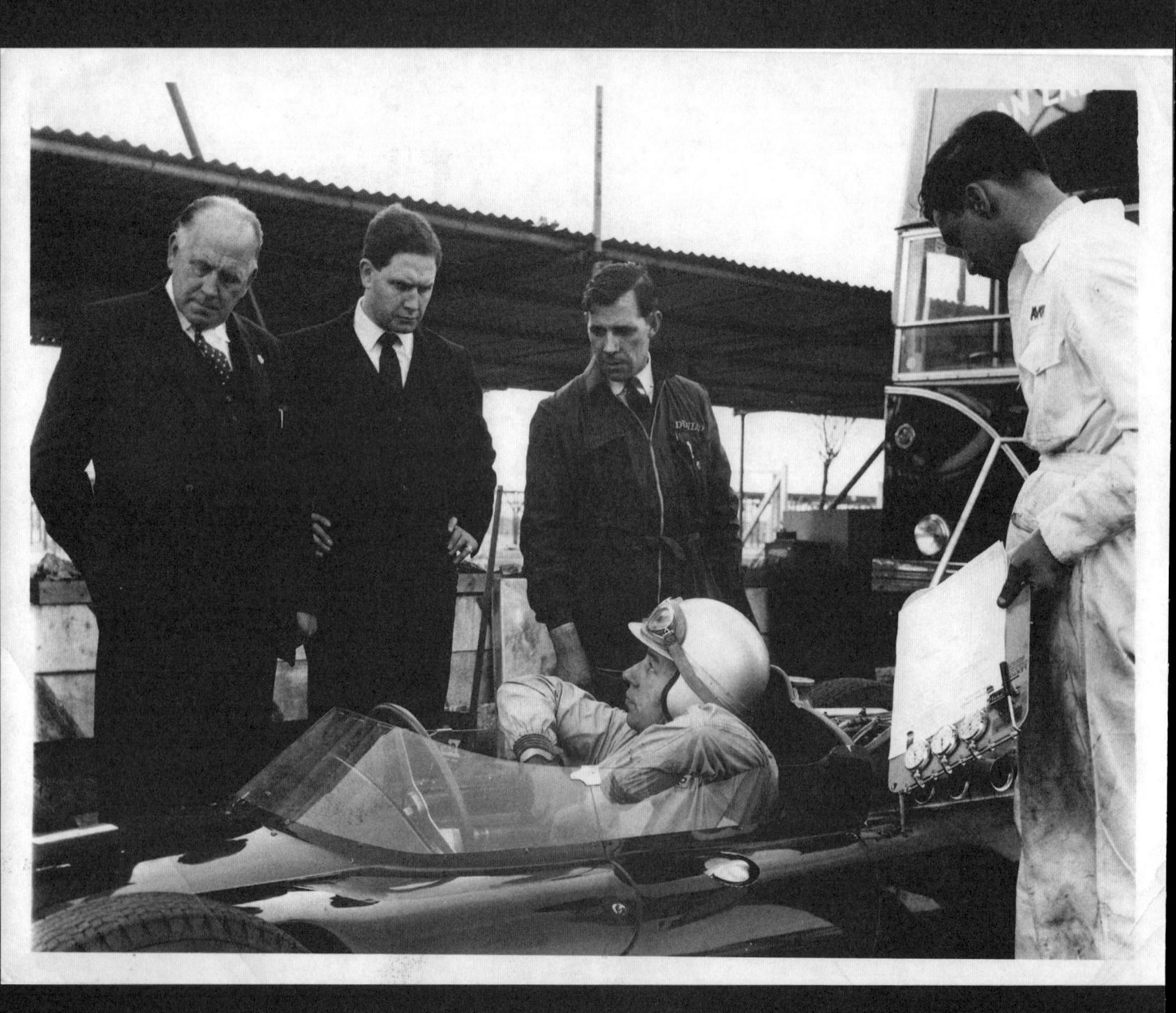

CHAPTER 9

My First Full F1 Season

When I got back to Hounslow, it was hard to recognize the Parnell workshop. They had cleaned it and repainted the whole facility, even the outside. The floor was painted gray, and you could almost see your face in it. Reg (as I was now allowed to call him) had hired a semi-retired World War II veteran named Joe as our janitor, and he did a great job with military spic-and-span. We were all issued white coveralls and we looked more like doctors than mechanics. I was given my own piece of bench, over in one corner of the shop, and settled right in.

We had acquired two new Cooper T53s, and Reg had signed John Surtees and Roy Salvadori to pilot them. The new Coopers were the latest in low-profile Formula One cars and looked great. I was very excited to be involved with Surtees in his first full year as an F1 driver, and to work for Salvadori, a legendary Le Mans winner, was an added bonus.

ABOVE: Roy Salvadori drove the Bowmaker F1 "Intercontinental" Cooper T53 to a smooth sixth-place finish at the 1961 British Empire Trophy race at Silverstone. (LAT Photographic)

We had also acquired a big Albion double-decked car transporter that had been used by British Racing Partnership, the team sponsored by Yeoman Credit the previous season, as well as a smaller truck that could hold all the other stuff we would need at race meetings and a Morris van for chasing parts. Surtees didn't like the old Yeoman Credit light green livery, and he and Reg had come up with a new color of green that had a lot of blue in it. All the trucks and the race cars were painted in the new green with dark red noses and stripes. They looked fantastic.

I was used for many different chores, from engine overhauling to parts fabrication. Whenever Reg wanted to try something new, such as putting a Maserati engine into a Lotus, I got the job, so I quickly loved working for him. The first order of business was to do a test at Goodwood with both the drivers, and Reg used it to get some publicity pictures taken for our sponsors.

With so many mechanics at Reg's disposal, and with spare engines in the truck, I was not needed at every race. It worked out well for me because I could have a little home life outside of racing. Don Beresford and I were the two leading fabricators, and much like I prepared engines, Don prepared gearboxes. That gave Reg the opportunity to try some things of his own. He bought a Formula Junior Cooper and told us he wanted to transform it into a special car for the next Monaco race. We fitted the chassis with an F1 drivetrain and suspension and special fuel tanks that intruded inside the space frame. Then we made a special, narrower body for it. Roy Salvadori tried to put his 6 foot, 2 inch frame into it and said, "This is very hard to get into!" So we called it the "VR," short for *Virgo Reluctarum*—a spoof on Latin, meaning "Reluctant Virgin." All racing mechanics are natural sex fiends, so it was only natural to make the connection. It was an interesting project, but it was never a serious contender in either 1961 or 1962, when we used it again without much success.

There were only eight FIA Grands Prix scheduled in 1961, but there were no fewer than 24 non-championship races, plus the Intercontinental series of five races for the 2.5-liter cars. Some of these non-championship races were scheduled on the same dates as others. A serious F1 team in those days had a choice of 37 races they could attend. Conflicts happened all the time.

Our first outing was in March at the Snetterton track in Norfolk for the Lombank Trophy, a mixed race for F1 and Intercontinental cars. I didn't go, but a strange thing happened that brought me into the picture.

I had prepared the engines for the Snetterton race and Reg had decided to have a test run at Mallory Park on the way to Norfolk. I had to stay in the shop to get an engine done for a car being readied for a race in Naples. In mid-afternoon, I was called to the telephone to speak to Reg. He told me the cars would not push-start, even when they towed them.

He said that fuel vapor was coming out of the intake trumpets and that the engines sounded weird. Was I sure I had timed the camshafts correctly? I told Reg that I was very confident that the engines were OK, but a thought occurred to me that he should check out. When Don Beresford had put the transaxles together, might he somehow have put the ring gear on the wrong side of the pinion? That would turn the engine over backwards when the gear was engaged as you pushed the car forward, and it wouldn't start. I suggested he put one of the cars in reverse gear and then push-start it. He gave it a try—and the engine started. The car then had one forward gear and four reverse gears. Don quickly reworked the transmissions, and they went off to Snetterton. I guess Don got such a razzing from everyone that Reg didn't even need to talk about it.

That was a great thing about Reg—he knew how to handle people. At one race meeting, before practice, I had put a brake pad in backwards on Salvadori's car and had to change it back after one lap. I was embarrassed, and Reg sensed it. He said, "Peter, I would give you a bollocking if I thought it would help, but you know you messed up! So the best thing I can do is say nothing because it'll make you feel worse. You won't do it again."

Jack Brabham won the Lombank Trophy in our Intercontinental Cooper entered by Tommy Atkins, followed by Cliff Allison in a Lotus. Surtees finished third, and after a pit stop to secure the engine cowling, Salvadori was fifth behind Henry Taylor in another Intercontinental Lotus. We had finished 1-2 in the Formula One class, and Roy had done the fastest F1 lap. Things were looking good for the Grands Prix.

The Easter Goodwood races were usually big in England because they gave the F1 teams a chance to flex their muscles before the World Championship started in earnest. But this year half the F1 teams had headed over to the French Pyrenees for the clashing Grand Prix de Pau. Easter Sunday fell on my 25th birthday, April 3, and I got a great present when Surtees won the 42-lap Glover Trophy for us. Graham Hill was second in his BRM, and Salvadori got third. There was an Intercontinental race for the Lavant Cup, and Roy was in the Lotus that had got back from New Zealand. Surtees managed fourth behind Moss, McLaren, and Hill, and Salvadori chased him over the line for fifth. The Intercontinental cars were about 3 seconds per lap faster than the new F1 cars, much as you would expect. It was a great weekend for Yeoman Credit, and their corporate chiefs, the Samengo-Turner brothers, were grinning ear to ear. I had a great birthday at the races. I was now living my dream of being an F1 mechanic.

I managed to miss the rainy Aintree 200, another non-championship F1 race later in April, because I had more engines to overhaul. The works Coopers of Brabham and McLaren got a 1-2 ahead of Graham Hill's BRM, and Surtees got fourth and Salvadori eighth after another unscheduled pit stop. Then, on May 11, Reg took me to London Airport and put me on a Comet airliner with Salvadori, and we flew to Rome for the Gran Premio de Napoli.

The organizers of the 1961 Monaco Grand Prix had decided to allow only the works teams to enter two cars. Teams like ours only had one guaranteed entry, and Surtees got the nod. That was why we went to Naples instead. Roy's car was taken down to Italy on a double-decked trailer towed by Reg's son, Tim Parnell, with his own Lotus 18 also aboard.

Roy had some friends with him, and they rented a car to get us to Naples. After a quick meal—my very first pizza—they dropped me at a hotel in Posillipo, near where the race was going to be held. I went to the desk to check in and the manager asked me if I wanted a room with or without a bathtub. I asked about the price difference, and he told me about £5 a day. I opted to use the communal bathroom and save money. The bellman showed me to a room and—lo and behold!—it had a tub. It also had a great view of Naples with Mount Vesuvius in the background. I was just about to celebrate my good fortune when two men came in and unbolted the tub, disconnected the plumbing, and took it all away, leaving me with just a washbasin and a toilet. When I checked to see where the communal bathroom was, there wasn't one. I was crushed!

ABOVE: Roy Salvadori gets a tow to the track for the non-championship Grand Prix in Naples. (Peter Bryant)

We had arranged for Roy to pick me up the next morning to go to the circuit, so I had a nice Italian dinner, with a little *chianti*, and went to bed. Next day we went to the circuit for practice. This was not going to be a walkover for Roy, but he established his presence in qualifying by being second fastest to Gerry Ashmore in a very quick Lotus 18 Climax. On the outside of the front row was a new Ferrari 156, driven by Giancarlo Baghetti. It was our first look at Ferrari's latest piece and the 120-degree V6 engine sounded like it was revving to a trillion rpm as it pulled out of the pits. We still had the old Climax FPF, and it only put out about 150 bhp at 6500 rpm.

Just before qualifying ended, Roy ran over a nail and got a puncture. We didn't have a spare. I begged him to try a set of rain tires we had brought, just in case. But Roy thought they would overheat like mad and be destroyed. He told me to give him the punctured wheel and he would return it next morning to a little garage where he rented space for me to work on the car that night. I had a few things to do, and one of them was to change the second gear ratio to suit the circuit better. So we towed the Cooper behind his rental car back to the garage, which was within easy walking distance to my hotel.

I was working away on the gearbox, watched by a little old Italian caretaker, when he pointed at the back wall of the garage and said, "Mousey Mousey." I looked over and there was an absolutely gigantic rat sneaking along the bottom of the wall toward a hole in the skirting. I looked at the old man and said in English, waving my finger, "No—it's a fucking great rat!" Later, Salvadori arrived with his friends to check out how I was doing, and the old man came over, pointed to the wall and said, "Fucking great rat." Roy and his friends looked at him in total astonishment.

Next morning we towed the car back to the track, and I put on the wheel that Roy had brought back. He said he hadn't been able to find another inner tube, but it had been vulcanized so it should be fine. I tried again to get him to test the rain tires, citing the fact that there were trees all around the track dropping all kinds of pith-soaked stuff, and it was getting very slippery. I said, "You never know, these rain tires could be just the ticket here!" He declined and told me that the repaired tire would be fine.

When the race started, Roy went straight into the lead, pulling away from the Lotus and the new Ferrari. Suddenly he appeared in the last turn before the pits straight with a flat right rear tire—the same one as before. The vulcanized patch had overheated and leaked air. Instead of immediately pulling into the pits so that I could change the tire, he ignored my frantic waving and went straight on to the end of the straight. The road made a left turn there, and he had to pull over after the car lurched to the right. I could see the car from the pit, so I grabbed a rain tire wheel, a jack, and a lug wrench, and ran as hard as I could up the track. When I got to the car, he was still sitting in it, and I started changing the wheel. Suddenly something hit me on the leg. Some Italian kids were pelting me with stones. That was a first in bad sportsmanship for me. I hurriedly finished the wheel, and Salvadori took off again. He ended up in seventh place, and in the process he did the fastest lap of the race. Baghetti won with Ashmore second and Lorenzo Bandini third in Centro Sud's private Cooper-Maserati.

When we got to the prize giving later that evening, Roy went and met with the officials to claim the money for the fastest lap. They told him they were going to give the trophy and the money to Baghetti. Roy had somehow obtained a copy of the timing tape, and it clearly showed he had done the fastest lap. It was obvious that the Italians weren't going to budge, but when it came time to call Roy up to get his money for seventh place, they gave him a giant trophy as well. I guess it was their way of compensating him for the fastest lap money he had lost. We bitched about it and said we would protest to the FIA, but it did no good.

We never returned to the Circuito de Napoli at Posillipo, but it had another F1 race the following year. I read in *Autosport* how Innes Ireland used those same Dunlop rain tires and cleaned up in the dry. Oh well. Everyone has 20-20 hindsight.

Meanwhile, in the opening World Championship race at Monaco, Surtees qualified 12th on the grid, but his fuel pump packed up in the race. It was one of Stirling Moss's greatest victories as he beat the Ferraris with Rob Walker's Lotus 18.

The 1961 season went by like a blur, with races everywhere and an unending stream of cars to build and repair. Between Surtees and Salvadori, there were about seven wrecked cars during the season. By the end of it, we were preparing cars by cutting off the good front end of one chassis and welding it to the good back end of another. Reg also bought a couple of wrecked cars to help with these expensive rebuilds.

One of the Grands Prix that sticks out in my memory was the Italian race at Monza. It was one of Salvadori's better races, and he got the last World Championship point of his career by finishing sixth. Surtees had an accident on the 19th lap but wasn't hurt. It was amazing how the drivers escaped serious injury in the 1960s, because they were basically surrounded by an aluminum bathtub full of gasoline, with no seatbelts or rollover protection to speak of. In fact, American driver Masten Gregory practiced (and was famous for) jumping out of cars should the need arise.

The first-lap crash at Monza involving Jimmy Clark and Wolfgang von Trips was one of the saddest for me, because I knew them both personally. Trips had got pole position for Ferrari, and it was his race to win or lose. When it happened, the cars flew into the stands, killing Trips along with 14 spectators. The officials should have stopped the race, but they let it go on.

Team Lotus were in the next garage to us, and after the race, the Italian paparazzi and fans mobbed the garage area. When we wanted to put away Salvadori's car, the only way we could clear them from our garage door was to throw buckets of water at them. They were standing on anything, including Surtees's car, to get a look at Jimmy in the next garage.

Jimmy and Colin Chapman left as soon as they could. In Italy, there were (and still are) laws that are very unlike anything in England or the United States. Because suicide is a mortal sin in the eyes of the Catholic church, you can't attend any function at your own

BELOW: John Surtees in the T51 Cooper leads off a star-studded field at the 1961 Silverstone British Empire Trophy race. (LAT Photographic)

BELOW: John Surtees in the non-championship Gran Premio Siracusa in April 1961. Note how close the spectators are to the cars. (LAT Photographic)

risk. Liability waivers are illegal. If there's a fatal car accident in the street, it has to be someone's fault, so the first thing they do is arrest everyone in sight. Until they find out what role spectators might have played in the accident, they can be held at a police station until that's resolved. The police questioned hundreds of people that day at Monza pending the investigation of the crash. Chapman and Clark were lucky to get away, but they couldn't go back to Italy for a long time, until a tribunal had cleared them of any wrongdoing and given them specific permission.

Ferrari's Phil Hill ended up as the World Champion with 38 points, and poor Taffy von Trips was the posthumous runner-up, with 33 points—he came very close. Our drivers finished 12th and 17th with only six points between them. One thing was certain. We would have a tough time in 1962 beating Ferrari and Porsche using Cooper customer cars with old Climax four-cylinder engines. Something had to be done.

But it had been an exciting year for me. I had attended five of the eight World Championship races and six others, plus four Tasman races—15 in all. My year ended when I prepared our Climax engines for the Tasman races, but I was given Christmas at home. Was I glad! One more missed Christmas, and I might have been in the doghouse forever...

In the off-season, Yeoman Credit became Bowmaker Finance, requiring new paint jobs for the trucks. But basically it was still the Samengo-Turner brothers in new colors. They were very nice people, and I was pleased that Reg still had their sponsorship.

BELOW: Jimmy Potton and I are seen working on the new Lola F1 car in this Bowmaker publicity picture. (Lola Heritage)

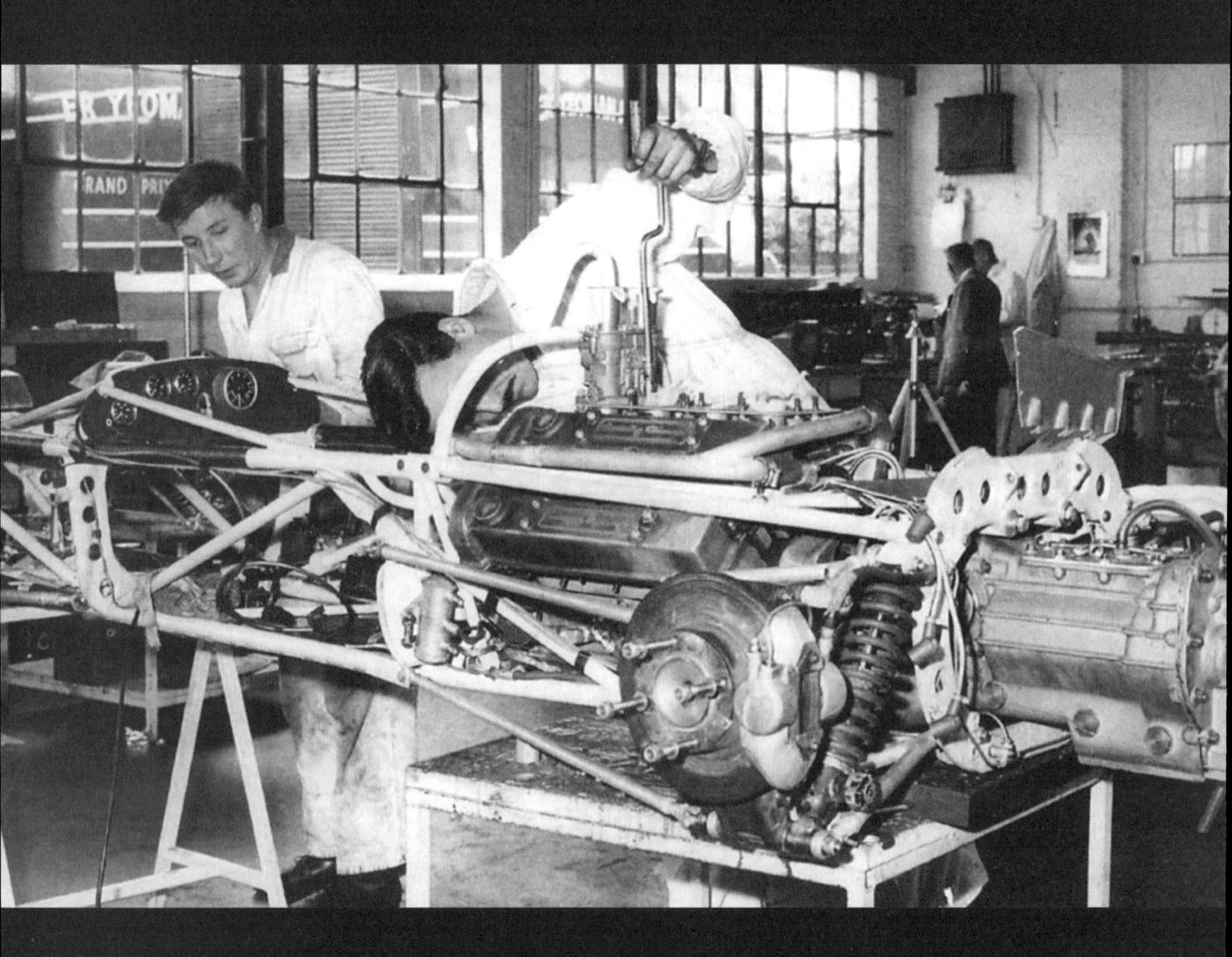

CHAPTER 10

A Long Season with Lola

In the fall of 1961, John Surtees, who lived near the Lola factory in Bromley, southeast of London, persuaded Reg Parnell to have Eric Broadley design and build a new car for our 1962 program. The Lola Mk 4 was Eric's first Formula One car, but he was already emerging as the nemesis of Colin Chapman of Lotus, because his sports-racing cars were having great success.

The plans were on the board before Christmas, with Tony Southgate doing some of the drawings. The chassis was to be a lightweight space frame, made of 18- and 20-gauge steel tube, using two of the tubes to carry the cooling water to and from the engine at the rear to the radiator at the front. The chassis wasn't welded together in the traditional way, because Eric liked to use nickel-bronze weld/brazing. The benefit was that it didn't require as much heat as welding, and besides keeping distortion to a minimum, it was much easier wherever you needed to make multiple tubes come together at a joint. Eric did a lot of the brazing himself. The chassis, which was painted bright yellow, was very light but seemed reasonably strong.

ABOVE: John Surtees tests the new Lola Mk 4 F1 car at Goodwood. (Peter Bryant)

Eric was also one of the first people to bolt the engine solidly into the chassis, making it a stressed member. The new car was designed to use the new 1.5-liter Coventry Climax V8.

Another new feature would be the first use of aircraft-type fuel cell bladders to carry the 26 gallons of gasoline safely while saving precious weight. There was a cell behind the driver's back and one over his legs, just ahead of the steering wheel. A new composites company called Specialised Mouldings, based nearby in Crystal Palace and headed by Eric's friend Peter Jackson, built the lightweight body parts. The Lola was very light, weighing a trim 1080 lbs. without gas or driver.

As one of Reg's fabricators, I was asked to go to Bromley and work with Eric to get the car ready. I was at the Lola factory a couple of weeks, and just like at Lotus, there was a pub across the street where we had lunch every day and played a little darts. Eric had a great sense of humor, and it was a real pleasure working with him.

The new Climax V8 was reputed to rev to more than 10,000 rpm and would require a new, five-speed gearbox. At that point, Lola did not have their own gearbox, and Reg Parnell awarded a contract to the Italian company, Colotti, to make one for us. The only problem was that Reg had to supply the gear banks, because high-quality steel was not available in Italy at that time. This required our truck to take the steel from England to Modena.

"Tug" Wilson was to drive the truck with Gerry navigating. Tug had been Aston Martin's transporter driver and was famous in a small way in racing circles for something he did at the Le Mans 24 Hours in 1955. When Pierre Levegh had the horrendous crash that killed more than 80 people, he was hurled out of his Mercedes-Benz 300 SLR and was lying on the track in front of the Aston Martin pit. In total disregard of his own safety, Tug ran onto the track and grabbed up Levegh's body. Tug was the kind of guy you could rely on in a fix.

When Tug and Gerry landed at the ferry docks in Dunkirk, they thought all they needed to do was hand over the usual bribes to the usual people and be on their way. But the French customs officers made a big fuss about importing steel into France without the proper paperwork. It took a personal effort from one of the Samengo-Turner brothers and Credit Suisse to put up a bond to allow them in. It took four days for them to get out of Dunkirk and on their way, but Tug Wilson came through again.

Tug came through when a life was at risk on another occasion—mine! He was the driver and I was co-driver of the big Albion transporter, which was so wide that six people could sit side-by-side on the front seat. It could carry six race cars double-decked. We were in France coming back from a race, and Tug was driving along one of those roads where they had what we called a "Death or Glory" lane—a third lane in the center of a two-lane highway. The rules were simple—whoever was in the overtaking lane first had right of way over the oncoming traffic. We were coming down a long hill and had picked up a lot of speed, and Tug moved into the center lane to pass another truck. Suddenly a truck pulled into the center lane out of the line of traffic coming towards us, so he was headed right at us. It was a game of "chicken," but we were going too slowly to pass the guy on our inside, and too fast to brake in time to tuck in behind him. Tug flashed his lights but the truck ignored him. So Tug began to inch over against the truck on the inside. We were in a right-hand-drive truck in a left-hand-drive country, and I was in the center of the road. When I could see the whites of the eyes of the driver coming at us, I threw myself to the right, down flat across the big seat. I heard an explosion, heard the sound of glass breaking, and felt a heavy blow on my ass.

Somehow Tug had pushed the inside truck over far enough that we almost missed the oncoming one, but the big driver's mirror on my side had been knocked off at a combined collision speed of around 130 mph. It came through my side window, hitting me on the ass. I looked up as Tug pulled to the side of the road. His face was as white as a sheet. I said, "How did you miss hitting him head on?"

He answered, "I don't know. It was a miracle, I guess!" Neither of the other trucks stopped. Ours had two big gouges down the left side. We cleaned up the mess in the cab

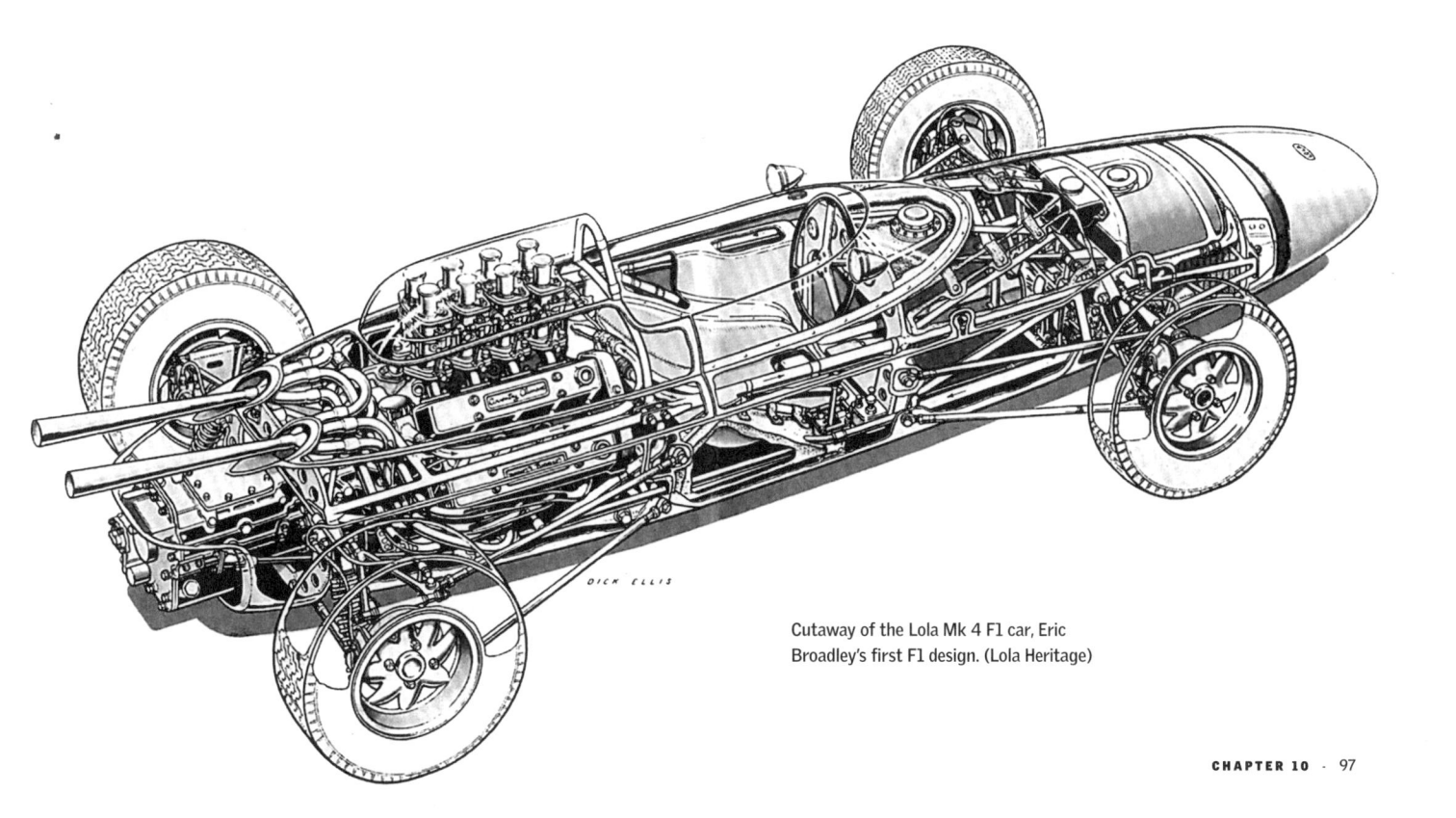

Cutaway of the Lola Mk 4 F1 car, Eric Broadley's first F1 design. (Lola Heritage)

and drove to the nearest café for a cup of tea to calm us down. I asked Tug how scared he had been, and he said, "My asshole went three penny-bit, half-a-crown, dustbin lid." If I had been driving, we would probably have died. Thanks again, Tug!

There was a big demand for the new Climax V8, and we had to wait our turn, so at first we raced the old Climax FPF engine. We ran Surtees in the non-championship Brussels Grand Prix and the Lombank Trophy at Snetterton to get the new car sorted out a bit, and received our first V8 in time for the F1 races at Goodwood over Easter.

The V8 was entrusted to Surtees, but Salvadori had the better day at Goodwood, although his Cooper-Climax had a fuel-feed problem in qualifying for the first race, the 21-lap Lavant Cup, which was only for the four-cylinder cars. He was in fifth position on the grid but, despite a spin, managed to get second place behind Bruce McLaren's works Cooper and was pleased with that. Later he fought his way up from 10th on the grid in the four-cylinder Lola to finish 4th in the main event, the 42-lap Glover Trophy race. Graham Hill set the tone for things to come by winning with the new V8 BRM from McLaren and Innes Ireland (Lotus).

Surtees, on the other hand, had a disappointing time. He qualified third for the first race but had a crash with a backmarker and retired with a broken nose section. It was my first time repairing fiberglass, but with some helpful tips from Jim Endruit, the chief mechanic at Team Lotus, I was able to get the car ready and fit the V8 for the Glover Trophy. Surtees retired with engine problems but showed great potential when he shared the fastest lap with Stirling Moss in the UDT-Laystall team's Lotus.

That race marked the end of Moss's career. He came into the pits with a sticking throttle. The mechanics worked on it and sent him out again, but he crashed when it stuck wide open and he went head-first into a grass bank. His head injuries put him out of racing forever, but luckily he survived to tell the tale. I felt sad about it because Stirling had won so many F1 races but never a championship, and was one of only a few drivers to beat Juan Fangio in equal cars. And he had done it with a Mercedes-Benz W196 in the 1955 British Grand Prix. That race was held at our next destination, Aintree.

Surtees persuaded Eric Broadley to come to the non-championship Aintree 200 in Liverpool to help in sorting out the handling of the Lola Mk 4, and it was not long before he had him working on the cars. Surtees qualified third but didn't finish after the intake valves got tangled up with the exhaust valves. Salvadori blew his four-cylinder engine in practice and then retired from the race with a broken throttle linkage.

During practice, I'd just finished adjusting the brake balance, and Surtees had just gone back on the track, when a young man emerged from the crowd of spectators and asked me what I had been doing. I explained how we had separate master cylinders for the front and rear brakes, and I had been adjusting the balance to increase the rear braking effort. He asked me a couple more questions, then if I liked the latest rock-and-roll sounds. I said I did. He thanked me for explaining things, told me his name was George, and invited me after the race to a nightclub called the Cavern where he and his band would be performing. He told me to bring as many friends as I liked. He had given out some passes to a few other racers and hopefully his favorite driver, Jimmy Clark, would come, too. After the race, the other guys were not interested, so I went alone. There were people from various teams there, and when the band started to play, I realized that the young man was George Harrison, and the band was the Beatles. After the show, Jimmy Clark, who had won the Aintree 200 with a Lotus-Climax V8, took us all back to a yacht he had been staying on over the weekend, and we partied until dawn. The race had been a bummer for our team, but the Beatles saved the weekend.

The next race was another non-championship F1 race at my second-favorite English track, Silverstone. Goodwood had always been my favorite, because it was where I had seen my first GP way back when. Surtees got a great third after qualifying on the front row, but it was obvious that an extra effort would be needed to get us involved in the battles between Graham Hill's BRM P57 and Jimmy Clark's fast Lotus 24. Salvadori had one of the 174 bhp Climax V8 FWMW engines in his car for the first time, but broke the front suspension when he was involved in an incident with Keith Greene, Maurice Trintignant, and Tony Shelly. He didn't even complete the first lap.

John Surtees told us at Silverstone how much he was looking forward to the first World Championship Grand Prix of the season, at Zandvoort in Holland, but he took the whole F1 entourage completely by surprise when he put our V8 Lola on pole position. Hill and Clark jumped him at the start, and he was also passed by Dan Gurney's new flat-eight Porsche, but he was doing pretty well when a front wishbone broke. He careened off the track through a fence, and went through a tent full of policemen eating lunch. Amazingly, he hit nothing during this journey except the barbed wire fence, which scratched his arm. In view of the wishbone failure, Reg pulled Salvadori out of the race. Another bummer!

I remember that race meeting well because we'd had to leave Hounslow without Salvadori's car. Only one of our V8 engines was rebuilt in time, so only one car was ready to load into the Albion transporter. I was given the job of driving the big truck from Zandvoort down to the airport at Antwerp to pick up the second car and Eric Broadley, who was traveling with it. On the way back, I missed the turn off the freeway to Zandvoort and had to drive the huge transporter across a short "floating bridge" over one of the many dykes we encountered. As I eased it forward onto the barge forming the bridge, the front went down about a foot and the bridge tipped up and strained the chains that were holding it down at the end. I decided to make a run for the other end as fast as I could go. Luckily the rear wheels were still behind the centerline of the bridge when the front wheels got to the road at the other side. But once the rears were past the centerline, the second half of the bridge dipped down and the rear wheels had about a nine-inch curb to jump. Luckily I was going fast enough to make it. We both heaved a sigh of relief. "Please don't tell Reg Parnell I did that with his transporter!" I begged Eric.

He smiled and replied, "Let's see how the rest of the trip turns out." I drove the rest of the way like an old lady.

Next, I found myself at the Monaco Grand Prix. I had always dreamed of being there and at last, here I was, standing outside the famous Casino, worrying if my £10 daily cash allowance would be enough. It wasn't easy to find a hotel room in Monaco to fit a £10 per diem, but somehow Gillian had come through. We were staying at a place called the Hotel Poste, over the top of a little post office down an alley near the famous Tip-Top bar. When we had finished work, we would usually wind up at the Tip-Top for a nightcap. Our nightcaps were usually short and sweet, because we never finished working on the cars before 2:00 a.m. or 3:00 a.m. The Tip-Top was almost opposite the Casino and had a piano. Gregor Grant, the editor of *Autosport*, liked to lead the British contingent with sing-alongs that went on into the wee hours.

We had made some extra-short nose parts for Monaco, and the cars looked kind of weird. Reg Parnell thought that opening up the nose air intake would help the cars cool better and might even help the driver for passing on Monaco's tight track. Reg was always looking for an edge. The attrition was high in the race, which Bruce McLaren won for Cooper from the Ferraris of Phil Hill and Lorenzo Bandini. Surtees finished fourth and collected his first points of the season, but Salvadori had a miserable time because he thought the springs on his car were way too soft and he just couldn't handle the corners well. When Bruce had won, there was a big party at the Tip-Top, and Keith Duckworth took great delight in leading the assembled mass of mostly English blokes in the rendition of his favorite pub song, "Swing Low, Sweet Chariot."

BELOW: Roy Salvadori comes flying past the temporary stands opposite the Casino at the 1962 Monaco GP. (Bowmaker Publicity)

CHAPTER 10 · 101

Reg had instructed Don Beresford and me to meet him at the garage at 6:00 a.m. the day after. Naturally we were a bit late—an hour late, to be exact! Reg was very annoyed. We were supposed to take Surtees's Lola back to England in a single-car transporter that he had bought from Jackie Lewis. In those days, whoever was first to get their engine to Coventry Climax for a rebuild was first to get it back—and with the Belgian Grand Prix at Spa just two weeks away, time was important. We promised Reg that we would get the car back the next day, or bust. He thought that was ridiculous, and no way could we get to Dunkirk and over the ferry in time. We said that if we did it we wanted the following weekend off. He agreed, and we left.

As we drove along the coast towards Nice, I told Don that I had never swum in the Mediterranean, and I was damned if I was going to get this close and not do it. We saw a beautiful beach and an empty parking lot. So we parked up and ran down to the water in turn for a quick dip. We didn't bother to dry ourselves off because it was hot and there was no air conditioning in the converted Ford van. We took turns driving and went all the way up to Dunkirk, stopping only for gasoline and sandwiches. The following morning we took the air ferry to Dover instead of the slow boat, and we pulled into Hounslow at about 2:00 p.m. Reg was staggered. He had flown back from Nice, and we'd almost beaten him home. We unloaded the car, took out the engine, and got it to Coventry Climax that evening. Only a Team Lotus engine beat ours back, and they had flown it all the way. We got our weekend off.

It was a weekend that the team all enjoyed except Don and me! There were two races scheduled, so Reg sent one group of guys to one and another group to the other. Surtees raced in the International 2000 Guineas at Mallory Park and won. Salvadori raced in the London Grand Prix at Crystal Palace, qualified first, and finished second to Innes Ireland's Lotus-BRM.

I took Sally, who was six months pregnant with our second try at a baby, to an event that was exactly the opposite of motor racing, namely the famous Hyde Park Sheep Dog Trials. It was a hot day, and we were seated on the grass near the Bowmaker van I had borrowed when she looked at me and said she was having labor pains. I rushed her to the hospital and they gave her a shot to stop another miscarriage.

Salvadori didn't go to the Belgian Grand Prix because his engine didn't get back in time from Coventry Climax. But Surtees did, and it was interesting to watch him go through Eau Rouge at full speed. Reg said it looked like he was taking the same line as he would on a racing motorbike. Clark in the new Lotus 25 and Hill in the BRM were making mincemeat of the rest of the field and even making the mighty Ferrari take notice. Clark won over Hill, with Phil Hill and Ricardo Rodriguez next for Ferrari.

The monocoque Lotus 25 was an awesome car, and Surtees began complaining that the space frame Lola Mk 4 was too flexible. It came to a head when at Surtees's insistence we jacked up one wheel and the other three stayed on the ground. It sure was flexing! That was when I first found out the importance of chassis stiffness. I guess all the cars except Clark's were flexing. In spite of not qualifying well, Surtees managed to get a couple of points by finishing fifth just ahead of Jack Brabham, who was no longer driving for Cooper and had bought a Lotus 24 of his own. When we got home, Eric Broadley made some much-needed modifications to the chassis.

The next two races were in France. The first was a non-championship race at Reims, where Surtees had fuel-feed problems in practice and went out of the race with broken valve springs, while Salvadori finished sixth. Reims was one of those places where the racers had fun after hours. There were two places to go—Bridget's Bar and the Jockey Club. I preferred Bridget's.

That year there was a famous party at Bridget's with a lot of racers there, including Colin Chapman and John Cooper. The story goes that Cooper climbed a tree in the garden and started peeing on Chapman, who thought it had started to rain. I remember everyone laughing about it when I got there. Some of the blokes picked up Cooper's Mini and wedged it between two trees on the sidewalk. Late one night, some other blokes carried Ritchie Ginther's little Fiat up the stairs of the Hotel Lion d'Or and put it outside his bedroom door. In the morning, he started it up and drove it down the stairway and out the front doors.

The organizers held a champagne reception at the Town Hall after the race. The lowly mechanics were never invited to it, so we missed John Cooper (after a beverage or two) conducting the Reims Symphony Orchestra!

The Bowmaker mechanics were staying in a cheap hotel on the rue Burette. We had a sweetheart deal from the manager. He said that if we let them use the rooms until 11:00 p.m., we could have them half-price. They would simply lock our luggage in a closet until then. One night we got back to the hotel a bit early and sat in the bar until we could get into our rooms. We found out that from 5:00 p.m. until 11:00 p.m. they were renting the rooms to prostitutes. No one complained, because they changed the bed linen and we couldn't tell what had been going on, and because we saved half our per diem.

After the race I was laid low by food poisoning—probably from a ham salad I'd eaten at the track. Reg and Gillian picked me up from the hotel on Monday morning to take me back to the workshop, because Reg had Surtees's engine in the trunk and wanted me to check it out before the Rouen race the following week. I was deathly ill all the way back. When we got to the ferry, Reg said, "I know what you need." He took me up to the bar and insisted on buying me a double brandy. He didn't believe I had food poisoning—he thought I had got drunk after the race and had a hangover. All I wanted to do was throw up and lie down. The brandy did help a little, although Reg wasn't finally convinced I had food poisoning until I threw up in his car on the London road.

I didn't go to Rouen, but the engine I checked over did, and Surtees used it to finish fifth. Salvadori blew an engine in practice, so we only had one engine left, a brand new one that Reg was saving for Surtees to use at the British Grand Prix the following week. The guys put it in Roy's car, but Reg persuaded Roy to pull out of the race at a given signal to save the engine for Aintree. Then Surtees had fuel-feed problems in the race and dropped several positions. Many other cars dropped out, and seeing all this attrition, Reg sent Roy out again to try and get a good finish. When Surtees started moving back up the field, Roy was again signaled to come in. Reg told the press that Roy's engine had lost its oil pressure. Roy was not happy.

Clark blew everybody's doors off in the British Grand Prix at Aintree with the fantastic handling of the Lotus 25, finishing a minute ahead of Surtees in our car. In turn, Surtees finished a minute ahead of McLaren in a works Cooper T60. The modifications to the Lola chassis seemed to have done the trick. Surtees's performance proved it was very competitive. Salvadori dropped out with no ignition spark before halfway. The Climax V8 used a new transistor-type ignition system and the transistor was housed in a "black box." It wasn't uncommon for the black box suddenly to quit working, and most teams had made a quick-release mechanism so it could be changed easily. They usually failed after the pre-race warm up. If you switched the engine off after revving it one last time, it could kill the black box.

For some strange reason, I liked going to the Nürburgring, even though the place had not been kind to me in the past. I guess I'll always fondly remember my adventures there the first time, at the 1000-kilometer race in 1960. Our trip to the 1962 German Grand Prix started literally with a bang when our transporter driver, Tug Wilson, tried to knock off the roof of the customs hut at the Belgium/Germany border crossing at Aachen. As he slowed so that we could show our papers, the windshield post of the huge Albion hit the edge of the hut's roof and skewed the whole thing about 4 inches. Luckily the Customs official was in another hut at that moment, so Tug backed up about 10 feet and, just as the guy walked up, approached the hut again. He passed us through, and as we drove away, we could see him looking at his little hut in bewilderment because it wasn't in line with the road anymore. We all looked at Tug. His face was bright red, but he'd dodged the bullet yet again.

The race was always very well attended, and they could spread as many as 300,000 people all round the 14-mile Nordschliefe circuit. They would only get to see each car 15 times, because that was the number of laps in the race, which still took over two and a half hours. But the place was massively popular because it had such a great atmosphere of history and tradition.

Ferrari showed up at the 'Ring with four cars. A total of 34 drivers tried to qualify for 30 grid positions, including Jack Brabham, out for the first time with his own new Formula One car. Graham Hill had one of the biggest surprises of his racing career when a big movie camera fell off the back of Carel de Beaufort's Porsche and hit his BRM, sending it off the road, luckily without serious damage. Hill later set the second-fastest time behind Dan Gurney's Porsche 804, but ahead of Clark's Lotus 25 and our man, Surtees. As had happened to me once before, it rained like crazy just as the grid was forming up, and they delayed the start for an hour. Just like Jackie Lewis in the 1960 German Grand Prix, Clark forgot to switch off the Lucas electric fuel pump and he ended up last into the South Curve. But he wasn't disqualified like Jackie had been—the F1 rules had now made on-board starters mandatory.

At the end of the race, Hill was in first place only a couple of seconds ahead of Surtees, with Gurney another 2 seconds back. It was an amazingly close finish for the 'Ring, and it proved again that the Lola was very competitive with Surtees driving it. Unfortunately, Salvadori wasn't having such a great season, and by no means all because of his driving. Surtees had only agreed to drive the Parnell Lola on the understanding that he always had the freshest engine. Salvadori very rarely saw a new engine in his car, and it showed in the results. I felt very sorry for Roy because he failed to finish seven of the season's eight championship races. He didn't even start in the U.S. Grand Prix at Watkins Glen because Reg gave his car to Surtees after he had crashed his own.

Roy equaled his best 1962 result—another second place behind Masten Gregory's UDT Lotus—in the first of two non-championship races in Scandinavia that followed the

Nürburgring, at Karlskoga in Sweden and Roskilde in Denmark. We had a mechanic who spoke fluent Swedish, so he went with Jimmy Potton to the Scandinavian races in the two-car transporter. I stayed home, working in the shop, partly because I was nervous about my wife's pregnancy. Our son, Paul, was born two weeks later, on September 10. I was there and I was thrilled by it. Seeing my son right after he was born was the biggest thrill I ever had until my daughter was born in America.

Reg wouldn't allow me to skip the Italian Grand Prix the following week. I wished he had. Behind a BRM 1-2 with Hill and Richie Ginther, both our cars had engine problems and retired within a lap of each other. It was curious, because this was the first race that Harry Spears of Coventry Climax attended with us, and I thought we did everything right, engine-wise. Like us, Harry was both surprised and disappointed. Monza is a long way to go from London for nothing.

When I got back to work after a short paternity leave, Reg called me into his office. In those days, this often meant trouble for me of some kind. Reg said he was going to send two Lola F1 cars to South Africa in December for two races in Johannesburg and East London, along with only two mechanics. I was the Climax engine man, so I was to go with Ray Lane. He added that he also intended to run two Lolas in the Tasman races in New Zealand and Australia, and I was to build five special, 2.7-liter Climax engines using the old 2.5-liter as a base. The additional 200cc would come from a special, stroked crankshaft with tungsten counterweights, and the 2.7s would be running on methanol, not gasoline. He told me I would leave on December 10, and after the South African Grand Prix, I would fly to New Zealand from East London and Ray would come home. I would then meet Jimmy in New Zealand, and we would get two cars ready for the first race at the new Pukekohe track near Auckland to be driven by Surtees and Tony Maggs, an up-and-coming South African driver who had been driving with Bruce McLaren at Cooper. I would finally come home after the last Tasman race in Melbourne, Australia—some time in February.

Ray Lane was a new team member, a nice guy and a very competent race mechanic who had worked for Formula 2 privateer John Campbell-Jones. He would be a good traveling companion. Reg planned to send the F1 Lolas and a Lotus 24 by air to South Africa, and two more Lolas and a spare Cooper by sea to New Zealand. He had bought the Lotus as a spare car earlier in the year, and I'd put a Maserati engine in it, then later a Climax V8 F1 engine. Now he had sold it to the reigning South African champion, Syd van der Vyver.

I didn't break the news to Sally right away about this trip. Frankly, I didn't know how!

Ray and I arrived at Jan Smuts airport in Johannesburg on December 10 and were met by a South African gentleman named Syd, who owned a Shell gasoline station on the Pretoria road near Kyalami, where the Rand Grand Prix was to be held. He took us straight to his garage, where our Lolas were still in their packing cases along with the spares and tools. He found out we had never been to South Africa before and said there were a few things to learn if we were going to enjoy our visit.

He told us never to ask his workers to do anything without first checking with him or Willy, the black foreman. He said most of his workers were from the Bantu tribe, and that Willy was kind of a Bantu chief and was very important to his relationship with the workers. Finally he said he would introduce us to them, and asked us to maintain a strict decorum while he did so. Willy rounded up the six men, and in their dark blue coveralls, they stood at attention in a straight line while Syd made this speech: "These gentlemen are Mr. Lane and Mr. Bryant from England. They are the white masters of the fast cars from across the big water. They are the guests of our government. Do not get in their way or ask them silly questions. Do not steal any of their equipment. If you do, they will go back to England and complain to the Queen. Then she will send special policemen to arrest those who did it. If they ask you a question, give them a polite answer with no lies. If you have any questions,

LEFT: Surtees leaves the pits at Kyalami for his qualifying attempt at the 1962 South African Grand Prix. (Peter Bryant)

tell Willy, and he will get their answers for you. That is all!"

Ray and I were taken completely by surprise. Syd assured us it was the right thing to have done and told us that if anything did go missing, we were to tell Willy and take no action ourselves.

We spent that afternoon unpacking Surtees's Lola and the Lotus 24, and getting them more or less ready to race. Then we went to the Hotel Capri, where they asked us who we were. We told them, "We are the white masters of the fast cars from across the big water."

One evening after finishing work in Syd's garage, Ray left his watch on the washbasin and didn't notice until we got back to the hotel, where we were sharing a room.

The next day, we asked Willy to help us find Ray's watch. Willy asked us not to tell Syd, and when we got back from lunch that day, the watch was magically back on the washbasin. We were never told who had taken it, but we did notice that one of the gas pump attendants had a black eye!

We delivered the Lotus to Vyver and pointed out that it was fitted with a new style of diaphragm clutch that only required a short action to disengage. We told him not to change the adjustment because, if he pushed the pedal too far, he could turn the pressure plate inside out. Well, he did mess with it. And that was what put him out of his first race after qualifying on the third row.

The Rand Grand Prix meeting was an interesting experience. I had never been to a segregated race before. They had separate sections for black and white spectators. The only thing a black man could do on a race car in South Africa in those days was operate a foot pump to blow up the tires for the Dunlop technicians. They had a giant foot pump and one stroke would give a pound more pressure. Only the white guy from Dunlop was allowed to operate the tire gauge. It was a totally ridiculous situation, I thought, but we had been warned to say nothing about it under any circumstances.

The race was won by Clark followed by Trevor Taylor in a 1-2 for the unbeatable Lotus 25. Surtees got a very creditable third in our Lola after a dice with another former bike World Champion, Gary Hocking, in Rob Walker's Lotus. Hocking would lose his life only a week later, practicing for the Natal Grand Prix.

We didn't do that race because we'd loaded everything back into the crates and had headed straight for East London. Surtees asked Ray and me if we would like a ride there with him, which meant driving across the Kalahari Desert. We thought we should go in case he broke down. It was a great safari! At one point, we came up to what looked like a speed bump on the desert highway. At the last second, John stopped the car. It was a gigantic snake, weaving its way across the road.

When we arrived in East London, John dropped us at our three-star hotel and left for his five-star one. We were still running on our £10 per diem and Gillian had found us a family-style hotel. The manager greeted us with a hearty handshake and started apologizing for the size of our rooms right away. It was Christmas, he said, and many families came to the southeast coast to enjoy the beaches, so he was full to the gills. He called my room the "Dog Box" because it was so small and said that, if I would stay in it until after Christmas Day, he would let me have it half-price. I readily agreed because all I was going to do in the room was sleep—what did I care if it had no windows?

The next day, we left the hotel to walk to the garage where our race cars had been delivered, and three little black kids met us outside. They were about nine years old and they had makeshift guitars made from one-gallon oil cans. They followed us all the way to work, playing and singing rock and roll to us as we walked. I gave them some money. Ray said this was a mistake, because now we would never get rid of them. What the hell, I thought, it's Christmas. Sure enough, they walked with us every morning until we left. When we said goodbye, we gave them a "bonus" and they cried. They were great little kids. The manager asked us how much money we had given them each day and, when we told him, he said, "No wonder they cried! You paid them more than I pay the room maids for a whole day."

The race at East London on December 29 was the first ever South African Grand Prix counting towards the World Championship, and obviously the last race of 1962. It was an anti-climax for our team. After Kyalami, I'd changed the main and connecting rod bearings, reground the valves, and reset the timing on Surtees's car, but it was all for nothing. He managed to get 5th on the grid, but Salvadori qualified 11th. In the race, Surtees went out with a broken oil pump, and Salvadori with a leaking fuel cell. It was his last F1 race for Reg Parnell. Clark lost the championship because of an oil leak and Hill cruised to the win and the title.

I didn't consider the South African adventure a total loss. We'd had a third place at Kyalami, and I'd seen the Kalahari Desert. The year was almost over and I was still a Formula One mechanic. I had actually been to the famous Monaco Grand Prix. To top all that, Sally and I had a new baby. I was not complaining. Life was good.

BELOW: At the 1963 New Zealand GP victory banquet, from left to right: Reg Parnell, Jimmy Potton, Tony Maggs, John Surtees, Peter Bryant, David Oxton. (Peter Bryant)

CHAPTER 11

An Epic Tasman Trip

The 1962 season was finally over, but the new one started straight away. I left Ray Lane to finish packing up all the gear we had brought out to South Africa before he flew home to England and, on December 30, I took the plane with all the racers who were going to New Zealand for the Tasman races. There was a whole crowd of us. It included Graham Hill, Jack Brabham, Innes Ireland, Bruce McLaren, and Stirling Moss, along with our own two drivers, John Surtees and Tony Maggs. I had a set of gears in a carry-on bag, a big box of Weber carburetor jets, and four anti-rollbars tied together with tape. In my suitcase were some of my special tools for working on Climax engines, including my degreed timing disc that bolted onto the crankshaft to time engines. I must have had about 90 lbs. of baggage.

Our first flight was to Nairobi, Kenya, for an overnight stay, after stopping briefly in Rhodesia to refuel. When we got to Nairobi, we all went straight to the Stanley Hotel. Our flight to the next stopover wasn't scheduled until 5:00 p.m. the next day, so we would have time to see the famous Nairobi game reserve. I woke up early and went down to breakfast. John Surtees was already at a table with some people, so I sat with Jack Brabham and his mechanic, Tim Wall. Jack asked me if I would like to go to see the game reserve with them, so we ate our breakfast and piled into a chauffeur-driven car that Rootes had provided for him.

The game reserve was incredible. We saw every kind of African wild animal, even lions, which was a rarity. At one point, a baboon put his hand though the window of the

ABOVE: I signal ready for the tow over the hill into Christchurch. (Peter Bryant)

car, grabbed Tim's camera, and wouldn't let go. Tim had to bite the baboon's arm to get it loose! I cursed myself for not owning a camera, and resolved to buy one at the next duty free shop. At another of our many stopovers on the way to New Zealand, in Aden, Jack Brabham helped me pick out a 35mm camera.

When we got to the airport for the next hop on our journey, East African Airlines declared that they would be weighing everything, including our hand luggage. It was obvious that everyone was over the 44-lb. baggage allowance, so we told them we would weigh in our baggage together, and they could divide the total by the number of passengers in our group. Luckily, the lip of the scales overlapped the platform it was mounted on, and as the bags were piled on, Innes Ireland and I put our toes under the lip to stop the platform compressing. The needle of the scales was flipping up and down like crazy, but the airline staff couldn't see what we were doing because they all stayed behind the counter. We finally got the needle to stop moving, and they took the weight and recorded it. We innocently waited for them to unload the scale, and we did it again. We did it four times and everyone also insisted on taking back their hand luggage, so they had no idea what had been weighed and what had not. They gave up, finally, and told us they wouldn't weigh any more bags.

When we finally boarded the aircraft, they'd upgraded us all to first class because it was New Year's Eve, so we sipped champagne on the flight to Karachi, via Aden and Delhi. Innes and I were old friends from my Lotus days and we sat together, chatting about my old racing buddy Britt Pierce, who had been his mechanic. On our approach into Delhi, the landing lights suddenly went off and we had to go round again. By then, we had drunk enough "champers" to calm our fears, and we just laughed it off. We arrived in Karachi just before midnight.

We were all booked to stay in the British Overseas Airways Corporation (BOAC) hotel, which was called Speedbird House, but first we had to clear Customs and Immigration. As we stood in line, word came back that we should have been immunized against yellow fever, because we'd stopped in Nairobi. This caused a panic! Several of us didn't have that stamp in the health certificates we had to carry in those days. Tony Maggs did have one, so Jack Brabham borrowed it, and six of us ran into the men's room and quickly made fake copies of the yellow fever stamp in our certificates. Jack was first done and he sailed through the line, but I had a problem. I'd used a fountain pen and the ink wasn't yet dry! Once the inspectors found a fake, they checked all the others very carefully. When it was all over, four of us had failed the inspection: Innes, John Surtees, Graham Hill, and me. So they marched us to a van to be put into quarantine for the night in a tin Quonset hut near the end of the airport runway. It was very hot, and the hut wasn't air-conditioned. Graham insisted on speaking to someone from BOAC. He explained who we were and asked them to get us some scotch or brandy to celebrate New Year's Eve. The BOAC guy knew that Graham had just won the Formula One World Championship, so he obliged with a bottle of each.

We settled down for a small, but not very quiet, booze-up. If anyone had ever told me that I would be at a New Year's Eve party with Graham Hill, John Surtees, and Innes Ireland, I would never have believed it. It was great! I felt very privileged to be in such company. Innes was a great storyteller. Being quite good at telling jokes myself, and very good at laughing at them, I can tell you that it was a whole lot of fun.

Graham told us how, having just become the 1962 World Champion, he had been disappointed with the accommodations on offer for our overnight halt in Nairobi. Apparently Sir Alfred Owen, the patron of BRM, was also a patron of Dr. Barnardo's, a charity for orphaned children all over the world. Owen had insisted that Graham stay at Dr. Barnardo's institution in Nairobi. So while we were all in the air-conditioned, five-star Stanley Hotel, he had been in a grass hut at Dr. Barnado's home.

The four of us finally fell asleep on some army cots at about 5:00 a.m. There were no guards that we could see, but we figured they had one posted outside the door. In the morning, they brought each of us two fried eggs, a piece of bread, and some coffee before taking us back to the terminal. They made us wait half an hour before the Indian health inspection officer informed us that the flight was going to be late, so we had to go back into quarantine. His uniform looked like he had slept in it, then rolled around inside a flock sleeping bag. Graham Hill hit the roof. "How dare you try to do this to us again?" he shouted. "You've brought us into the terminal building and made us wait nearly an hour surrounded by people with all kinds of diseases! Look at that man over there! He's got flies swarming round the open sores on his mouth! And look at yourself in the mirror! You're filthy! When was the last time you washed? You're the one that should be quarantined, not us. Now take us to the transit lounge so that we can be with our friends and protected from all these sick people." Graham had a military-type moustache and could have been an army officer. I guess he scared the pants off the guy because, the next thing we knew, we were in the transit lounge.

The plane, a Boeing 707, arrived and Reg Parnell was on it, with several other racers. I slept so long that I missed landing and taking off again from Singapore. Whenever I went to a new country in those days, I ran into the gift shop and bought a souvenir to remind me of the experience. I blew it that time.

Our next stop was Darwin, Australia. As it came in to land, the aircraft was weaving from side to side. We found out later that it had ruptured a hydraulic line in the tail rudder control system. They didn't want to unload the plane at first, but eventually relented, adding that passengers who wanted their suitcases could have them. So I asked for mine. I'd worn the same underwear and shirt for nearly two days, and felt a bit yucky, to say the least. After we'd been in the lounge about two hours, they announced that they needed some parts that weren't available locally. We were to be taken to a local hotel for the rest of the morning and they would fly in another plane that evening to take us on to Sydney, still about 2000 miles away. This was becoming a truly epic journey. By that time I was so jet-lagged I had no idea where my body clock was. They put us into the Fanny Bay Hotel for a few hours. I was in a dormitory along with a bunch of people, including two of my roommates from Karachi. Innes and Graham amused themselves by throwing shower rings at the big electric ceiling fan to see how far they would ricochet. Often they would fly off and hit one of us; they thought that was great fun and laughed like crazed idiots. The jetlag was beginning to affect everyone.

I went for a swim and it was like diving into molten lead. It was 115 degrees Fahrenheit with 95 percent humidity. If you listened carefully, you could plainly hear the termites eating into the wooden hotel structure. The hotel owner told me they had to rebuild the hotel every four years, section by section. I could never have lived in Darwin for very long.

Finally, they took us back to the airport and loaded us onto a new 707, and we set off for Sydney. I have a ton of relatives there, but it was my first visit. My father's brother had emigrated from England and had raised six kids, who by then had started to create a new line of Aussie Bryants. I wouldn't have time that trip to meet with them, but maybe I could later in the tour. I called Uncle Bob just to say hi, and he was delighted and surprised to hear from me. We stayed over at the Hotel Wentworth near Sydney Harbor Bridge, and I got to walk around a bit. It felt good to be on the ground for a few hours and actually sleep in a bed.

Next morning, Reg woke me early to tell me he had managed to get me an early flight to Auckland, so I should move my ass and pack. It was still the holiday period, so he had been lucky to find even one open seat to Auckland that day. I was surprised that Reg gave it to me, but it was now January 3, and the race was on January 5. If the drivers got to the circuit by Friday, they could still qualify, but only if the cars were ready, so I was needed there right now. The aircraft was a Lockheed Electra. I got on with a bit of trepidation, because they had been falling out of the sky on a regular basis. I was nervous all through the flight, but finally I arrived in Auckland.

Jimmy Potton was there to greet me like a long-lost buddy. It was evening, and we went straight to the Station Hotel and into the bar for a cold one. I was sipping my beer when something hit me in the back. It was a very drunk Kiwi bloke and, as he turned to say something to me, he puked all over me. I ran to the bathroom to wash myself down and then went to my room for some fresh clothes. I took the soiled clothes down to the front desk to get them dry-cleaned, and when I got back to the bar, the guy was very apologetic. He insisted on giving me £10 to pay for my cleaning. The bartender remarked, "Why don't you buy a charity raffle ticket for this nice transistor radio?" So I did. We had another beer and went to bed. At 2:00 a.m. my phone rang, and it was the bartender. "Come up to the bar, mate, and get your radio—you've won the raffle." Being jet-lagged, I couldn't sleep, so I went up and picked up the radio. The guy who had puked on me was still there and insisted on buying me a beer, telling everyone how he had brought me luck. I told them why I was in New Zealand, and the puker asked me if he should come out to the track and vomit on our car for luck. I wondered if the name of the track—Pukekohe—figured in the equation some way.

Pukekohe meant "hill of the koekohe," New Zealand's native mahogany tree. The Franklin Racing Club and the New Zealand Grand Prix Association had built the track themselves for the amazingly low cost of £50,000, and it was very nice, too. The first non-championship race of 1963 was named the New Zealand Grand Prix, and a few of what the Kiwis called "internationals" were entered, including the freshly crowned World Champion. Graham Hill was going to race the new Ferguson P99, a revolutionary, front-engined, four-wheel-drive car with a 2.5-liter Climax engine. Jack Brabham had one of his own BT3 cars, equipped with a 2.7-liter Climax similar to the engines in our Lolas, which were to be driven by John Surtees and Tony Maggs. Bruce McLaren also had a 2.7 Climax in his own 1962 Cooper T53, while another NZ driver we had our eye on was a young guy named Chris Amon, driving Bruce's ex-works Cooper T53. The previous time I had been in New Zealand, he had done amazingly well racing a 250F Maserati against the more modern rear-engined cars.

We were all running methanol fuel, with giant, 52mm Weber side draft carburetors.

LEFT: "Lucky" Jimmy Potton gets a speeding ticket in New Zealand. (Peter Bryant)

ABOVE: Kiwi journalist and McLaren secretary Eoin Young (hanging on rail) and mechanic Barry Grouby join two unidentified women in the ship's pool on the way to Australia. (Peter Bryant)

ABOVE: My uncle Bob gets back the hat he left in England at the Sydney docks in an official "handing over" ceremony. (Peter Bryant)

What the others didn't know was that Reg had two top-secret engine tweaks that would make all the difference.

When I had been building our engines from scratch, Reg had taken the wet-sleeve cylinder liners to a fire extinguisher company to have them "Parkerized." This was a graphite-type coating that was plated onto the surface of the cylinder walls. When you run an engine on methanol, it washes the oil off the cylinder walls, and that accelerates the bore wear and reduces the lubricating efficiency of the oil, which also gets burned more quickly by the engine.

Our other secret weapon was dry ice. The weather promised to be hot and humid, so Reg and I planned to buy up all the dry ice we could find the day before the race. The fuel was always supplied in five-gallon jerry cans, so it would be a simple matter to surround the cans with dry ice under a tarpaulin and bring the fuel temperature way down before we put it in the car. This would have two benefits: the engine would run cooler and make more power, and it would keep the cockpit nice and cool. Running the cars on methanol was a nuisance in one respect because if they were going to be standing around for a while, you had to drain out all the fuel at the end of each day and run some gasoline through the fuel system. If methanol was left in the complex Webers for very long it tended to turn to jelly and gum up the works. Being able to cool it way down made up for that.

We kept the secret weapons very, very secret. No one knew about the liner treatment, even at Coventry Climax where they had dyno-tested the engines prior to installation in the cars.

About 30 cars had been entered in the race, but not all were F1-type single-seaters. It was a strange sight to see such an assortment of sports cars and specials practicing with F1 cars from all eras, including an old Super Squalo Ferrari and even a Jaguar-powered Maserati special. Reg Parnell had brought over one of last year's Tasman Coopers as a spare car and ended up loaning it to a young Kiwi named Jimmy Palmer. Jimmy had entered a Formula Junior Lotus 20 but knew it was not a potential race winner against cars like ours. It was a last-minute thing, but after only an hour of practice in the Cooper, Jimmy did an amazing qualifying time that put it ninth on the grid. He was thrilled, because race day would be his 21st birthday and now he had a good chance. I wasn't quite as thrilled—all it meant to me was another potential engine to maintain on top of the other stuff we had to do.

Surtees got to the track on Friday, put in a few laps, and recorded the second-fastest qualifying time, just behind McLaren. It was really hot, and it looked like it would be a race of high attrition. After qualifying, both Surtees and Maggs needed their cylinder heads retightened to keep the head gaskets intact. Brabham made the third-fastest time ahead of Maggs, Hill in the experimental Ferguson, and Amon. The difference between the fastest and slowest qualifiers was so vast that the organizers decided that some of the slower cars would run in a supporting race. This meant that there were 17 cars on the grid with a time difference between fastest and slowest of around 10 seconds.

On race day, a crowd of 45,000 people made their way into the track to sweat, drink, sweat some more, and watch a race that would be what the local press dubbed "a bit of a debacle." John Surtees won the 75-lap New Zealand Grand Prix with our dry ice–cooled Lola Mk 4. I was totally thrilled because he did it with an engine that I had personally built from the ground up. It was the greatest moment in my racing mechanic's life so far, and getting a really big thank you from the legendary Reg Parnell was a bonus worth more than I could ever have wished for.

Maggs over-revved his engine and bent a valve early on in the race. In second place was a local driver named Angus Hyslop in a 2.5-liter Cooper, the only car on the same lap as Surtees. Palmer was more or less tied for third place with Hill, who then conked out on the penultimate lap. It was a great birthday for Jimmy. An old front-engined Lola Mk 2, with a 1400cc Ford engine, was fourth, driven by another local lad, John Hinstead. That tells you how bad the attrition was. Only seven cars were running at the end, and Surtees was really just coasting around. Amon's Cooper was the seventh car, after numerous pit stops to try and fix a faulty magneto.

The other three races in New Zealand weren't much fun for Surtees, but Maggs did pretty well after I'd rebuilt his engine with a new piston and valves. At the next race, on the little 1.1-mile track at Levin, Tony got second place behind Brabham and just ahead of Ireland, who was now driving the four-wheel-drive Ferguson. John dropped out after only one lap with gearbox problems.

The highlight of practice at Levin was provided by the antics of Bruce Abernathy. Bruce was a former New Zealand motorcycle dirt track speedway star, and he decided to have some fun. He painted his old Formula Junior Cooper purple and wrote "Noddy Car" on it—after a popular British children's cartoon character who drove a little car with a bell on it, wore a little red pointed hat, and had a best friend called "Big Ears." He painted big white circles that were slightly offset from center on the four tires, and wore a red pointed hat over his crash helmet. Somehow he did all this after taking the car through tech inspection. When practice started, he shot out onto the track to the complete amazement of everyone, and actually turned in some quite good laps. Sadly, the organizers didn't see the funny side and excluded him from the race.

Next day, we loaded the cars on a ferry to Christchurch for the Lady Wigram Trophy race. When the boat docked at the South Island port of Lyttelton, Jimmy and I once again enjoyed the opportunity to climb into the Lola F1 cars. We were towed up a hill outside the port and then coasted five miles or so down a steep hill into Christchurch. We just let the cars go as fast as they wanted, relying on the brakes if anything happened. We could coast silently past other drivers at quite high speeds, and it must have really spooked them.

Tony finished third in the Lady Wigram race, behind McLaren and Brabham. John had gearbox problems again and retired halfway through. He was very disappointed, and so were we. He and Tony had both been on the front row of the 4-3-4 grid, with John milliseconds slower than Brabham on pole, and Tony fourth outside McLaren.

At Teretonga, amazingly, the front row of the grid was exactly the same. McLaren won again, but this time Tony was second behind his former teammate, ahead of Ireland in the Ferguson. Unfortunately John had fuel-feed problems and finished ninth, but he salvaged something when he won a six-lap sprint for the fastest eight cars (from a rolling start) at the end of the day.

The New Zealand portion of the Tasman was over, and right after Teretonga, Jimmy and I loaded all the stuff into the crates and put them on a boat to Australia. We had planned to fly, but instead we traded in our Pan Am tickets for ship tickets and went with the cars on a three-day cruise to Sydney. We had plenty of racers for company on the boat, including Chris Amon and Eoin "Buster" Young, who was now officially involved in Bruce McLaren's career as his "secretary" and was traveling with Wally Wilmot, Bruce's mechanic. The addition of Bruce Abernathy, Jimmy Palmer and his dad Barry Grouby (a mechanic for Kiwi driver Tony Shelly), and the Ferguson mechanics Bill and Malcolm turned the voyage into a real party experience. It was a wonderful change from the racing activities, and we all had a great time drinking a few beers and singing in the ship's piano bar.

Two people met us in Sydney. My uncle Bob was on the dock to welcome me, and in a brief but moving ceremony, I gave him back the hat he had inadvertently left in England on his last visit. I promised to come to his daughter's house for a barbecue the following weekend. The other was Laurie O'Neil, a wealthy friend of Reg Parnell. We were going to be housing the cars in his garage, called Cannington Propriety. The O'Neils loved racing and collected classic cars. They had wonderful facilities and were very helpful. We had a lot of work to do.

The following Sunday, Jimmy and I found our way to my cousin Jean's house on the outskirts of Sydney for a family barbecue. It was great to see my cousins again after nearly 20 years. We all stood around in Jean's unfenced backyard, drank a few beers, and ate some "chooks" (Aussie for chickens). The fire was dying down, and a couple of the kids were attempting to revive it. I wasn't paying much attention until I heard a scream. One of the little boys had been pouring kerosene from a quart measure onto the dying ashes. Suddenly flames had run up the kerosene and set fire to the can. He dropped it and it bounced on the edge of the barbecue wall and spilled flaming kerosene over another boy. It was he who had screamed. Now he was running into the great outback!

Without thinking, I dropped my beer and ran after him. He was about 11 and running like he was on fire—which he was! I never was a very good runner, but I dived at his feet and brought him down. I rolled around on the ground with him to put out the flames. They took him to the hospital with second-and-third-degree burns over 40 percent of his body. He was in bad shape. His mother couldn't thank me enough for catching him, and we all went to the hospital and waited until he was stabilized.

Jimmy and I went back to work next day and followed his progress by phone. Many years later, in 1997, my wife and I visited Australia to help celebrate Uncle Bob's 97th birthday. That little boy was now 6 feet, 4 inches tall and had a family of his own. He gave me a big hug, and I asked him to stay well away from the barbecue.

The first race in the Land of Oz was the Australian Grand Prix, held for the first time just outside Sydney at Warwick Farm, a horse-racing track that had been converted to hold motor races as well. It was as hot as hell, and we did the same trick with the dry ice. Even so, the heat got to John, and he lost the lead to Brabham. He drove the fastest lap in a mighty attempt to catch Brabham again but had to settle for second place with McLaren third. The heat was also too much for Tony, and he started getting dizzy, so he came into the pits for a bucket of water to be thrown over him. We weren't expecting him, and the only place to dip a bucket was a horse trough. I could see pieces of chaff in the murky brown water but I filled a bucket and threw it all over his face and chest. He shouted for more, so I refilled the bucket and this time poured it slower so some went down his back. He tipped back his head and opened his mouth, and I poured some down his throat. It must have tasted like shit because it sure smelled like it. He pulled down his goggles and finished the race. Afterwards he never mentioned the crappy water, and neither did I.

We did two more races on the Australian mainland, and one in Tasmania, at Longford.

LEFT: The cars leave the ferry at the port of Lyttelton on New Zealand's South Island before being towed into Christchurch for the Lady Wigram Trophy race. (Peter Bryant)

BELOW: Bruce McLaren holds the Lady Wigram Trophy after winning 1963's last Tasman race at Teretonga. He shares the roof of the pace car with runner-up Tony Maggs for a lap of honor. (Peter Bryant)

Being a beer drinker of some finesse, I particularly remember the coldness of the beer served in the hotel where we stayed for the race at Lakeside, near Brisbane. In New South Wales in those days, the pubs shut for dinner between 5:00 p.m. and 7:00 p.m., but here in Queensland, they shut at 6:00 p.m. for the night. However, if you were a guest staying in a pub, you could drink after-hours. In the tropical temperatures at that time of year, we needed a cold beer after work. The glasses were kept in the freezer, and the beer was almost frozen when you tried to drink it. At first it seemed too cold, but amazingly it went down even faster!

At the Lakeside circuit, near Brisbane, it rained cats-and-dogs every afternoon. The Ferguson P99, with Graham Hill back in the cockpit, finally showed the value of four-wheel drive and ABS in the rain. The car had a new kind of anti-lock braking called the Dunlop "Maxaset" system, which Harry Ferguson had imported right from the airplanes on which it was used. The P99 just ran away from everyone in practice. But after all the rain, the race started in the dry, and Surtees pulled out another win for us, with Hill in second place. Defending Australian Gold Star champion Bib Stillwell was third with his Brabham-Climax, ahead of 19-year-old Chris Amon in his Cooper. Reg Parnell was really impressed by the youngster's driving. Maggs and McLaren both failed to finish with water-related ailments.

ABOVE: Reg Parnell takes the helm of Laurie O'Neil's boat during a cruise of Sydney Harbor. (Peter Bryant)

Before we traveled to Tasmania, we unfortunately lost the services of John Surtees, who returned to Europe to sign a contract to drive for Ferrari. The rest of us enjoyed the opportunity to get on a ferry again for the overnight trip over from Melbourne. Thirteen of us "slaves" bellied up to the ship's bar that evening, with each one buying a round of 6-ounce beers. I went to bed happy that night—as far as I know.

The track at Longford was made up of public roads closed for the weekend to allow us to race for the South Pacific Trophy. McLaren won this race after Brabham's car caught fire with Stillwell second. Maggs qualified well but was sprayed by hot oil during the race from a crack in one of the Lola's fore-aft chassis tubes. After several pit stops to clean his goggles, he finished sixth. Jim Palmer was fourth with our Cooper. Amon was a delayed seventh this time, but Reg kept asking Jimmy and me what we thought of him. We always said he looked bloody good considering his age and equipment.

We had one more race to do, at Sandown Park in Melbourne, and I couldn't wait to get home. Since November, I'd worked at eight races in three separate countries on two continents. I had packed and unpacked those giant crates until I could almost take no more. I figured I would get home about March 17. I wondered if I still had a wife and how my son was doing. My mail from England kept missing me. I needed to go home badly.

Reg hired Masten Gregory to drive Surtees's Lola at Sandown. Although I'd known Masten a long time, he'd never driven a car I worked on. He gave us a surprise when he came to the garage for his seat fitting. He was sitting in the cockpit when he suddenly jumped up into a standing position and threw himself sideways onto the floor. I thought the car must have caught fire! He put another string of red licorice in his mouth and said, "Don't worry, I always check out the escape route when I drive a different car." Then we began the process of modifying the seat to suit his weirdly shaped ass. A couple of rolls of sponge rubber behind the upholstery failed to satisfy him, so I removed the seat and put a box of Colotti gears in the lower back area to get an idea of what he needed. Amazingly, he said, "That's great! If you can shape the seat like this, I'll be fine." I looked at Jimmy and we laughed. Masten passed round his packet of licorice to celebrate. I took out the box of gears, formed an aluminum piece, and covered it with some foam. He loved it.

McLaren won again, with Brabham second and Maggs third. Masten qualified our other Lola seventh but worked it up to fourth until two laps from the end, when a half shaft broke. Masten was pushing his car over the finish line as Brabham came slowly past and he reached out to give Jack a high-five. Jack drove over his foot. I told Masten a World Champion usually charged extra for that. He was classified seventh and Amon ninth. Reg again loaned our Cooper to Palmer, who retired with gearbox problems.

It took us all next day to pack up, and we left the following day to fly home via an overnight stop in Hong Kong, and another nervous flight from there back to England on an untrustworthy BOAC Comet. When I finally got home, my reception wasn't as friendly as it might have been, especially when I complained how cold it seemed. Sally said, "Well, that does it! You have no idea what cold is! While you were racing around the Antipodes in your shorts, we had to have the cat put down because it refused to go outside to pee in the frozen dirt and I couldn't have it peeing in the house near Paul. You'd better find us somewhere warm to live soon, or we'll go on our own!"

BELOW: Chris Amon at his first Formula One race for Reg Parnell at Goodwood in 1963. He finished fifth—a great start. (LAT Photographic

CHAPTER 12

Farewell to Formula One

When the Bowmaker finance company stopped sponsoring Reg Parnell Racing at the end of 1962, he decided to finance the team himself. John Surtees, who had finished fourth in the World Championship behind Graham Hill, Jimmy Clark, and Bruce McLaren, was offered a drive by Scuderia Ferrari and decided to take it. You can't blame him for taking the opportunity. It has been and probably always will be every driver's dream to drive for the most prestigious Grand Prix team in history.

Reg had Tony Maggs, but he again asked Jimmy Potton and me what we thought of Chris Amon as a potential driver. He was only 19 years old but had shown outstanding talent in the Tasman races with older cars. We endorsed his choice, and Chris came over to England.

Reg also asked Mike Hailwood, the motorcycle king of the Isle of Man TT races, to drive for us in selected races. He invited New Yorker Peter Revson to use our racing facilities to house his Formula Junior car while he did the European series, and he also rented out workshop space to New Zealander Tony Shelly for his F1 Lotus 24. Arnold Stafford—the ingenious engineer who had made us a gearbox input shaft at the 1961 New Zealand Grand Prix—was Tony's mechanic.

ABOVE: Chris Amon in the Mk 4 Lola at the 1963 French GP at Reims. (LAT Photographic)

It promised to be an exciting Formula One season, with Jimmy Clark and Graham Hill again going head-to-head for Lotus and BRM respectively, along with competition from Surtees in a new Ferrari. We felt that if Amon lived up to his potential in our Lola Mk 4A, we could do fairly well.

On Easter Monday, Amon made his debut in the Glover Trophy race at Goodwood, which was won for the British Racing Partnership team by Innes Ireland in a Lotus 24. Bruce McLaren's Cooper was second, and in our Lolas, Tony finished third, and Chris did a pretty good job and came in fifth. He had qualified seventh next to American Jim Hall in BRP's other Lotus-BRM, which finished just ahead of him. Reg was tickled pink with these results.

Chris came to the attention of Basil Cardew, a journalist for a very widely read British tabloid, and he asked him where in New Zealand he came from. Chris answered, "Bulls."

Cardew said, "Well, if you're going to take that attitude, I won't bother you with any more questions." And he walked off in a big huff. We were all laughing when Reg told Chris, "You need to answer that question with something like, 'A small town called Bulls.'"

Our next race was the Aintree 200—another non-championship event, but this one was different because Hill and Clark were going to be there in their works BRM and Lotus cars. Hill beat Ireland by 10 seconds, with Clark third. Chris again finished in the money in sixth place, ahead of the second Team Lotus car, driven by Trevor Taylor.

After the race, Reg asked me to stop by at his farm, Wallfield Farm, near Findern in Derbyshire, to rebuild a four-cylinder Climax engine for Tim, his son. Tim was going to Ireland to race in a small event that paid good money, but his engine was broken. Belgian driver André Pilette and his son, Teddy, were going to compete in the same races, and they joined us at the farm. After a good night's sleep, I had time to tear down the engine before we all went to a local pub for lunch. We were sitting by the window when we heard brakes screeching and looked up in time to see a car skidding in the rain. It hit a dump truck that had pulled out of a farmyard right into its path, and careened onto two wheels, throwing out the driver through the open door. We all ran to see if we could help, but it was no use—the driver was dead in the road.

We trudged back to the pub to pay our bill. When we got back to Tim's house, one of his cows had decided to have a calf. I looked out the window of the shed and saw Tim and his laborer putting a rope around the tiny front legs of the partially born calf, and then pulling like hell on the rope. Suddenly it was all blood and afterbirth and all the other nasty stuff that goes with calving. I was a city slicker! I had to quit for a while, so I went into the house, and Tim's wife made me a cup of tea.

A local policeman arrived to find out what we had witnessed at the scene of the accident. After about an hour, I went back out to the shed and finished the engine. At dinner that evening, Tim asked me how I liked life on a farm. I told him it was not as serene as it had been cracked up to be—in fact, there was far too much violence and carnage for a nice young man like me! Next day, I was quite glad when Reg picked me up, and we went back to the race shop in suburban Hounslow.

The next race was the BRDC International Trophy at Silverstone. Amon could only qualify 13th (right alongside Jim Hall again) with the same time as Jo Bonnier in a Cooper-Climax. Bonnier went on to finish fifth in the race behind Clark, McLaren, Taylor, and Ireland, but Chris went out after only eight laps with gearbox problems. Our Colotti boxes were getting worn out and the gears fatigued. It was really time to get some new ones but they were not available, so we kept replacing gears as they wore out. Our Lolas were still fast in qualifying, but we were losing races because of component failures. Reg started talking about buying some new Lotus chassis to replace them.

To add to Reg's disappointment, Tim Parnell drove his own Lotus in the International Trophy but blew up his engine!

For the opening round of the World Championship, at Monaco at the end of May, Reg had decided to loan a car to the veteran French driver, Maurice Trintignant. Maurice was a real nice man and a pretty good driver, but he was beginning to show his age a little. Nevertheless, a former champion of France commanded good starting money in Monaco. Maurice was not used to the Lola's gearbox, and in the first practice session he missed a shift, over-revving the V8 Climax enough to bend a few valves. I begged Reg to let me fix the engine, but Harry Spears was there from Coventry Climax, and he put the kibosh on it.

It was Chris Amon's first time at Monaco, and he liked it all a lot, including the nightlife. He did quite well in the same session but decided to have a late night in the Tip-Top Bar with Buddy, one of our newly recruited mechanics. He showed up late for the second day of qualifying. Reg took one look at his bloodshot eyes and gave his car to Trintignant for the race. I really believe Chris could have gone faster than Maurice, even with a hangover, but Maurice carried that all-important cash in his back pocket, and that did it. So that was how Chris lost his first chance to race in Monaco.

We were staying at a small hotel in Eze-sur-Mer, on the coast road towards Nice. We often drove the cars from rented garages to the tracks and back in those days, and it was always a great experience for us mechanics. On race morning, I jumped into the Lola to drive it along the lower *corniche* the few miles to Monaco. On the way, we had to go through a tunnel. As we approached it, another car came out its mouth, and I realized I was on the English (wrong!) side of the road. I just had enough room to swerve before we had a head-on crash. It shook me up quite a bit—if I'd crashed the car, I don't think Reg would have ever forgiven me. In the race, Graham Hill and Richie Ginther delivered a 1-2 finish for BRM, and only seven cars finished. Maurice was not among them because he went out with an oil leak after 34 laps.

Next day, there was another "mechanics' Grand Prix" to get all the engines back to Coventry Climax for rebuilds. We made it in record time again, but in this case Reg didn't give us any extra time off. Meanwhile, until he left for the next race, Chris Amon had to stay at Reg's farm to "get fit," as Reg put it. Personally, I felt sorry for him, but I think he enjoyed farm life, so it was really no hardship.

June was crazy, because we had races only a week apart. For the Belgian Grand Prix at Spa-Francorchamps, Reg had Amon and a Belgian driver, Lucien Bianchi. We booked into in a small hotel very close to the track in a village called Trois Ponts (Three Bridges). We had the small transporter that carried two cars, and there were only three mechanics present—me, Ray Lane, and the infamous Buddy. And it was Buddy who insisted on driving the transporter up a steep ramp that led out of the parking lot. Almost as soon as he started up the ramp, the cold engine stalled. Buddy slammed on the brakes to stop the truck rolling back, and the inertia made the two race cars try to break out the back door. The one on the upper deck did just that, and with its rear wheels still held by the rearmost wheel chocks, it flew out and came to rest with its nose on the road. The nose fiberglass was broken, the radiator support was bent, and it looked pretty bad.

A top window of the hotel opened and out came Reg Parnell's red face. "What the heck is going on?" he yelled. Then he saw the broken car. "Who's driving?" Buddy sheepishly admitted his crime. Reg said, "Well, no more driving for you! Peter—get that car to the track and fix it. I'll be along shortly." With the help of the hotel staff, we lifted the car back into the truck, and I drove to the track. Luckily it was a clean fiberglass break, and I had made it look OK by the time Reg arrived.

It rained a lot the first day, so practice was limited. Chris became famous as the youngest driver ever to qualify for a Grand Prix, and with his local knowledge, Lucien also did OK in qualifying, although he was a couple of seconds slower. In the race, it rained some more, and Jim Clark won easily for Team Lotus. Chris had another engine problem, and Lucien crashed heavily in the rain at the end of the Masta Straight after colliding with Jim Hall. He hit so hard that the radiator was torn off and it flew through the window of the nearby farmhouse. We had to buy it back to pay the farmer for the damage.

Lucien recovered from his injuries, but it took some time. I loved Spa for its location but hated it for its danger in the rain. As things turned out, I never went there again.

We rushed back to England to get the cars ready for our next effort in Holland two weeks later. Reg was cutting back severely on expenses since losing Bowmaker's money, so I was the only mechanic he sent to Zandvoort. I drove the truck alone. The Dutch resort was wet and windy and everybody had problems, especially with blown sand jamming the throttles open. We only ran one car there, but there was a second chassis in the transporter ready for the French Grand Prix the following weekend.

The 1961 World Champion, Phil Hill, was now driving for the new ATS team, which had been formed by Carlo Chiti and five other engineers who had walked out of Ferrari before the start of the season. The ATS engine was pretty good, but the cars were very rough around the edges. They were in the same garage as us, and the night after qualifying, Phil came up to me and said, "Peter, may I ask you a question?" We walked over to the ATS car. The mechanics had left for dinner, and Phil pointed to the left front wheel: "Do me a favor and feel that bearing slop." I wiggled the front spindle, and sure enough, the bearing was very loose. I quickly checked it out, scared that the ATS guys would come back and catch me screwing with their car. The large inner wheel bearing outer member should have been a press fit in the upright, but it was loose. The whole bearing assembly could spin when you turned the wheel. I showed Phil the problem and scurried back to work on my own car. I had the Lola almost loaded and was getting ready to leave by the time the ATS guys got back from their dinner. I never knew the outcome of their conversation with Phil, but I did hear his distinctive American voice in rather serious discussion with Ingeniere Chiti about those front wheel bearings.

Chris showed promise in practice and qualified our Lola in 11th place, just behind Ludovico Scarfiotti's Ferrari. But the race was another anti-climax when Chris had to retire again, with a broken water pump. Early in the race, Phil Hill had a nasty moment when the left front wheel came off as he entered Tarzan, the big first turn. We were in the pit next to ATS, and it was not long before Phil arrived, carrying the severed front wheel complete with broken spindle. He shouted some words I can't repeat here, hurled the wheel over the pit counter, and stormed off. Obviously the ATS mechanics hadn't fixed the problem. Hill's relationship with ATS was at a real low. They didn't go to the next race at Reims, and Phil accepted a drive there in Scuderia Filipinetti's Lotus-BRM.

After the race, John Surtees's personal manager, David Yorke, asked me to have a drink with him at the Bowes Hotel, where I was staying. He said he had something to discuss. Although John was getting on pretty well with Ferrari's young technical boss, Mauro Forghieri, he was apparently having a tough time with the team manager. David told me that John was making plans with Ferrari to contest some big sports-car races in California and at Mosport, in Canada, around the same time as the U.S. Grand Prix. Ferrari had agreed to provide a car, but Surtees would have to provide his own mechanic to prepare it at the factory in Maranello. Would I be interested in working for John on this project?

I told David Yorke that when the time came to make a decision, I would discuss it with Reg Parnell, and we left it at that.

Next day, I set out for Reims for the French Grand Prix. I had a rear tire blow out on the freeway, but luckily I got the truck stopped without incident. I was just about to start jacking it up to change the wheel when the Team Lotus transporter pulled up and out got Jim Endruit, Colin Riley, and the guys. They told me to get out of the way, and in no time, they'd changed the wheel for me and put the tools away. I started to thank them, and they said it was their job to beat me on the track, not the highway. I was very moved by their help and generosity. The wheel weighed 85 lbs., and it took 400 ft. lb. of torque to tighten the lug bolts, so I hadn't savored doing it on my own. Colin would later come back into my life when I joined the Carl Haas Can-Am team in 1968 and he was Chuck Parsons's mechanic.

Reims 1963 was a very good event for Reg Parnell Racing. I was staying with the BRM guys at the same cheap hotel on the rue Burette, again letting them rent out my room to a hooker during the daytime to save money. We had our cars housed in a Simca garage opposite the hotel. After practice, we would work half the night preparing the cars, and Louis Stanley, BRM's team principal, would drop in after his dinner for a tour of inspection. He was always accompanied by his wife, Jean, who was the sister of the BRM owner, Sir Alfred Owen. She always had an amazing bouffant hairstyle and wore very expensive, very bright pink or pastel-colored dresses and coats. As she walked past the cars being worked on, a brush flick of dirty cleaning kerosene would sometimes head her way—accidentally on purpose. I bet her cleaning bill was enormous. Whenever they came along, it was a big waste of the mechanics' time because they would tie up Cyril Atkins, the chief mechanic, with silly questions. It was very amusing, and we razzed Cyril about it at every opportunity.

After work, and to kill time before we could get back into our rooms at 11:00 p.m., we would head over to Bridget's Bar for a beer or two. One evening the club was visited by the local *gendarmerie*, armed to the teeth and looking for so-called Algerian terrorists. It was really their way of trying to scare the British tourists! As they walked past one of the BRM boys, he reached out and touched the trigger of a Sten gun—and it fired! Everyone threw themselves on the floor, and in the confusion, while the *gendarmes* were yelling at us poor tourists, Ray Lane ran outside and opened the trunk of the Citroën the *gendarmes* had parked there. He grabbed the lug wrench, undid all the wheel lug nuts, and threw them away.

The police closed the bar, so we were all on the sidewalk when they came out to leave. They jumped in the car and it went a few yards, and then the wheels all wobbled and fell off. Everyone cheered. Tim Parnell happened to be standing the closest to the car, so the *gendarmes* put him in handcuffs and marched him off to jail for "questioning." We all followed, and when they took him inside, we started chanting, "Let Tim go! Let Tim go!" The hullabaloo woke the whole town, and the mayor showed up to see what was happening. One of the French racing mechanics told the mayor that the police were holding Tim and that if he wasn't released right away, all the Formula One mechanics would strike, and there would be no French Grand Prix. They released Tim, and we went back to our hotels in triumph.

Back at the track, Masten Gregory came up after the first practice session and said he would like me to meet a friend of his from California. He introduced me to Mickey Thompson, who told me he had heard good things about my mechanical abilities with rear-engined race cars, and would I be interested in relocating to California? Masten would be driving for him in the 1964 Indy 500 and wanted an experienced F1 mechanic on the car. I told him I was very interested and gave him my address in England so he could send me a proposal. Suddenly a *gendarme* asked Mickey where his pit pass was, and not speaking French, Mickey asked Masten to intercede. The policeman ignored Masten and grabbed Mickey by the arm to eject him from the pits. That was the wrong move. Mickey punched the *gendarme* on the nose. The next second, three more *gendarmes* grabbed him, frog-marched him backwards to their paddy wagon, and took him off to jail. I guess Masten was later able to square things with the police, but Mickey had to leave town.

Sunday was another very hot and humid day, but this time I avoided the ham salad that had poisoned me the year before. Reg Parnell had again rented our Lotus 24 Climax to Maurice Trintignant who surprised us by out-qualifying Chris Amon's Lola Mk 4A for 14th spot on the grid, with Chris 15th of the 19 cars in the race. Jimmy Clark was on the pole in his Lotus 25 with Graham Hill alongside in his BRM P61. The race starter was a fat little Frenchman named Toto Roche, who was a famous idiot. He liked to walk slowly in front of the grid with the starter's flag behind his back, and then suddenly spin round, jump in the air and wave the flag. All the drivers hated Roche's antics, and Graham Hill told me that they used to aim for him. But he would always get out of the way by the skin of his teeth, as all the mechanics cheered.

This time, for some reason known only to himself, Toto used a red flag, which was supposed to be used only to stop the race. It really spooked the BRP guys. Innes Ireland ran into the back of his teammate Masten Gregory, which put Innes into the pits and meant that Masten eventually retired with gearbox problems. Clark won easily, and Tony Maggs, now driving for the works Cooper team, beat Hill to take second place. Our guys did great. Chris finished seventh and Maurice eighth, a lap down after a quick pit stop. He pulled into the pits, jumped up in the seat, and took off his right shoe. He told me in French what was wrong, and for a moment I looked at him blankly. I had in my mind that *steak chasseur* was horsemeat so I thought he said his horse was hot, but actually it was his shoe (*chaussure*). I removed my right shoe, and he put it on and took off again. It turned out that there was a small pinhole in the footwell bulkhead, and hot air from the radiator had heated up the sole of his shoe to more than 200 degrees.

We were very satisfied that we had finally finished two cars in the top ten. We weren't the only ones. Next morning, as we drove the truck out of Reims, a car passed us and waved us down. It was Maurice. He had raced to catch up. He thanked us profusely for a great ride and gave us a bunch of French francs as a bonus. I went back to Hounslow with instructions to put a BRM V8 in one of the Lotus 24 chassis. I wondered what plans Reg had for it.

At Silverstone, Reg gave "Mike the Bike" Hailwood another ride in our Lotus 24 Climax. Mike was a real cool guy. Man, could he ride a motorbike at the Isle of Man TT races! He drove an E Type Jaguar with sheepskin seat covers, always wore the latest fashions, and always had the latest gadgets like miniature radios. The race was on Chris Amon's 20th birthday. He was determined to do well again, and he did, finishing seventh, with Mike eighth. Jim Hall was sixth in his BRP Lotus 24, seemingly confirming that the Lotus was faster with the BRM V8 than the Lola was with the Climax V8. Clark won the race with the Lotus 25, John Surtees was second in a Ferrari 156, and Graham Hill third again for BRM. It looked like Clark was going to be the champ this year.

It was a very hot race, and Chris got out of the car afterwards and lay down on the ground with heat exhaustion. As I was pouring cold water on him, Reg again told him, "Amon, you're unfit!" I thought Chris had done great—definitely as well as could be expected with our outdated cars. There was no time for anyone to do anything about his fitness, anyway, because we had a race at Stuttgart the next weekend and the German Grand Prix the weekend after that. We left for Germany only three days later.

I think Reg got onto Chris about his fitness because he couldn't find anything else to complain about. He sincerely wanted only the best things to happen to Chris and felt obliged to treat him like he treated his own son. He was always on Tim to straighten himself up a bit.

The non-championship Solitude race, near Stuttgart, was great for Jack Brabham, because he achieved his first victory, driving one of his own cars. But for us it was a big disappointment. Chris qualified eighth, but both he and Mike went out with engine problems. It gave me a lot of work to do before the Grand Prix at the Nürburgring a few days later.

Reg told Chris to ride with Ray and me to the 'Ring, to get there early and learn the circuit. Poor Chris had to ride from Stuttgart to Adenau sharing the only passenger seat in the truck with Ray, sitting on the engine cover for half of the time. He had never been to the 'Ring before and obviously needed to drive as many laps as possible, so I got Arnold Stafford's wife to give me a lift into Cologne to rent a car. It was a Ford Taurus, which Chris quickly nicknamed a Ford Tortoise. As we worked on the race cars, Chris did lap after lap of the 14-mile track. At the end of the first day, he gave the mechanics a ride back to Adenau via the whole length of the track, and scared the pants off us. I had never been through the Karussel so fast. We were amazed how quickly he had learned the circuit and knew the names of all the corners and features. I knew Reg would also be very impressed when he arrived.

To set up the F1 cars as best they could during the practice sessions, the drivers again used a short portion of the track, leaving the pit-lane, going round the South Curve, and coming back to the pits via the back entrance. Once they were satisfied with the fuel mixture and handling, they would do the short piece, then go across the start line at speed to get one full lap recorded, and then return via the back door. Even so, Reg only allowed Chris three full laps of practice and qualifying each day for fear of wearing out the car, but as he became used to the track Chris lowered his lap times in big increments—as much as 20 seconds. He ended up 14th on the grid, just behind Dan Gurney in a Brabham and ahead of Trevor Taylor in a works Lotus 25. I was certainly not alone in being very impressed with young Chris Amon on his first visit to the Nürburgring. Even then, it was a very treacherous track, and in view of the increasing speeds of the F1 cars, one badly in need of revising.

The race was a disaster for the two Kiwi drivers. On only the third lap, Chris's Lola had a steering arm break on landing at the *Flugplatz* ("flying place"), ending up in a ditch on the right side of the track. A barbed-wire fence nearly decapitated him, so he was lucky to escape with minor injuries. Bruce McLaren was not so lucky. On the very next lap, at the very same place, his steering also broke. He crashed on the other side of the road and was knocked unconscious when he was thrown out, seriously injuring both his legs. Moments later Willy Mairesse crashed his Ferrari 156, killing an ambulance attendant who was trying to help Bruce. "Mad Willy" injured an arm so badly that it ended his career.

When I saw how Bruce's Cooper T66 was rolled up into a ball, I was amazed he had even survived. There were seven accidents in all. Clark, who had won four races on the trot, had recurring engine problems in his Lotus-Climax, and finished second to the Ferrari of Surtees, who finally scored his first Grand Prix victory.

We had three weeks to get ready for the non-championship race at Zeltweg, in Austria. We took one Lola for Chris to drive, and he qualified it sixth, behind Clark, Brabham, Jim Hall, and Innes Ireland on the four-car front row and splitting Jo Siffert's Lotus and Jo Bonnier's Cooper on the row behind. No doubt about it, Amon was getting faster and faster. The heat caused all kinds of problems and thinned the field, and late in the race, Chris had our Lola in second place behind Brabham—until lap 70 of the 80-lap race, when he came into the pits with low oil pressure. Reg sent him out to drive a very slow lap and park up just before the finish line so that he could stutter across it when Brabham took the checkered flag. This he did, and he was classified fourth behind Tony Settember's Scirocco-BRM and Carel de Beaufort's old Porsche. It was disappointing, but it was still a good result, and Tim Parnell finished sixth with his Lotus-BRM. Young Jochen Rindt made his F1 debut at Zeltweg in an old Ford-powered Cooper and naturally the Austrian press were all over him. He did well to qualify 12th, but the engine broke in the race.

Then it was straight to Monza for the Italian Grand Prix, where Clark's victory sealed the championship. As it turned out, this race marked the end of the Formula One season for both me and Chris—but for him, it was almost a permanent end. The organizers decided not to use the banked portion of the track, and thank goodness for that. After the previous race I had attended there, Tony Maggs had told me how the cement ribs across and under the banking surface caused the car to buck, as if it were trying to throw him out.

We had two Lolas at Monza, with Mike the Bike back in the second one. Mike qualified 18th and fought his way up to 10th in the race, but by that time we were down to one car. Chris's car had an experimental Climax V8 that had more horsepower than we had previously seen. In the first practice session, he had a huge crash coming out of the second Lesmo turn and was almost thrown out of the car, breaking three ribs. He was hanging unconscious from the cockpit and some bastard stole his wristwatch. How low can you go?

Chris had certainly had quite a baptism in his first year of Formula One. He is one of the finest people I have had the pleasure to meet, and he was the smoothest driver I have worked with. But he was also the unluckiest. A Grand Prix driver needs to have luck on his side, and although he later raced for Ferrari, he just couldn't win with one of their cars. When he was driving for them their engines had the worst reliability ever, but as soon as he left to drive for March, Ferrari's luck changed. Later he won the 1971 Argentine Grand Prix for Matra, but it was the last time it was run as a non-championship race! So Chris is now in the Formula One history books as the driver who competed in the most World Championship Grands Prix without a win. As we say in the United States, this is a dirty shame!

After driving a Lotus 25 for Tim Parnell in 1964, Chris told me that he now realized how tough a job it had been for John Surtees to coax a win out of our Lola Mk 4. He said the aluminum monocoque Lotus was light years ahead of it. When John had complained about the lack of chassis stiffness at Spa in 1962, he had been right on the money with what was needed from a race-car chassis to be competitive. I stored that upstairs.

ABOVE: At his farm near Bulls, New Zealand, a mature Chris Amon holds the steering wheel that he bent out of shape wrestling with our Lola during his big accident at Monza. (Eoin Young)

After Monza, John Surtees asked me again if I would go with him to Maranello and then on to America and Canada for the sports-car races that David Yorke had mentioned. I spoke to Reg about it. He told me that any mechanic who had a chance to work for Ferrari and didn't take it was throwing away a great opportunity. He added that if it went somewhere for me, I deserved it. If not, I would be welcomed back the following season.

As soon as the Lolas were ready for the next Grand Prix at Watkins Glen, I said goodbye to the lads in Hounslow and to Reg Parnell, and flew to Italy to help John Surtees—and Ferrari.

BELOW: The Ferrari 250 P at Riverside. To spare Surtees's feet, I added a small duct to help get air into the footbox. (Chuck Queener)

CHAPTER 13

Wowed in America

Where were you when Kennedy was shot?

Whenever Harry Mundy, a brilliant British engine engineer and technical journalist, used to meet Jimmy Potton and me at the Formula One races, he would berate us for not joining the British Racing Mechanics Club. We thought it was just a bunch of old-timers, sitting around and spinning tales. We would laugh and tell him we didn't need to join a club to become F1 mechanics, and besides, we didn't qualify because we had never been riding mechanics at Brooklands in the good old days. Finally we found out that Mike Costin was the president and the meetings were really interesting, with reviews of technology and so on, so we joined.

The first annual dinner and dance I attended was at the Criterion Restaurant in Piccadilly, London, in November 1963. There were three big racing affairs in England each Christmas, and this was one of them. Most of the current Grand Prix drivers showed up, and the featured speaker was Graham Hill. It was a lively, black-tie affair, and as usual, everybody was on their worst behavior. As Sally and I arrived and began to walk up the stairs, two large silver serving trays came flying down the carpet towards us. We dodged out of the way, because riding on the trays were Innes Ireland and another guy who had challenged him to a race. This was definitely not going to be one of those stuffy affairs, then. The booze was flowing freely.

We walked into the bar to order our drinks, and the place suddenly fell silent. I thought we must be in the middle of some kind of practical joke. Then I noticed a TV behind the bar and everybody staring at it in stunned silence. The BBC announcer was saying, "President Kennedy succumbed to massive brain damage and was pronounced dead on arrival at the Parkland Memorial Hospital in Dallas."

This terrible news put a damper on the whole affair. We Brits considered Jack Kennedy to be our newest hero, partly because of the Cuban missile crisis and his magnificent management of the outcome. So now, whenever anyone asks me where I was when Kennedy was shot, I tell them I was at the annual BRMC dinner dance, watching Innes Ireland slide down the stairs on a tray.

John Surtees arranged an air ticket into Milan for me, and he drove from Modena to meet me. He had the concept version of the newest Ferrari Dino, and we drove back to Modena at very high speed. I remember thinking on the way that, for a cockney kid with a grammar school education, life didn't get much better than this. Here I was, being driven in a Ferrari by the number-one Ferrari race driver, to work as his mechanic at the Ferrari factory, so that I could fly to America with him and help him race a Ferrari 250 P sports-racing car. Nobody at my school would have believed it! I felt very proud of myself.

We checked in at the Hotel Real Fini in the via Emilia, and John took me to dinner that evening to talk about the project. He said he would pick me up every day and take me to the factory to work on the car. He introduced me to all the key people, including the engineering boss, Mauro Forghieri, and engine designer Valerio Colotti.

I already knew some of the Formula One mechanics, and they were very helpful. I was shown how to overhaul the gearbox and the clutch, which was mounted behind the rear cover of the transaxle. I liked that idea, because with a few special tools that they supplied, you could easily remove and inspect the clutch plates without pulling the gearbox off. The only thing I didn't like was the way that the slave cylinder was used to bleed the hydraulic clutch. It had a pump on top of the fluid reservoir where the fill cap was normally mounted. I thought that wasn't necessary and could screw up and cause the clutch to slip. But I reasoned that Ferrari was smarter than me, so one day I would be told why they did it that way.

Finally I was taken into the inner sanctum of the engine shop and shown how to time a V12. I was in race-car heaven at last!

One of the Ferrari mechanics I knew was named Vecci, and he and his colleagues were getting the F1 cars ready for the U. S. Grand Prix. One evening, they took me to their favorite watering hole in Modena, a club where they were all members. Vecci explained that Ferrari was a union factory and that all the mechanics were members of the *Federazione Impiegati Operai Metallurgici nazionale*—the Italian metal workers' union. The club sold beer real cheap, had a big TV for watching sports, and other nice benefits. I asked Vecci what was required to become a member and how much it cost. He told me it was free, but you had to be a card-carrying member of the Italian communist party. That explained why the Scuderia had so often stated that strikes by metal workers at the factory had stopped it from participating in races—all the mechanics were communists. Vecci hastily explained that most of the guys didn't give a damn about the *Partito Comunista Italiano*, but they liked the cheap beer.

Another evening, John and I were seated on the outside patio of the hotel having dinner, when an elegant couple stopped by to say hello to John. It was Alessandro de Tomaso and Isabelle, his tall and beautiful American wife, who had actually raced and entered cars under her maiden name, Haskell. They were taking their poodle for a walk. John told me that when Alessandro took out the dog by himself, some of the Italians used to make snide remarks about him being married to an American woman. But apparently she was fairly rich and that may have helped when he started his business, which had just produced its first road car, the Vallelunga. The remarks soon died away. He was an extremely talented engineer and later showed me an F1 gearbox he had designed with the rear suspension mountings integral to the box and bell housing casting. I believe it was the first time anyone had done that.

The last thing we did was to take the Ferrari 250 P car out to Ferrari's private test track for John to check it out. I had never seen Fiorano before, and it was really interesting. I didn't realize that they measured the oil pressure in kilograms per square centimeter so, when we started it up, and the gauge showed only 10, I wanted John to stop the engine before we damaged it. John laughed and pointed out my mistake. I was relieved and said I felt a bit stupid. John said, "No problem—we've all done that one!" The car worked great, and I got a ride around the track with John.

I had a great experience working at the factory, but it was over all too soon. I found myself packing up spare parts and tools into some oblong boxes, with gray and red stripes, for shipment by air to New York with the car. The F1 team was doing the same thing. I was looking forward to New York because for the past couple of weeks I had consumed a whole bunch of *zamponi* (stuffed pig's leg) and drunk nothing with dinner but the local wine *Lambrusco*. This seemed to be the staple diet of most Modenese. A New York steak would be a very welcome change. Vecci told me he was looking forward to having something he called "egg and egg." It turned out he meant the Haig & Haig brand of Scotch whisky.

David Yorke met me at Idlewild (now Kennedy) Airport, and we checked into the Forest Hotel on 48th Street, near Broadway. It was in the heart of the famous theater district and very close to Times Square. Next morning, we went over to Luigi Chinetti's Ferrari dealership on Eighth Avenue to check out the car, which had already been picked up from the airport with all the spares. The F1 cars were there, too. As we separated the boxes of F1 parts and sports-car parts, I noticed an extra box.

It was announced that we were all going to Luigi's favorite café for lunch, and my mouth began to water at the thought of that steak. We needed three cabs to get there, and I jumped into the first one. Vecci and the F1 mechanics grabbed the extra box and jumped into a station wagon, and we all met up at the Casa Rex. The mechanics presented the box to the owner, who was an old friend of Luigi's. They had smuggled it into America as a surprise for them both. He pulled out large packages of *zamponi* and bottles of *Lambrusco*. He poured out some wine and hurried off to the kitchen with all the *zamponi*. My face fell. Fortunately the owner came over and asked me if I would rather have a steak, and later Vecci got his "egg and egg."

Strangely, there were three 250 P Ferrari sports cars in Chinetti's garage. I found out that Pedro Rodriguez would be driving one at Mosport Park for Chinetti's North American Racing Team. Nobody seemed to know who would be driving the second NART car. Chinetti had two factory mechanics who worked in his repair shop on customers' cars, and they would be going to Mosport, too.

I spent a few days getting our car ready at Luigi's dealership and I got to spend some time with his son, Coco. He had recently married the richest woman in America, Mamie Reynolds, the heiress to the Reynolds Aluminum fortune. Wanting to see as much of America as possible, I asked Luigi if I could ride with the three race cars up to Canada in the cab of an 18-wheel rig he had gotten from John Tulp, his old buddy who owned a trucking company. He agreed, so I got to see Niagara Falls on the way.

When we got near Oshawa, Canada, we checked into the Canadiana Hotel and took the cars to a local garage to inspect them for damage from the trip. Chinetti's two mechanics looked theirs over and left. I had noticed them busy doing something under the front hood cover of a rear-engined car so, being nosy, I opened the cover on Pedro's car and—lo and behold! Where the spare wheel would normally be kept under Le Mans rules, they had secretly added an auxiliary gas tank. We had the spare wheel.

I quickly took some measurements, made a sketch, and went back to the hotel to find John and David. I asked them how long the race was going to be, and whether we had enough fuel capacity. The race would be nearly 250 miles. I did some calculations on the fuel usage, based on information on the V12 that John had from the factory. We would be about four gallons short to go without a pit stop. John wasn't surprised that nobody had said anything. I wondered if we would have done the same if the roles had been reversed.

Somehow David found somebody who would make us an extra tank from my sketches, and it showed up at the garage the next afternoon. Luigi's mechanics saw me modifying the spare wheel platform to hold the tank and asked me what I was doing. I told them we didn't have enough fuel capacity, so I was adding another tank. Perhaps they needed an auxiliary tank? If they did, I said, I could get another made by tomorrow. They smiled and told me they would be OK. We all knew the playing field was now level.

Driven superbly by John Surtees, our Ferrari 250 P was the fastest of the 38 cars in qualifying for the Pepsi Cola Canadian Grand Prix, lapping 0.8 seconds faster than Pedro Rodriguez. John was leading when he came into the pits with clutch slippage problems. I couldn't figure out why, but the plunger in the top of the clutch cylinder had somehow got released from its locked position, allowing the clutch cylinder to activate the clutch throw-out bearing, causing it to slip. Instead of staying in the car and telling me what the problem was, John jumped out to fix it himself. I suggested that he should get back in the car, put it in gear, and hold the brake while I simply cut the hydraulic pipe that went to the slave cylinder. But this would have meant that he had no clutch for the rest of the race. He opted to retire the car.

So the 100-lap race was won for NART by Rodriguez. Lorenzo Bandini raced the other NART Ferrari, but he got into an accident and didn't finish. Graham Hill warmed up for his F1 victory at Watkins Glen the following week by finishing second with Ian Walker's little yellow Lotus 23, ahead of Dennis Coad in a Lotus 19 and Don Devine in a Scarab.

Next day, I flew from Toronto back to New York and spent a day or so working on the car, which had been taken back to Chinetti's overnight by truck. Before the next race, at Riverside, I fitted a new clutch and put a stop on that cylinder plunger so it wouldn't operate any more. It worked fine, and we never had clutch problems again.

Pedro paid a visit and told me that he would have a different car for the *Times* Grand Prix at Riverside. He was going to drive a Genie made by Joe Huffaker in San Francisco. It was powered by a big Ford stock-block V8 and, reckoned Pedro, would probably blow the wheels off John's little 3-liter Ferrari. I was suckered into a bet of $10 that John would out-qualify Pedro.

That week, America was listening to radio broadcasts of the baseball World Series games. Sandy Koufax and the L.A. Dodgers won the first two games in New York against the Yankees. The Dodgers won two more games in a row, and Koufax pitched a no-hitter in the fourth game. All this was taking place while I was in New York, and then in Los Angeles, and I never even watched any part of a game—not even on TV. I missed historic moments in American sports.

When I arrived in Los Angeles, David and I went to a Ferrari dealership owned by Otto Zipper on Olympic Boulevard, near Santa Monica. The head sales guy, Orin Brown, invited me to stay at his house near Santa Monica Pier for the duration of my time in Los Angeles. He even loaned me a beautiful Chevy Nova wagon. The house had a remote control TV—I'd never seen one before. I fell in love with California and remembered what Sally had said about the English weather. I decided there and then that if Mickey Thompson ever did get around to offering me that job in Long Beach, I would take it for sure.

Meanwhile, John had flown down to Mexico City for the Formula One Grand Prix, so I was at liberty to do some sightseeing in my meager time off from preparing the 250 P. Orin was great, making me maps and telling me how to get to interesting places. He took me to a restaurant called The Cheerio, where I had my first-ever taste of prime rib, cooked medium-rare. I'd never tasted any meat like that in my life.

The entry for the 1963 *Los Angeles Times* Grand Prix at Riverside was fantastic—a Who's Who of American sports-car racing. The fastest five in qualifying were Jim Hall in his "all-plastic" Chaparral-Chevrolet; Dave McDonald and Bob Holbert in Carroll Shelby's "King Cobras," which were Cooper Monacos with big Ford V8s; Dan Gurney in one of the Ford V8 Genies; and Roger Penske in his Zerex Special. Powered by a 2.7-liter Climax engine, which had been based on a wrecked F1 Cooper and was supposed to be a two-seater, but the passenger would have had to be a midget! The next five were Pedro Rodriguez (Genie), A.J. Foyt (Scarab-Oldsmobile), Lloyd Ruby (Lotus-Ford), Roy Salvadori (Cooper Monaco), and Skip Hudson in the other Chaparral.

Surtees qualified the Ferrari 250 P in 11th position, so I lost my 10 bucks to Pedro and learned there was nothing in Europe that could beat a decent car with the power produced by American cubic inches. The race was over 200 miles of the 2.6-mile short circuit, so we needed the auxiliary fuel tank again. I also had to put an extra fresh-air duct into the footbox of the 250 P because John had burned his foot the previous Sunday in Mexico. Hot air from the radiator had gone through a small hole in the front bulkhead and put so much heat into the metal throttle pedal that it had burned a hole in his shoe. On top of that, he had been disqualified from the Grand Prix because he had had a push-start in the pit-lane, so he wasn't very happy.

Other names racing at Riverside included Richie Ginther, Rodger Ward, Jerry Grant, Augie Pabst, Tim Mayer, and Dick Thompson, not to mention foreigners Jimmy Clark and Graham Hill in Lotus 23s. It wasn't surprising that 82,000 people came along on race day. There were TV and movie stars in abundance, which really helped jazz up the activities. I was thrilled to death when Dan Blocker of *Bonanza* fame invited us to share dinner with him and some other cast members at the famous Mission Inn. Dan had entered a car dubbed the Vinegaroon (after a scorpion) and had a stunt man drive it in the race.

It was very hot, and the attrition was incredible—cars were dropping out like flies. John finished fourth, just ahead of Jimmy but behind Pedro in the Genie. Penske was second, but there was no catching Dave MacDonald. He drove the tires off that King Cobra and lapped the entire field. It made me really interested in what the Americans were doing with big engines in English sports-racing chassis.

I got the Ferrari ready to go to Laguna Seca for the last race, but John's foot needed time to heal, so he canceled the trip, and I flew home to England.

I was so impressed by the way everyone had treated us at Riverside. It was very different from Europe in that everyone wanted to help us and nobody asked for anything in return. I remember one friendly American named Chuck Queener who noticed that the Ferrari team was a one-man band and asked how he could help out. I told him I had to put an air duct through the nose and into the car. He went off and found me all the stuff I needed, including some spray paint. He never asked me for any money and wouldn't have taken it anyway. He loved racing and just wanted to help out. Many years later, I met up with Chuck at the Amelia Island Can-Am Reunion. He was the editor of the Amelia Island Concours program and a right-hand man for Bill Warner, its patron and organizer.

Another helpful guy was a California Highway Patrol motorcycle rider named Tom Hooker. He provided us with a cooler full of water and cold drinks and helped to keep our little pit enclosure clear by putting a rope up and asking people to stay out of my way as I worked on the car. I was very impressed by it all and determined to go back to the United States as soon as possible.

I had the option of going back to work for Reg Parnell. But on January 7, 1964, Reg was rushed into surgery in London with a ruptured appendix and peritonitis and didn't come out of it alive. Along with his family and many, many other people who knew him, I was devastated by his death. I get tearful even when I think about it now, more than 40 years later. I owe Reg so much for all the excellent challenges that he presented, all of which helped me understand what makes race cars go faster. Besides being one of my racing heroes as a driver, he had to be the best man at tuning racing cars I had ever met. He will be in my heart and memories forever. He had personally made me into a decent Formula One mechanic, and I will always be in his debt for that.

BELOW: Mickey Thompson looks on as Masten Gregory pits his revolutionary Indy car at a pre-race tire-test day at Indianapolis in 1964. (Indianapolis Motor Speedway Photo)

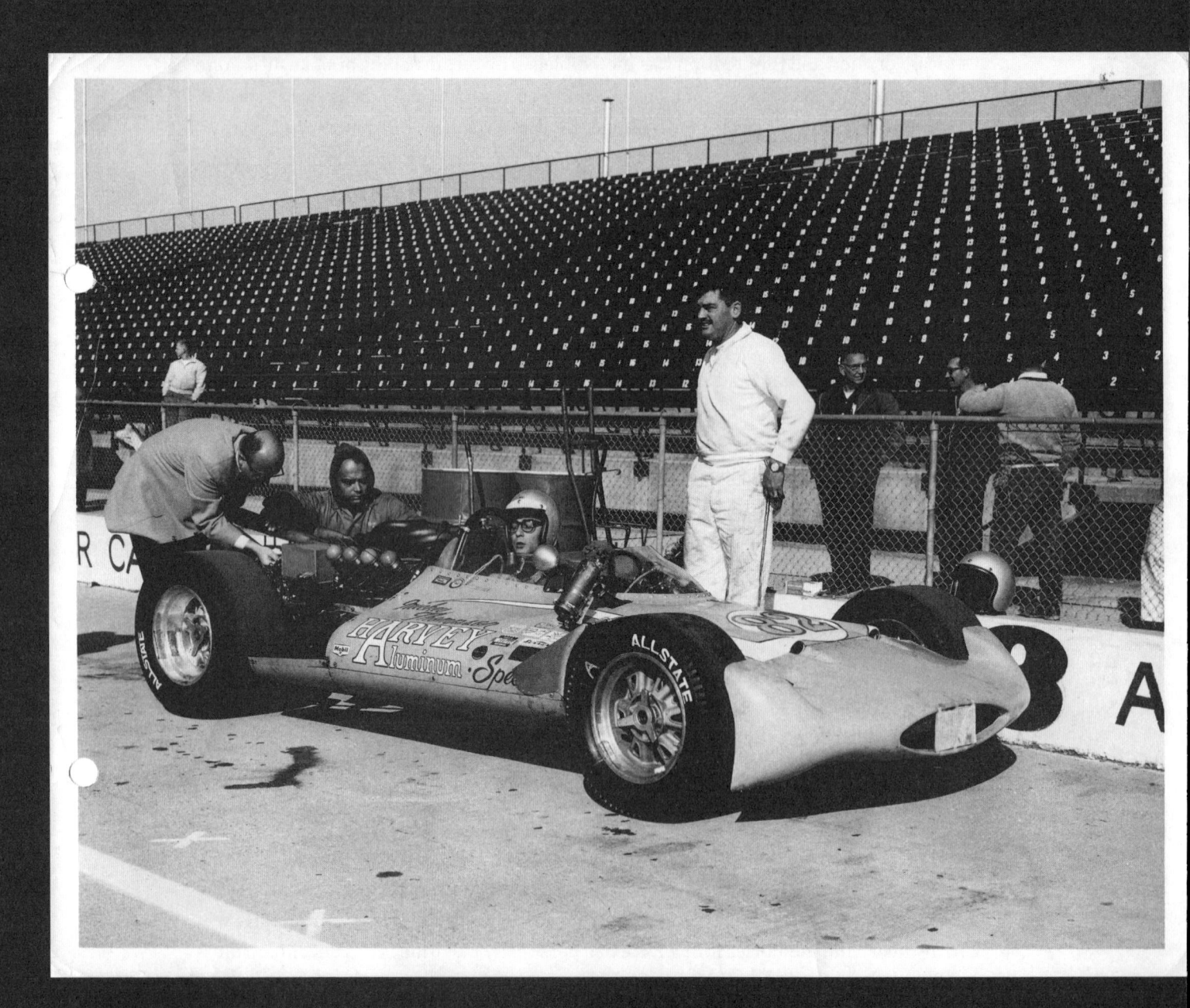

CHAPTER 14

The Road to Indianapolis

I had only been back from America about a month when, in January 1964, I received a letter from Mickey Thompson. After being introduced to Mickey by Masten Gregory during the 1963 French Grand Prix at Reims, I'd bumped into him again briefly at Riverside at the *Times* Grand Prix, and we'd talked some more about a job for me preparing his Indy cars in Long Beach, California. You had to give Mickey Thompson his due. He was one of the world's most accomplished speed record holders, with literally hundreds of records to his name, and he was also very innovative as an Indianapolis 500 entrant. In 1962, he had entered three unique, low-line cars with very small wheels, driven by Dan Gurney, Chuck Daigh, and Englishman Jack Fairman, although only Gurney had qualified. In 1963, he had made two even lower cars with even smaller, 12-inch diameter wheels, and had tried to get them qualified along with the three 1962 cars. Duane Carter had qualified a 1962 car and Al Miller a 1963 car.

ABOVE: This publicity photograph shows Mickey Thompson and mechanic Paul Nicolini with his 1964 Indy car. The aerodynamic body shape was unique at the Speedway. The car's engine had not yet arrived from Ford when the shot was taken. (Mickey Thompson Publicity)

Masten had been one of the 1963 non-qualifiers but Mickey had again asked him to drive at Indy in 1964. Masten told me that if Mickey did ask him again, he would like me to prepare the car, and that was why he'd introduced me to Mickey at Reims. As his other driver, Mickey had chosen Dave MacDonald, the young, very fast Californian I'd watched dominating a strong field in the Riverside sports-car race.

Mickey's letter laid out the terms of my employment. For working in California and on the road, I would receive $2.65 an hour for a 40-hour week, plus time and a half for any hours over that. This was amazing to me, because I'd never been paid overtime in my life for working on racing cars. And I would also receive a percentage of any prize money as a bonus, plus my air fare from London to Los Angeles and help getting my Alien Registration card from the U.S. embassy in London.

At that time, I was one of the highest-paid racing mechanics in England, on a salary of £1100 Sterling a year. That calculated out to about $1.25 an hour for a 40-hour week—and no overtime was ever paid to English racing mechanics in those days.

European racing wages then were not very good in general. Innes Ireland once told me that he received less than £2000 a year to race Formula One cars for Team Lotus. Other drivers, like Roy Salvadori, who was a savvy businessman, could drive their earnings up to about £20,000 with endorsements from Shell and other companies.

I talked it all over with Sally. We were living with her mother in a tiny, rented flat in an antiquated, 100-year-old house in Muswell Hill, north London, backing onto Highgate Woods. The toilet was in a small closet in the kitchen. We had a small refrigerator with a freezer that could only hold two packets of frozen peas. We had some old furniture that her mother had given us when we got married, but we didn't have the "luxury" of having our own telephone. Sally had quit full-time work to look after two-year-old Paul, and was working part-time in an employment agency that she had managed before having the baby. We couldn't afford to own a car, and the way things were going, it would take years before we could afford to buy a house. We didn't need much incentive to move to America, because our lifestyle was frugal, to say the least.

I told Sally that I'd visited the homes of other race mechanics in California, and they were paid enough to live decently. I told her this was our chance to emigrate to America for a better life, and she readily agreed. So I applied for our visas. I'd also been offered a good position in Surfer's Paradise, Australia, where I'd worked for Reg Parnell with John Surtees and Tony Maggs, and we had also applied to emigrate there. We considered that either of these places would give us a better chance to improve our lifestyle and our children's prospects. The American visas came through first, and that settled it. I accepted Mickey's offer.

On April 10, 1964, I boarded Pan Am Flight 01 at Heathrow to fly to Los Angeles. The plan was that Sally and Paul would follow when I got back to Long Beach after Indy. I figured I would save enough money before the end of May to be able to afford their air tickets. When

I got on the flight that day, I had the grand sum of $40 in my pocket, and that would have to get me through until payday.

Charlie Jackson, one of the guys who worked for Mickey, met me off the flight. He told me he was a mechanic and a "gofer" for Mickey. I'd never heard the word before, so he told me he was mainly used to go for things. I would learn a whole lot more new expressions before long. Normally, whenever I went to a new country, the first thing I learned was how to swear correctly.

Charlie had volunteered to house me until we went to the Speedway in May. He was single, and we would be sharing his two-bedroom apartment on Linden Avenue in Long Beach. Boy, was I grateful for that! The rent was only $75 and Charlie said he didn't need any until the following month, so that solved one of my immediate money problems. Years later, Linden Avenue would form part of the famous Long Beach street circuit, used for Formula One and Champ Car races.

Next day, we went to Mickey's workshops on Santa Fe Avenue in Long Beach, near the docks, and I met the rest of the crew. Mickey's right-hand man was Fritz Voight, who ran the shop. Born in Hawaii, Fritz was a straight-talking jack-of-all-trades, and working on race cars was only one of them. The others had all agreed to work for Mickey only through the Indy 500, which was a common practice in those days. Paul Nicolini was a lead mechanic and fabricator and the nicest person I met. Another mechanic was Neil, whose real occupation was a meat cutter in a supermarket. Then there was Fred Sinclair, who was from Indiana and loved racing, and was hired as a temporary fabricator.

Once at the Speedway, they told me we would be joined by some volunteers who would be helping out in the pits. They wouldn't receive any pay—they would just do it for the love of it. I couldn't figure why anyone would want to work for nothing, but the Indy 500 did that to guys all the time. They just wanted to be part of it all!

When I had worked on racing cars in England, it was one mechanic for each car. Here we were going to have two mechanics for each car. I thought we were really lucky, but what did I know? I was just a "limey rookie"—well, that's what I heard one of them say.

I spent my first day looking over Mickey's Thompson-Ford race car in total fascination. It was strange, to say the least. It was a very simple space frame chassis with a huge, overhead valve V8 in the back. There was a single large fuel bladder, holding about 44 gallons, on the left outside of the frame in a fiberglass body shell supported by the fill neck, which was anchored to the inside frame rail with a loop of steel tube and a small bracket.

The only bottom support for the fuel cell was the molded fiberglass body housing and a flat thin magnesium plate beneath the tank, braced by two steel straps hanging from the top rail of the frame. The chassis didn't appear to have much torsional stiffness. When I thought about the crashworthiness of the car and the fact that the whole gas tank was being restrained by just a little fiberglass and a mounted fill neck, it worried me.

I asked who had designed it, and was told it had been John Crosthwaite, a former Team Lotus engineer. Mickey had changed it quite a bit in the two years since Dan Gurney had driven it at Indy with the small wheels fitted. Since then the United States Auto Club (USAC) and the Speedway had told Mickey that he had to use larger rims if he wanted to run again in the 500. So Mickey had gotten Sears, Roebuck to sponsor the car, and special wide tires were made to Mickey's specs. They were the widest tires and rims I'd ever seen on a race car. I was surprised at first, but it made a lot of sense when you considered the power we had. Traction was quite important.

ABOVE: This side profile shows the lines of Thompson's fully enclosed body Indy cars outside the garages. (Peter Bryant)

Probably the biggest surprise was the all-enveloping, fiberglass bodywork. The wheels had fenders over them—an Indy first. Mickey had made it look like a center-seat sports car and the body was quite artistic and curvy. Unfortunately this would cause aerodynamic problems that would surface at the Speedway, but our three cars, in their red-white-and-blue paint jobs, sure looked different.

Stranger still, there was a bell crank arm fitted to the steering pinion shaft, just after the shaft emerged from the front of the rack and pinion housing. This arm had a link that went over to another bell crank. In turn, this was linked to a rod running alongside the right-hand lower frame rail to a third bell crank. In turn again, this was linked to the inner ball-joint near the right rear upright at the wishbone A-arm. This car had steering control of the right rear wheel! Mickey said he wanted to test it and see if it helped if a rear wheel steered as well as the fronts.

When the driver turned the steering wheel to the right, the right rear steered left—that is, until the driver gave it more than half a turn, and the bell crank on the front of the rack went past center. Then the rear wheel would turn in the opposite direction! I thought it was really tricky, but I didn't like it at all. It made no sense to me! I reasoned that once you had entered a corner and were steering in the correct direction, you wouldn't get much help from one of the rear wheels turning suddenly in the opposite direction. In fact it could be disastrous.

Another surprise was the overhead camshaft Ford Indy V8. I'd seen V8 engines before, but never with the exhaust coming out of the top of the engine where the intake manifold normally was. The exhaust system looked like a big bunch of spaghetti snaking out over the back end of the car. This car was very different from any I'd worked on before.

Mickey asked me what I thought of the car and I told him he should stiffen the chassis because it was way too flexible. I said the front end wouldn't relate to the rear end if we tried to increase the roll stiffness of the chassis/suspension system. I was used to drivers sitting alongside aluminum gas tanks in Formula One cars, but I'd seen my first fuel bladder when Eric Broadley had put one in the Lola F1 car, so the bladder alongside the cockpit on the left side didn't worry me. The way the filler neck was connected to the top inside frame tube worried me a bit, but I said nothing about it. But I did say he should disconnect that bell crank thing and abandon the rear-wheel steering. Mickey replied that the first car was going to Phoenix for a test that weekend, so he couldn't change the chassis, and it was then going straight to the Speedway so that Dave MacDonald could take his rookie test. But he agreed to disconnect the rear-wheel steering until he could test it himself at the Speedway. He added that I would get a chance to change some things after we got to the Speedway. I said OK and went to work helping the mechanics put the cars together.

This was a Saturday, and Mickey invited me to dinner with his family that evening, and then to the Lions drag strip in Long Beach. He then took me to another building and showed me the Challenger, the four-engined car in which he'd run 403 mph in at the Bonneville Salt Flats. There was no doubt in my mind after seeing that car that Mickey was a very brave man. Just to steer the Challenger required the driver to put his hands under a chassis crosstube to grip the wheel. There was almost no steering lock, and you could barely see out the small front windshield. The noise from the four engines must have been deafening, and how those tires got any traction on the Salt Flats confounded me.

We went to his house in the hills near San Pedro Harbor, and he introduced me to his wife, Trudy, and his son, Danny. Trudy served up a great dinner. Later, at the Lions drag strip, Mickey introduced me to his sister, Colleen, and her husband, Gary Campbell, who handled all his PR for him. In addition to being the inventor of the "slingshot" dragster,

BELOW: After hitting the wall at Indy, Masten Gregory's titanium car gets towed back to the pits. (Peter Bryant)

Mickey was one of the original founders of the facility.

Bravery very soon appeared to be an American trait. I was staggered when I saw my first slingshot dragster. The driver sat right behind the clutch bell housing and the differential, with his legs over the top of the axle half shafts. I remember thinking that if the bolts holding the axle to the chassis failed, it would turn over and take off his entire male gender cluster!

The noise was deafening when they went off the line, and the stink of fuel vapors took your breath away. The mechanics rebuilt the engine after each run and threw parts away as if they cost nothing. In those days, the organizers didn't require full scatter-shields, and I saw a blowup that sent a large piece of blower housing flying towards the grandstand. I made a mental note not to sit in the stands at drag races. When the blower blew up, the engine spewed oil onto the track and caused a delay. Mickey was the event promoter and he figured he needed to do something to amuse the crowd, so he jumped into his Corvette and did "doughnuts" all the way up the track. The smoke was thick and the crowd loved it. Mickey loved it, too. He was in his element—show business and racing all in one.

About a week later, we loaded one of the cars on a trailer behind Mickey's pickup truck, and he took Fritz and Fred with him for the test at Phoenix Speedway in Arizona. The rest of us continued putting the other cars together. One of the space frames was made up of titanium tubes and had titanium suspension components. I'd never worked with titanium before and became intrigued with it.

The golden rules of working with titanium were simple. You could do almost anything to it that you could do to steel, except the bending and welding. When it was bent, it sprang back 20 percent. Titanium had to be welded in a completely inert atmosphere because if it got over 1100 degrees in air, it picked up the hydrogen and became embrittled. Paul Nicolini did the welding using a heliarc machine with argon gas shields to keep the air away from the hot metal, and he taught me how to do it. It was very interesting and would prove to be invaluable later in my career, when I designed and built my own titanium Can-Am car, the Ti22.

I wanted to go to the Phoenix test, but it was Mickey's program, and this was the car that would be raced by our rookie driver, Dave MacDonald. I'd been hired mainly to work on Masten's car with the titanium chassis. By now I was dying to see how these weird cars handled. The chassis were so flexible that if you held the rear end rigid, you could twist the front end with a wooden broomstick. I resolved to fix that as soon as I could. It was no way to go racing. How the hell could you tune the chassis?

For Masten's car, I made up some titanium frame reinforcement pieces in advance and made sure that Paul packed all the stuff he would need to weld them in place when we got to Indy, including the heliarc machine. At first, the other guys didn't want to take it because they said they could hire people at the Speedway to make parts. I convinced them it wasn't a good idea for other people to know if we had problems with our car. They might speak to the drivers about it, and we didn't want to have to deal with that. So everything we thought we might need was loaded on a big Ford F350 pickup truck and trailers.

The day we left for Indianapolis was a seamless continuation of the previous day, because we'd worked all night long. Racing was like that. If you had two years to put a car together, you would still end up working all night on the last day. It was about 4:00 p.m. when our little convoy finally set off from Long Beach.

I traveled with Neil in a red Ford station wagon that belonged to Mickey's wife. The family used it to tow their ski boat, so it had a hitch and we were trailing the titanium car. We left the back seat clear for sleeping, and Neil insisted on taking the first driving stint. He had cadged some diet pills from his wife and said they would keep him awake through the night, so I crashed out on the back seat. Only half an hour later, he woke me and said he was falling asleep at the wheel—would I take over the driving chores for an hour or so? We weren't even out of L.A. yet! He gave me one of those diet pills, and we changed places on the fly so as not to lose sight of the F350 truck. The truck was driven by Paul and Fritz, with Fred in the sleeping compartment above the cab, and our third race car on a trailer. Meanwhile, the first car had already arrived in Indianapolis, towed behind Mickey's pickup truck.

We'd decided to drive straight through to Indiana, taking turns in the F350's sleeper compartment. But this was my first real American road trip, so I really wanted to stay awake to look at the scenery. We were going up the famous Route 66, and I'd never seen it before.

I got my wish! I ended up driving nearly all the way to Gallup, New Mexico, before I was relieved. I saw more of Route 66 than I really wanted to see in one day. Those damn diet pills worked like crazy on me and like placebos on Neil. We filled up with gasoline, Fred took over, and I fell asleep on the back seat of the station wagon. Somehow, after sleeping all the way to Albuquerque, that crafty bastard Neil had got himself in the sleeper of the other vehicle.

Soon after Albuquerque, we encountered a problem. As I pulled the station wagon into a gas station, the brake pedal went to the floor. I pumped furiously, and miraculously we stopped before we creamed someone's car. The brakes had simply run out of fluid from lack of maintenance. It scared the hell out of me. "Why didn't someone check that before we started out?" I asked the others. They just laughed.

"Don't sweat the small stuff!" Fritz said. "You didn't crash, and it's over, so forget it and get on." I loved America from the moment I arrived. It was the only place I'd been where people who had a problem said, "There has to be a better way than this!" In contrast, the English seemed full of regrets and thought that life was similar to weather—there was nothing they could do about it.

Finally, we pulled into the Indianapolis Motor Speedway and parked up in Gasoline Alley. Curious people immediately ran to examine the race cars on the trailers. "That Mickey Thompson sure likes to do things different," was a fair summation of the comments I heard. I was from Formula One, and I knew you got ahead of the opposition by finding something they hadn't done and doing it yourself. That was also Mickey's philosophy because the Thompson-Ford cars were totally different from all the others.

Most people were curious about the shape of the body and the big tires. In those days, having gone over 400 mph at Bonneville, Mickey was considered a speed hero by Americans, and that didn't escape the attention of the marketing people at the Speedway. Next day, we were the big story in the local paper. Mickey loved any kind of publicity, good or bad. We were bombarded with questions and comments about the cars. They looked spectacular, and that was all it took.

Qualifying hadn't even started, and there was all this publicity. I just hoped we could live up to it. A.J. Foyt and Parnelli Jones were in their prime, and they were both here in front-engined Watson-Offenhauser roadsters. Rear-engined cars had just started to creep into the Indy field but were already beginning to outperform the roadsters. The established Indy folk referred to them as "Funny Cars," a name that wouldn't stick until it came to rest in drag racing. We had rear-engined cars, but so did Jim Clark and Dan Gurney, driving brand new Lotus-Fords. Jack Brabham had a rear-engined Brabham-Offy, and Rodger Ward a new, rear-engined Watson-Offy. If Mickey was going to win, it would have to be a superhuman effort. Since I hadn't been to the 500 before, I approached it like just another race—get the cars qualified as high on the grid as possible, get them started in the race, bring them to the finish in the money.

The 1964 Indy 500 was most definitely not going to be just another race. It would turn out to be a horrific experience, and it would change my life forever.

BELOW: Dave MacDonald tests the Thompson race car at Indy. Tufts of wool were stuck to the bodywork so that Mickey Thompson could judge its aero performance from photographs. There was no data acquisition in those days! (Mickey Thompson Publicity)

Dave MacDonald, El Monte, Calif. rookie driver, maneuvers his Mickey Thompson, Sears-Allstate Special through one of the four turns at the Indianapolis Motor Speedway in preparation for the 500 mile Memorial Day classic.
MacDonald qualified the car with a four lap average of 151.464 mph, the second fastest rookie to make the race.

CHAPTER 15

Portents of Disaster

I was really impressed by my first sight of Gasoline Alley at Indianapolis. I had never seen a racing facility so well equipped and organized. All the garages had polished linoleum floors and enormous four- and five-tier Snap-On tool boxes. The other mechanics would invite their buddies over to laugh at my little English tool box! Every kind of machinery we could desire was freely available, like the latest in alignment equipment from the Bear Company, set up in several stalls. All the support companies, like Autolite, Champion, and Firestone, had beautiful shops with everything needed to support their products. A daily highlight turned out to be a free beer at 6:00 p.m. in the Autolite sparkplug store.

Once the cars were in our garage, Mickey handed me four white shirts, four slacks, and a jacket with red and blue stripes down each arm and leg. My name and "Mickey Thompson" were embroidered on the front pockets of the shirts and the jacket, with "Sears Allstate Special" in very large letters on the backs. I'd never seen such blatant commercialism in racing before and I said to Fritz Voight, "I'm not wearing these in public! I'd feel like a walking billboard."

ABOVE: Indy 500 veteran Eddie Johnson easily put Mickey's second car into the field during the second week of qualifying at the 1964 race. (Indianapolis Motor Speedway Photo)

Fritz laughed so hard, I thought he would bust a gut. He said, "Peter, stop being a stupid, stuck-up limey for five minutes and think about it." He explained how Indy racing was all about money, whereas Formula One in those days was a rich guy's hobby. He told me that almost 100 cars were sometimes entered for the 500, but only 33 could qualify, and the lowest-finishing car would get $4000. Cars that did qualify were all sponsored to help defray the enormous expense of providing the chassis and engines and keeping the team at Indianapolis for the whole month of May. He asked me who I thought could afford to put up all that money themselves.

There would be 400,000 people in the stands and in the infield, added Fritz, and they would all be rooting for one car (maybe two). Most of them would give their eyeteeth to have one of these uniforms and would probably sleep in it if they had one. He'd had letters from about 500 people offering to pay to be on the pit crew as tire changers or refuelers or signalers. We would be on show the whole month of May and people wanted to see us in our uniforms. The race would be televised in every country that had television. We should wear them when we went out to a restaurant for dinner, because we needed to advertise the Sears name and support our sponsor, and we should be proud and happy to do it. Now—what was that about not wanting to wear the uniform? My face went red, because I knew he was right. I apologized, and he slapped me on the back and said, "By the way, keep your eye on that jacket if you take it off. It cost $150 and, if you lose it, you'll have to pay to replace it."

ABOVE: This 1947 De Soto was the first car I ever owned—and it only cost me $50. (Peter Bryant)

Up to that time, the only Formula One team to have had commercial sponsorship was the Yeoman Credit Racing Team I'd worked for in England. They'd raced the cars without any advertising or decals on them. The Europeans considered product decals ostentatious. They mostly painted the cars in their national colors and had a badge on the nose with the maker's logo on it. That was it. Drivers and mechanics wore plain coveralls unless they were the brown ones supplied to the Ferrari guys or the light blue ones supplied by Dunlop, which was the only European manufacturer that made racing tires at that time.

Formula One also trailed Indy racing in terms of safety features. There were certainly no fire-resistant driving suits. In the 1960s, Formula One drivers didn't even wear seatbelts and a small rollover bar behind the driver's head and an on-board fire extinguisher were the only safety precautions. The extinguisher was about six inches long and was usually emptied to save weight, anyway. Most F1 cars had aluminum gas tanks (without safety bladders in them) surrounding the driver's body and legs. Getting in a crash often involved getting into a fire. Compared with the contemporary Indy cars, the F1 cars were death traps.

We left the track and went to a private residence in Speedway, the local town. Mickey had arranged for us to stay there in a converted garage, which was now a dormitory complete with a shower and lockers for our clothes. In those days, finding hotel space for the team in Indianapolis would have cost a fortune. For the qualifying and race weekends, room prices tripled. We wouldn't be spending much time there anyway, except to sleep, so it was OK. We went to the Speedway early every day and had breakfast and ate most of our meals in the cafeteria near the end of Gasoline Alley. It opened at 6:30 a.m. and served decent food.

Having driven one of Mickey's cars at the Speedway the year before, Masten Gregory didn't need to pass the rookie test. By the time we got there with the other two cars, Dave MacDonald had already passed his test and could take off the rookie stripes. Masten was to drive our blue car (the one with a titanium tube frame and suspension), Dave would drive the red car, and the white car was a spare until after both cars were qualified.

The USAC people had banned the small wheels and tires Mickey had used in 1962 and 1963, and told him to use his own wheels of at least 15-inch diameter or the standard, 17-inch Halibrand wheels used on all the roadsters. Mickey made no bones about hating USAC officials with a passion, but it was their motor race, and he had no choice but to do it their way. Nevertheless he refused to run the standard Halibrand rims and Firestone tires. His tires were specially made for him by Armstrong Rubber Company and labeled as Sears Allstate tires. They were the widest tires ever seen at the Speedway. Most tires in those days were about 8 inches wide but these had 11 inches of tread width at the front and 13 inches at the rear. Mickey wanted to win any way he could. He had a few good ideas and a few crazy ones, but I really liked those tires.

It intrigued me how they'd been constructed so that they didn't bulge out in the middle of the tread when inflated. The answer was that the Armstrong engineers had learned a new technique for laying them up, called "bias ply." They brought the cords that formed the foundation for the tread across the tire at an angle of about 25 degrees, instead of straight across. Nowadays they use steel-belted radial tires to control the bulge.

Meanwhile Team Lotus showed up in Gasoline Alley with some special tires made by Dunlop that had an interesting, asymmetrical tread pattern. In the race, those tires would prove to be the team's Achilles' heel.

We were joined by Bill Rosokovsky, who was a volunteer for the month and was going to help our team where he could in the garage and change wheels in the pits. He was built like a body builder. With his horn-rimmed glasses, in fact, he looked a lot like Clark Kent, so I nicknamed him "Superman." Many years later, he would change his name to Bill Marcel and become Mickey's business manager.

Practice for the Indy 500 took place every day up until the first weekend of qualifying. Each evening, at 6:00 p.m., they posted the lap times of each car and a sponsor gave a prize to the fastest. Everything was good for prizes, from money to a free car wash for a year. It was mostly one of three or four drivers who won. A.J. Foyt did well in his roadster but didn't win as many as Bobby Marshman, who looked really good in a Lotus-Ford on Firestone tires. So did Jimmy Clark and Parnelli Jones, the previous year's winner driving a roadster for J.C. Agajanian. Initially both our drivers took it easy, trying to feel out how the cars behaved at speed.

It didn't take long for Masten to notice that his car was "darting" under braking at the entrance to turn 1. I went down there to watch with Mickey, and we were startled to see how bad it was. If we crouched down low and looked at the nose of the car, we could see it was also lifting a fair amount due to the aerodynamic setup. In fact, because the weight of the car was so offset to the inside where the gas tank was, it looked like it was lifting the outside front wheel almost off the ground. This might have been partly due to the stiffness of the front anti-rollbar. I told Mickey that I thought the car had "bump-steer" and he said, "What's that?" I explained that it happened during vertical chassis movement when the front wheel toe-in changed due to the geometry of the steering arms in relation to the steering rack position. He asked if I could fix it and I said I could, but there were other things that needed fixing too. I told him that the chassis needed stiffening and the geometry of the suspension probably needed to be altered, because the wheels had too much camber change as the body moved up and down. This could cause the wide tires to lose contact with the road. He said we didn't have time for all that before qualifying, so I should just fix the bump steer and he would fix the aerodynamic problems.

When we had the cars back in the garage, I took out a Dunlop optical wheel alignment kit that Mickey had bought in England. It was the first in the United States and no one in the team had ever even unpacked it, let alone used it. They didn't really know what it was. They all watched with interest as I took it out of its oblong case and assembled it. You used it by putting the ends of two horizontal prongs against the front wheel rims on opposite sides of the car, and sighting down the optical instrument to the cross-hairs target on the other side. You could then adjust a dial that showed what toe-in or toe-out the wheels had.

I took out the suspension springs and put a jack under the chassis. Then I took readings of the toe change as the chassis went up and down. I was really surprised to find that they toed out an inch for every inch of wheel movement. Wow! That was bad! With bump-steer like that, I wondered how the drivers even kept the cars in a straight line.

By relocating the steering rack, I found I was able to eliminate the bump-steer completely. We moved the steering rack on all the cars overnight and rechecked the bump-steer on all of them.

Next day, Mickey put some wool tufts on Dave MacDonald's car and sent him out to run some laps as a photographer took pictures with a long-range lens. Mickey looked at the pictures and took some aluminum sheeting to make the air intake for the radiator smaller and lower in an attempt to prevent the car from lifting.

Both our drivers liked the car better but still complained about oversteer. Then, just before the first qualifying weekend, disaster struck. Masten spun and hit the wall, wrecking the blue titanium car.

He wasn't badly injured, although he said his leg hurt a bit, and he had very severe bruising of his ribs where the seatbelts had held him. But the crash really shook him up. He was upset and angry about it. He told Jack Brabham that the Thompson-Ford was the most lethal, evil-handling car he'd ever driven—and promptly quit. Brabham said later that the car must have been pretty bad, because nothing ever scared Masten Gregory.

I was wishing that Masten had stayed around at least until I'd had a chance to sort out his car. It was thanks to Masten's efforts that I'd gotten this job in the first place, and I felt he should have waited a bit before giving up on the team. He never said how bad he was hurting from the impact with the wall, but he rarely complained. His wife had been at the Speedway every day, although she wasn't allowed in the pits because of the "No Tits in the Pits" rule that was imposed by the Speedway in those days. She was French and had never heard of such a thing, so she didn't like "those Speedway people" at all. I wondered how much input she had in Masten's decision to quit.

I must admit that my first impressions of the 2.5-mile Speedway were not very favorable. Like other Europeans who came out of road racing, I thought it was totally unforgiving for one simple reason—the wall! It ran all the way around the outside, and if a driver made even a small mistake, he had to hit the wall. Most road courses had maybe 30 feet of grass or a run-off with room for the car if it left the track. If the driver had a problem, he didn't hit something straight away, or run into the spectators. Even today on a walled oval, a car that has hit the wall has a good chance of being hit by another car, because the driver simply can't get out of the way.

A few days earlier, Jim Hurtubise, the young American driver, had lost control of his Watson-Offy roadster coming out of turn 4 and started to spin down the track at high speed. I was standing near the chain-link fence that separated the pit tool box area from the walkway in front of the grandstand. Mickey was out at the edge of the track, standing inside the pit wall, which was only about two feet high. When he saw Hurtubise spinning down the track towards him, he ran past me, and in a single bound leapt over the five-foot chain-link fence as if it was only a foot high. I was amazed. He laughed nervously and said, "Amazing what a little fear can help you to do."

When Masten quit, it came as a big shock to Mickey. He took me to the coffee shop that evening and said, "Foyt is doing 157 mph, and we're struggling to do 147 mph. That won't even get us qualified. How long will it take you to make all the changes we need to get these cars up to speed?" I told him that if I started right away doing the geometry studies for the suspension and he could get the necessary parts made, I was willing to work flat-out over the next few days. At that rate, maybe we could be done in time for qualifying on Saturday. He said, "In that case, start now!"

When Sears, Roebuck had delivered the tool boxes for us to use in the pits, they were packed in giant cardboard boxes, and I used them for drawing paper. I made compasses out of welding wire—wrapping one end round a pencil and making a small loop to use with a nail as a pivot—to lay out the arcs prescribed by the suspension arms during their travel up and down. I found that the front suspension had about 2 degrees of camber change for every inch of vertical chassis movement, which I figured was way too much for those fat tires.

So I designed some extensions for the front uprights that in effect set the A-frame mounting points further apart, and lowered the camber change to less than half a degree for each inch of travel. I dug out the reinforcement tubes I'd made to stiffen the titanium car, and then duplicated them in steel to stiffen the chassis of the other cars. I also did a geometry analysis of the rear suspension and made some changes there too. I didn't stop working for three days and nights, thanks to Mickey's inexhaustible supply of "bennies," or Benzedrine tablets.

We discussed what he'd found out with the wool tufts in the aero tests and concluded that the lift at the nose of the car was helped by the airflow under the front fenders. While I was working on the suspension problems, Mickey had the crew cut the tops out of the

ABOVE: In a free moment at the Speedway, Paul Nicolini took me to see the Borg Warner Trophy. It was by far the biggest I'd ever seen, so he took my picture standing next to it. (Peter Bryant)

front fenders in an attempt to allow the air to escape.

Late one evening, when all our tails were dragging from sheer fatigue, Mickey came into the garage and started to skip a rope in front of us. He was saying, "Look at me! I'm an old fart compared with you young guys—so get your asses in gear and get finished with these cars!" Then he disappeared for a while, but repeated the act an hour or so later. This time, Paul Nicolini followed him to see where he went. He watched him getting ready to sleep in his Corvette and reported back to us.

"I'll put a stop to this crap," said Fritz. In New Mexico on the way to Indy, he'd bought some M80 fireworks to use at home for the 4th of July celebrations. He and Paul waited until Mickey was fast asleep and then threw four of them under his car. BOOM-BOOM-BOOM-BOOM! We could hear the explosions from the garage. An M80 firework had almost as much power as a small stick of dynamite, and the car rocked from the concussions beneath it. It scared the living daylights out of Mickey, and he leapt straight out of the car and ran. Fritz and Paul returned to the garage and described the scene. We all laughed, and when Mickey came in with his face as white as a sheet, we laughed some more. "Now, that's what we call stimulating!" said Fritz. "It was so much better than watching you jump rope." To give Mickey credit, he took it really well.

I spent the rest of the night sorting out the correct springs to put on the car. Now that the chassis was stiffer, we could see each corner weight on the scales and work out that it would take different spring rates at each wheel to balance the car in the turns. When we'd previously put the scales under each wheel, the sag in the chassis had effectively adjusted the weight reading at each wheel to try and equalize them. I was very happy that we now had a chassis stiff enough so that the anti-rollbars would work properly instead of twisting with the whippy frame.

The next day was Friday, and I'd not slept one wink since the previous Tuesday night. Mickey had Dave MacDonald test the car in an open practice session. When Dave returned to the pits, Mickey had a big grin on his face and told him he'd driven a lap at almost 155 mph—more than enough to qualify. I felt really good knowing that I'd been able to get the car to go significantly faster and, even more important, that the handling was much safer.

The tire temperatures indicated that a little more chassis tuning was still needed. Dave said the car now had a little understeer, which I thought was what you needed at the Speedway, but he said he could do 160 mph if we could take some of it out. He was used to hanging out the back end of the sports cars he drove, and preferred a slight oversteer characteristic. Mickey wanted him to drive as smoothly as possible, because oversteer was dangerous on a track like that.

Everybody was very happy now that our lap speeds were closer to the fastest cars. I remember well the moment when Mickey finally grinned at me and said, "OK, limey, you've done well, so how about I take you out tonight and buy you the biggest steak you've ever had?" I murmured something about waiting to celebrate until after we'd qualified, walked into the garage, and collapsed. The next thing I remember was being woken up early on Saturday morning. Fritz said I'd been like a little rag doll when they carried me to the house from the car and just stuck me into bed, clothes, dirt, and all.

During qualifying practice on Saturday, Mickey played around with the springs I'd selected and slowed the car down a bit, to just above 153 mph. But it was good enough for 14th place on the grid on the first day of qualifying, at 151.46 mph for the three-lap average.

Mickey said that part of our newfound speed had come from the use of nitromethane in the methanol fuel. Mickey liked to "tip the can" (as they called adding nitro) but Ford disapproved because, if you added too much, it could blow up the engine. I don't think it made much difference to the times, because it was the handling that controlled the speed around the turns, and everyone was fast on the straights. The times around turn 1 and turn 2 were a good measure of whether you had a good car, and ours were beginning to creep closer to the better ones.

Dave was really happy to make it into the Indy 500 on his debut, but I told Mickey that if he'd let me make a smaller anti-rollbar for the front, Dave could have gone faster. And I was a bit annoyed that Mickey had messed with the settings. I was stunned when he apologized and said he should have left the springs alone. It wasn't like Mickey to do that sort of thing, so he obviously didn't want to discourage me. He took me to lunch at the Speedway café and told me he wanted me to design a four-wheel-drive car for next year's 500. He suggested I take a good look at Andy Granatelli's four-wheel drive Ferguson/Novi Special. It had qualified 22nd, driven by Bobby Unser. Mickey thought 4WD was the way to go in the future. He was always looking ahead.

Now that Masten had left, Mickey had to find a driver for the second car. He talked to several, including Al Miller and Duane Carter, who had both driven for him at the Speedway before. Eventually he settled on Eddie Johnson, who was very experienced at Indy and was known as a conservative driver who stayed out of trouble. On the second qualifying day, Eddie set off to drive a few exploratory laps during open practice. On his second lap, the bracket holding the exhaust tailpipe in place fell onto the track and he was black-flagged for dropping debris.

In those days, the Speedway itself was totally controlled by a man named Clarence Kagel. His official title was track supervisor, and he came up to Mickey in front of everyone in the pits, handed him the bracket, and told him that he'd just talked with USAC, and unless we put a steel mesh cage around the engine compartment frame, we couldn't run the cars any more. I think he made all the Ford-powered teams do it, but Mickey was livid. He looked at Kagel and said, in a loud voice: "One of these days, I'm going to buy this place and fire you, you stupid son of a bitch!" Kagel just walked away—which made Mickey madder than ever.

While we took the cars back to the garage and wrapped the engine compartments in chicken wire, Mickey ran out to a local toy store and found a rag doll with the name "Ratfink" on its chest. He wired it to the cage so that it looked out under the engine. You could see it easily. When Kagel saw it, he was furious and told USAC that unless Thompson removed it, he would be banned from the Speedway. Needless to say, Ratfink won the day.

Eventually Eddie got the white car qualified at 151.9 mph for 24th place on the grid but actually faster than the time done by Dave. Eddie did one lap at 153.4 mph, and I was very impressed that he'd done it with so little practice. Mickey said it was his experience that made the biggest difference, and it was possible that Eddie would end up beating Dave.

As you can imagine, I was very happy when Masten Gregory did come back for one last try at qualifying in the rebuilt titanium car he'd crashed. After a short practice session, he made a final qualifying run at 12 minutes past 5:00 p.m. on the last day of qualifying. Understandably, perhaps, he didn't make it into the field, but at 146.038 mph, he was fast enough to be listed as the second alternative if any cars dropped out. But none did.

Masten would try his luck again at Indy in 1965, qualifying a BRP-Ford entered by George Bryant, who had briefly been married to Masten's mother. He retired with engine problems, winning $9600. Bryant (no relation to the author) had been involved with the British Racing Partnership (BRP) team, for which Masten had driven Formula One cars in Europe. Although he went on to try to qualify again, this would be Masten's last Indy 500.

There were 61 entries in 1964, and they included several interesting approaches to designing the perfect Indy car. The most unusual was the brainchild of Henry "Smokey" Yunick, stock car tuner *par excellence*. He had built a car that looked like a motorcycle sidecar outfit, with the driver sitting in the sidecar trying to control the whole thing. All the heavy stuff was on the outside of the track, with the driver lying right alongside the engine and transmission. Bobby Johns made a brave attempt but missed out on qualifying when he spun out on the last lap. Even Mickey's old buddy and expert driver, Duane Carter, proved unable to qualify Smokey's car. The previous year, in the last minutes of qualifying, Duane had qualified Mickey's Harvey Aluminum special 15th. If he couldn't make Smokey's car work, it probably couldn't be done. So Smokey disgustedly left the track, and I was sorry to see him go. Smokey later donated the car to the Indy 500 Museum, which was a lot better than ending up as one of the famous blocks of compressed scrap metal in his garage. He put cars he didn't like through the compressor at his local junkyard, and enjoyed kicking them as he walked by.

The evening after final qualifying, Mickey took everyone to a nice steak house for dinner. I was on top of the world because it was obvious that Mickey was happy he had brought me over from England.

Masten Gregory · 1964 · Indianapolis Motor Speedway

CHAPTER 16

Carnival and Calamity

Pole position for the 1964 Indianapolis 500 was taken by Jim Clark in a Lotus-Ford on Dunlop tires. Bobby Marshman was second in a similar car on Firestones, and Rodger Ward completed the front row in another rear-engined car from the famous Watson team. A.J. Watson was the man who had made the best roadster chassis, but after four Indy victories in seven years, he was now switching to rear engines. It was a sign of the times and spelled the end of the roadster era.

On the second row, Parnelli Jones and A.J. Foyt (the eventual winner) had the fastest of the Watson-Offenhauser roadsters alongside Dan Gurney in another works Lotus-Ford. Dave MacDonald was very happy to line up his Thompson-Ford in the middle of the fifth row, ahead of drivers like Johnny Rutherford (Watson-Offy), who was just behind him on the grid alongside Eddie Sachs (Halibrand-Ford), who had almost won the 1961 race.

Both our drivers were ahead of Jack Brabham in his own Offy-powered rear-engined car. This also pleased Mickey, because he'd heard how Masten had described our car to Jack before we'd had a chance to rework it. Most people credit Brabham as the Formula One driver who had started the rear-engine revolution at Indy, and to out-qualify him was no mean feat.

Race strategy was going to be extremely important, because the pit stops would play a big part in the outcome of the race. In recent years, some cars had managed to do the race with only one stop for fuel, and that was a big key to winning. We only had room in our fuel tank for 44 gallons, so after qualifying was over, Mickey decided to switch the engines from methanol to gasoline. This would give the cars much better fuel mileage, but of course, the engine would have less power. Mickey figured that our cars could pick up valuable positions if they needed one fuel stop fewer than the cars running on methanol. He reasoned that race speeds were always slower than qualifying speeds, so power wasn't really such an issue.

The decision meant that we had to remove the fuel cells and clean them out very thoroughly, because the methanol we'd been using didn't mix well with gasoline.

After qualifying was over, it was mandatory for the teams that had made it into the race to tear the cars down. USAC demanded to see paperwork certifying that all the critical parts of the suspension had been crack-detected and certified. So we had another thrash to get the cars back together for the final practice on what is customarily called Carburetion Day. Then as now, this took place on the last Thursday before the race and was a free practice. It was a last chance to check out the cars after they had been rebuilt and to tweak the handling.

It was a good day for us, although it was very tricky trying to reset the Hilborn fuel-injection systems for gasoline. Meanwhile Dave was enjoying himself as a top candidate for Rookie of the Year. There was a rookie on the row in front of him, a road racer named Walt Hansgen who was driving a unique car for its designer, Joe Huffaker, and Kjell Qvale, the British car importer from San Francisco. The rear-engined Huffaker-Offy had hydraulic suspension from the British MG. There were five more rookies behind Dave, and he was determined not to let any of them past, saying that he planned to get by Hansgen as early in the race as he could.

As race day dawned, we'd worked through the night again. Very early in the morning, Paul Nicolini took me up to the top of the infield grandstands to watch what he called the re-enactment of the Oklahoma Land Rush. At 6:00 a.m., they opened the gates for hundreds of cars that had been standing in line all night for the infield parking. I'd never seen anything like it. They drove straight across the golf course in a big cloud of dust to get to their favorite spots. Many of them parked up and quickly erected their own mini-granstands, made from scaffolding, in the back of their pickup trucks. But they were forced to take them down by officials because of an injury the previous year. It was amazing to see it all happen.

Indy was not just a race—it was a happening. There was even an exclusive club for beer drinkers who listened to the race on the radio while they drank their barrels of beer in the infield. If any member of the club actually saw a racing car, they threw him out of the club. There were reputed to be 60 temporary jail cells set up under the stands to house anyone rowdy enough to attract the notice of the security people, but this wasn't true. If anyone was arrested, they were taken straight off to jail.

Eventually the race cars were all pushed out onto the track, and I'd never witnessed such a show. The place seemed to be filled with marching bands as they paraded the drivers for the fans. All kinds of stuff happened, including the customary introductions of famous people, before Vic Damone sang "Back Home in Indiana." Then we had the national anthem and the famous directive: "Gentlemen, start your engines!"

To our dismay, Eddie Johnson's engine wouldn't fire properly. Mickey himself frantically fiddled with the injection system and anything else he could bang with a wrench, but it refused to start and stay running. Finally an engineer from Ford named Danny Woo, who was their fuel-injection guru, ran up and somehow got it fired. We all breathed a sigh of relief as the cars drove off for the parade laps. Dave's car sounded fine and that was a big relief. As the cars started the parade laps, thousands of balloons went up in a giant, multicolored cloud.

I was given a trackside job as Dave's pit signaler as an honor for all my help. I wasn't sure if that was the best place for me, because the pit wall looked like it could be a very dangerous place, being so close to the track. I don't mind admitting that I was really scared when the green flag waved. I ducked down on my knees behind the inner track wall as the cars thundered by. There was a lot of dust and crap on the track, and it all flew up in the air like a fog. Frankly, rather than being a fun experience, it was terrifying, and it wasn't until all the cars had passed that I got up off my knees and peered over the wall, looking for them to come by again.

As they were on their second lap, I had just heard the announcer say that Dave MacDonald was moving up through the field at a great rate—when it happened. Dave had passed several cars on the first lap and according to Len Sutton, a driver who was following him, he tried to duck inside the other rookie, Walt Hansgen, in turn 4 and simply lost it. The car spun facing backwards, then forwards, and hit the inside wall hard on the left rear. We all saw a big fireball go up into the air near the end of the pit entrance wall. The burning car bounced back onto the track, and Eddie Sachs's car T-boned it. Sachs was killed instantly.

USAC stopped the race, and I ran up to the accident scene. It was over half a mile away, and it seemed to take forever. By the time I got there, the firemen had put out the fires—I'd never seen firemen get to a race car that fast. I felt totally helpless and very upset. They were starting to get Dave out of the car and he was in terrible shape, barely recognizable with his nose burned away. A photographer ran up to take a close-up picture and that really angered me. I yelled in his face, "Piss off!" I told him he should be ashamed of himself for even wanting pictures of that. He shrugged and walked away.

I looked closely at what was left of the car. It was burned up quite a bit, but the steel flange that located the fuel filler cap on the left side was still in place, and so was the cap. The big impact with the wall had broken the right-side suspension and pushed it all against the bodywork. The body had been ripped away and had taken a big part of the fuel cell with it. I guessed that when that happened, the frame metal hit the wall and caused sparks that ignited the gasoline. Then I saw how Sachs's car had T-boned it and realized that no tubular space frame chassis could possibly have been strong enough. This car hadn't been designed for crashes like modern cars are. Dave MacDonald was an unfortunate victim of his era. He died from his injuries and burns a short time later.

OPPOSITE: The wreckage of Dave MacDonald's car sits in the garage in Gasoline Alley. (Peter Bryant)

Right then and there, I vowed never to come to Indy unless it was with a car designed to survive impact with the wall in a crash. At that moment, I hated the place. I blamed Dave's death on the unforgiving nature of the track design. Everyone knew racing was dangerous, but I felt that something could have been done to make it a little safer at the Speedway. Accidents like that still happen there, but advances in car design have enabled drivers to survive them. It took nearly 40 years for them to install a "soft" wall to reduce the impact violence. But I guess we all have perfect hindsight, and in spite of the danger, Indy is and always will be the biggest racing spectacle, and one of a small handful of races that drivers most want to win.

I went back to the pits. Mickey had gone to the infield hospital to see Dave. Meanwhile Eddie had pulled in with his engine running badly. After the red flag, no one was allowed to work on his car until the race was restarted. Unfortunately he would end up doing only six laps under the green flag before retiring with a broken fuel pump. I think it could have been repaired, but none of us had any interest in the race anymore.

I was very upset and disappointed that it had ended this way. Dave had wanted to win his first Indy 500 and he had been a racer who died doing something he loved. I thought this was a whole lot better than some of my childhood friends, who had died from a Nazi bomb during World War II. But I felt really bad for his wife and family.

The atmosphere in our garage was sad, to say the least. They had brought in the crashed car, and we had to lock the doors to keep out the press. Some people came in from Sears, Roebuck to offer Mickey their condolences, but he had stayed at the hospital with Dave. The next day, we loaded everything up on the trailers and went back to California with a tarpaulin covering the wreckage.

The day after we got back, we all went to Rose Hills Cemetery in Los Angeles for Dave

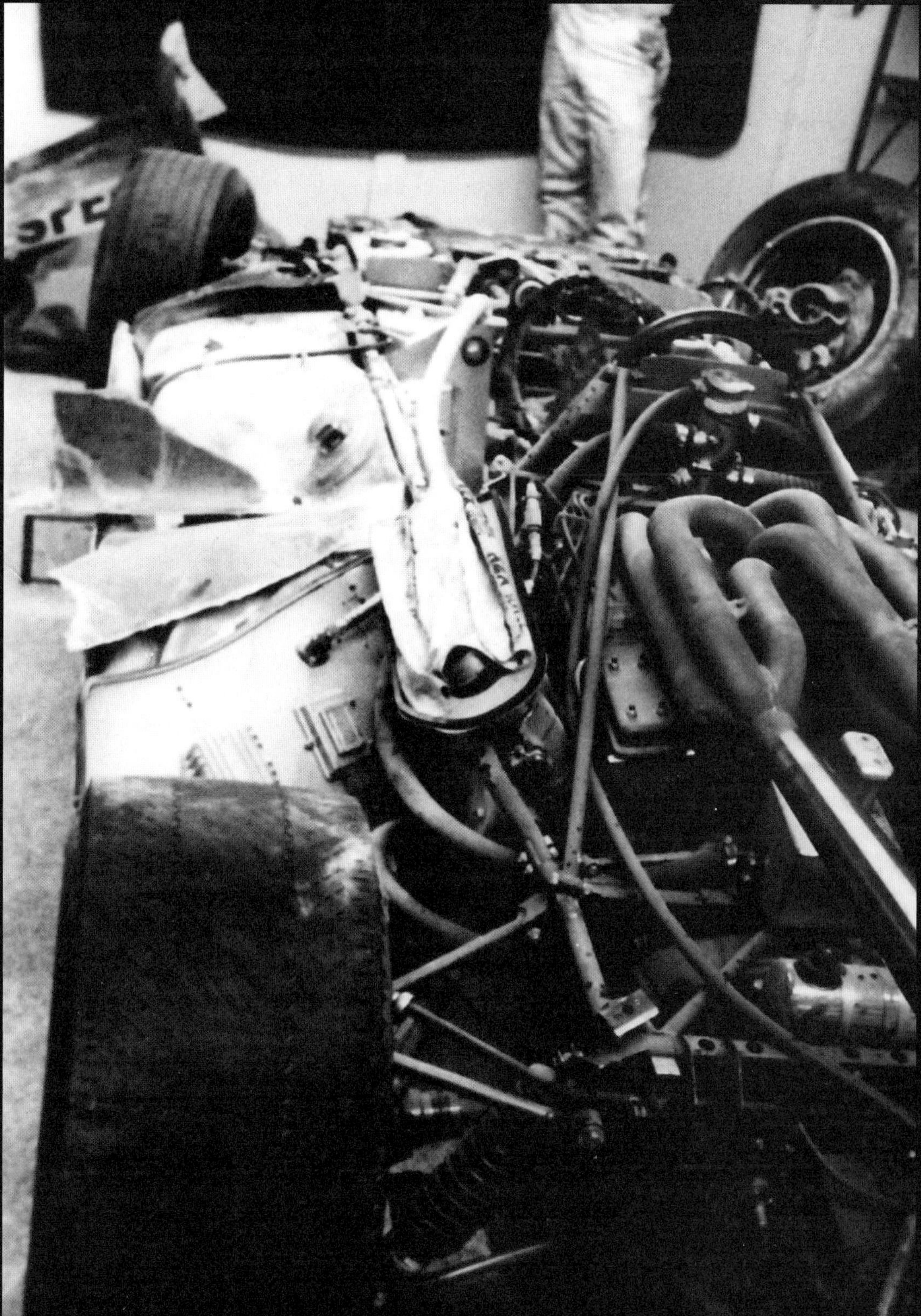

MacDonald's funeral, and heard Mickey say a few words for him. We had to stand outside the church because it was so crowded. Standing just in front of us was Dan Blocker, one of the stars of the TV show *Bonanza*. He was still in his cowboy costume and had obviously run out of the studios to get there. Next to him were race-car driver Skip Hudson and another guy I didn't recognize.

After some of us had gone down to the chapel to pay our last respects, I overheard this other guy saying to Skip Hudson that he'd heard there had been over 100 gallons of gasoline in the Thompson car, and it had been nothing short of a bomb waiting to blow up. On top of that, he continued, its handling was so dangerous that several drivers had turned down offers to drive it. I waited until the service ended, and then grabbed the guy by the arm as he was leaving. I said, "I don't know who you are, and I don't really care. What I do care about is people spreading false rumors about that crash, and saying things that aren't true. There was less than 44 gallons of gas in the car, and it was handling well enough for Dave to pass seven cars on the first lap. Dave died because he wanted to lead and win the Indy 500 and couldn't wait to do it, and no other reason."

He looked surprised and said, "We were only chatting, and no harm was meant, but I apologize if I upset you. My name is Gordon Martin, and I'm the motoring correspondent for the *San Francisco Chronicle*. Here's my card. I would really like to interview you for an article about Dave MacDonald."

Fritz Voight stepped in and said, "Not today, if you don't mind. Goodbye."

I was destined to run into Gordon Martin on many other occasions, and we eventually became friends. Seven years later, he would be the journalist who put together the press conference in San Francisco introducing the Shadow Mk 2 Can-Am car that I designed.

Back in Long Beach, Mickey laid off all the other crew members except Fritz, who was his shop foreman. He couldn't lay me off because he was an obligated sponsor of a registered U.S. immigrant and had agreed to keep me in work or support me financially for at least 18 months.

Mickey asked me to prepare the car that Eddie Johnson had driven at Indy for an attempt at a speed record—500 miles at 200 mph—on a giant, 6-mile circle at the Salt Flats in Utah. I got the car ready and he managed to get Goodyear to make some special spiked tires for better traction. One day he came in and told me he had canceled the attempt, without offering any explanation. In July 1964, I found work with Carroll Shelby's racing team in Venice, California. I didn't want to be a burden to Mickey and really wanted to work in a racing team. At that time, the Shelby Cobra factory in Venice was the busiest in the United States.

Twenty-four years later, on March 16, 1988, Mickey and Trudy Thompson were brutally murdered in their own driveway. More than 13 years after that horrible event, after incredible perseverance on the part of Mickey's sister, Colleen, and her husband, Gary Campbell, Mickey's former partner in a stadium racing venture, Mike Goodwin, was arrested and charged with the murders. The Thompsons had sued Goodwin and won a civil judgment against him. Police alleged that Goodwin had then hired two hit men, who have never been found, to murder them. After spending four years in jail, having the case dismissed and being charged again, Goodwin was finally brought to trial in Los Angeles in November 2006. Early in 2007, he was found guilty and given a life sentence without parole.

I really owe everything I have ever been able to accomplish in America to Mickey Thompson. I am permanently in his debt. In my eyes, and in many other people's eyes, too, he truly was an American hero.

BELOW: Publicity photo of the Shelby American workshops at their home in a former hangar at the Los Angeles Airport. That's me at the left working on the grindstone, with mechanic John Olson behind me. The Mustang GT350 production line can be seen at the rear. (Shelby Publicity)

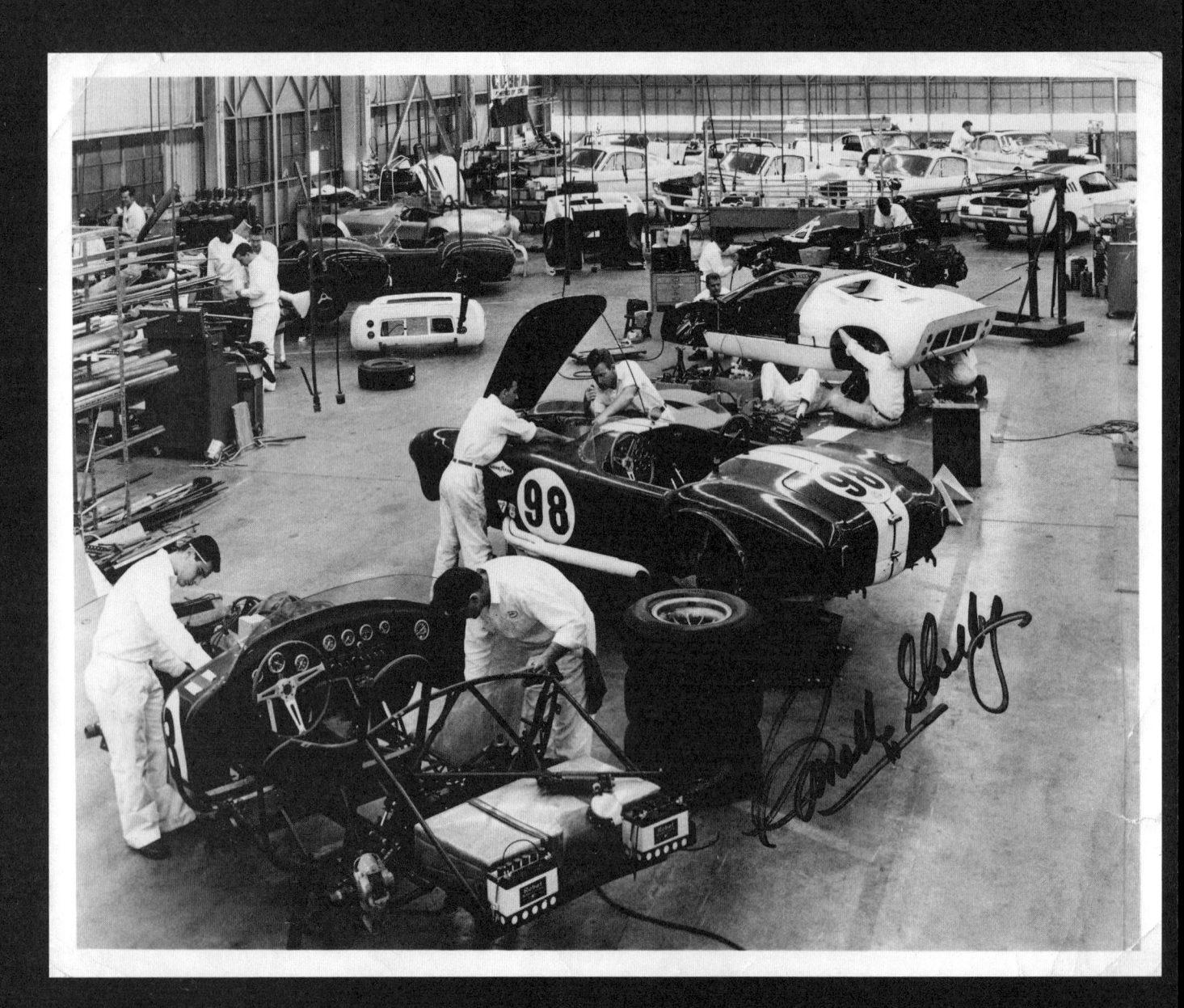

CHAPTER 17

A Circuitous Route to Can-Am

It was July 1964 when I went to Shelby American for an interview. I expected to be questioned by Carroll Shelby, who had offered me a job when I had been working for Reg Parnell in England. Instead an English chap named Ken Miles interviewed me. He seemed totally unimpressed by my Formula One credentials but said they could probably use me to help prepare their Cooper Monaco V8 sports-racing cars for the big *Times* Grand Prix at Riverside. He offered me about $3 an hour and I started work on Shelby's King Cobras.

The first thing I noticed about the other mechanics was that very few had any road-racing experience. They had either been hot-rod enthusiasts or metal fabricators somewhere. The employee turnover was incredible—people were coming and going like lightning. Jack Hoare, one of the engine builders, lived near me in Long Beach, and we shared rides and became friends. My 1947 DeSoto, which I had bought from Fritz Voight, had finally blown up, and I welcomed getting a lift for a few days. Then I bought a used Mercury Monterey with an electric gearshift. I rebuilt the engine, and we used that.

ABOVE: Shelby manager Al Dowd looks over the GT40 I prepared before loading it onto the plane for Le Mans. In the background, a line of Cobra 427 chassis wait on blocks for engines. (Shelby Publicity)

It appeared that Shelby had put people in charge of everything based on their administrative abilities, rather than their race-car knowledge. The shop manager was Buck Allen, and the foreman was Jack Balch. Neither of them knew anything about race cars, and Balch was in the army reserve. He behaved like he was our sergeant, and we were his new recruits. So no one took any notice of him!

One week, Balch brought in a red smoke grenade that he had stolen from the army, and put it on the desk in his little glassed-in office. It didn't take long for someone to set it off and shut the door. He ran in, grabbed it, came out into the shop, and threw it as far as he could. Unfortunately it landed in an area where all the brand-new seats and upholstery items were stored and dyed everything a nice shade of red. I have no idea how he explained that to the powers that be.

Fortunately for Carroll Shelby, he did have some talented mechanics who could do a good job preparing a car—guys like the Agapiou brothers, Charlie and Kerry, and Bill Eaton, whose nickname was "Big Five" because of the size of his hands. Those three were also from England. There was a talented guy from New Zealand named John Olson, and a very good American fabricator named Phil Remington. John Collins, who also worked there, later had his own shop, building replica McLarens. By the end of 1964, Shelby had a pretty good staff, mainly due to attrition.

I was given the task of building a prototype Ford GT350 Mustang for Jerry Titus to drive. They also assigned a staff engineer from Ford named Chuck Cantwell, and we got along fine. We also received a prototype Mustang from Ford, with independent rear suspension, but it never did handle as well as the original one we built, mostly because there was far too much compliance in the rubber bushings, and not enough inherent roll stiffness. I believe the secret to the great handling of our GT350 Mustang was the use of leaf springs in the rear, coupled with the addition of a traction bar to help the "bite" going out of corners.

The leaf spring may be antiquated, but it has a property that coil springs don't have. If set up right, it resists rebound as well as jounce, and this amounts to helping the suspension resist roll under cornering. This is because as the inside wheel lifts during roll, the spring tries to resist it and delays the roll a few milliseconds. Not many people know that. When they see leaf springs, they think they are inferior to coils, whereas in fact they can be superior in certain applications.

Christmas Eve at Shelby American was livened up when Buck Allen put some clear moonshine in the office water cooler. Chuck Cantwell used to come down every day from his office upstairs to get a drink from the water cooler and check out the action in the shop. That day, he got quite a shock when he took a big swig from the paper cup and discovered how everyone was getting high working on Christmas Eve. To his credit, he never told the management. Carroll Shelby had gone to Texas for the holidays, so he never found out that we were playing football in the back lot on his time that day. I had no idea how potent that moonshine was. Jack Hoare had to stop on the way home under a freeway overpass so I could throw it all up. I never drank moonshine again.

I went to races with the Cobra team at Laguna Seca and Riverside. I also attended a couple of test sessions, at Willow Springs with Bob Bondurant in the King Cobras and at Riverside with Ken Miles in a 427 Cobra. Bondurant was a great test driver, but Miles wasn't. At Riverside, "Side Bite" (Charlie Agapiou's nickname for Miles, who talked out of the side of his mouth) did a few exploratory laps and started adjusting the shocks and anti-roll bars right away. We kept track of all the changes, and then went to a local café for lunch. After lunch, he made some more adjustments and went faster and faster, giving the impression that he was improving the car's handling with all these changes. At about 4:00 p.m., he declared it a successful test, and we loaded up the car and went back to the shop. When I analyzed the changes he had made since lunch, I discovered that the settings were exactly the same as they had been when we had arrived at the track. What happened was that as Miles did lots of laps in the afternoon, he got more and more acquainted with the car's handling and went faster by correcting the things that were screwing it up—namely, the changes he had made in the morning. I told Buck Allen about this, and he never asked me to go testing with the team again!

About a year later, however, I tested again with Miles for Ford, running the open-cockpit Ford X1 at Sebring under contract from McLaren, who had built the car in England. Miles screwed up the test when he tried to run a lap without shifting gears. He said, "Well, Peter, it's supposed to be a semi-automatic gearbox, so I thought I'd try it out." He cooked the oil in the torque converter. All the gears were stained dark black by the overheated oil, destroying all traces of previous wear patterns that we'd been measuring painstakingly at 10-lap gearbox teardown intervals. Miles was a great Cobra driver but a lousy tester. Unfortunately he was killed in August 1966, testing the prototype Ford GT "J-car" at Riverside. It was a great loss because, in races, he could drive the wheels off any car.

Shortly after Christmas 1964, Carroll Shelby was awarded the new Ford GT40 program, in addition to his own Cobra Daytona Coupe, and we moved from Princeton Street in Venice to a former Pan Am hangar at the West Imperial Terminal of Los Angeles Airport. The hangar was really needed because the GT350 Mustang had been so successful that Ford wanted Shelby American to go into limited production with it, and so Shelby needed more room. I got the job of preparing a Ford GT40 for the 1965 Le Mans 24 Hours.

At about the same time, Shelby hired a new man, Carroll Smith, to take charge of anything that was going to Le Mans. I didn't envy him that task. Later I found it amazing when he became such a successful race-car preparation guru. Charlie Agapiou gave him the nickname "Scattershit" because his office was always such a mess he could never find anything.

I was the only guy working at Shelby American who had been to Le Mans before, and I didn't want to go back there any time soon. In those days, I didn't see Le Mans in the same light I did Formula One racing and, besides, I had just brought Sally over to America with little Paul. I didn't want to leave them alone in Long Beach for three months, especially considering that she couldn't yet drive a car. So when the time came for the team to leave for France, I was laid off. Shelby American had been an interesting experience, but I hadn't learned much there compared with working for Reg Parnell.

I wound up moving to Connecticut for a year to help Jerry Willets and an old friend, company founder Walt Boyd. Walt had been Peter Revson's mechanic when Peter raced in Formula Junior in Europe in 1962. They had just started a new company called Motorsport Design Corporation (MDC). They needed an experienced racing mechanic, so Walt tracked me down at Shelby American and asked me to go and work for him. He promised moving expenses and help finding accommodations. I had no other offers in California, so we went. Sally was apprehensive about moving 2,000 miles just to change jobs. Sally, Paul, and I ended up renting the top half of a small two-story house in Ridgefield, Connecticut, for a while.

ABOVE: Kerry Agapiou (left), Ron Butler (center), and engine builder Jack Hoare (right) work on the Cobras. (Peter Bryant)

At MDC I met Mac Tilton, who later became one of the most successful race-car component suppliers in America, and I started getting involved with McLaren sports-racing cars and the United States Road Racing Championship (USRRC). Coincidentally MDC also made great torsion bar–suspended race-car trailers, and McLaren used them in the Can-Am. I spent a lot of my time running their dynamometer, tuning engines.

We prepared a McLaren M1B for John Cannon, which was sponsored by Dan Blocker. John was driving this car a couple of years later when he won the 1968 Laguna Seca Can-Am race in the rain. He was a very talented driver and unfortunately lost his life in an air crash

ABOVE: The works Cobras fill the front row at the start of an SCCA race at Laguna Seca. Ken Miles won the race for Shelby. (Peter Bryant)

years after he quit racing. We also prepared a Porsche 906 for Peter Revson's brother, Doug, which they drove together in the 500-mile USRRC race at Road America. Doug later went to Europe to race in Formula 2 but sadly lost his life in a racing crash at Zolder in Belgium.

Another client of MDC was a young driver named Mike Goth. He'd raced a Cobra, a Brabham Formula B single-seater and a Lotus 23 in club events, and in May 1966, he bought a McLaren M1A with a Chevy V8. Mike was pretty fast and entered the car in the USRRC and the Can-Am Series events that followed. I was recruited from the MDC staff to go with him to the races and look after his car. Mike had a good third in the USRRC race at Bridgehampton but was basically learning what big-bore sports-car racing was all about, and only finished two of the six Can-Am races that season. But it was good experience for me, and I started to understand what was happening to the car as it was put through a race.

I was at the last Can-Am race in Las Vegas when my old friend Charlie Hayes came up to me to talk about his car's handling. I had walked round the track and looked it over before practice, and had seen the problems of racing on the three-mile airfield circuit, which had several surface changes from tarmac to concrete and back. Charlie was complaining about what he thought was a steering problem in one particular corner. As he talked and I asked questions, suddenly it was like a moving picture had started in my head. I could see the car cornering and the suspension moving, and I saw the rear wheels leave the track at a junction of two surfaces. I told Charlie that I thought the rear wheels were coming off the ground, and suggested we make a large spoiler flap and put it on the back of the bodywork to help keep traction. We found a place selling plexiglass and made two spoiler flaps overnight, one for his McLaren and one for Mike Goth's. They were immediately about three seconds faster around the lap.

I had found the true value of downforce. When I coupled that with other stuff I'd learned about aerodynamics from Mickey Thompson, I began to realize its importance to the performance of a car during cornering.

As well as those three McLarens, I also worked on a McKee clone called the Hamill, for Ed Hamill of Illinois. I went to several races with all of them and experienced what a challenge it was to race the older production McLarens against the factory team's latest cars and the Lolas. It was tough going. None of those drivers was of the caliber of the Grand Prix drivers they were racing against in the Can-Am, but with his Chaparral 2E, Jim Hall had won at Laguna Seca, showing everyone in sports-car racing what could be done with some ingenuity. I desperately wanted to work with a front-runner if I was going to be involved in American sports-car racing.

After a year or so in Connecticut, the weather reminded me of why I'd moved from England to California! As the winter of 1966–67 approached, I moved my family back to Garden Grove in California and got employment with Bill Thomas, of Cheetah sports-car fame.

My first job for Bill Thomas Race Cars consisted of putting a 427 Chevy engine into an E Type Jaguar. When I finished that job, Bill gave me the task of building a dragster for Hayden Profit to race. Next I prepared two Camaros, which were to have been sponsored by a Chevrolet dealer in Chicago in the Trans-Am series. But when the sponsor didn't come through with the money, they were sold.

ABOVE: The GT40 is loaded up for a shakedown run before I say goodbye to it, and to Shelby American. (Peter Bryant)

I liked Bill, and we became good friends. While I was working for him in 1967, two major personal events took place. My daughter Elizabeth was born, and Sally and I bought our first house, in Santa Ana.

Halfway through that year, Peter Revson called me about going to work on his Can-Am car. It was a Lola T70 owned by Peyton A. Cramer, whom I had met at Shelby American, and was to be sponsored by Dana Chevrolet. The Lola T70 had won five of the six Can-Am races in 1966. Peter had some good Formula One experience in Europe and was much faster than those club racers I'd worked for. I figured he could give the other Lola drivers a tough time, like defending champion John Surtees in the works T70, Dan Gurney, Mark Donohue, and George Follmer, not to mention Bruce McLaren and Denny Hulme in the works McLarens. In fact, I was sure my wish had been granted: I was going to be working for a front-runner.

And this is where my Can-Am Challenge saga really began.

BELOW: Denny Hulme's McLaren leads Mario Andretti's Honker and the Dana Lola of Peter Revson at the 1967 Riverside Can-Am race. (LAT Photographic)

CHAPTER 18

Can-Am Reality Check

Like the American participants in the Can-Am Challenge Cup, the professional European teams quickly noticed that it paid more money than Formula One. When John Surtees won the inaugural series in 1966, he took home over $76,000—more than the total prize money on offer in all that year's Grand Prix races. The word spread that the tracks in this new championship were paved with gold.

Peyton Cramer reckoned he stood a good chance of winning some of that moolah when he formed his new racing team. The Dana Chevrolet shop was located in downtown Los Angeles, which for me was not too bad a commute and much better than working in Connecticut. Cramer had purchased two new Lola T70 sports-racing cars for Peter Revson and Lothar Motschenbacher to drive. A private sponsor of the team was Dan Blocker, so our paths crossed again. Our engines were prepared at Traco Engineering, the top American Chevy engine builders. In those days, you could buy a 6-liter small block race engine putting out nearly 500 bhp for about $5000. If you were successful, running a Can-Am car in 1967 could be quite lucrative.

ABOVE: The Dana rig arrives at Elkhart Lake for the opening race of the 1967 Can-Am season. At the center, mechanic John Ward (in white) and I (in blue jacket) can be seen with hair still wet from our unplanned swim along the highway in Wisconsin. (Tom Schultz)

I was really looking forward to having an exciting season. I had known Lothar for a couple of years. He was a competitive driver and a factory-trained Mercedes mechanic. With his meticulous preparation, he had finished well in many races in the USRRC in his own McLaren. I was pretty sure I could learn something useful from him. Lothar worked on his own car with an assistant known as "Sparky." I did all the work on Peter's car with the help of a mechanic named John Ward.

I had met Peter Revson for the first time in England, at Reg Parnell's workshop. Reg had rented out some space for Peter and his mechanic, Walter Boyd, to prepare a Formula Junior Cooper for a championship that was run on the support bills at Grands Prix. Unfortunately they picked a new Holbay engine, which was still very much at the development stage. The two of them spent hours and hours trying to get the dry sump oiling system to stop puking oil all over Europe's premier race tracks. So Peter didn't have a lot of fun that year. He was a very wealthy young man, an heir of the Revlon cosmetic corporation but not pretentious in any way. He was very happy to clean the oil off the Cooper's bodywork or sleep in a sleeping bag on the floor of "Gertie," his old diesel truck, under the ramp holding his car—sometimes with its oil dripping on him! Gertie smelled very strongly of diesel fuel. The radiator hose had broken on the way to a race, and after they'd fixed it, they'd realized they had no water. So they'd refilled the radiator with diesel. When Gertie got hot, she absolutely stank.

I hadn't seen Peter drive in the United States much prior to the USRRC in 1967, but he'd done half a dozen Formula One races for Reg Parnell in Europe. I figured I had a potential star driver, and it was my job to make his Lola competitive with the factory T70 of John Surtees, along with the McLarens of Bruce McLaren and Denny Hulme.

The place for me to start was the aerodynamic setup, so I immediately had some spoilers made for the front and rear of the body. Then I made some extra-strong anti-roll bars and fitted some stiffer suspension springs. After many all-nighters, John Ward and I finally loaded up the double-decker transporter and headed out for the opening Can-Am race at Elkhart Lake, Wisconsin. Lothar would meet us there. His mechanic had disappeared into the sunset one weekend, because we had to work on a Sunday. Sparky was a free spirit, having been an assistant to the rock group The Loving Spoonful.

We were on the freeway in Wisconsin when suddenly an old Oldsmobile in front of us made a sharp right turn and disappeared into the countryside. Then the Olds abruptly reappeared and shot across the freeway right in front of us. It went down the slope of the grassy median and up the slope on the other side, which launched it into the air across the freeway lanes coming the other way, narrowly missing an 18-wheel truck. Then it disappeared into a field of tall ripe corn. We stopped, figuring the driver had had a heart attack or something, and ran across the freeway and into an alley of broken corn that the Olds had made. The path took a right, then a left, and ended at the edge of a gravel pit filled with water. The front of the car was in the murky water, with the hood already submerged. The car was at a steep angle and sinking at an alarming rate. There were two women and a little girl on the back seat, and they were screaming for help. John and I ran up to the car and he grabbed the rear bumper. "I can't swim!" he yelled.

I ran into the water alongside the car and yanked one woman through a rear window and into the water alongside me. Then I pulled her towards the bank, and John let go of the bumper and grabbed her. Then I seized the little girl by an arm, and pulled her out too. By then, the water was filling the car through the open rear window and the older woman screamed: "I can't get through!" The door was locked, and I yanked up the unlock shaft by the tip. As I pulled the door handle, the car slipped completely underwater. It seemed forever before I could reach inside for the woman, and by then we were both submerged. Her arms were flailing about, and I ended up with a handful of her hair. I pulled her out by her hair and kicked the doorsill to get to the surface with her in tow. John had walked into the water up to his chest and helped me pull her onto the bank. She was about 70, and she hadn't missed many meals. Her dress was halfway up her body and the driver of the 18-wheeler helped her to stand up and straighten herself out. "These men just saved your lives," he said to her. "Don't you have anything to say to them?"

The old woman looked straight at me and said with a sob, "My purse is on the back seat—can you get it for me?"

John and I started to laugh as we walked back to the transporter on the other side of the freeway. We grabbed some dry clothes from our bags and went behind the truck to change. We drove on to the track and just made it to technical inspection.

Next morning, we saw a headline in a local paper that said, "Mystery Truck Drivers Save Family." The story was about two truck drivers rescuing a daughter, mother, and grandmother from drowning in a gravel pit, and leaving before anyone could get their names.

I'd already made several modifications to the Dana Lolas. As well as the shiny aluminum front and rear spoilers, I'd also lowered the ride height a little. But there was still plenty to do, and I worked 56 hours without sleep before the race started.

This race was considered the first of a new golden era for sports-car racing in North America, and 32 cars were entered. After what seemed an incredible struggle to get our Lolas up to speed, Peter qualified in eighth place, just three-tenths slower than Surtees in the works car. The two new McLaren M6As of Bruce and Denny showed us all up by qualifying two seconds faster than Dan Gurney in his All American Racers Lola T70, and five seconds faster than us. If it was any consolation, we were faster than Jim Hall in his Chaparral 2G, who lined up ninth, just ahead of Lothar in the other Dana Lola.

The result was a big win for Denny's McLaren, after Bruce dropped out after only six laps with low oil pressure. Newly crowned USRRC champion Mark Donohue finished second in Roger Penske's Lola, with Surtees third and Hall fourth. Peter had the rear suspension break after 31 laps and was forced to stop, but Lothar managed a ninth-place finish for the team, three laps down.

We wearily loaded up the cars afterwards, and Dan Blocker invited us all to join him for dinner at the hotel after we'd cleaned up. I went to my room and climbed into a hot shower. The next thing I knew, it was 6:00 a.m. and I was waking up. When I went down to join the team for breakfast, Dan sat opposite me and asked me, "How are you feeling this morning?" I told him I felt great but I was very sorry I hadn't made it to the dinner last night, and I hoped he didn't think I was rude. He laughed and said, "Peter, when you didn't make it down, I came to your room to look for you. The door was locked, and there was steam coming under it, so I got the bellman to let me in. You were curled up in the shower with hot water pouring all over you. You looked like a little broiled crab. We put you to bed and left you to sleep. I figured that anybody who fell asleep in the shower needed his rest!" Dan was a real nice person.

The rest of the six-race Can-Am season didn't go well for the Dana Chevrolet team. It was the era of cracked cylinder heads and broken gearbox and suspension parts, and we had six more non-finishes. The only highlights were a fifth place for Lothar in the second round, at Bridgehampton, followed by a fourth for Peter at Mosport. I remember that race because I persuaded Peyton Cramer to hire Charlie Agapiou to help me prepare the car. We worked all night as usual, but that time it paid off, because Charlie was an excellent mechanic.

But then we had two DNFs at Laguna. Before the fifth race, at Riverside, I lowered Peter's car as far as it would go without grinding off the chassis. I used the stiffest springs and anti-rollbars I could find, and the car was handling pretty good, but the chassis was getting weaker. Even though the season wasn't yet over, the chassis had less than 1800 ft.-lbs. per degree of torsional stiffness, so it was just twisting. There was no point in trying to stop it rolling with even stiffer bars.

We even suffered the ignominy of being disqualified from the last race in Las Vegas when Peter was running fifth because we had to push-start him in the pit-lane, which was against the rules.

I felt frustrated for both Peter and me. He drove the wheels off his car and was sometimes faster than Surtees in the works-supported Lola. Peter was over half a second quicker than Big John both at Riverside and in Las Vegas, where Surtees won. The races were over about 200 miles, and unfortunately, Peter tried so hard that he crashed on a couple of occasions.

We ended up with Peter only scoring 11 points all season, and Lothar only 12 points. But we knew we'd pretty much gotten all we could get with customer cars and engines because at Riverside, Lothar and Peter qualified with an identical time. The two of them always qualified well, but we had nothing to offer that could challenge Team McLaren. Bruce and Denny finished 1-2 in the championship, with Surtees third.

How were we going to win a Can-Am race? The only Americans building race cars at that time were Dan Gurney and Jim Hall, but Gurney's All American Racers (AAR) hadn't built a Can-Am Eagle, and Hall's Chaparral didn't sell cars. A couple of open-cockpit Ferrari P4s hadn't been successful, so England was the only place to buy a new Can-Am car. And yet we had learned that if we were going to win, buying a production race car wouldn't do.

I reckon Peyton Cramer felt the same way because after the last race, the team was disbanded, and the Lolas were sold. Once again, I was looking for work.

BELOW: The start of the last USRRC race to be held at Riverside in 1968. Lothar Motschenbacher (11) leads Skip Scott (26) on the left, while Mark Donohue (behind the pace car) leads Peter Revson (52). (Peter Bryant)

CHAPTER 19

On the Learning Curve

I had no real job prospects after the 1967 Can-Am had finished until Colin Riley, an old friend from Lotus, came to my rescue. Colin put me up for a job helping to prepare a new Lola, owned by Carl Haas and to be driven in the 1968 USRRC and Can-Am races by Skip Scott. Charlie Parsons was to be the team's number-one driver, and Colin was his crew chief.

Carl Haas, one of the nicest people you would ever want to work for in auto racing, had just become the Lola Cars distributor for the United States and had put the team together with sponsorship from the Simoniz wax manufacturer. It was apparent to everyone that Carl firmly believed "Chuck" Parsons was a hell of a race driver. Charlie had a deformed leg as a result of a serious injury as a child. Most people would have said he could never be a good driver with that handicap, but Charlie persevered until he became one of the best American sports-car drivers of the sixties. I believe his determination was his greatest strength, and he loved what he was doing. Most great

ABOVE: The Simoniz Lola T70 Team at the 1968 USRRC race at Kent, Washington. It was a 1-2 finish for Skip Scott in number 26 and Chuck Parsons in number 10. That's me leaning on the car, with Parsons at the far right in the blue jacket and Colin Riley in the center. (Ike Smith)

men are backed up by a great woman, and Charlie's wife, Sherrie, was among the greatest. Her presence helped Charlie to focus better. Much like Charlie, Carl too benefited from the loyal support of his wife, Bernie. Many racing wives grow to hate racing, because it does so much to test their marriages. And yet, when they do support their racing husbands, it makes for less pressure, and the relationships can become even stronger.

The Simoniz team had just got back from Mexico City, the first USRRC race of the season, and Carl had just fired the English bloke who had been sent over from the Lola Cars factory to help. Apparently he was an obnoxious type of guy who, instead of helping, tried to take over—a control freak. According to Ike Smith, one of Carl's long-serving mechanics, Carl had told him, "Ike, take this 50 bucks—go to downtown Mexico City and buy a jackass so we can ride this asshole right out of town!" With the Lola expert gone, they hoped I could sort out the new Lola Can-Am cars. Maybe I got the job because I'd helped to make Peter Revson's Lola car pretty fast the previous year.

I was hired to prepare Skip Scott's car, but I spent plenty of time working with Chuck Parsons and all the guys. At first, the four mechanics were Colin Riley, Ike Smith, Gil Munz, and me. For the Can-Am, we were joined by Fred Nething, who had been a mechanic for Lothar Motschenbacher, and some temporary helpers who came and went during the season. Carl had set up a facility in Highland Park, a northern suburb of Chicago. Most of the rest of us were from California, and we all stayed in the same motel when we were working in Chicago—a Howard Johnson on Touhy Avenue.

When the races were held on the West Coast, Carl had a workshop in Burbank on the same industrial estate where Al Bartz prepared our Chevy engines. That was where I joined the team.

The plan was to compete in all the 1968 USRRC races and then the Can-Am Challenge Cup with two cars. The USRRC had already been reduced to not much more than a preamble to the Can-Am and gave the teams an opportunity to test themselves against the other American competitors. The 1968 USRRC started in Mexico City in March and culminated in the last of nine races at Mid-Ohio in August. Then the Can-Am started with another race in the Midwest, at Elkhart Lake, on September 1 and ended in Las Vegas in November. It was a grueling schedule of 15 races that would test the endurance and spirit of any team. It meant being on the road a lot—I think we drove 45,000 miles that year in pickup trucks towing open trailers.

We planned to run Lola T70 Mk 3B cars in the USRRC and switch over to the latest Lola T160 for the start of the Can-Am. I was hoping that the experience I'd gained with Dana Chevrolet in 1967 would prove invaluable to my new team. If we were going to beat the other Lola customer cars and the works McLarens, we would need to develop our cars beyond their inherent design capability. That would be quite a challenge, but for me, the big question was: Would Carl Haas and his team allow me to mess with their new cars?

> **OPPOSITE:** The starting grid is assembled for the start of the 1968 Bridgehampton Can-Am race. Mark Donohue won, followed by Jim Hall in second after both McLarens suffered rare engine problems. (LAT Photographic)

The first part of the Simoniz team's program was very successful. Both Skip Scott and Chuck Parsons did very well. They finished first and second in that order at Bridgehampton, and then second and first on the Pacific Raceway at Kent, in Washington state. The main opposition came from Mark Donohue in Roger Penske's McLaren M 6B. He won some races but he also had some DNFs, usually when his engine blew. When we had a DNF, it was often due to the cylinder head cracking and consequent overheating. The cracking was caused by Bartz enlarging the intake and exhaust ports in order to improve the power output of the

ABOVE: Chuck Parsons (left) and Skip Scott (right) wear the laurels after winning the 500-mile USRRC race at Elkhart Lake in 1968. Squeezing in at the far right is owner Carl Haas, who seems to have dropped something behind Skip. Behind him is mechanic Gil Munz. (Peter Bryant)

Chevrolet engines. We didn't have the cylinder head development choices they have today.

The best memories I have of being part of that great team were the events surrounding the penultimate round of the USRRC, the 500-mile race at Road America, where all the teams had to use two drivers per car. There was a lot on the line as we approached the race. Going to Road America, Donohue led our men in the championship with 36 points, with Chuck at 25 and Skip at 24. We had a team meeting to discuss the best strategy to ensure Chuck maximized his points score. Carl would spare no expense to see that happen.

It was decided to qualify Chuck to drive both our cars in that race. We would modify Chuck's regular Lola with enough fuel capacity to do the entire race with only one pit stop—our attempt for an outright win against the faster McLaren of Donohue. Because the rules said that no driver could drive for longer than three hours without rest, we couldn't just have our two regular drivers switch cars at halfway, so Carl hired Sam Posey to start Chuck's "long-distance" car. If it was still strong at halfway, Chuck would take it over, and Sam would spell Skip.

It was no simple problem to get a Lola T70 to go 250 miles nonstop. We solved it when I made some special "fill necks" that went from the filler flange on top of the bodywork down to the top of the chassis tub to connect to the fuel bladders. These fill necks were actually big tubes that necked down at each end to couple to the car. By expanding the capacity of the big connecting tubes so that they each held about two gallons, we picked up enough fuel capacity—and it was perfectly within the rules. We also borrowed a quick-fill refueling rig from George Bignotti of Indy car-racing fame to give us a fast pit stop.

We knew that only one tire, the left rear, wouldn't go the 500 miles on this track. The final touches to help us beat the Donohue car were knock-off wing nuts on the left rear wheels, in place of the customary four lug nuts, so that we could change that tire as quickly as possible. In those days we didn't use air wrenches, and a wheel change could lose a lot of time.

Well, the race didn't go to plan for very long. Everything started to go crazy after only 11 laps when the engine in Posey's "long-distance" car blew up. It should never have happened, but rev-limiters hadn't been invented, and neither had the computer. Our potential Donohue-beater was out. Thankfully, before halfway, so was Donohue with engine-related problems. We could relax a little. Charlie took the last stint in the car started by Skip and went on to win the race, but not without drama. In the last 20 laps, the car started leaking oil, and we kept bringing it in to refill it. But we were so far ahead at that time that we could take our time to ensure a finish. At the end, we were still six laps ahead of the nearest competitors, who were Bob Nagel and Ed Lowther in a Mk 7 McKee-Chevy.

My fondest memory of Carl Haas and the Simoniz team that weekend at Elkhart Lake came after the race, when Carl invited us all to dinner at the Siebkens resort to celebrate our success. It was an intimate affair, with only team members and some of their families present. After a very nice dinner, and Carl presented each of the mechanics with a beautiful Gallet chronograph watch. On the back he'd had engraved our names and the words "Simoniz Special USRRC 1968." I still have mine and I treasure it. It was the first time in my entire racing life that anyone I'd worked for had showed this kind of recognition for a job well done. I was really moved by Carl's gesture.

I went to another memorable dinner at Siebkens when Dick Gail, the representative of the Champion spark plug company, invited some of the more successful USRRC teams to a big dinner there. There was a giant table set up and the champagne flowed. Donohue's co-driver for the 500 was a successful Chicago lawyer named Jerry Hansen, who had been driving when the engine blew in the Penske McLaren. It was his birthday, and he was seated at the head of the table, regaling everyone with his stories. Suddenly a young waitress came out with a big chocolate cream cake. As Dick led us all in a chorus of "Happy Birthday," the sweet young thing made it right up to Jerry but then appeared to trip. The cake went right into his beaming face and splattered all over him. There was silence for about five seconds until everybody realized what had happened. Jerry had been "caked" by the Siebkens professional cake-thrower—the best-kept secret of the famous resort. Once more she'd successfully done her thing, to the delight of everyone present. We all howled with laughter, and Jerry took it quite well, really.

Unfortunately for our team, Donohue won the last round of the USRCC at Mid-Ohio, with Skip third behind Lothar Motschenbacher's McLaren, and Chuck parked with an oil leak. So Donohue was the champion with 45 points, Skip second with 37 points, and Chuck third with 34. That was the last USRRC—the following season, there was just the Can-Am.

We took delivery of our Lola T160s for the 1968 Can-Am but now Team McLaren arrived in North America with the new M8A, and swept the board again. The new Lola couldn't compete on either pace or reliability. Our best result with it was a fourth for Chuck in the final race in Las Vegas. (For any reader wanting to know more about the race results, I can highly recommend Pete Lyons's excellent book, *Can-Am*.)

LEFT: A rare photo of me actually working on Skip Scott's Chevy engine, in this case tuning the Lucas fuel injection system. (Ike Smith)

Faced with McLaren's dominance, at the end of the season Carl Haas decided to scale back his Can-Am effort for 1969 to a single car driven by Chuck. The move left Skip without a drive, and me without a job.

Parsons and Scott were pretty close in terms of driving ability, and I honestly believed they both got the most out of the Lola chassis and the Bartz engines. But it didn't take a genius to figure that it would take a better car and engine combination to take on the likes of Team McLaren and win a Can-Am. I began to think about the specification that would be needed for a car to do just that.

The first item on the specification would be a full monocoque chassis with at least 10,000 ft.-lb. per degree of torsional stiffness. It was obvious that the customer Lola and McLaren chassis didn't possess that kind of torsional strength. The second item would be a body totally designed for maximum aerodynamic downforce. And a custom-made engine couldn't hurt, either.

And I started thinking of ways to raise the money to build such a car.

CHAPTER 20

Two Little Words . . .

When Skip Scott realized that he wouldn't be asked to drive for Carl Haas in the 1969 Can-Am, he told me he wanted to do the Formula 5000 series instead and asked me if I would be interested in preparing the car. I told him I hadn't been invited to return by Carl Haas, either, and was therefore available. I was fearful that I'd missed out in the dreaded game of "musical mechanics" that always took place between seasons—when the music stopped, all the empty slots would be gone. By that stage, I was delighted to be offered any kind of racing job. It meant paying the bills for at least another season and more racing for me.

Skip introduced me to Ernest Kanzler Jr., who was the owner of a marine products company called Autocoast. Ernie turned out to be one of the most fascinating people I'd ever met. He was the adopted son of Ernest Kanzler, a powerful man in the American automotive industry. He was a member of the Ford family, a close friend of Edsel Ford and Henry Ford Sr., and had been in charge of the production of the Model A Ford car at the Fairlane plant.

Ernie Kanzler Jr. was also an exciting guy in his own right. He could afford to be, too, because his father had endowed him with a very nice trust fund. Besides having a good education, he was very creative. He had talent in the fields of architecture and marine design and was an accomplished sculptor. He designed the house that the famous movie animator Walter Lantz built in Bel-Air, California, as well as his own in the same neighborhood. He designed a small wooden car, powered by a lawnmower engine, for kids of all ages to drive, and sold it in kit form through the mail. He'd started his Autocoast boat company in Costa Mesa and was building a prototype cabin cruiser called the Marauder. He wanted eventually to build a low-volume classic-type sports car. Ernie was a man on the move. I liked him instantly.

When we met at his house in Bel-Air, Skip gave him a rundown on my racing background, and I gave him a copy of my résumé. After he'd read it, he told me I was just the man he was looking for. Not only would I be preparing a car for Skip to drive, but he had a few other products and ideas of his own that I could help him with. In return for my faithful services, I would receive a generous salary (more than generous by racing standards) and company benefits. One of these was the use of the *Sally*, his 40-year-old, 10-meter racing yacht, which was anchored at the "Stuffed Shirt" dock in Newport Harbor. His only question was: Would I be available to start work right away? I was ecstatic but I kept my composure long enough simply to tell him—yes, I was!

As soon as I started working for Ernie, I realized that he was a different type of employer. It was not uncommon for him suddenly to announce that he'd reached a good stopping point for the day, he was going out on the *Sally*, and anyone who wanted to join him would be more than welcome. He was a good father to his kids, and they spent hours at the workshop, riding on the wooden cars and just making stuff. I was also able to bring down my own young son, Paul, to ride the wooden cars. Working for Ernie was a nice change of scene from the usual life of a racer.

With Ernie's blessing (and checks), I went straight ahead and purchased a Gurney Eagle Formula 5000 chassis, an engine from Al Bartz, the respected Los Angeles race engine builder, and a Hewland transmission. I was soon preparing the car for testing.

I met a rather mysterious man one day at the Bartz engine place. He was tall and kind of sinister-looking, with a beard. Al Bartz introduced us. His name was Don Nichols, and his card said he was with Advanced Vehicle Systems. He seemed pleasant enough but obviously didn't want to discuss what he was doing. All I could glean was that he was building some kind of top-secret car. It would turn out to be the small-wheeled Shadow Mk 1 Can-Am race car, designed by Trevor Harris. Don Nichols and Shadow would one day write another chapter or two in my racing life.

It was March 1969, and the Can-Am races loomed on the horizon, but I was out of it now and going full blast to come up with some way to give the Eagle an edge over the Formula 5000 competition. Meanwhile, Skip was lagging behind a little in his commitment to arrange the sponsorship that was needed to campaign the car Ernie had bought and was preparing for him.

One day, Ernie told me something I didn't want to hear. He said, "Skip Scott has failed to satisfy me that he can support the cost of putting the Formula 5000 car on the track for the season, and I'm afraid that I won't let him out of the deal we have. If he can't provide sponsorship to cover the expenses of racing the car, I'll have to make other plans for it, perhaps even sell it."

I was stunned that I might be out of work again. My heart jumped in my chest and, luckily, I was speechless for a moment. Otherwise I may have jumped the gun and said the wrong thing. His next words would prove pivotal to my career. He said, "What do you suggest we do if Skip doesn't come up with something in the next week?"

My mind flashed back to my dream of returning to Can-Am racing with a car that could take on the McLarens and Lolas. I also recalled something that Ernie had said when we first met. I reminded him of it, "Ernie, you've said you would like to build a car of your own and make your own mark on the automotive scene. Why don't I sell the single-seater and start designing a Can-Am car? It's only March, and the Can-Am season doesn't start until June. I've already spoken to the Titanium Metal Corporation of America, and they'll give me all the material and as much technical help as I need. We could use the money we get from selling the formula car and build a competitive Can-Am car with the Autocoast name on it, and your name on it. And it would knock people's socks off!"

Ernie grinned from ear to ear. Almost without hesitation, he uttered two little words—four letters in total that changed my life forever.

He said, "Do it!"

I blurted out, "OK." We shook hands, and Ernie patted me on the back. "Right, then, knock their socks off," he said. And he smiled again, because he could see I still hadn't regained my composure. I felt about 10 feet tall and I promised Ernie he would own the fastest American-built car in the Can-Am.

That evening, I went home and told my family what had happened. I still couldn't really believe it. Ernie had made the decision in a wink of an eye. It hadn't required one iota of salesmanship on my part. The key must have been that this would be an Autocoast car with a clear Ernie Kanzler identity.

Do it! Those were the most exciting words I had ever heard.

200 - CAN-AM CHALLENGER

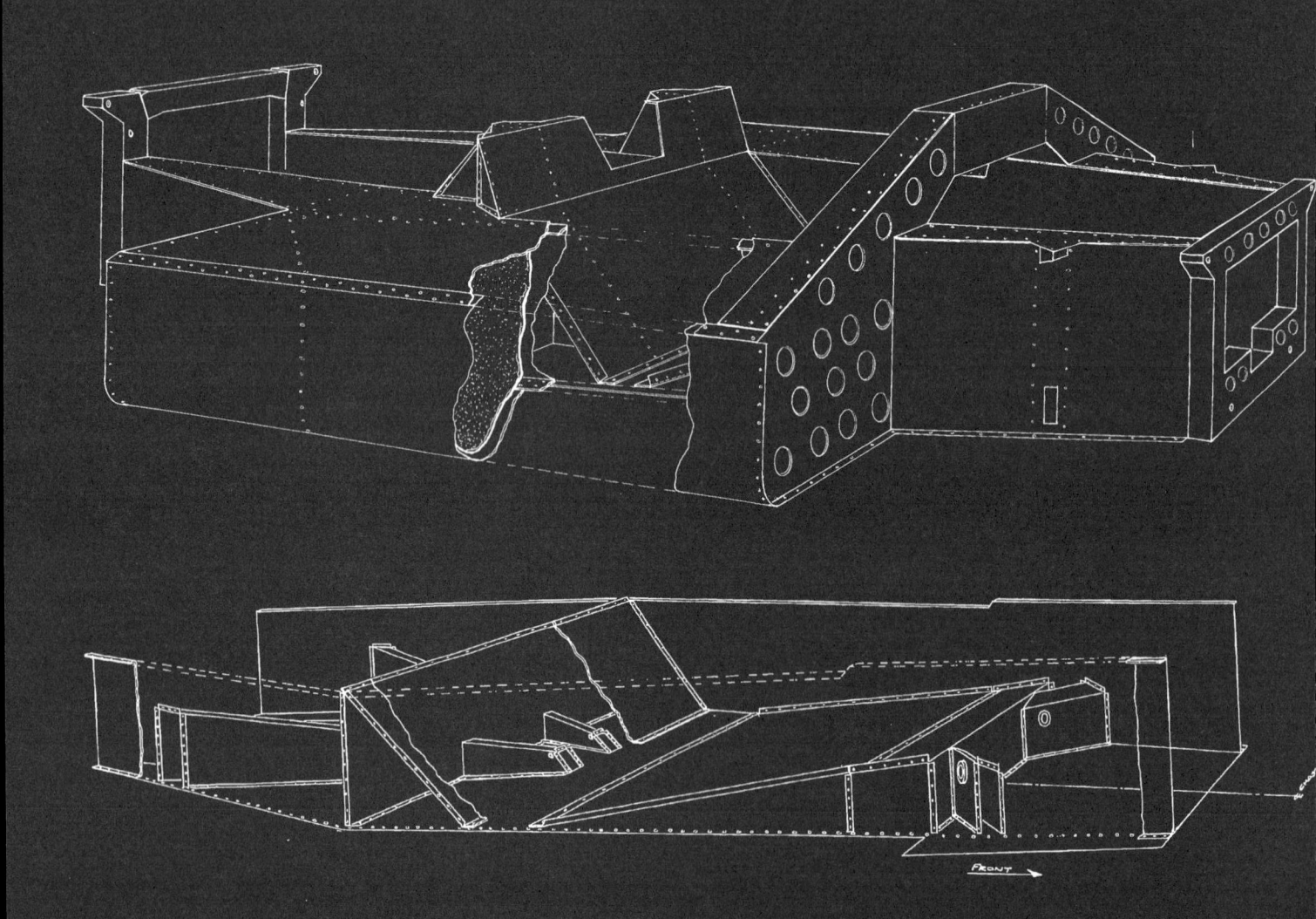

CHAPTER 21

Understanding the Problem

In the Periodic Table of the Elements, the chemical symbol of titanium is Ti, and its atomic weight is 22. When, in early March 1969, Ernie Kanzler handed me such a wonderful opportunity to design and build a titanium Can-Am car, I already knew it was going to be called "Ti22." Many people seem to think the car was called the Autocoast, but that was the name of Ernie's company, which was the sponsor. I made a plan for the design and build program, and got down to work. Every day, I worked from 7:30 in the morning until noon planning the work, chasing parts, and organizing the program. After lunch, I got on the drawing board and worked on the chassis design. I never did feel very creative before lunch.

From the outset, my design philosophy was to create a ground-effect car. The task at hand was to build a car that could beat the McLarens. The taskmaster was the clock.

ABOVE: The Ti22 body male tooling is ready for mold making in 1968. (Al Willard)

Working on a racing car is a way of ensuring that you never have any time to do anything else until it is time to race it. Then, when it is out on track, you spend your time thinking of all the things that you could have done that might have improved it, and waiting to find out what the driver has found out about it. Then you plan what work you have time to do before it has to go back on track again to generate more work. Even when you have finally run out of time and have to roll it onto the starting grid, you find yourself wishing they would put off the damn race until tomorrow, because that way you could make one last, race-winning modification. Racing cars are monsters that perpetually create work.

And they can present problems that are harder to solve than a Rubik's cube. You never stop identifying new problems to solve—in fact, you chase them. If you can be the first to discover a new problem and you can solve it—well, you'll be ahead of the game.

Plenty of race mechanics do an excellent practical job of preparing their car to survive a race mechanically. The problem is that many don't know how much they don't know! It takes real understanding to make a car go faster—handle better—than its inherent capability. The best mechanics have an understanding of why the car behaves the way it does, and then can make adjustments that can change it for the better. One important asset in solving problems is the power of logical thinking. Whenever anyone asked how I knew that a change I made to a car would improve it, I'd tell them I had a fantastic grasp of the obvious!

Race-car design, however, is something else again. It demands a complete and proper understanding of vehicle dynamics. That understanding must include all the contributing factors, and it can really only come with education and experience.

Until the late sixties, people tended to think that the most important aerodynamic quality of a racing car was its capability to pass efficiently through the air with the least resistance, or aerodynamic drag. Airflow was viewed as a nuisance. By 1968, many designers were starting to understand that airflow could be a positive tool in making the car more stable.

I figure Jim Hall must have seen the first wing used in racing about the same time we all did. It was pictured in a magazine, and it was mounted on a Porsche. Being pretty damn smart, Jim probably realized quickly that it had not been exploited to its full potential. He then did a very clever thing: he invented a moveable rear wing, and mounted it directly to the rear suspension uprights. In aerodynamic terms, Jim Hall's Chaparral then had the best of both worlds.

He could use the wing at its most aggressive angle of attack for optimum traction in cornering. The wing would be pushing down where it was needed most—right on the tire contact patch with the road. On straights, the driver could reduce the angle of attack with a lever, for minimal drag.

This is not to say that everyone else was unaware of the value of downforce. In USRRC racing, everyone had already started using front and rear spoilers. They had a downside in terms of increased drag, but the handling improvements through medium and fast turns more than offset the loss of straight-line speed. But Jim Hall's solution was much better than everyone else's and in 1968 everyone in the Can-Am began to use upright-mounted wings—a sign that we were all beginning to understand the problem.

The Sports Car Club of America reacted with alarm at the prospect of a big increase in the performance of the already powerful Can-Am cars and announced a ban on high wings. Effective 1970, wings could be only 31 inches high. That was why the Ti22 was conceived as a ground-effect car.

In view of the SCCA's restriction, I had to find a way to increase traction using the airflow over and under the body. So I set out to make the whole car a wing. This meant that I would have to increase the suspension stiffness to allow the downforce on the body to push as hard as possible on the tires, without being used up in merely compressing the coil springs. Since the tires would effectively now become a component of the car's suspension, I wondered if they might get too hot.

I hadn't yet arranged a tire supply, so I telephoned Goodyear and spoke to Teddy Lobinger, their trackside Can-Am support guy. We had become friends over the previous couple of years, and he had watched the results of my chassis-tuning efforts for Carl Haas. Teddy had a good working relationship with Goodyear's racing boss, Larry Truesdale. I told him I was going to build a car for the Can-Am and Ernie was going to sponsor it. He told me I could count on tire support from Goodyear, and if the car went well, maybe even some financial help in 1970. When I told Ernie, he was delighted, so I resolved to get more help from other suppliers, with parts if not money.

I'd had a couple of experiences that pointed the way to applying the theory of ground-effect to auto racing. One had been in 1965, when I was working in Connecticut. I was at a club race with Mike Goth and his Formula B Brabham, and Mike needed a second or so off his lap times (nothing new there!). The Brabham came with an underpan that fitted snugly around the gearbox and swept up and away at the back to meet up with the engine cover mount. After a gear ratio change when we first got to the track, there wasn't enough time to put the underpan back on the car, so we left it off for the first practice session. When we put it on for the second session, the car went nearly two seconds quicker. Mike attributed the quicker lap times to the ratio change and his improved track experience, but I wasn't so sure. Without telling Mike, I removed the underpan again before the last session. Mike went almost as fast as he had before, but complained that the track was getting slippery with oil. I put the pan back on for the race. He won it and said the car had handled great.

I realized that what happened to the airflow under the car had a very significant effect on its roadholding. It was also apparent that when the ground clearance under the front of the car was lower than at the back, the car stuck to the road even better. The conclusion I reached was that when the airflow could speed up as it went under the car, it sucked the car down towards the track surface. So my idea for the Ti22 was to stop the air from spilling off the sides of the body until it got back past the rear wheels, thus creating large amounts of downforce. I also wanted to build in some rake upward in ground clearance from front to back.

OPPOSITE: Al Willard and I install the rollbar mountings. (Ti22 Publicity)

I decided on a unique body shape for the Ti22, using raised sides to form air dams in order to keep the airflow going over the upper bodywork. If I could get the upper airflow to push down on the body hard enough to drive the car lower to the ground, it would force the underbody airflow to speed up and exit faster out the back —much like squeezing a wet bar of soap between your fingers. To help this happen further, I drew the car with a ride-height two and a half inches from the ground, with a rake up to the rear underpan of about an inch.

The reasoning behind the low ride-height was simple: "Proximity Sucks!" I wanted the car to be sucked towards the track surface. In order to maintain its position relative to the ground, the suspension had to be very stiff and the car would need lots of anti-rollbar to stop it rolling. In essence, I was making a big, powerful kart. I figured I would get some criticism from the driver about that, and realized I would need someone who liked to "hang the back out" to work with my ideas.

The new rules barring high wings from Can-Am racing wouldn't come into force for the 1969 season, so I reckoned I would find out sooner than anyone else how it would go in 1970. In fact, I planned on mounting an external wing on the rear uprights for the last two races of 1969, so I could test the car with and without a wing. I also designed an adjustable spoiler for the extreme rear edge of the upper bodywork, for trimming and balancing the car. I shaped the front fenders like chisel points so that the airflow had less choice of which way to go as the car's nose cut through it. This was a Can-Am first, because most designers rounded off the tips of the front fenders for styling purposes. I put exit vents at the top backside of the front fenders to vent the high-pressure air out of the wheel arch, and angled back the side of the chassis tub sheet metal to help.

I'd taken a look at the Lola and McLaren tubs and noticed that the fuel tank portions of the tubs were basically rectangular. To simplify the shapes of the fuel bladders, there were stiffening "doublers" above and below the tank cavities, but no diagonals going from front to back. I decided that I had to have diagonal tub members to help the torsional stiffness. To this end, I also tapered the inner side of the monocoque as it went into the footbox. The additions would increase the weight of the monocoque a little, but the increased torsional stiffness would compensate for it. As a result, my design required fuel bladders that were irregular in shape, instead of oblong.

    I'd noted that neither of the other chassis were true monocoques, because they had frame-type bulkheads made from steel tubing. Weight-wise, using steel tube wasn't the most efficient solution. If you unfold a one-inch-square tube made out of one-sixteenth steel, you have a lump of steel four inches wide. It didn't take much math to figure out that, if I used a lot of that tube in the bulkheads, it would all start to get pretty heavy. So I determined to make the first true monocoque sports-racing car, with no tubes in the chassis whatsoever.

Lastly, I drew the bottom outer edges of the tub on a tight radius, instead of rounded. Again, this helped to make the tub stiffer and to optimize the airflow under the car by creating more flat surface there.

All this downforce I was making would inevitably increase aerodynamic drag, but I would compensate for this with a bigger, more powerful engine—I hoped! The engine would be based on the 430 cid (7.02-liter) Chevrolet block that was being made for Chevrolet by Reynolds Aluminum Company and only sold to Can-Am teams.

ABOVE: Dennis Toomey (left) and Al Willard (right) installing the bodywork to the chassis for the Mk 1 Ti22. At the center is "Mitch," who helped make the body molds, and whose last name still escapes me. (Ti22 Publicity)

As the chassis layout progressed, I was able to fix the critical dimensions of the car. The wheelbase would be 94 inches, the overall length 150 inches, and the overall width 74 inches. The height at the top of the rear spoiler would be 32 inches. I planned to use 15-inch diameter wheels, 11 inches wide at the front and 16 inches at the rear.

Once I had the low camber change suspension geometry designed, and the fundamental chassis packaging done, I laid out the monocoque and then hired an architectural engineer named Al Willard to help with the drafting chores. We double-checked everything. We made a full-size mock-up of the chassis in plywood to check it for stiffness and driver function, and then used that as a basis for the fiberglass body plug—the tool used to make the molds for the body panels. We built the body mold plug in only two weeks from start to finish. We worked until at least 10:00 p.m. every night and, for a break, we would often go to the local pub for a quick pint of beer and dinner, then go back to work.

You would think that guys who worked with each other for 14 hours a day would want to get home to the family, or at least get away from each other for a spell, but it was exactly the opposite when we were designing and building the titanium car. It was our group obsession. Having a beer together was our group therapy. It gave everyone a chance to air his opinions about what was happening. Anyone could say anything they wanted about what was going on. It was a great communication time and helped a lot. When I worked for Colin

Chapman at Lotus at the beginning of my racing career, we "blokes" had a cash allowance to buy dinner if we worked overtime. We had our pint and our dinner in the pub next door run by Colin's father, and spent most of the time talking about work. So I found out very early that the more time a team spends together, the better the communication—and the better the car. I guess either Chapman was smart, or his father was. Either way, his father ended up with the dinner allowance!

Our Ti22 team grew to four with the addition of Dennis Toomey, who helped us make the body molds, and a guy I can remember only as "Mitch." He was a former Gurney team member who was a real craftsman and worked on the chassis fabrication. It was amazing how we all became engrossed in building the car. It was like a drug—we couldn't wait to get back on it the next day. One Sunday, Al Willard's wife arrived at the workshop with their kids and a big hamper of food. It was Memorial Day, and we'd all forgotten it was a public holiday. So we all stopped work and listened to the Indy 500 on the radio while we had a picnic lunch.

Very early in the program, I had a taste of Ernest Kanzler Sr.'s lifestyle that also shed some light on Ernie Jr.'s. He often talked about the days of his youth, when he would drive a sort of Quarter Midget race car up and down Grandpa Henry Ford's

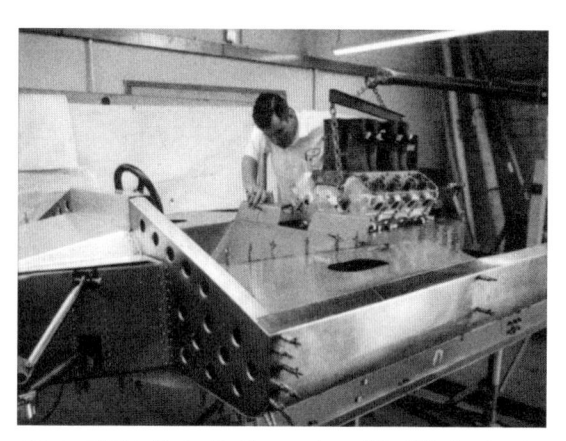

ABOVE: Al Willard helps the Chevy engine and the Ti22 chassis get acquainted. (Ti22 Publicity)

driveway in Grosse Point, Michigan. The annual 12 Hours of Sebring sports-car race was coming up, and I persuaded Ernie we should be there. The purpose of the trip was to talk to candidates to race the new Ti22. The Sebring race was a high-profile event and I hoped to find a driver with an international reputation, and not only because that would mean he was quick—it would also assist me in finding sponsorship. Ernie told me the trip would give him an opportunity to visit the family house on Jupiter Island, in Hobe Sound, near Palm Beach. I didn't know how exotic a piece of real estate that was until we got there—and getting there was almost a disaster.

We were booked on Eastern Airlines with connections to Palm Beach through Atlanta. We were sitting on the connecting aircraft to Palm Beach waiting to take off in Atlanta when a stewardess told us we were wait-listed on that flight, so we would have to give way to people who had confirmed seats. It was no big problem, she said, because she could put us on a flight that would get us to Palm Beach ahead of them. We could claim our baggage when our original aircraft came in a few minutes after our new one. So Ernie and I trotted onto the other plane. We arrived in Palm Beach and were waiting for the aircraft with our bags to land—only it didn't! It had been hijacked to Cuba—with our bags aboard, but luckily not us. We filled out the lost baggage claim forms and rented a car.

We finally got to Jupiter Island at about 2:00 a.m., and we were bushed. We were greeted by three servants who had waited up for us. One escorted me to a room and brought me some pajamas. After some hot cocoa, I went to sleep. Next morning, my clothes had been cleaned and pressed and were waiting for me on hangers in the wardrobe. I was very impressed. It seemed they could judge exactly what time I would wake up, because there was hot coffee in a jug by the bed for me, and it wasn't in a Thermos! I dressed and found my way downstairs to the dining room. There must have been 15 or even 20 rooms in the house—it was big. The butler sat me down in the family room to wait for Ernie with some orange juice from the breakfast buffet that was being set up. I couldn't imagine them cooking a buffet for just the two of us, but they did.

Ernie took me to the Jupiter Country Club for lunch and renewed his acquaintance with some old family friends. It was like wading in wealth. Having come from poor working-class stock in cockney east London, and almost fresh off the boat, I felt more than a little self-conscious. They soon put me at ease and I enjoyed a great lobster lunch. What impressed me most about them all was how comfortable they were with me. If this had taken place at some exclusive country club in England, my slight cockney accent would have raised a few eyebrows. Here I was readily accepted and made to feel comfortable. I liked that. These Americans certainly weren't snobs.

The house was fantastic, with a fresh-water swimming pool in the back yard and a man-made seawater pool, carved in the ocean rocks that refilled every time the tide came in. Ernie explained that his half-brother, who spent most of his time in charity work, usually occupied the house in the summer. Ernie later sold his share in the house to his brother and spent the funds building a new house on Harbor Island in Newport Harbor, California, that resembled a lighthouse. He gave the *Sally* yacht to the Newport sea scouts and bought himself a very nice old cabin cruiser.

We drove on to Sebring and I introduced Ernie to some of my racing friends. He got along with James Garner so well that he promptly bought one of his racing Lola GT team cars for his collection. Ernie loved fast cars and had a real nice supercharged Alfa Romeo from the thirties that he liked to drive at speed on Mulholland Drive.

The renowned racing journalist Chris Economaki invited Ernie and me to join him and a few friends for dinner near Sebring that evening. Ernie sat next to America's 1961 World Champion, Phil Hill, and I could tell that he really enjoyed himself. Phil is a great ambassador for auto racing and his love for old cars gave him and Ernie something in common. As I thanked Chris for inviting us, I said the evening had done a lot to encourage Ernie in his racing ventures and I really appreciated his support. Chris and I had always enjoyed a great story-telling relationship and he is always excellent company. Going to Sebring was a big help in introducing Ernie into the greater racing fraternity.

We went to the 12-hour race the next day and Ernie watched it right through to the end. I kept expecting him to suggest leaving, but there was no way once he had met some of the drivers and owners. He took a particularly keen interest in the Ferrari team because he owned a Ferrari and loved everything about them. He was a totally immersed in the experience. It sure looked like he was thoroughly hooked on racing and I just hoped his enthusiasm would stay at the same level until we got the new car going. It hadn't been a perfect weekend, because I hadn't finalized a deal with the driver I went to Sebring to meet. I had written to David Yorke, an old racing friend in England, whose opinion about race drivers I really respected. David, who had been a team manager for John Surtees and was now with the works-supported JW Gulf Ford sports-car team, had told me to take a look at an up-and-coming driver who was on the team and was also racing in Formula One for BRM. His name was Jackie Oliver.

Jackie won the Sebring 12 Hours with Jacky Ickx in one of John Wyer's GT40s. Like us, he left right after the race so we ran out of time to talk with him. We were only at Sebring for a couple of days before the race and it was impossible for us to get pit passes. The best view we had was in the small space above one of the Jim Garner team's boxes. I hated that I had no chance to interview Jackie and I had to write to him to get a relationship started. When the negotiating was finished, Jackie had agreed to drive the Ti22 for all expenses plus a minimum of $1000 a race, or 40 percent of all prize money we won, whichever was the greater.

All we needed to do now was build the race car!

BELOW: The very first publicity picture of Bob Bondurant testing the Ti22 at California's Orange County Raceway in August 1969. (Ti22 Publicity)

CHAPTER 22

From Concept to Reality

Luckily for me, I had worked with titanium before—when I had first come over from England in 1964 to work with Mickey Thompson. He had gotten some sponsorship from a local aluminum and titanium manufacturer named Harvey Aluminum. Mickey was a big-time innovator and started making everything he could from their products. He made the first titanium and aluminum connecting rods for drag racing engines, and the space frame chassis of one of the cars he built for the 1964 Indy 500 was made of titanium tubes. I thought at the time that if he'd made a monocoque chassis and then substituted titanium for the standard steel in the bulkheads, it might have been better. Later, when the opportunity came for me to use titanium, that's just about what I did. As titanium is only 56 percent of the weight of steel in comparable sections, it saved a lot of weight. But using titanium isn't as easy as it sounds, because of the unique properties of the material.

Titanium is the ninth most abundant element in the earth's crust and the fourth most abundant metallic element in nature. Titanium metal is made from a mineral ore called Rutile. Major deposits are found in Australia, Canada, Finland, Norway, South Africa, and the United States. Rutile is common in beach sand near continental coastlines, where erosion and wave action have elevated concentration of the mineral. Most commercially available Rutile comes from Australia's black sands, but it's also found in India, China, Russia, Sierra Leone, and Sri Lanka.

Titanium's atomic number (22) ranks it as one of the lightest metallic elements, and its atomic weight is 47.90. It has the highest strength-to-weight ratio of any of today's structural metals. That's what makes it so good for racing cars.

Titanium is weird stuff. It isn't magnetic and it's corrosive-resistant to some basic compositions like seawater. They use titanium for seawater valves in nuclear submarines.

It doesn't rust, and when you try to bend it in sheet form, it springs back 20 percent. On top of all that, I'd learned from working with Mickey that it can't be welded or heated in the normal atmosphere. Beyond a certain temperature, it picks up the hydrogen from the air and becomes extremely brittle. So if you want to weld it, you have to put it into an inert atmosphere such as argon gas and keep the air away from it until it has cooled off. Otherwise, whatever you just made could become hydrogen-embrittled and simply crack or break when stressed or impacted.

Pure titanium isn't the ultimate form of the material; to increase strength, it's made into various alloy forms by adding other metals, such as aluminum and vanadium. The strongest titanium alloy at that time was called 6AL4V, which uses 6 percent aluminum and 4 percent vanadium.

It was Skip Scott who helped me get a contact in the titanium business. He told me that the Titanium Metal Corporation of America (Timet) in West Caldwell, New Jersey, had once offered to make some race-car parts for him, but he'd never bothered to take them up on the offer. It was tricky stuff to deal with, and they hadn't been interested in putting up any money to cover the additional costs of testing. When we'd started to put the Autocoast Formula 5000 car together for Skip, I called and spoke to Timet about our program and they were very keen to be involved in racing in some way. They told me they'd made the masts for the America's Cup yacht, *Intrepid*, and said they would like to make some automotive parts. They sounded like interesting people and they were offering to help with the fabrication of the welded parts, so I became a lot keener to use titanium than I'd been previously.

Working with Timet meant I now had the opportunity to build a car with a monocoque chassis in which I could use titanium that I could get for free—plus help with the fabrication. I would have to be pretty stupid to pass that up.

I took my chassis drawings to Timet and went over them carefully with their technicians. They made a few suggestions and I left them to make some components for me. I was scared that I was asking for too much, so I only asked them to make one set of chassis parts, except for an extra set of suspension control arms for spares.

Without Timet, working with titanium would have been a tough learning curve for us to overcome in the time we had. Timet did make one small mistake, but on reflection, it was really my fault. They were asked to build the front footbox bulkhead, which incorporated provisions for mounting the brake and clutch master cylinders and the pedals. I'd designed the car to be right-hand drive, like most Can-Am cars, because most tracks ran clockwise, and the driver is located better if he's on the inside of most of the turns. Laguna Seca was an exception, but it wasn't worth the complication of trying to make the car good for both ways. When Timet built the bulkhead, they assumed we'd made a mistake and moved the pedal mounts to the left-hand-drive configuration without checking with us. We didn't want to upset them, so we added a second set of mounts for the pedals on the other side. At the first race, at Laguna, a journalist asked me what the other set of mountings was for in the footbox. I told him we might switch the car over to left-hand drive for the next practice, to give the driver an advantage. He was very impressed by our thoroughness!

I soon found out how tough it was to work with titanium, compared with steel or aluminum. Not only did it spring back when you bent it, but it was difficult to drill holes for rivets and chewed up the expensive hole punches we bought like they were made of wood. If I was going to get this car done in time to race in the Can-Am in 1969, I would need additional help from someone who was experienced with this stuff to make some of the other parts, like the pedals.

I didn't have far to go. Conveniently, California was the aerospace hardware technology capital of the free world. I decided I needed some help from one of the high-tech fabrication companies working on the NASA moon program. I checked with a friend who worked for Atlantic Missile, and he told me they farmed out a lot of their work. He recommended I talk to Murdock Inc. of Gardena, who had made the titanium tools the astronauts would use to get rock samples that year after the first moon landing. A titanium brake pedal wasn't exactly the same as a titanium rock shovel, but knowing how particular those space guys were, I bet that titanium shovel was made with fantastic tolerances and quality.

Next day, I called Murdock and made an appointment to see their PR guy. He was really sympathetic to my cause, but declined to help due to pressure of work. He did offer me a factory tour, turning me over to the plant supervisor. That was fine with me, because he was the guy I'd wanted to talk to in the first place.

This guy, Larry, turned out to be about my age—and a car nut. When I showed him the pictures of how the Ti22 would look when it was finished, he flipped out and took me to lunch. We went to one of those businessmen's places and had the required five martinis, or the equivalent in beer. We had a great lunch, and became almost like blood brothers. I remember thinking—boy, these aerospace guys can drink!

When we finally got back to the plant, it was about 3:00 p.m., and Larry gave me a tour and showed me all the tricks they used when working with titanium. I told him what the PR guy had said about the company not having enough time to help me out with a few parts, and he laughed and said, "Just give me the drawings and specifications. I'll work it in for you if I have to do it myself." All he wanted in return was a Murdock decal on the car.

Later, when I figured out the value of the hydraforming and fabrication work that Larry had quietly done at Murdock and the time it saved us, I felt eternally grateful to the love affair between man and machine that makes people into car nuts.

Meanwhile Don Zimmerman, our liaison engineer at Timet, suggested I talk to Hi-Shear Corporation in Los Angeles, who made titanium fasteners. George Wing, the owner, was a racing fan and perhaps they would sponsor us with fasteners. What a great contact that turned out to be. We saved a whole bunch of weight by using his special, lightweight "six-wing" nuts and bolts for all the fasteners holding the car together, plus the engine and gearbox.

On August 23, we had all the chassis tub parts made and were ready to assemble. That was a big milestone in our quest. We had a calendar on the wall and Al Willard made a note on it that said: "At 2:10 p.m., the first rivet was put into the race car." A little later, I added another note: "At 2:18 p.m., the eighth rivet was drilled out and replaced, so at this rate it will take over four years to finish the tub." We all laughed.

At 2:30 p.m., the compressed air line blew out and stopped the riveting until we could fix it. We'd made and pre-fitted all the panels together and pre-drilled the 590 rivet holes. We were going to bond the panels together, as well as rivet them. We had to do it in sequence because the shelf-life of the two-part adhesive was only about four hours—after that, the adhesive would gel and we wouldn't be able to squeeze the panels together with the rivets. We worked almost nonstop until 6:00 a.m. the next day, when the tub was finally finished. Then we went home to rest, because it took 24 hours for the adhesive to cure fully. This didn't mean we could take the 24 hours off—we came back at 4:00 p.m. that day and carried on working on the car.

Once we had the chassis design configuration totally sorted out, I did a half-scale drawing of the body. Paul Lamar was an aerodynamic consultant who specialized in tweaking race cars, and we'd talked about him making wings for us on several occasions. I asked him to come in and take a look at the body design. His help later on in the program, assisting us in evaluating the effects of various changes to the aero configuration, was invaluable. He was also a great help in getting a rear wing made in time for the 1969 Riverside Can-Am race.

One of the many niggling problems involved in building a new race car is security. You really don't want the opposition to find out what you're doing. You also need to keep it out of the papers until you're good and ready—otherwise you might see one of your innovations exposed prematurely to your competitors. On top of that, hearsay is a way of getting facts distorted. A big part of the problem is dealing with suppliers. You need them to know what you're doing in order to get their full cooperation, but some of these vendors deal with your competition, and love to tell their customers little secrets.

When we took the body plug over to Wayne Hartman's fiberglass factory to get the body molds made, Wayne asked me if I wanted him to keep it confidential. Naturally I did, and I told him, "If someone should see it, don't say what it is or who it's for!" If they didn't know it was a Can-Am car, and they didn't know who owned it, there wouldn't be very much they could say about it except, "I saw this sleek-looking thing being built at Hartman's. I don't know what it was or who it was for, but it was nice." It would sound like a flying saucer!

I had several objectives for the Ti22 suspension design. I wanted to have as little as possible going on to interfere with the traction at the tire contact point on the track surface. So I took great pains in the geometry to minimize the disturbances during vertical suspension travel and during steering. Mainly to assist the aerodynamic functions, I also took great pains to minimize the vertical movement itself. "Recovery" was the name of the game in road racing. You couldn't drive hard around a right turn in an "S" bend until you and the car had fully recovered from driving hard around the preceding left turn. Very stiff springs were going to be needed to counteract the downforce from the body that would try to compress the suspension. It would also take some pretty stiff anti-rollbars to keep the car flat on the road. To maximize the advantage of the ground-effect, I wanted the ride-height to stay as constant as possible at all speeds. The end result would be a suspension that was as stiff as a board.

I had been told that Jackie Oliver liked to hang the back out a bit when he drove, and I liked that. I didn't want a driver who would try and finesse the handling to death, demanding subtle changes to suit his sensitivities. This car was going to be like a big, brutal kart with lots of horsepower.

The chassis was going to need lots of torsional stiffness. Cars with flexibility in the chassis between the front and rear suspension systems don't handle the same way twice. They are unpredictable and hard to drive. So I took great care in the design of the monocoque to be sure to mount the suspension assemblies to a solid foundation.

One location where the typical monocoque lost structural stiffness was the cavity on each side of the tub where the fuel tanks went. Usually each fuel tank was a big, oblong, aluminum box. I put in a diagonal chassis stiffener that went from the inside front vertical corner of that cavity to the outside rear corner, resulting in much-increased torsional stiffness of the tub. This design split the cavity into two triangular shapes, and created two drawbacks: it complicated the fuel cell installation and plumbing, and increased our overall weight due to the extra weight of the installation and the chassis stiffeners. But when we looked at the weight we'd saved from using titanium bolts, as well as the fantastic gain we'd made in structural strength, we concluded it was well worth doing.

There were five separate fuel tanks in the car, with bulkheads between them. When the Goodyear engineer who was going to make the fuel cells saw our drawings, he asked: "Do all these fuel cells go in the car?"

On September 9, we tested the tub for stiffness by trying to twist it end-to-end through the suspension mounts. When we reached loads in excess of 10,000 ft. lb., without the chassis twisting any part of a degree, we stopped the test. I figured that was enough. If we'd continued until the tub twisted at some extreme load, there might have been a loud bang, signaling that we'd "gronked" the tub. There was no point in that. Besides, I'd never seen a chassis as stiff as this one in all my years in racing. Better to quit while you're ahead, right?

We were now racing against the clock to get the car to the Laguna race in October. As the car took shape, the excitement built. It had now become a blinding compulsion to get the car finished, and I was spending more and more time at the shop. Everything else was secondary to me. How my family put up with it was a constant mystery to me, but they didn't complain. In fact, on the rare occasions when they saw me, they actually encouraged me.

This magnificent obsession takes hold of all of us when we get involved in building race cars, and those of us who suffer know it by various names. I used to call it "The Disease." Don Zimmerman was really impressed by our focused determination to finish the job. So he decided that if we could do it, he could too. He started showing up at the shop after he got off work and watching us feverishly building the car, helping out where he could. Pretty soon he found the pace very tiring, and it was making it difficult for him to focus on his own work the next day. I explained to him that he could only keep up this mad schedule if he had The Disease. He couldn't dedicate 100 percent of his time to the race car, so he couldn't catch The Disease properly. The Disease must dominate your life. If you have other commitments apart from racing, of course, you can still catch a mild form, but it's more of a fascination for race cars than a full-blown obsession like ours was. Once you have it, it will be with you in one form or another for the rest of your life.

Many people have thrown their other personal lives out the window after catching The Disease. Divorce is one of its more serious side-effects, and I'm sorry to say it can also be fatal. Many race mechanics allowed their health to deteriorate because they neglected anything that distracted them from their work.

In my days in racing, the most common treatment to alleviate the symptoms of The Disease was alcohol. On the Monday mornings after races, it wasn't uncommon for race mechanics to wake up with real big hangovers. They now have drugs to cure obsessive-compulsive behavior, but nothing can cure The Disease.

After a few beers, I sometimes liked to indulge in a little show business. I would jump up on the stage and do impersonations of Louis Armstrong, Billy Daniels, and George C. Scott. Funnily enough, it only happened after I'd had a few pints. I'd discovered back in England that I could sing, and had entered a few talent contests, and even won. But once I got hooked on racing, there wasn't time for singing. No way could I do both properly—and I didn't relish the thought of spending the rest of my life in a drunken stupor just to make a living. But now and then the old urges come back. Besides, I felt that getting up and doing my showbiz thing was only fair—people in show business often indulged in racing, didn't they? Incidentally, there was some real talent in racing in those days, like Pete Biro, the official photographer for Goodyear, who was (and still is) a great magician. There was always a piano player in the crowd, so a good old sing-song was a frequent occurrence for the mechanics after races.

For our engines, we got help from Bill Thomas of Anaheim, California, an engine builder who had good connections at Chevrolet. It was almost impossible to get the good racing stuff from Chevrolet without a good contact, so I asked him to build the engines for us. We specified the new Reynolds Aluminum 390 cylinder blocks, and Bill somehow persuaded Chevrolet to sell us two. We built two 427 cid engines—with one small mistake in each!

In my overzealous mission to save weight, I decided to use the crankshaft-mounted dry-sump oil pump system that Jim Hall had previously used on Small Block engines in the Chaparral. It would save us about 5 lbs. over the segmented-type external pump. But because we were building Big Block engines, we had to grind down the nose of the crankshaft that went through the pump gear, because the pump was inside the timing chain cover. We had the crankshaft ground down, but we couldn't get it rehardened to the original specification. We had it shot-peened to stress-relieve the machined part, and thought that would be good enough. We would pay dearly for that mistake later.

The engines put out good horsepower, and once we found out how to run them in on the dyno, we even managed to stop wearing off the cam lobes whenever we started them up! The radical high-lift camshaft lobes would wear flat when the engine was started for the first time, unless you ran it up to over 3000 rpm as soon as it fired. Unfortunately, it took us a couple of camshaft changes and some telephone time with Chevrolet to get that little gem of information. Bill did a good job on the engines and almost right from the start we were reasonably competitive with everyone else in terms of horsepower. That's not to say we had enough power—you never have enough!

When we bought a Hewland five-speed gearbox and a selection of gear ratios, we only had one small component left to get to help our car's traction. A Chicago engineer named Pete Weismann had invented a new limited-slip differential we knew as the "Weismann Locker." At that time this was a little known tweak that made a big difference to a powerful Can-Am car. It did one thing very well. It ensured that the power always went to the wheel with more traction, whereas most standard rear axles would power up the wheel with less traction. If both rear wheels were turning at the same speed, it applied the power evenly to both of them. Denny Hulme told me later that without that locker, he had a tough time handling the power of the McLaren and was lost without it.

It cost $1000 to buy one, but that wasn't the trick. The trick was in getting Pete Weismann to make one for you. He only made them in batches to special order. There's no doubt in my mind that at that time he made the best differential in the racing business. Pete later went on to build Can-Am, Indy, and Formula One gearboxes for many manufacturers, including the contemporary McLaren F1 team. His work is good example of the quiet contribution made to race car development by good old Yankee know-how. Maybe, when the auto historians give engineering its proper due in their halls of fame, Peter and his father will have their day in the sun for their significant contribution to good racing.

In late September 1969, the car was fully assembled, with the body on for the very first time. We'd worked another all-nighter because we only had two weeks to go if we wanted to make the Laguna Seca race. Jackie Oliver was insisting that he would only race the car after testing it first. So we'd set a deadline to have the car completed and on its wheels.

It was a big moment for us. Our perspective of the size of the car had come only from the drawings, or as it sat on the 30-inch-high stands we used to assemble it. When the big moment came for us to lower the completed chassis to the floor, it was a weird and wonderful experience. The lowered chassis seemed to melt into the floor. It was so low you had to kneel down beside it to do any work on it. Then we put the white-and-blue fiberglass body on it, and stepped back. I was totally overcome, and tears came into my eyes. Our emotions were already a bit ragged from the fatigue of working all night, and the reality of it hit me. Only the births of my children, Paul and Elizabeth, had ever come close to that level of emotion for me.

We all took turns sitting in it for about half an hour, and then we locked it up in the garage and everyone left to go home for a few hours' rest. I got halfway home and decided to go back for one more look. I woke up about two hours later, sitting in the cockpit, thinking I was dreaming. I pinched myself to be sure. Yes, the Ti22 was a reality at last!

Next day, we weighed it. It weighed 1348 lbs. dry (without fuel and other fluids). I figured we'd saved a bunch of weight with the titanium. Next we would get a lighter body made. The prototype body could have been much lighter, but first things first—let's get the Ti22 out on the track!

BELOW: I steer as Al Willard supervises the unloading of the Ti22 for its first Can-Am race at Laguna Seca. At the right are journalist Paul Van Valkenburg (with beard) and racing aerodynamics expert Paul Lamar (in sunglasses). (Dave Friedman)

CHAPTER 23

On Track with the Ti22

The afternoon after we'd finally assembled the first Ti22, we took the car to Orange County Raceway, where Bob Bondurant had his race driving school. I'd asked Bob to drive the car for us on its shakedown run. I'd hired Deke Houlgate, a well-known PR expert, to handle the PR chores for Autocoast, and Deke had his photographer there.

I was really nervous about what Bob would think of the car. He drove it for only a few laps, and was just getting used to it, when the oil pressure dropped to almost nothing. Bob told us that as far as he'd been able to tell, the car worked fine, and he would be pleased to race it whenever we liked. I was upset that the oil pressure had acted up, to say the least. It could blow our chances of running our car in the Laguna Seca Can-Am, because we didn't have the second engine ready yet. It meant taking the engine out and giving it back to Bill Thomas to fix, so we took the car back to the workshop. We had only just finished putting the car together. Now we were taking it apart again. This was definitely a real race car!

Luckily, Deke had got a few photographs for his press kit, so he started to generate some pre-race publicity for Autocoast. When word got out about

ABOVE: McLaren mechanic Tyler Alexander and I enjoy the joke about the candle factory that burned down—now it was a whole new ball of wax. (Dale Von Treba)

this mysterious titanium race car, the telephone started ringing off the wall with journalists wanting more details. One of the press guys who called said he had something to do with the *Times* Grand Prix at Riverside, the next Can-Am race after Laguna Seca. He said his name was Harley Tankum and he wanted to know if it would be OK if the *Los Angeles Times* motor-racing reporter called me about the car—some guy named Shav Glick. I broke up laughing. I said Harley Tankum sounded like the name of a motorcycle, and Shav Glick

CHAPTER 23 · 221

like an electric shaver. I told him it was funny, but I didn't have time to be involved in any bullshit with some fictitious reporter, so he should tell whoever had put him up to this stunt that it hadn't worked. I was about to hang up when he asked, "Would you prefer to speak to Glenn Davis? He's the director of special events for the *Times* and has organized our end of the race." Glenn Davis was the legendary football hero from West Point. I was curious to see how far this bullshit would go, so I agreed to speak to the next guy.

It was all for real. Was my face red! Davis patiently explained about the need for advance publicity, how important it was to get people to buy tickets and go out to Riverside to see the race, because it was all for charity and helped raise thousands of dollars. I later became personally acquainted with Glenn Davis, and he was very quiet-spoken, a real nice person and the perfect choice for such an important job.

The Monday before the Laguna race, after racing for BRM in the U.S. Grand Prix, Jackie Oliver arrived in Newport Beach to be fitted in the car and test it. I drove over to the Newporter Inn to pick him up. On the way back to the shop, he pumped me for information. He was really curious—and a bit nervous, I think—about what he called "this titanium stuff." Was it as strong as steel? Was the car safe? What were my credentials as a car designer? I got a bit twitchy myself when he asked me that! Luckily David Yorke had told him about the work I'd done in Formula One and in the USRRC with John Surtees, so I didn't have too tough a time with that.

My biggest surprise was Jackie's size. I'm 5 feet, 9 inches, and he was shorter than me by about 3 inches. I was delighted, and not only because there would be a small weight advantage. He would fit into the car easily, and the last thing we needed was to be modifying the chassis tub to get some wide-ass driver into it. I amused myself thinking that it was amazing how such a small driver, in such a short time, had gotten such a big reputation for having such a big foot—on the throttle, that is! I told him what I was thinking, and he laughed. That was good. He had a sense of humor, so we would get along great.

At the shop, Jackie went over the car with a fine-tooth comb. He couldn't get over the big weight difference between steel and titanium. We showed him the results of the chassis stiffness test, and I guess that satisfied his natural apprehensions about "this titanium stuff." I told him the landing gear main struts of the Boeing 747 that had brought him across the Atlantic were made from titanium and that the aircraft could carry as much fuel as the total weight of a Boeing 707. I guess that helped put the matter to rest, because he stopped asking questions about it.

The following Tuesday, we took the car to the Willow Springs track, north of Los Angeles, and Jackie tried it out. We had a few throttle and fuel surge problems, and the engine was blowing out a little oil from the crankcase breathers. But Jackie announced that he liked the feel of the Ti22 enough to race it at Laguna. "Oh, and by the way," he added, "some driving mirrors might come in handy, for when we're in traffic."

After the test, Jackie took off for Monterey with his wife, Lynn, and we went back to the shop to fix the problems and load up our own trip there. We had a list of things to do as long as my arm, so there was at least another all-nighter ahead if we were going to get to the track in time for any practice on Friday.

The urgent problem was the fuel surge system. To save weight, again, I had designed the system to do away with the aluminum surge tank that we had all used in the past. The Ti22 system consisted of the series of fuel bladders inside the tub, interconnected with one-way check valves. The objective was to get the fuel into the engine pump via an integral surge tank, which was a small triangular portion at the rear of the left-side fuel bladder. If the integral surge tank was full, the fuel would run through a passage in the top of the tank and return into the forward section. This was to ensure that we got all the fuel out of the tanks. It was called a "surge system" because the fuel went from one tank to another when it surged due to acceleration or cornering. For some reason, my new system had problems when the tanks were below half-full. I found a faulty check valve going into the surge tank portion, replaced it, and figured the problem was solved. I would be proved to be wrong about that, too.

All too soon, it was 7:00 a.m. on Friday, October 10, 1969. We'd worked all night to get the car ready. The Ti22 was on the transporter and ready to go, and Dennis Toomey had volunteered to drive Ernie Kanzler's motor home. When I say "ready to go" I mean "almost ready" because race cars are never really ready to go. Ours wasn't because we still had to install the rear view mirrors. I figured I could do that at the track. I thought about getting in the motor home and sleeping on the way, but I couldn't let the Ti22 out of my sight, so I went in the car transporter. Later I was glad I did, because Dennis had a tough time with the wind blowing the motor home all over the road on the interstate and didn't arrive until practice was over. For us, it would be a seven-hour drive if everything went smoothly, which would have got us to the track at about 2:00 p.m.

Not to be! We were going 65 mph up the Pacific Coast Highway, near San Luis Obispo, when the right front wheel came off the transporter! We lurched to a shaky halt about 15 feet off the highway. The truck was new, and we found out later that the wheels had to be retightened after the first 100 miles. We were lucky we didn't go over a cliff—if it had been the left front instead of the right, I think we would have. Consequently we got to the track at about 2:15 p.m.

Both Bob Bondurant and Jackie Oliver may have test-driven the Ti22 and liked it, but it had never been raced before. Boy, was I nervous! I soon lost my jitters in frenzy of unloading in the Laguna paddock and trying to get the car on the track for practice. While we were resolving the myriad of little preparation problems that all new racing cars have, I was thinking that I was one of the luckiest people on the planet. I had only been in America a little over five years, barely long enough to become a U.S. citizen, and I had already reached one of my major personal goals—to design and build a racing car for international competition. I was going to run my Ti22 car in the Can-Am, and I figured that this day was going to be the highlight of my racing life.

The eight hours that the Ti22 had spent on the transporter was a new record for someone not to be working on it. We didn't remember the last time any of us had taken a day off, and before this race started, none of us would get more than two hours of continuous sleep. The weird thing was that we looked on feeling tired as a nuisance that had to be overcome. The Disease was in its most virulent stages, and we must have looked like zombies.

We unloaded the car amid a big crowd of curious spectators and media guys asking questions about it. Colin Chapman was among them. After winning the U.S. Grand Prix with Jochen Rindt, he'd flown across America from Watkins Glen to take a look at the Can-Am en route to Mexico. He was looking curiously at the titanium rollover bar that we'd taken off the transporter. I told him to go ahead and pick it up. Our aerospace friends had made the bar for us, and it was the same SCCA-mandated wall thickness and diameter as the steel ones everyone else used. Colin expected to need two hands to lift it, and I'll never forget the wondrous expression on his face as it almost flew up into the air when he grabbed it. We both laughed, and he said, "Peter, I think you're onto something with this titanium. Can I get it in England?" I told him he probably could, through an exotic metal dealer. He wished me luck with the new car and said he would be investigating titanium further.

We finally made a rope barrier around our pit and were able to start preparing the car. The first job was to install the driving mirrors and warm up the engine. The tires we had on the car were not the latest specs, but we would take care of that after Jackie got in some laps. The tech inspectors were kind enough to come over to the car to look at it and gave

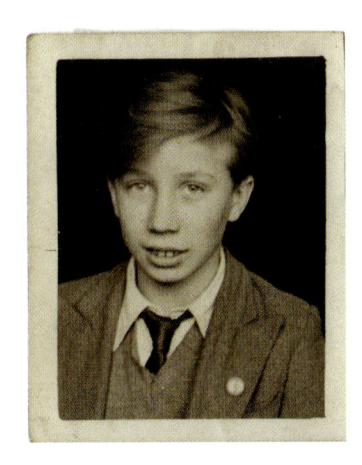

ABOVE: This is a photograph of me around the time I became seriously interested in cars as a teenager. I was 15 years old when my father signed me up as an apprentice automobile mechanic at the Gladwell & Kell repair garage in Clerkenwell, London. (Peter Bryant)

RIGHT: I officially became a racing mechanic in 1959 when I went to work for a privateer named John Ewer. Here I tend to his Lister Corvette's temperamental engine with support from Dave, a mechanic who worked for another Lister racer named Ron Brightman. I had to be careful not to drop any nuts or bolts in the Silverstone paddock's long grass. We worked continuously on the cars—the norm in those days. (Peter Bryant)

BELOW RIGHT: This is the official program from the Goodwood event that I attended in 1953 at age 16. The entry list comprised some of the greatest racers of that time, including Juan Manuel Fangio, Mike Hawthorn, Stirling Moss, and Roy Salvadori, and the exciting atmosphere sparked my lifelong passion for racing. (British Automobile Racing Club)

ABOVE: Fellow Parnell F1 mechanic Jimmy Potton and I relax between the Lolas driven by John Surtees and Tony Maggs during the 1963 Tasman meeting at Sandown Park in suburban Melbourne, Australia. (Peter Bryant)

ABOVE: A big crowd, unprotected by any safety barriers, turned out at Pukekohe to watch the 1963 New Zealand Grand Prix. Here, John Surtees in our Lola (far left) gets the jump on pole man Bruce McLaren, as Jack Brabham tries to get between them alongside Angus Hyslop and Tony Maggs in our second car. (Bruce Sergent)

BELOW: Exhausted after the 1963 Australian Grand Prix at Warwick Farm, Tony Maggs sips a Coke to take away the awful taste of the filthy water I had thrown over him to fight the blazing heat. Refuse from the horse trough I took the water from still covers his face. (Peter Bryant)

BELOW: The official team qualifying picture from the 1964 Indy 500. I'm on the left next to Mickey Thompson (center) and Fritz Voight (right). Dave MacDonald is at the wheel of the Sears Allstate Special. (Indianapolis Motor Speedway Photo)

BELOW: The Shelby American Ford GT40 I prepared passes a herd of GT350 Mustangs on its way to the plane that would take it to Le Mans in 1965. In France the car raced as No. 1, driven by Bruce McLaren and Ken Miles, and it led in the early running, but on lap 45 it succumbed to gearbox failure. None of the GT40s finished in 1965 due to engine and transmission failures. (Shelby Publicity)

ABOVE LEFT: That's me leaning on James Bond's famous Aston Martin at an SCCA Race at Laguna Seca in 1965. With me on the left is fellow Shelby American mechanic Kerry Agapiou. (Peter Bryant)
ABOVE RIGHT: Ron Butler (left) and I (center) get in Shelby engine builder Jack Hoare's way as he tweaks the Cobras at Laguna. (Peter Bryant)

RIGHT: Having a laugh in the Riverside pits with the Haas Can-Am team in 1968. I brandish a cigarette at mechanics Fred Nething (in sunglasses) and Colin Riley, as Sherrie Parsons (left) and Bernie Haas (right) watch from their lap-timing positions atop the pickup truck. At the far right, Chris Amon, visiting America to drive a works Ferrari 612P, is unimpressed. (Ike Smith)

BELOW: Chuck Parsons (left) and Skip Scott (right) wear the laurels after winning the 500-mile USRRC race at Elkhart Lake in 1968. (Peter Bryant)

OPPOSITE: This proof sheet shows Al Willard, Dennis Toomey, and Mitch working to fit the bodywork to the chassis of the Mk 1 Ti22 in 1969. The Ti22 was the first car in any series to use all-titanium monocoque construction. Titanium was also used extensively in the suspension, rollbar, and anywhere that it could be substituted for steel. (Autocoast Publicity)

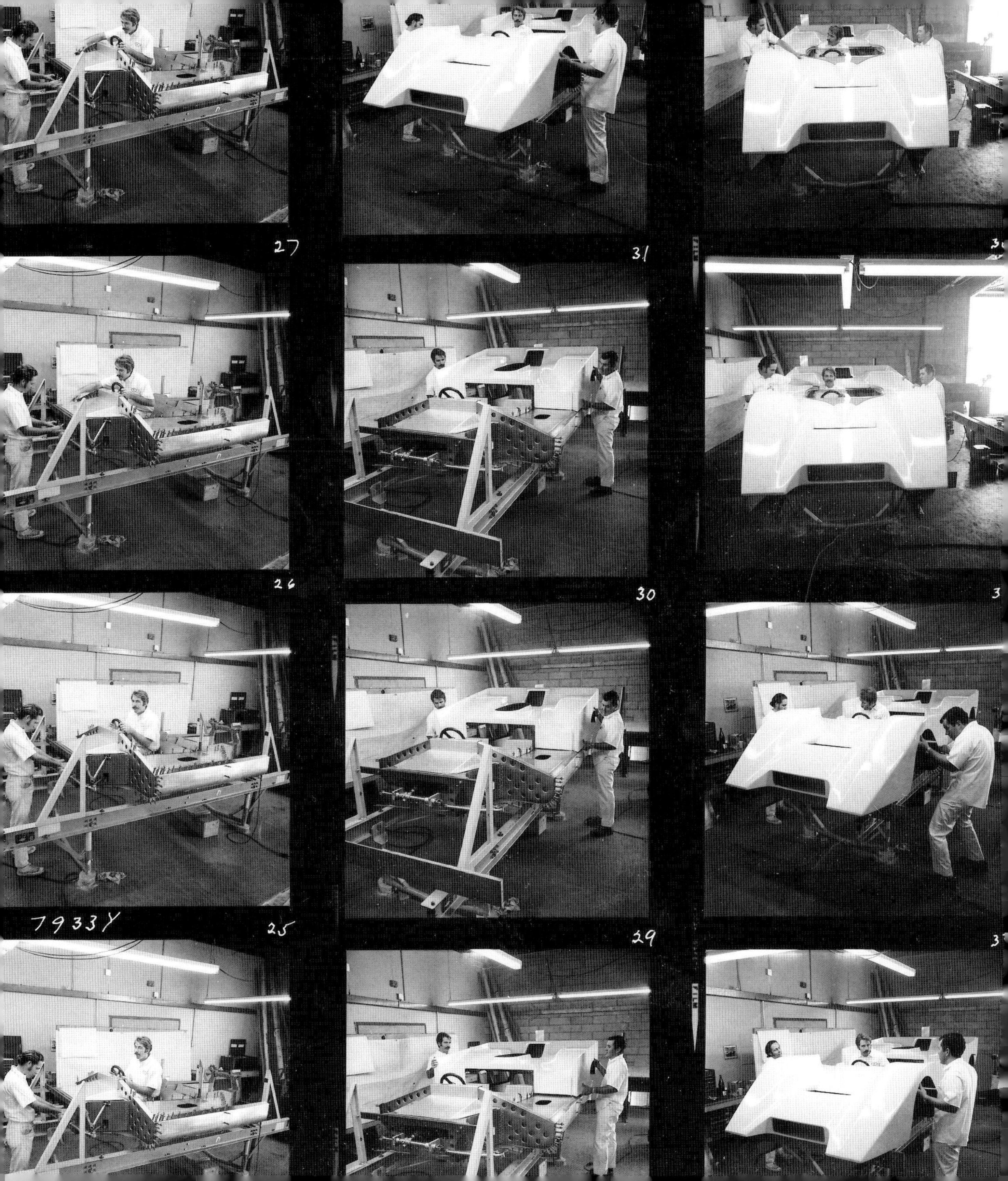
27
31
26
30
7933Y
25
29

ABOVE: The Bruce and Denny Show: Bruce McLaren leads Denny Hulme at the Riverside Can-Am race in October 1968. Could I really expect to beat them? (LAT Photographic)

LEFT: Jackie Oliver (upper left) watches as I warm up the Ti22's engine for its debut at Laguna Seca in October 1969. I am very nervous at this point because the man opposite me in the dark suit and sunglasses is Colin Chapman—head of Lotus cars, and my former boss. Note the car's side fins—a new aerodynamic feature that had yet to be proven. (Dave Friedman)

BELOW: Another view of the Ti22 at Laguna Seca. (Pete Lyons)

OPPOSITE: The Ti22 takes a turn at Mosport during the first Can-Am race of 1970. Jackie Oliver finished second to winner Dan Gurney after a long battle with Gurney's McLaren M8D. (Pete Lyons)

ABOVE: Jackie Oliver in the Ti22 is set to pass the Chuck Parsons Lola at Riverside's turn 8 in 1969. Note the difference in front ride-height between the two cars. (Bob Tronolone)

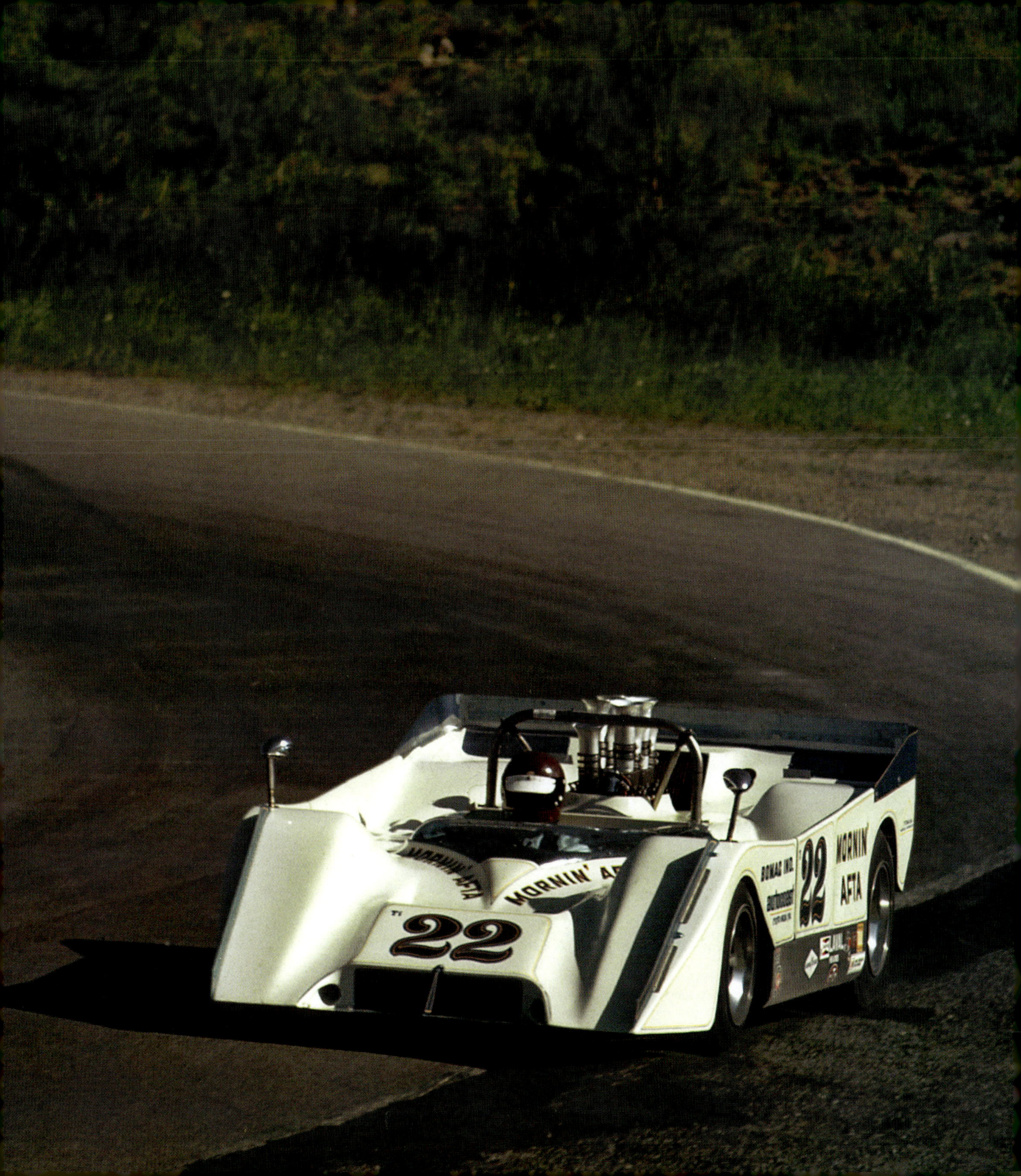
MORNIN' AFTA
22
MORNIN' AFTA
22
MORNIN'
AFTA

ABOVE: "Right out of the box!" The Ti22 Mk 2 runs fourth behind the two McLarens and Peter Revson's Lola at the start of the 1970 Laguna Seca race. (Pete Lyons)

ABOVE: With Jackie Oliver after taking second place at Laguna. He gave me his silver Can-Am medal as a souvenir. (Peter Bryant)

RIGHT: Shadow sponsor Universal Oil Products (UOP) made stickers and patches and gave them to fans at the races. (Bob Tronolone collection)

BELOW: A sight not often seen at the start of a Can-Am race in 1971: Jackie Oliver in the Shadow leads Denny Hulme in the McLaren at Elkhart Lake. (Pete Lyons)

LEFT: Jackie Oliver chases Jackie Stewart's latest Lola in the 1971 season's final race at Riverside. (Pete Lyons)

BELOW: The "mess of snakes" exhaust system on the turbo Mk 3. The hastily prepared car didn't make it into the 1972 Riverside race. (Pete Lyons)

ABOVE: NASCAR star Bobby Allison tests the second Mk 3 Shadow car at Riverside in October 1972. This was the only time that Bobby drove a sports car, and he absolutely loved it. (Mike and Pat Smith)

it their seal of approval—an SCCA Can-Am decal. The first milestone was accomplished, because the Ti22 was now officially a Can-Am car and could go onto the track for practice. Jackie slowly drove it out of the garage and accelerated up the pit lane. It was a lump-in-the-throat, fingers-crossed, but very proud moment.

We watched the Ti22 disappear over the hill and got ready to start taking the lap times—but it didn't complete the lap. The throttle was sticking, and we had to fix it. We massaged the throttle butterflies and got it back on the track just before the end of practice. Jackie did half a dozen laps but never did get up to full speed. The brake pedal felt spongy, so the brakes needed bleeding. The throttle was still acting up. The oil breather was blowing out so much oily vapor that it went on the exhaust pipes and smoked like the engine was on fire. There was a list of work to do, and it meant another all-night session. Luckily, Bill Thomas had sent us Bob, one of his engine men, in case we needed help. Boy, did we need help!

Jackie was unbelievably patient with us and the car. He was risking a serious accident every time he drove it with a sticking throttle. We had to fix that, or withdraw from the race. Bruce McLaren and his team were in the pit next to us. He came over and asked me if there was anything he could do to help, so I told him about our throttle problems. Bruce went back to his transporter and returned with the latest in throttle cables and Gary Knutson, his engine development engineer. Gary painstakingly explained how to dismantle the eight throttle butterfly valves in the intake manifold and modify them to work properly.

Bruce was a truly great sportsman. He told me he wanted the Ti22 to go well in the race and would help us any way he could. He wanted to compete with us on the track—not in the garages!

The Bruce McLaren Motor Racing team was dominating the Can-Am. In fact, it had become known as "The Bruce & Denny Show." Between them, Bruce McLaren and Denny Hulme had won five of six races in 1967, four of six races in 1968, and eight of eight races so far in 1969. The latest McLaren M8B appeared to be invincible. But it was still tough for me to regard Bruce as an enemy because he was such a considerate man and a good friend. If he had it, Bruce would give you any part you needed so you could race against him. My take on it was that you raced with Bruce, not against him. Later at Laguna, he even sent over a couple of mechanics to help us.

One of the keys to Bruce's immense success was his chief mechanic, Tyler Alexander, an American who had met Bruce through his relationship with American driver Timmy Meyer.

Meyer had been tragically killed in a racing crash, and Bruce was so impressed with Tyler that he asked him to take over as his chief mechanic. Tyler was totally dedicated to Bruce and his meticulous work was paying huge dividends. Tyler has a great sense of humor, and we shared a lot of jokes together. He still works in R&D for McLaren in England.

The works McLarens were not the only problems. There were other new cars at Laguna that weekend, and other very classy drivers. Like Jackie Oliver, Bruce McLaren, and Denny Hulme, Formula One drivers John Surtees, Mario Andretti, and Jo Siffert had flown in from Watkins Glen. Surtees, the 1966 Can-Am champion, was at Laguna to drive the new Chaparral 2H, which was equipped with by far the biggest wing ever seen in auto racing. Andretti was driving the Holman & Moody team's McLaren M6B, which had a giant, 494 cid (8.1-liter) Ford V8, and Siffert was in the Porsche 917PA. In addition, Chris Amon was assigned a third McLaren M8B when his Ferrari 612P hit engine trouble, Dan Gurney was in his modified McLaren he called the "McLeagle," and Peter Revson was in a new Lola T163. I had previously worked with half these drivers and knew how tough they would be to pass on this twisty, 1.9-mile course. We were in for a tough time.

I had arranged to use the facilities of a local Chevrolet dealer, and when it was getting dark, we loaded up the car and set off for the workshop there. When people refer to The Longest Day, they're usually talking about D-Day, when the Allies landed in Normandy during World War II. But for me the longest day of my life will always be October 10, 1969. It actually started on October 9 and went on until October 12. It was more than 90 hours long and it was the most exciting day of my life.

We arrived at the garage and unloaded the car. By now, we were feeling a bit washed out, to say the least. But we had a long list of things that needed fixing on the car. We sent out for the staple dual-purpose food that was used by many racing mechanics—Kentucky Fried Chicken. We called it dual-purpose because you could use the first piece you ate to wash your hands—the fatty skin was very effective in removing grease. Then we worked all night. I don't remember how, but we ended up back at the track next morning for the Saturday practice sessions in clean clothes. I guess at one point we must have gone to the hotel for a shower.

Saturday practice revealed more fuel surge problems, and we hadn't stopped the engine from puking oil over the exhaust headers. Jackie never did get a clean lap without the engine cutting out from fuel starvation, and we never got a qualifying run. Jackie was very patient with us, and when the stewards of the race offered to let us start from the

ABOVE: Colin Chapman points out the titanium content in the Ti22's chassis and suspension to Mario Andretti. (David Friedman)

CHAPTER 23 · 227

back of the grid, he agreed to have another go in the race. This really spurred us on to fix the problems, and we worked another all-nighter—running on pure enthusiasm. We each looked like something a dog had thrown up.

I finally figured out there was blow-by from the pistons. The scavenge oil pump wasn't powerful enough to create a negative pressure in the oil pan, so it blew the oil out of the breather. Our fix was like using a Harris Tweed jacket to cure dandruff. We made an oil catch tank to collect the vapors blowing out of the breather, took a hose from the side of the tank, and connected it into the oil pan right near the scavenge pump inlet. It worked like a charm—the oil in the catch tank was sucked right back down into the pan. We also found that the check valve in the fuel surge tank was sticking open and letting the fuel surge away from the pick-up under braking. We fixed that, too.

When we left for the track on race day, we were fairly confident that the titanium car would finally show its potential. Ernie Kanzler had arrived at the track before us and was in the motor home cooking bacon and eggs for breakfast. With him were his wife and two kids and my wife and two kids. He'd chartered a small plane to fly them in from Los Angeles. Everybody was excited.

We got the car into the race warm-up session, and Jackie did about three laps without stopping. Wow! We began to think we had the problems licked when he came into the pits with oil smoke billowing off the hot exhaust—again. The pipe from the breather had vibrated out of the catch tank, and the vapors were pouring over the exhaust pipes. Bruce McLaren lent us some fiberglass, and we bonded up the whole thing so it couldn't come loose again.

Jackie suggested that even if things didn't hang together in the race, we could still get some useful test time in race conditions, taking the opportunity to optimize the handling of the Ti22. This made us all realize that we were expecting a bit much if we thought a virtually untested car would actually finish a race first time out. It was also asking a lot of Jackie to get it anywhere near the front of the race. He was starting in 31st position—dead last. Laguna Seca was a tight, tough little track. It was going to be a bastard to get by anyone, let alone the whole field. We had no chance at winning or even finishing in the top 10 from that grid position. We only had one thing in our favor—we didn't have to worry about anyone passing us. There wasn't anyone behind us!

The moment of truth finally arrived. The cars disappeared over the hill from the start line in a roaring, dusty mass for the pace lap. Something terminal happened to the Chaparral's

LEFT: Jackie Oliver and the Ti22 dice with Dan Gurney's McLeagle at Laguna Seca in October 1969. (Dave Friedman)

engine, and they red-flagged the race. After the restart, as the cars came into sight from behind the hill, everyone was watching the leaders except us. Was our Ti22 still running last? It was not! Jackie was racing up through the field and had already passed eight cars! He kept on passing cars on almost every lap. To us, after all the problems in practice, it was almost unbelievable that this could be happening. By halfway, he was racing in the top 10!

By virtue of his tenacity and driving skills, Oliver had got the Ti22 up to seventh place in 33 laps when he came into the pits. I leapt almost into the car to find out what was wrong. Jackie shouted that the throttle pedal linkage was broken. I dived down inside the cockpit and looked at the pedal. The little titanium nut that held the cable to the pedal had come loose and fallen off. We fixed it, and Oliver went back into the race. It took only a few minutes but the fastest cars—Bruce and Denny, en route to yet another 1-2—were lapping in just over a minute, so we lost about six laps. When the checkered flag fell, Jackie was still racing. He finished in 13th position.

We were certainly not too disappointed, and neither was Jackie. We were all amazed that he even finished the race. He put his heart into the drive and overcame all the setbacks, including getting his head jerked back against the rollover bar at least four times a lap when the engine cut out. He said it was like being on a roller coaster ride when it happened, and made him feel seasick. He did a fantastic job in bringing that car home in its first race.

Ernie was totally delighted with the result. Our families gathered around us, thrilled by the whole experience. Lynn Oliver had big tears rolling down her cheeks.

That evening, at the prize-giving ceremony, Bruce McLaren collected the winner's trophy and said in his speech, "I think what Peter Bryant and his crew have done is remarkable. They've built a straightforward race car and finished first time out. The car ran very well indeed. It's a tribute to the team and the driver that it beat some of those multi million dollar teams that were going to come out here and blow us off!" I will never forget that compliment from Bruce. I still have the original press clippings with the quote. Whenever I feel a bit down, I look at them and give myself a lift.

OPPOSITE: A serious-looking Bruce McLaren and Denny Hulme answer press questions after their 1-2 finish at Laguna Seca. (Dale Von Treba)

Jackie Oliver said he would be available if we wanted him to drive in the next Can-Am, at Riverside. After all he'd been through, I'd reckoned I would have to beg him to get him back in the Ti22. I promised to make changes that would improve the driveability and roadholding.

Next morning, the telephone rang in my hotel room at 6:30 a.m., and Ernie was on the line. He said, "I have plane tickets booked to take us back to Orange County. Would you like to come with us, or would you rather rest and go back with the truck?" I didn't need to be asked twice—I hated traveling in trucks. John Holman of Holman & Moody sat next to us on the plane to Santa Ana. We'd met years before, when I was on a Ford test program in Sebring with the Ford GTX. He was very complimentary about the titanium car, and I could see Ernie beaming with pride.

Ernie dropped me at the workshop and said, "You've done everything you said you would do for me, and you should be rewarded for it. If I increase your pay by half, would that be enough? I don't know what good designers should be paid." For the second time since I'd met him, I was speechless—which doesn't happen very often. How lucky could I get?

Ernie Kanzler, the Autocoast team, and all our supporters made a miracle happen at Laguna Seca that October. And Ernie showed himself to be the best employer and friend I'd ever had.

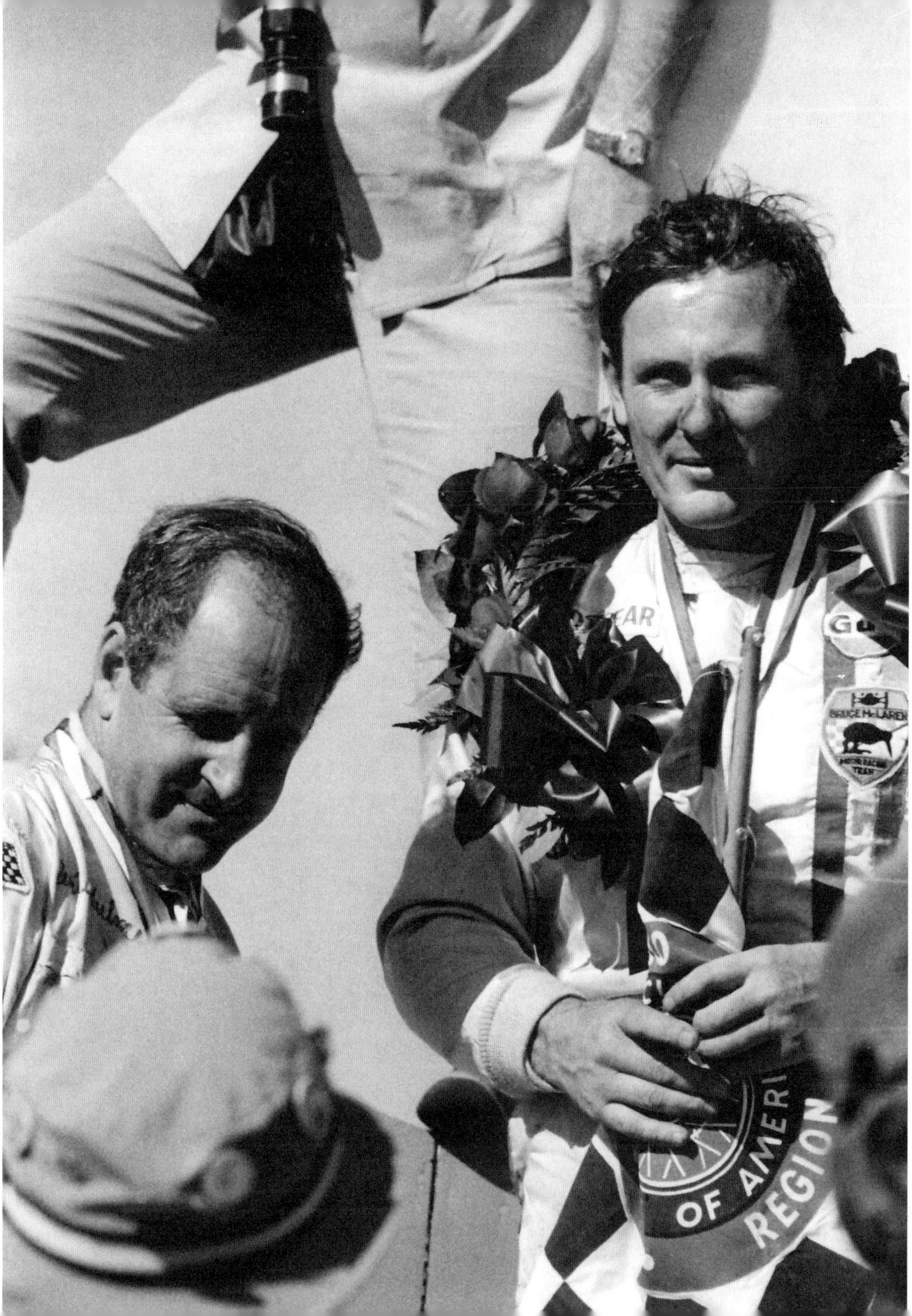
BRUCE McLAREN
OF AMERI
REGION

BELOW: After the first practice session at Riverside in 1969, we removed the rear spoiler and added Paul Lamar's wing to reduce drag and increase downforce on the tires. (Bob Tronolone)

CHAPTER 24

On the Pace at Riverside!

After that amazing debut at Laguna, we had two weeks before the next round of the Can-Am, the *Los Angeles Times* Grand Prix at Riverside Raceway, also in California. But once the car had returned to our shop, we had only about seven days before we would be loading it up to leave again.

The first American sports-car race I had attended had been at Riverside in 1963, when I was a mechanic on a Ferrari 250 P driven by John Surtees. That race was also a *Times* Grand Prix, and I remembered how tough it had been. We'd finished fourth of only about seven cars that ran the distance. It was a very grueling race and was hard on every part of the car. Even at that time of the year, temperatures could reach 95 or even 100 degrees. Just finishing the race would be an almighty task.

ABOVE: Showing barely any roll at all, Jackie goes flat out through turn 3 at Riverside. (Mike and Pat Smith)

The very first *Times* Grand Prix in 1958 had been won by Chuck Daigh in the Scarab sports car, built by Lance Reventlow, and the race carried a lot of tradition. The big, powerful Can-Am cars were great crowd-pleasers, and the race was supported every year by over 80,000 spectators. It raised a lot of money for charity, thanks in a big part to the efforts of director of special events, Glenn Davis. This year, it was going to be the most important sports-car race in the history of racing in California. There were 40 cars entered—one of the biggest fields ever in a road race, and nearly twice as big as most of the contemporary Can-Am events.

Riverside was a very different kind of track than Laguna Seca. It was 3.3 miles around and had some very fast turns, some esses, and a long, fast back straight with a kink leading into a 180-degree, 90 mph last turn. It wasn't as hard on the brakes as Laguna, but very much faster. It would require the ultimate compromise in aerodynamic tuning, because we would need lots of downforce for the turns (especially turn 9), but low downforce for the big straight. I decided to replace the rear spoiler we'd used at Laguna with a high wing on the rear uprights, like many of the other cars had. I also cut away the rear underbody part of the rear fenders to allow the airflow to exit more easily from under the body. This would increase the traction for minimal drag, meaning better speed at the end of the straight—a good trade-off for this track. I asked aerodynamicist Paul Lamar to make us a rear wing, and he started on it right away.

We pulled out the engine, sent it back to Bill Thomas for reconditioning, and put in the second motor that he'd built. We went over the car with a magnifying glass to find any small cracks or problems. It was good, so we put it all back together. Then we worked on the surge problem by building a separate surge tank, and reconfigured the fuel system. We replaced every titanium fastener in the car, remembering that loose throttle cable bolt.

Meanwhile the *Times* held a reception and dinner to promote the race at the Jolly Knight restaurant in Garden Grove, and invited the press and most of the team managers and drivers. It was my first night out since the Ti22 project had started. I was invited to bring Jackie Oliver, but he was in Mexico for the Formula One race, so his wife, Lynn, agreed to come in his place. Lynn had been "Miss Players" when Jackie drove for Team Lotus, and the press were so busy drooling over her that I had a nice, undisturbed, and interesting evening, chatting with the co-founder of the new March Engineering company, Max Mosley (who is now the president of the FIA). A couple of the press guys did tear themselves away from Lynn long enough to ask me about titanium—the metal that took men to the moon that year. I had a small piece in my pocket, along with a piece of steel the same size. They lapped it up. Next day Shav Glick of the *Times* wrote a very informed article and instantly made me into a local celebrity.

When the time came for us to leave for Riverside, we had another mechanic on the team named Alex Groundsel. We'd completely rebuilt the Ti22, but there was no time to test again. We needed all the track time we could get during the practice sessions for Jackie to learn the circuit and for us to tweak the car. We got to the first open practice session late on Thursday, but unfortunately the new rear wing wasn't ready. We'd gotten the mounts ready for bolting it to the rear uprights, so installing it would only take five minutes—once it got there.

The car went reasonably well on the first day, but the new 454 cid (7.5-liter) engine developed an oil leak. We wasted precious track time trying to fix that and loosening up a stiff steering rack. We immediately ordered a new rack from Gordon Schroeder in Los Angeles, in case we couldn't make it work better. But we ended up with very little practice and another all-nighter in the track garage.

In qualifying on Friday, Denny Hulme was fastest in his McLaren M8B, followed by Chris Amon in the V12 Ferrari, Dan Gurney (McLeagle), Mario Andretti (McLaren M6B Ford), Bruce McLaren (who had engine problems in his M8B), Peter Revson (Lola T163), and Chuck Parsons in Carl Haas's modified Simoniz Lola T163. Jackie qualified eighth. We were happy to be faster than Jo Siffert's Porsche 917PA and John Surtees's Chaparral, but I knew we could do much better. I wanted that new high wing to arrive from Paul Lamar's fabrication shop in the worst way.

I remember talking to Cosworth Engineering founder Keith Duckworth about Mario Andretti's big Ford V8, hoping for some insight as to its potential for us to use in 1970 instead of the 427 Chevy. He said, "Peter, that intake manifold design is so bad they've had to put arrows inside the ports to show the fuel mixture which way to go!" I guess someone at Ford listened in to him, because Cosworth ended up being bought by Ford.

The Saturday qualifying sessions turned out to very dramatic. We spent a lot of time on the new rear wing. We soon found out that if we tilted it up to increase the angle of attack and, therefore, the downforce, it created a whole lot of drag, slowing our speed on the straights. We needed to add side plates like the McLaren wing had, but we weren't sure if the wing could stand the extra loads. The skin of the Lamar wing was only about 20-thousandths thick, and it seemed very fragile. So we tweaked the wing as it was—and, as the English newspaper, *Motoring News*, reported, "Oliver shook up the troops in the titanium car, improving its times dramatically." We started to get excited about the possibilities for Jackie in this second race for the Ti22.

But something happened in the final qualifying session that properly jangled our frayed nerves. We'd just put on a stiffer rear anti-rollbar when we noticed a small stream of oil running down the side of the block, near the oil pressure line outlet fitting. The fitting was leaking. It only needed to be screwed in just a bit tighter, but we couldn't turn the fitting one complete turn without it fouling part of the chassis structure. Really, we needed to unbolt the engine and lift it an inch. We only had 45 minutes left. What to do? We quickly decided to take the car back to the garage in the paddock, clean around the fitting with acetone, put a ring of epoxy around it, and let it cure just enough to stop the leak. So Jackie did a partial quick lap to see if the rollbar change had worked, and then came in so we could fix the leak.

Stirling Moss was the Can-Am "commissioner" for the series sponsor, Johnson Wax, and came over to the garage just as we finished with the epoxy and put the body back on. We had the car jacked up so that we could periodically go under it and check if the epoxy was hard. Time was running out fast, so we hoped no one screwed up the track with oil before Jackie could get in a flying lap to try for pole position. We kept checking the epoxy, popping in and out under the car. Stirling asked me what we were doing, "Is this some secret qualifying tweak to get the pole at the last second?" I gave him a conspiratorial grin and answered, "Yup!" Stirling ran back to tell the announcer what he thought we were doing.

We let the jack down with only 10 minutes to go. Jackie drove out of the paddock, and we had time for two flying laps. The second one took 1:36.23. Phew! What a lap! The works McLarens were in the 1:34s, and Amon's Ferrari, which was fitted on the Saturday with a new, 6.9-liter V12, had done 1:35.09. Jackie went fast enough to get us fourth place on the grid, just ahead of Gurney, Andretti, and Revson.

Jackie Oliver's fantastic qualifying attempt was a very nice surprise to all of us, and especially me. I hadn't even thought about how people would react if we could blow off a few important doors. I was on Cloud Nine. Here I was, a mechanic with no formal education except a few night school classes, and I was the designer of the fastest American-built car on the grid! Within five minutes of the end of qualifying, the Riverside PR people asked Jackie and me to go to the press box in the stand for interviews, and I was up there so long I started to get concerned about getting back to the car. I guess I love to talk—someone once told me that if I was asked what time it was, I would tell them how to make a watch.

Everyone in the media raved about the car. Deke Houlgate wrote a nice piece for the press telegram and told me it couldn't have come at a better time, because Jackie's performance in the Ti22 had breathed new life into the Can-Am. Chris Economaki from *National Speed Sport News* said, "Peter, you've reached a new status in auto racing. I'm the chairman of the Martini & Rossi Driver of the Year Awards, and I'd like to invite you to our event in Los Angeles next week as our special guest." Chuck Barnes of Sports Headliners, which represented major sports figures in sponsorship, invited me to go to their annual Christmas party at the Roosevelt hotel in L.A., the same evening as the Martini & Rossi lunch. But the most satisfying compliment came from Chuck Parsons in the garage, "Well, Peter, I have to give you credit. You said at my party at Laguna last year that one day you'd build a car that would blow our doors off, and you did it! Congratulations!" Laughing, he added, "What took you so long?"

I guess it took a while for us to realize what we'd achieved in only two races. Ernie Kanzler was delighted again, and said so. He insisted on getting to the track early on race day to cook us all breakfast in his motor home. We both had a very dedicated crew to thank. No one can do something as complex as build a competitive car without good teamwork. Not one person had ever complained about the long hours—I was very lucky to have found such people.

That evening, Jackie Oliver and I were invited to attend the SCCA event at the Holiday Inn in Riverside, where we were staying. The trouble was that I knew we had a lot of work to do on the car, so I asked the crew if I should go. They said, "Yes—but don't stay out all night!" Jackie and I were treated like movie stars, and it felt good, but at 9:00 p.m. I went back to the garage and spent the rest of the night working on the car.

I was going over the day's events in my mind, and it occurred to me that everyone had been asking about the titanium, but almost nobody had noticed the aerodynamic differences of our body shape relative to the other Can-Am cars. Almost nobody had asked why the Ti22 had a chisel edge to the front fenders, or why it had fences running down each side of the body, or why the rocker panels were so square. Only one person had asked me about the side fences—Bruce McLaren! I had a problem not revealing all to him, because he was such a nice guy. I told him the simplest truth—they helped increase the downforce, as he might expect they would. He smiled and said, "You're a tricky bugger, Peter." I'd met Bruce years before when he was driving for the Cooper Formula One team with Jack Brabham. Like Jack, he was a great listener. Neither of them missed many tricks.

Next to us in the garages at Riverside was an old-model McLaren that was way back on the starting grid. The owners were a lawyer and his wife, Vickie. They called their team Ecurie Vickie, and we became quite friendly during our night-time preparations. I didn't know yet that he would play an important and fateful part in my life the following year.

Race day dawned very bright and sunny. We double-checked everything on the car, crack-tested the ring gear and pinion on the Hewland gearbox, and put an extra epoxy seal over any seam where oil could leak.

Don Zimmerman of Timet had invited the corporate president to the race. If he liked what he saw, we might get more support the following year, perhaps even some much-needed sponsorship. Goodyear's head of racing, Larry Truesdale, spent a lot of time talking with Jackie, and that pleased me no end. Larry and Goodyear could make our 1970 program a lot easier financially, as well as provide tire support. That could be a big plus in trying to attract sponsors. We had a lot on the line, and it was almost as much as we could do to contain our excitement.

The Ti22 performed well in the morning warm-up, while Siffert's Porsche sprang an oil leak, Gurney's McLeagle lost engine oil pressure, Chuck Parsons had an exciting moment with a sticking throttle on his Lola, and Surtees's Chaparral 2H started misfiring badly. Happily for them, they all got their problems fixed in time to make it to the grid. There were a lot of important racing visitors because the Mexican Grand Prix had been run the previous week (and won for McLaren by Denny Hulme). Many of the participants had dropped in for a look, including Jack Brabham, Frank Williams, Keith Duckworth, and Mike Hewland. Movie stars like James Garner and Paul Newman were also there, and it was a fan's delight. They milled around the cars and stars to get autographs and photographs. I'd never seen so many people on a starting grid.

Finally, the grid was cleared, and the cars sent off for two pace laps before the rolling start. Amon's Ferrari failed to start on the starter motor as required by the rules, but a race official signaled for the car to be push-started. From the 40 cars that had practiced, only 35 were permitted to start, and the slowest car had qualified almost 22 seconds slower than pole position. This meant that the leaders would be lapping the backmarkers within five laps of the start. I think the organizers liked that because it added more drama to the race.

Hulme led from the green flag and immediately set a fast pace. He was trailed by McLaren, Amon, Gurney, Andretti, Parsons, and Oliver in our car. Jackie seemed to be losing speed on the long straight, but then he could make up a bunch of time in turn 9. We got some comfort from the fact that the Ti22 was handling very well, but we were mystified by his loss of straightaway speed. There was already a lot of oil on the track, and it was making it difficult for everyone. Jackie was being patient—he knew he had to finish to win.

Then poor Chris Amon was black-flagged and drove into the pits. His team manager, Bill Gavin, ran to the officials to find out why. They allowed Chris back out, only to show him another black flag. They said he'd had a push at the start. His race was done. I thought it was stupid. Once they'd let him start, they should have let him continue and figured out something later. Instead, it robbed the fans of some exciting action and the only Ferrari. I'd been Chris's mechanic in his first Formula One season, and we were good friends, so I felt very sorry for him.

LEFT: With the McLarens and Amon's Ferrari already past, a surprising fourth-place qualifier named Jackie Oliver (number 22) leads Dan Gurney (48), Mario Andretti (1), and the rest of the pack on the pace lap at Riverside. (Autocoast Publicity)

Meanwhile the race had settled into yet another Bruce & Denny Show, only this time it was Denny and Bruce. Gurney was four seconds behind Bruce in third place, ahead of a fierce battle between Parsons, Oliver, and Andretti. After 25 laps, much to our chagrin, Jackie limped into the pits with broken rear suspension—a really big disappointment. We didn't want to tell the press that a piece of titanium had broken loose at a weld, because it might have embarrassed the president of Timet, so we told them the differential had broken.

Bruce McLaren also had a suspension break, and he crashed heavily at 150 mph, injuring a corner worker, but luckily escaping injury himself. The very next lap, Frank Gardner crashed Alan Mann's Ford Special due to another suspension failure but was also uninjured. The rash of suspension failures on other cars eased our pain, but we knew there was a flaw and accepted the blame. It would have been pretty stupid for us to blame the high curbs and the bumpy track when one of our welds had failed. You can't solve problems if you can't recognize them. We vowed we would be more than ready for the next race in Texas in a couple of weeks.

We discovered later that we'd been losing about 75 bhp due to a worn camshaft lobe, which explained why the Ti22 was so slow on the straight. Jackie had done an exemplary job in making the car go as fast as it did.

Hulme went on to lap the entire field. It was one of his best drives in the Can-Am.

He never eased up and averaged over 120 mph for the race. Jackie might have been able to get second place if the Ti22 hadn't broken, because Parsons finished second ahead of Andretti, with Gurney, who had an ailing engine, and Revson behind them. Endurance had yet again been a big factor at Riverside. Chuck kept up a decent pace and finished without incident, and ended up on the podium.

Even before the engine problem we had in the race, the Riverside Can-Am had indicated a basic flaw in our engine program—not enough power! We needed to take control of that situation if we were going to beat McLaren in 1970. I vowed to start immediately to seek out a likely recruit to run an engine shop for us. I liked the look of Gary Knutson, who worked for McLaren, and started a dialog with him at the prize-giving that evening. Early next morning we were back at the shop and tearing into the car.

The Tuesday following the race was the day of the Martini & Rossi Driver of the Year awards and the Sports Headliners bash. I'd arranged to meet with Larry Truesdale and was going to try for a cash commitment from Goodyear for the next season. I invited Ernie to join me, but he had some family matters to attend to. Ernie loaned me his car to drive, saying, "I can't have you driving up to the Ritz Hotel in that clunker of yours!" Chris Economaki was the master of ceremonies and guiding light for the Martini affair. Their Driver of the Year award winner had been picked in a poll conducted by the auto-racing press. It was a prestigious award and highly coveted. The event was by invitation only, and I felt very flattered to be included. Chris introduced me to several important people and sat me down in front of the rostrum at a table with Bill McCrary, the head of the Firestone racing division. Stock-car racing ace Lee Roy Yarbrough was also at our table and was one of the contenders for the award. He told me he would love to try an Indy or Can-Am car, and gave me his card for future reference. Chris began the proceedings by introducing Count Rossi and then welcoming the guests—including me. He was very generous with his comments and I felt myself blushing. I'd never done that before! He then announced that the winner was Yarbrough, who gave a great acceptance speech. The fact that Chris had seated me with the winner of the award reinforced my feelings of self-worth no end. It gave me a lot of confidence ahead of my chat with Larry Truesdale later, and I owed Chris a big thank you for that. After all, I wasn't a sophisticated guy—I was a really just a cockney bloke who had a lot to learn when it came to politicking.

The lunch finally wound down, and I went over to the Roosevelt Hotel for the Sports Headliners function that evening. There were all kinds of athletes and other sports people there, and I was taken round and introduced to a lot of them, including football hero OJ Simpson. Chuck Barnes gave me his card and invited me to his office in Indianapolis next time I was in town. I made a mental note to take him up on that—what a great contact to have if you were seeking a sponsor! Someone gave me some champagne, and just as the George Mitchell Boys Choir started to sing, Larry Truesdale walked up to me and said, "Peter, shall we go to the Hanalei Restaurant in Hollywood for dinner, and talk some things over?"

I really wasn't ready to leave just yet but readily agreed. He'd been described as the most powerful man in American auto racing, and I couldn't afford to piss him off. I drove to the restaurant at top speed and found him on his second martini. His companion was Barry Galloway, who had been introduced to me at Riverside as his associate. I naturally assumed that Barry worked for Larry. I ordered a scotch and water and listened eagerly to what Larry had to say, "Let's get right to the point. In addition to tire support, how much do you think Goodyear should pay you for next year's Can-Am? Bear in mind we already sponsor McLaren, along with several others."

Wow—that was certainly direct. I must have looked nervous. He told me to relax and take my time while he went to the bathroom. I took a sip from my glass, and Barry told me not to be nervous, because they weren't going to bite me. When Larry came back, I jacked up my nerves and said I thought we should get about $150,000 for the season—thinking I would start high and let him beat me down. Then I went to the bathroom to let him talk to Barry in private. When I got back, our food was there and Larry said that his budget had been cut back for the coming year, but he felt an obligation to help me due to the excellent work I'd done and the friendship we had. He said he was going to give me $50,000 for the 1970 season, plus tire support.

I was overjoyed. I would have been happy with anything at all. The tire support alone was worth more than that. I thanked Larry so profusely that his face went red with embarrassment. He waved me to silence and told me I deserved it, or I wouldn't have gotten it! We shook hands, but he didn't mention drawing up a written agreement. He simply told me I should expect the first check, for half the money, some time in January, and the balance after the first race.

I don't think my feet touched the floor when I walked out of that restaurant. Next morning, I told Ernie what had happened, and he said, "Great work! Let's celebrate—we'll go sailing." It sounded like a nice idea, but I declined and went to the shop to see how the car was coming along.

CHAPTER 25

College Football Wins in Texas

The last Can-Am race of 1969 was scheduled at Texas Speedway on November 9. Again, we had only a week before we had to leave for College Station, the nearest town. The Texas race was a fill-in fixture for the cancelled Las Vegas round, and as the track was brand new, I personally thought that everyone did a fantastic job getting it on. But somebody really goofed on the scheduling, because it was on the same day as the college football game between Texas Tech and Texas Agricultural College. Not being familiar with college football, I knew nothing of the rivalry between these two teams. It was a big annual bash and famous for the largest bonfire in the United States on the night before the game. I soon found out about it when I tried to book hotel space. We managed to get Jackie and Lynn Oliver into the local Holiday Inn, but the crew and I had to be 70 miles away, near Bryan. Luckily it was a straight shot, and we could do it in about an hour and 15 minutes. What this would really mean in terms of precious time was two hours less sleep—if we were lucky enough to get any at all!

We did arrange to move into the Holiday Inn the night after the race, because the prize-giving was going to be there. As this was the last race, there would be money handed out, as well as trophies. We hoped to get some of that, even though we would have done only 3 of the 11 races.

The track was a brand-new superspeedway, and they'd used part of the infield to make a combined road and banking circuit. There was a ramp at the transition from the infield onto the banking, and that could cause the cars to bottom out like crazy.

We repaired the broken titanium suspension parts and reinforced them. We also changed engines and performed a post mortem on the Riverside motor. I got onto Bill Thomas to find out why it had lost a camshaft lobe. Chevrolet said it sometimes happened when you first started the engine on the dyno after a rebuild and told us to be sure to check the valve clearances during practice and before the race. I called my buddy Gary Knutson at McLaren about it. He said the trick to avoiding it was to put plenty of molybdenum disulphide or similar grease on the lobes after the cam was installed in the block, rev the engine above 3000 rpm as soon as it fired, and then hold it there for several minutes. If this didn't wipe off the cam lobes, they would probably be OK. I reckoned this all meant that there was something wrong with the pushrod geometry or the cams themselves but had no time to go into it. It was common practice in overhead-cam engines in England to slightly angle the face of the cam lobes, so that the cam followers (tappets) rotated when the engine turned over and the cam pushed them. This prevented wear in one place on the followers. We desperately needed to do some engine development.

Our transporter left for Texas with our three mechanics at the last possible minute, and I flew down with Jackie and Lynn the next day. The Texas track facilities were great, with waterproof and well-lit garages for us to work in. That was important, because the weather in Texas was unpredictable at that time of year.

We spent the first practice session playing with the fuel mixture and trying to make the chassis work without bottoming out on the ramp between the banking and the infield. On the banked section, the cars got up to some very high speeds before diving down onto the infield section. I took a dislike to the Texan climate. It was humid as hell one minute, and the next it would suddenly cool like it was going to rain. I had big trouble getting the right fuel-air mixture to handle the atmospheric changes. In those days, there were no computers with oxygen sensors and feedback systems to help in adjusting the fuel mixture. I only had one of the first calculators with three levels of memory. It cost $460. Now a bank will give you one just for opening an account.

We used to do plug cuts to get the air-fuel mixture tuned. You needed to see the color of the sparkplug insulators at peak power—if they were white, it meant that it was too lean, and dark brown meant too rich. You looked for the best compromise. It was bit dicey, because the driver had to get the engine up to maximum power rpm, then cut the engine and coast into the pit. If your pit was near the pit-lane entrance, it was easy. But if you were a long way down, it could be a problem—we often had to run out to the car and push it in. Champion's Can-Am guys were Art Sparks and Dick Smith, who ran the company's research facility and dyno in Long Beach. They were considered the best in America at reading plugs. I was always skeptical about the process and tended to favor running on the rich side of the line.

The problems with this method were that the driver had to be good at doing it, that you had to start with new plugs but with some constant laps on them, and that it was a big nuisance for the mechanics. They were constantly taking out old plugs and putting in new ones. This was only done when the engine was hot, and we all had "idiot marks," or burns, on our hands and arms where we'd accidentally touched the hot exhaust pipes. Every time the car came into the pits for suspension or tire pressure adjustment, we always checked at least one plug. It was a good precaution to avoid burning a hole in a piston—the result of running too lean. It wasn't the most popular job among the mechanics. Whenever I suggested we should check a plug, everyone seemed busy doing something else. Many teams had their own engine men who did it all the time, but our engines were built at Bill Thomas's racing shop, so as a former Formula One engine man I assumed that responsibility myself.

We were a small team with only two races under our belt, and it was becoming more and more obvious that we needed a full-time engine man. But where to get one as good as Gary Knutson? I'd managed to secure the services of Mike Lowman, a very experienced mechanic I'd met when he worked for Dan Gurney. He and Al Willard were my entire crew in Texas, because Alex Groundsel had to go back to his other job.

Three people could maintain a Can-Am race car, but it was tough with all the "gofer" stuff we needed to do, like taking wheels down to Goodyear and having them mount some tires. It seemed almost ludicrous because, after our Riverside qualifying success, we were now considered by the media to be the top American challenge to the McLaren team—and there were really only three of us and a driver. In my English way, I laughed about it. The "American challenge" was really just three blokes and one chap! But it was true that the Ti22 car was paid for with good old American bucks by a real American, and it was made in America with American technology with lots of American know-how and parts.

If I look at the personnel requirements in modern race teams, I'm amazed at how specialized it has become, and how we did it with so few people. No wonder the costs are so high these days. I reckon the development of the computer has also had a lot to do with increased specialization and costs. But that was then, and this is now.

We had two problems in qualifying at Texas. We couldn't get the engine to put out enough horsepower, and we couldn't find the fast suspension setup for Jackie. I put that down to the difficulty we had going from the infield to the banked oval. Our car was very ride-height sensitive and needed a nice, flat track surface. But the uneven Texas track created two suspension problems that together made the Ti22 tough to drive fast. First, as soon as one side of the car was raised up on the transition ramp, it lost ground-effect and flicked sideways. And second, we had to run it too high to stop the ramp grinding off the chassis tub.

But the biggest problem was the engine. Its performance was way off. I thought we might have scuffed a piston in one session, but short of tearing it down, there was no real way of knowing. It also was oiling its plugs a bit, so I couldn't read the mixture on plug cuts.

Nevertheless, Jackie qualified sixth, a tenth of a second slower than Peter Revson in a Lola T163. Ahead of us on the front row, the powerful McLaren-Ford of Mario Andretti had out-qualified both works McLaren-Chevrolets and surprised everyone, thanks to his incredible driving talent and the torque of that big V8 pushing him over 200 mph on the banking. We never saw 200 mph all day. Denny Hulme was alongside Mario, in front of Bruce McLaren and Chris Amon in the Ferrari. We hadn't done too badly, considering our engine situation.

Jack Brabham had joined the fray for this race, driving Alan Mann's Ford Special. He qualified just behind us, alongside Chuck Parsons's Haas Lola. It was a tough field to beat, although among the disappointed people was Texas's own Jim Hall. Stand-in driver Tom Dutton clouted the wall and cracked the monocoque on the Chaparral 2H, forcing Jim to withdraw it.

We decided to switch engines for the race and hoped to get the mixture right in the warm-up. We finished work at about 2:00 a.m. and shot back to the hotel for 40 winks.

Returning to the track on race day was absolute murder. I thought it was going to be a great turnout for the Speedway. Wrong! When we finally did get to the track, we expected to see packed grandstands, like at Laguna and Riverside. The stands were almost deserted. All the roads to College Station had been jammed with football fans! Nothing but nothing stood in the way of that legendary rivalry between the Tech and the Aggies—not even world-class auto racing.

The race started out fairly well for us. Andretti seized the lead at the start, but Hulme was right with him, followed closely by McLaren. When Mario's engine expired, Jackie got our car up to third, with Brabham close behind, but our luck ran out there. The engine started to smoke and finally Jackie came into the pits with a burned piston. Our team and Holman-Moody were not alone in having an engine problem. So did Amon's Ferrari and Revson's Lola, and the biggest surprise was when Hulme's engine blew up about seven laps from the finish, handing McLaren the win. George Eaton was second in a McLaren M12, Brabham third in the Ford, Jo Siffert fourth in his Porsche 917. My old buddies Chuck Parsons (Lola T163) and Lothar Motschenbacher (McLaren M12) finished fifth and sixth.

Bruce's unexpected victory gave him the Can-Am crown, and he totally deserved it. His cars had won every race of 1969, finishing 1-2 on no fewer than eight occasions.

At the prize-giving that evening, master of ceremonies David E. Davis Jr., the editor of *Car & Driver* magazine, observed, "I don't know who scheduled this race for this particular weekend, but I've seen more people at a streetcar derailment in Detroit." He then presented Bruce with the Johnson Wax Trophy, and Bruce's team won over $300,000. In only three races, I learned a lot about what it would take to win the Can-Am Challenge Cup, and I wanted to get my hands on some of that money the following year. I quietly vowed somehow to find my magic engine man and win that trophy.

But our 1969 season wasn't yet over. We'd been invited to one more race—the second annual "Can-Jap-Am."

BELOW: Jackie Oliver leading the field in the Ti22 at the misty start of the 1969 Mount Fuji Nippon Grand Prix race. (Al Willard)

CHAPTER 26

Teppanyaki and Pole, Please . . .

The extra race after the 1969 Can-Am series had finished in Texas was a second invitation event organized by the Nippon Auto Club of Japan, with help from excellent organizers like Burdette Martin of the Sports Car Club of America, who was to be the chief steward. The press nicknamed the race the "Can-Jap-Am," and it was scheduled for November 23 on the Fuji International Speedway, in the foothills of the spectacular Mount Fuji volcano.

We were told that it would be run under the same regulations as all the previous Can-Am races. This made sense only at first glance, because these things are never that simple. In the previous races, for example, if you lost a piece of your front bodywork, you had to replace it or be disqualified. So the serious teams carried a spare nose wherever they went. This is OK if you have a nice, big truck, but if you're packing up to race in Japan, you're going to need to put a very big crate on the airplane. I asked Burdie Martin if they were going to enforce this rule, and he repeated, "The same rules will apply as all other Can-Am races." That short statement ended up costing the organizers a fortune in extra air freight charges.

Apart from that, the logistics went off great. We got the car ready and packed up enough stuff to do what we normally do. We took a spare engine and a spare gearbox and nose section. We took 20 new tires, including two sets of rain tires supplied by Goodyear after Texas. We had a lot of stuff to pack, but we finally got it delivered to Japan Air Lines freight at L.A. Airport.

On travel day, everyone boarded a JAL Boeing 707 to Tokyo, with only a fuel stop in Hawaii. I sat next to my old buddy, Chuck Parsons, who promptly set a happy tone by telling me a joke, "This guy goes to the doctor and tells him, 'Doc, every time I sneeze, I have an orgasm.' The doc asks, 'Are you taking anything for it?' And the guy says, 'Yeah. Pepper.'"

Pretty soon, the joke had swept through the plane and everyone was laughing. It was quite a funny joke, but the funniest thing was that the Japanese crew and passengers all started laughing, too, without knowing why.

We drank a few beers, ate some food, and told more jokes until we got to Honolulu more than six hours later. The landing terrified us all when the plane bounced at least four times. Chuck said to me, "After that, I need a mai tai! Care to join me?" We went to the airport lounge with Chuck's wife, Sherrie, had at least two of their great maitai cocktails, and got back on the plane feeling pretty good all round. Those cocktails were great sleeping potions. We slept almost the whole way to Tokyo, until they woke us up for breakfast. It was sushi and seaweed. The omelette that followed the seaweed was rubbery. A guy who could have conjured up a plate or two of bacon and eggs could have made a killing.

After getting down to the Fuji race track, about 100 miles from Tokyo, we were all booked into the same golf hotel, called the Hakone Kanko Resort. There was a shuttle bus to the track, and we were all anxious to find out how our equipment had survived the trip. The first thing we saw on arrival at the garages was the entire Toyota team doing morning calisthenics, including the five drivers. In those days, I don't think you could have gotten any American to do jumping jacks first thing in the morning—not to mention singing the company song—even if you offered a bribe. Toyota was deadly serious about winning this race and had entered five cars with V8 engines. I was introduced to Hidemasa Tadaki, the team manager, and he politely wished me good luck.

We need not have worried about the condition of our cars. They were all in separate garages under strict security, and looked exactly as they had when they were in our shops ready to leave. I was amazed at the care that had been taken with them. I remembered one Formula One race when the cars were airfreighted to New York from England, and then trucked to Watkins Glen. Obviously our cars didn't have tie-down hooks, like passenger cars, so the truckers tied them down to the trucks with chains. We had to rebuild all the suspension wishbones. What a relief to discover that my titanium wishbones didn't need welding up again.

Fuji Speedway was so high up the mountain that for half the morning it was in the clouds. It was cold, damp, and foggy, and reminded me of England. Our first run on the track was in a rental car. There was a big, sweeping right-hander at the end of the very long start-finish straight, which kind of corkscrewed downwards. On the outside of the track at that point was a sheer drop over a cliff, guarded only by a chain-link fence. It scared the pants off me. If a car had a tire blowout there at the kind of speeds we could generate, it would certainly end up in a ball at the bottom of the cliff. I immediately found Burdie Martin, and with Jackie Oliver and several other drivers, we begged him to ask the organizers to reverse the direction of the race, so it went counter-clockwise. That bend would then be on an uphill climb to the long straight. To our amazement, the organizers readily agreed, and we all went back to our respective garages happy. We unpacked our stuff, checked over the Ti22, and went back to the hotel at dusk.

The hotel had a *teppanyaki* room, where people sat on the floor with pillows behind them, ate *tempura* (deep-fried seafood and vegetables), and drank *sake* around a long, low table. A picture in the lobby showed some kind of tea ceremony in there, with geisha girls kneeling at the table in kimonos. The hotel had arranged a *teppanyaki* dinner for the 30 or so visiting Can-Am people. Chuck Parsons called us all individually in our rooms to tell us not to forget to wear our kimonos, which we would find hanging in the wardrobes, because they were supplied by the hotel for ceremonies just like this. I wasn't falling for that one! The kimono in my room was a bathrobe, and it said so on the wardrobe door! So at 7:00 p.m. I went down and walked into the room. Our group was wearing normal clothes, but there was also a group of American tourists, some of them wearing kimonos. After a few minutes, Jackie and Lynn Oliver arrived—and they were the only ones who had fallen for Chuck's ruse. They looked at us and asked us why we were being so rude, not following the Japanese tradition. Just at that moment, the tour guide at the other table stood up and said to his group, "I hope you all enjoyed the *teppanyaki* tonight. I'll meet you all at 8:00 a.m., and please don't wear your bathrobes to breakfast!" We all howled with laughter, Lynn's face went as red as beetroot, and Jackie's face had a very rueful look. It looked like this was going to be a fun trip. Needless to say, we never let either one of them live that down.

Next day, we started practice in the afternoon, after the clouds had almost dispersed. One of the most interesting things we saw was wing-tip vortex flow. We were in the clouds, and as the Ti22 went past at speed, you could see a vapor trail coming out sideways from the end of the high-mounted wing, extending 12 or 15 feet. We obviously needed endplates on the wing, because we were probably losing downforce due to that. But we were fast anyway, and I figured we weren't hurt by it very much. If we made endplates and put them on without testing them, we could screw up the balance of the car. So we left well enough alone.

Jackie and I decided not to show our hand to the Toyota guys, so we broke the lap up into pieces. Fuji was much like Laguna Seca in that you could observe different parts of the track from the back of the pits. It was pretty simple to time the Ti22 from different points to different points, and find out where the difficult bits were. So we put sequences together and never did a full lap at our maximum speed until qualifying began. Lynn Oliver was good at keeping track of things, and it worked well, using four stopwatches.

The factory Toyota team's 303 cid DOHC engine was a real screamer, and it impressed everyone. It seemed to rev higher than any engine I'd heard since being in Formula One. But they also had spies everywhere, which was less impressive. One guy stood next to our car with a rolled-up race program in his hand, with several rubber bands round it. It was concealing a camera, and he took lots of photographs while another guy distracted us. It was really obvious that they wanted all the fine details of the car. I got fed up with this spying bullshit and finally said to Mr. Tadaki, "This is our last year's car, so I'll make a deal with you. You give me Toyota engines and money for next year, and I'll give you a full set of the drawings." He blushed a little, smiled, and said in perfect English, "The press here wants to know everything, Mr. Bryant." After that, they stayed out of our garage—or at least they did when we were there.

For our part, of course, we found the new Toyota-7 very interesting. Its main feature was that 5-liter V8, but it also had a rear wing made of a silk-type fabric and fastened to the sprung mass.

The drivers from the Can-Am races included Chuck Parsons, Peter Revson, and Gary Wilson with Lolas, and Lothar Motschenbacher, John Cordts, and several other McLaren drivers. John Cannon was there to race the special McLaren-Ford that Mario Andretti had driven in the Can-Am, and I knew it had lots of power. It was now owned by Charlie and Kerry Agapiou, who had been ace mechanics with the World Championship winning Cobra team. And John was no slouch as a driver, having won a Can-Am race in the rain at Laguna Seca. The five Toyotas were really an unknown quantity, so it promised to be an interesting race.

Qualifying was spread over two days, and we stuck to our strategy of not quite putting a lap together until the last session. With half an hour left, Jackie did a very fast lap, and our watches indicated that he was quickest of all. We had almost a whole second over the best Toyota, but the PA announcer didn't say we were fastest—he just kept on saying how fast the Toyotas were. With 15 minutes to go, I ran up to the timekeepers' box, determined to get our time posted. Burdie Martin was there, so I told him what was going on and showed him all the lap times we'd taken. I said that if the Japanese didn't intend to acknowledge our time or wanted to dispute it, he should find out now. Then we would do one more quick lap as he watched over the official timekeepers' shoulders. He said to go ahead and do the lap now. So I ran back to the pits and sent Jackie out to do another quick one. That did it. They announced Jackie's fastest lap just before the end of the session. Then they presented us with flowers. We were all very happy as we worked on the Ti22 until they kicked us out at 8:00 p.m.

When we returned to the track race morning, it was drizzling. We had rain tires, but we hadn't tested in the wet, so we put them on for the warm-up. Jackie said they didn't seem to help much, because the track was not awash, and its surface was fairly abrasive. He pointed out that if it dried out during the race, as it tended to do as the sun rose in the sky, we would have to stop and switch tires. We had no equipment to do that very quickly, so a little gamesmanship was going to be necessary.

When the time came to grid the car, we left the dry-weather tires on and took the car, the wet-weather tires, and our tools to the starting grid, and waited in the drizzle. The drivers were introduced to the large crowd that was now filling the stands, and we all got more flowers as a bunch of bowing and grinning was done all round. With five minutes to go, we jacked up the car and pretended to undo the wheels, as if to change the tires. We were on the pole, so everyone was watching us, and some immediately followed suit, including Cannon and Parsons and a couple of the Toyotas. But then we stopped and let the car down with the dry tires on it. The drizzle eased a bit more just before the flag dropped and the race started.

Jackie was passed by a Toyota going into the first turn, but it was a kamikaze move, and Jackie went round him on the exit of the turn as he tried to gather it all up again. The Toyotas could scream past us on the straight, but they lost it all in the turns. A couple of them crashed out of the race. One tried to elbow past Jackie on the back straight, but he would have none of it and dropkicked the Toyota into the toolies. He could play rough if he needed to!

That seemed to settle things down, and soon Jackie started lapping backmarkers. One Toyota was hanging on pretty good, but as the Ti22 got lighter, and the road dried, Jackie went quicker and quicker. He had an enormous lead when disaster struck. He stopped on the track right in front of our pit. I ran to the wall, and he shouted, "Something's broken in the engine." But the engine was still running and sounded OK. I leapt over the pit wall onto the track and looked down the front of the engine, past the intake stacks where they came out of the body top. The nose of the crank had sheared off, and the vee belt was loose. I gave Jackie the cut engine signal, and he clambered out of the car. The crowd applauded him, and he gave them a wave. I was sick about it because we had been so close to winning a race.

A Toyota-7 driven by Minoru Kawai was the winner, with Cannon second, and Motschenbacher third. Jackie was classified ninth. They made the race finishing order announcements, and after more bowing ceremonies, an official asked if he could have a word with me and Burdie. He said that because we'd taken over so much stuff, the freight bill for the race was going to be $44,000 over budget. He asked if we would mind if some of the non-essential stuff, like spare body parts, came home by sea. I told Burdie that they shouldn't have insisted on the strict application of the Can-Am bodywork rules. Everyone agreed that it had been a mistake to make everyone ship extra body parts, but it was too late now. So we agreed to allow some stuff to go home by sea, but not the car or the spare engine.

Next day, we were all taken by bus to the New Otani Hotel in Tokyo. At about 3:00 p.m., I went up to a suite where they paid us all our prize money in cash. With lap money and other bonuses, we got a tidy sum for our trouble. I paid Jackie his share, gave the mechanics their bonuses, and made plans for going home. Before flying home to England, Jackie agreed to race for us again in 1970 if I could keep the team going.

Chuck and Sherrie Parsons and Peter Revson decided to fly back on a different airline and stop over for a day or so in Hawaii. I decided to join them. I called Sally and asked her to bring the kids and meet me there, but she said it was too short notice and I was to get my ass back home. I then called Ernie Kanzler and made my report to him. He expressed his happiness about having the fastest car in Japan, and agreed that the engine failures had to stop. He offered to talk to John Holman about possible candidates for the engine job.

When we got home, I put the prize money in a new Autocoast account that we'd set up for the racing program, and started planning for the 1970 Can-Am season. I felt good about bringing back some money, and with the funds coming from Goodyear we would have a good chance of covering our expenses the following season. All I needed now was to get a major sponsor on board. That really would secure the future of the Autocoast racing team for at least one more year. I didn't realize how tough it would be to find a sponsor, and what I would go through to get one.

I wasn't disappointed with our performance in 1969. Everyone I met told me we'd made a real difference to the Can-Am series, and they were looking forward to watching us race in 1970. When I look back now, it seems totally amazing that we designed and built a competitive car, raced it four times, and spent less than $150,000 doing it.

BELOW: What a thrill! In 1970 I finally got to test my own car during the filming of a Texaco TV commercial set up by Bob Bondurant at Orange County Raceway in California. (Peter Bryant)

CHAPTER 27

Testing Times

Our short 1969 racing season was over, but my workload was about to increase dramatically. We needed to get ahead if we were going to beat the McLarens. Besides finding an engine man and setting up an engine development department at the shop, I decided to build a second-generation titanium chassis, which would use the engine as a stressed member. In the few races we'd done, I'd learned a whole bunch of new aerodynamic stuff that would help us with the new aero rules. Added to these tasks was finding a major sponsor. As they say in Texas, I was going to be as busy as a one-legged man in an ass-kicking contest.

Early in 1970, I tried to recruit Gary Knutson to do our engines, but he was happy with McLaren in a new facility they'd opened in Livonia, Michigan. Gary suggested I talk to Barry Crowe, an English mechanic he'd worked with at Chaparral. Barry was interested in moving from Texas to California, so I hired him to run our engine program.

Ernie Kanzler relocated us to two connected workshops in Costa Mesa. I liked the arrangement because I could have a small front office in one building for a reception area and clerical stuff, and a similar room in the other building for the drafting office. No one could get into the drafting office without going through both buildings, so we had privacy for our new program. With the help of Al Willard, I started laying out the plans for the new car.

I hired a fabricator to make tooling and parts as we developed drawings. On the advice of Timet's liaison man, Don Zimmerman, I decided not to ask the company for any help beyond supplying us with titanium. I wanted to try "hydraforming," which was then a new aerospace process, to make the titanium chassis bulkheads. It works by heating the metal to make it easier to form, and using hydraulic pressure and rubber in a press to "push" the metal sheet around an aluminum form block.

Meanwhile Deke Houlgate put me back in touch with Sports Headliners, the agency representing professional athletes for sponsorship and endorsement deals. Burt Shear there said that for about $2500 they would generate some literature to help in securing sponsorship. They would do everything else at their own expense; in return I would give them 20 percent of the money they raised. I figured it would cost about $50,000 for a full-time person, so I gave them the go-ahead. The brochure they produced was absolutely beautiful. I liked it a lot, and so did Ernie. Armed with this new marketing tool, they started banging on doors, and so did I.

We had a lot of testing and development to do with the first Ti22 car, because we needed to race it until our new car was ready. We were spread a bit thin, even though our staff had grown and now consisted of two race mechanics, a fabricator, a draftsman, an engine man, a secretary, and me. Sharon Barnes, our Girl Friday, did all the office chores including the book keeping and payroll work. Her husband, Jack, was as big a race fan as she was, so he helped out a lot too.

Ernie was still footing the bills, and I was going through the money we'd won the previous year like crap through a goose. I asked a friend, Bruce Junor, whose management skills I respected, what I could do to make things easier. He pointed out the simple fact that I wasn't just a race mechanic any more. I was trying to run a small business, but I had no business training whatsoever. He told me Loyola University did a 12-week seminar called Small Business Management that taught management and planning techniques. It cost $250 and was the best money I ever spent on education. I came out of it with much better abilities in problem-solving and decision-making. Best of all, I now knew how much I didn't know! I was able to keep the balls in the air without dropping one as often as I had before.

The new car design progressed, and with some general tidying up, the Ti22 Mk 1 was ready for testing. Now that high wings were banned for the 1970 Can-Am, I needed to resume examining the trade-off between downforce and drag. Finding the most efficient way to increase the downforce was important, and the engine power output was a factor. On a track where the straightaways are not very long, you can overcome increased drag with increased horsepower.

Barry Crowe certainly helped us out there. He found out that the Mercury outboard engine company made a special crankshaft that would increase the swept volume of our 430 cid (7.02-liter) engine to 497 cid (8.02-liter). It meant we might pick up as much as 100 bhp—I liked that idea a lot. We were looking at the possibility of 750 bhp in a car weighing less than

1500 lbs. In a naturally aspirated race engine, 100 bhp per liter was a realistic goal in those days. Modern Formula One engines get more than treble that amount of horsepower.

I contacted Convair Aviation in San Diego, the American importers of carbon filaments from Courtaulds in England. McLaren was already using carbon filaments in their bodywork components, and it was no secret how light and strong they were. McLaren wove them into "string" and crisscrossed them over the inside of the body panels to make them stronger, so they could use thinner fiberglass to make them lighter.

The engineering boss of Narmco, the company that had given us the urethane epoxy for bonding titanium sheet to aluminum sheet in the Ti22 chassis, told me that he thought Convair would be more than happy to give me a couple of pounds of filaments in exchange for an endorsement. I said I didn't think it would be enough. He laughed and said, "A couple of pounds of carbon fiber will cover your desk to a height of about two feet." That's what a lightweight material carbon fiber was.

Narmco were experts in the new field of advanced composites and supplied carbon fiber in "pre-preg" sheet form—impregnated with epoxy to avoid the laborious lay-up process that was then used to make fiberglass bodywork panels. He added, "If you make some Hydrocal molds of your bodywork, we can use a pre-preg sheet, put them in a vacuum chamber, vacuum bag them to suck out the excess resin, and make the whole body weigh less than 30 lbs. total." I tried to figure out how to make molds economically with Hydrocal, a proprietary gypsum material much like plaster of Paris. I would dearly love to have a body that weighed only 30 lbs. instead of the 85–95 lbs. we were so proud of. I was planning on making the new body four inches wider to improve the traction and handling, so I could do with some weight-saving to help offset the weight of a wider car. But I estimated the cost of making the Hydrocal molds at over $10,000, and that was out of my reach. So we did the same as McLaren and laid up the fiberglass as thin as we dared, adding the carbon as reinforcement. We saved about 20 lbs.

I'd found out very early in life that you couldn't solve problems if you didn't recognize and understand them. I figured "invention" was creating problems, and "engineering" was solving problems. The new era of auto-racing aerodynamics was all about downforce because we'd finally worked out that race cars spent more time cornering than going in a straight line. The old problem—trying to come up with a streamlined shape that slipped through the air with minimal drag—had become redundant.

The first part of the new problem was finding a way to measure the downforce on the body at a constant speed. To this end, Paul Lamar loaned us his ride-height measuring device, which measured changes in the length of the shock absorbers as the car was driven. To calibrate the system, you added weight in 50 lb. increments to the chassis near the shock and measured the shock travel, taking into account the ratio of wheel movement to it. A cable was connected to the lower end of the shock with a spring-returned slider block that held a piece of pencil lead contacting paper. The paper was dragged over a flat surface between rollers by an old windshield wiper motor. Once on track, the driver pushed a button to start the rollers, and the lead made a line on the paper that moved sideways as the ride-height changed. The distance it moved gave us the shock travel.

Our plan was to drive the Ti22 Mk 1 at a constant 100 mph at Riverside, and measure the front and rear shock travel on one side of the car. Aero downforce testing is tedious work and doesn't really require the services of a Grand Prix driver. What does require a good driver is confirmation testing after you've made the changes, so that you can really optimize the aero devices. We always did before and after testing when we made aero changes. I used Bob Bondurant and John Cannon because it was too expensive to keep bringing Jackie Oliver over.

The testing was very revealing. We found out just how effective fences on the edges of the front fenders were in increasing downforce at a relatively low cost in increased drag. In the original Ti22 design, we hadn't put a "splitter" below the radiator air intake. We added one in testing because it was just common sense. The airflow had to make up its mind to go under or over the bodywork, and a flat sheet of aluminum at the very bottom of the nose helped it to decide in favor of going over the top.

The testing revealed that it was no problem to get over 700 lbs. of downforce at only 100 mph, and that it was easy to trim out the balance between the front and rear downforce with small tabs and fins. So we configured the aerodynamics of the Ti22 for two different types of tracks—"fast" and "slow." We defined tracks with lots of straight road as fast, and tracks with lots of curves as slow. You couldn't use all the available horsepower to reach high speeds on slow tracks, so you might as well use it for downforce to increase cornering performance.

Under the 1970 Can-Am rules, wings had to be fitted directly to the chassis (whereas previously they could be fitted to the wheel uprights). This change was significant because it would add a lot of drag. Under the old rules, the body could be fairly "slippery" to minimize the drag induced by the upright-mounted wings, which put the downforce directly onto the tires. That was basically all you were trying to do—increase the tire adhesion in turns. The new rules also said that the underside skin of the wings could be no more than 31 inches off the ground. This created another problem because it meant the rear wing would be much closer to the body, so it wouldn't function as well in the turbulence coming up from the body appendages and the engine cover. We found that we could get as much rear downforce from a small spoiler lip as we could from a low-mounted wing. So for 1970 we decided just to use a spoiler on the rear.

With our aero development work and the new engine program, we started reducing the testing lap-times of the Ti22 Mk 1 at Riverside until they were very comparable to the McLaren times at the previous race there.

Meanwhile, the tough search for sponsorship was ongoing. In those days, there was a springtime NASCAR race at Riverside, and I got a call from Larry Truesdale of Goodyear to meet during the event. Larry greeted me with a firm handshake. During the Can-Jap-Am the previous November, the president of the Nippon Auto Club had given me his personal cap, dark blue with his name on the back and gold braid on the front, and I presented it to Larry as a souvenir. His face went bright red. Then he told me that because Firestone was no longer competing in the Can-Am, Goodyear had trimmed his budget, and he couldn't give me the $50,000 he'd said he would. The amount was to be cut in half. I nearly passed out! He could see I was upset and said he was very sorry, and would see if anything could be done later in the year. Meanwhile, he gave me a check for $16,000 to start with. The money I'd bought back from Japan had made up some of the shortfall, and my mother had once told me never to look a gift horse in the mouth, so I took the check and thanked him. But I knew it was going to be tough explaining this to Ernie Kanzler. I decided not to tell him until I had a sponsor. The search now took on a whole new meaning.

Our testing program was useful in this regard. Burt Shear persuaded NBC television to do a segment on "The Titanium Car" on their half-hour *Close Up* program. We made camera mounts so that they could show the car and driver from all angles on the track, and they were delighted with the results. Piers Anderton narrated, and NBC did a wonderful job of explaining the Ti22. They gave me a copy of the show on 16mm film, and we used it in our sponsorship effort. But it didn't help much, because it came too late in the day.

In May 1970, I managed to set up some appointments to see the Gatorade people and a couple of other prospects at Indianapolis. I told my secretary not to tell Burt Shear or his people, because I didn't want to give them 20 percent of any money that I found myself. But somehow they got wind that I was going to Indy, and Burt followed me there to "assist."

He turned up almost everywhere I went, until I persuaded him to do his own thing and double our chances of finding a sponsor.

I spent hours at Indy with Gulf Oil's PR man, Rick Holt, trying to convince him to add us to their list of sponsored teams, which included the Mirages at Le Mans and McLaren in both Can-Am and Formula One. Rick and I had become very good friends at Can-Am events, and he lived at the Balboa Bay Club in Newport Beach with his wife and kids. Ernie Kanzler had his yacht, *Sally,* moored nearby at Newport Harbor, and I invited Rick to come sailing a couple of times. Rick's father was the movie star Tim Holt, and his wife was Senator Barry Goldwater's daughter. He was an avid racing fan and a good friend, but he said there was no way Gulf would sponsor us too. I know he tried very hard.

I asked Larry Truesdale to introduce me to sponsors in his Speedway Hotel suite during his daily cocktail hours, on the chance they might be interested in getting involved in another form of racing. But to no avail. Very disappointed with my efforts, I flew home the day after the first weekend of qualifying. I'd exhausted every possibility and could only hope that Burt would come through. I had less than a month to get the car ready for Mosport on June 14, and we still had a final test at Orange County Raceway to do with Bob Bondurant driving.

That was when the sponsorship debacle really started. As I walked into my house, Sally greeted me and said, "I just got off the phone with Burt Shear, and you have to go to Miami straight away. You have to meet a new sponsor he found at Indy. Here's a phone number." You could have knocked me down with a feather. While I got on the phone, Sally repacked my bag. The number belonged to a company called Bomac Industries, and a man named Peter Melnick told me he had met with Burt and wanted to sponsor the Ti22 for the whole 1970 season. There was a ticket waiting for me at the Northeast Airlines counter at Los Angeles Airport, and I should get the first available flight. The last thing he said was, "Don't you want to know the name of the product that will be sponsoring your car?" I felt pretty stupid for not asking. "It's a brand-new product called Mornin' Afta. It's a hangover remedy, and we want to get plenty of TV exposure through the Can-Am." The first race of 1970 was going to be televised live on ABC's *Wide World of Sports*. It appeared Burt Shear and his partner, Bobby Frankel, had come through.

I was really excited. I was proficient at designing and building racing cars, but I was a real greenhorn when it came to business. This was a deal that had been found by Burt and Bobby, and I was glad they were going to handle the contract arrangements. I figured all they would need me for would be a publicity photograph when Melnick handed me the check.

I took off again within an hour of arriving home. I was pleasantly surprised to be handed a first-class ticket that had been left for me. A note suggested that after my arrival I should go to the Miami Airport Inn and wait for Peter Melnick to contact me.

In the morning, I got a call from Melnick, who said we would get together for dinner. I was a bit miffed about the waste of time—I could have flown that day and still made a dinner meeting. I had a lot going on at the shop and would have liked to be home for at least one night with my wife and kids after the Indy trip. But I decided not to complain. You can't piss off the guy who is going to sponsor your car.

So I worked on the plan for our final test before leaving for Canada. I made a note of the things I needed to ask the sponsor and a small checklist of things that Burt needed to cover in the deal. Burt called at about 1:00 p.m. He'd checked in and wanted to meet for lunch to go over the deal. He told me he'd met the sponsor at Indy and he had a contract ready to sign. He mentioned an amount of $10,000 a race for the whole series of 10 races.

In hindsight, I was very naïve in those days. Ernie had some of the finest legal people in America at his disposal, and all I needed to do was to ask him for help. This wasn't my first mistake. I would soon make some even dumber ones in my self-appointed role as the team's business manager.

I finally got to meet Melnick. He was extremely courteous and friendly, and put me completely at ease about his intention to sponsor the Ti22. I was immediately comforted by his sincerity and relieved that he was such a nice guy. To this day, I genuinely believe he liked and respected me.

Next day, Melnick said that he had some things to do and asked me to come along. He made a number of errands and took me to his office, which was surprisingly small, and then to his home, where his wife made coffee, and we chatted about racing. He had a nice house, but nothing too luxurious—in fact, it was much like mine in California. He seemed like a pretty ordinary guy, not a wealthy entrepreneur who could afford to sponsor a racing team. I asked if he was just getting Bomac going. He said he had just secured the distribution rights for Mornin' Afta for several states and was getting things under way. He gave me a case of the product and said it was so fantastic that Bomac would soon be in a much larger facility. He hoped to have a much better sponsorship arrangement with me in 1971. He dropped me back at the hotel and said that the first check for $10,000 would be delivered to California within a week.

I flew to L.A. the next morning more than just happy. I was so up I could have probably flown back without a plane!

BELOW: At Mosport, Mike Lowman and I talk to Jackie Oliver as Al Willard listens intently from the other side of the Ti22. The Goodyear technicians at the left are taking tire temperatures. The square hole at the back of the car is for intake air to the engine oil cooler, while the round holes on either side of it take in brake-cooling air. (Dave Friedman)

CHAPTER 28

Head to Head with McLaren

We had one more test to do before the first Can-Am race of 1970 at Mosport Park, Canada. It was during that test that I might have screwed up the best chance of sponsorship I ever had.

Bob Bondurant had a very special pupil at his high-performance driving school that day—movie star Paul Newman. He and Bob were already good friends after working together on the movie *Winning*. Bob had just got out of the Ti22 when Newman walked up. His eyes lit up when he saw the car, and he asked Bob to ask me if he could drive it for a lap or two. Being ultra-protective about damaging the car only two weeks before the first race, I said all I could do was ask Bob to give Newman a ride.

Can you imagine anyone better placed to sponsor us than Paul Newman? He might even have bought into the team the way he did much later with Carl Haas in the CART series. Sometimes I still ask myself, "What if?"

Paul allowed us to strap him into the car and tie his arms with duct tape to the rollover bar behind the cockpit to stop them flailing around in the corners. After a couple of quick laps, Bob came into the pits with a grinning Newman. He said he loved the car and the experience, and warned me, "One day, I'll get to drive this car."

That was a prophetic statement. Newman did drive a Ti22 the following winter at Ontario Motor Speedway for a TV special he made about his racing experiences, called *Once Upon a Wheel*.

Meanwhile, the first race loomed closer. Our new sponsor sent us some Mornin' Afta decals, and we put them on the car and spent money on PR and materials, although we hadn't yet received the first $10,000 sponsorship installment. It didn't cross my mind that they might not send it—why would someone fly me all the way to Miami if they weren't serious? The day before our transporter was due to leave for Mosport, Peter Melnick called to say that the check would be personally delivered that day.

The check arrived later that morning. I endorsed it, gave it to my secretary, and asked her to pay it into the bank account I'd opened after the Can-Jap-Am. Ernie Kanzler had been pretty distant for about a month because he was going through some tough times in his personal life. He'd moved out of his house in Bel-Air and was living in a condo on Newport Bay.

I saw Ernie next day and told him about the check. You could always tell when Ernie was pleased—his face lit up, and he grinned from ear to ear. I suggested that we spend a couple of grand of the money for some PR at the race, since it was going to be televised on ABC's *Wide World of Sports*. I went back to my office and called Deke Houlgate about doing some PR for us at Mosport. He was way ahead of me. He'd received some product from Bomac and had already put together press kits to take to the race. He'd even called a PR buddy in Toronto and hired a model to be Miss Mornin' Afta during race week.

The Wednesday before the race, Deke and I flew into Toronto on Air Canada from L.A. We went straight to the Canadiana Hotel in Bowmanville, and then to the garage where the car was to be housed when we were not at the track. In those days, most tracks had no garage lighting or security for working on the cars overnight, so most of us rented space in local garages. Automobile dealers were usually accommodating because having famous race drivers around was good for publicity. The car wasn't there yet, so we went back to the hotel. Deke went out and rented a mobile house trailer for the weekend to use as press hospitality center for Bomac and Mornin' Afta. I thought it was a bit excessive, but Deke assured me it would really help in creating the best image because in those days there were virtually no press facilities at the track.

Next day, our race car arrived, along with Debbie Molina (our Miss Mornin' Afta) and our driver, Jackie Oliver. That evening we were invited to the Toronto town hall for the mayor's reception welcoming the race teams to Canada. Like the race itself, the reception was sponsored by the Molson beer company. We sat opposite the mayor and Stirling Moss, in his role as the "commissioner" for the series sponsor, Johnson Wax. Being a legendary driver and very easy to talk with, he was a great spokesman for the Can-Am series. The soup had been served, and we were having a nice chat with the mayor, and when a waiter came up, told me there was a long-distance call for me in the lobby. It was my secretary, Sharon. She told me that the bank had just called to inform us that there were insufficient funds to clear the check from Bomac. I told Sharon

> **OPPOSITE:** The Mosport pace car leads the two McLarens of Gurney and Hulme, followed by Peter Revson's Lola and Oliver's Ti22. George Follmer is behind Jackie in the Mk 1 AVS Shadow. (Pete Lyons)

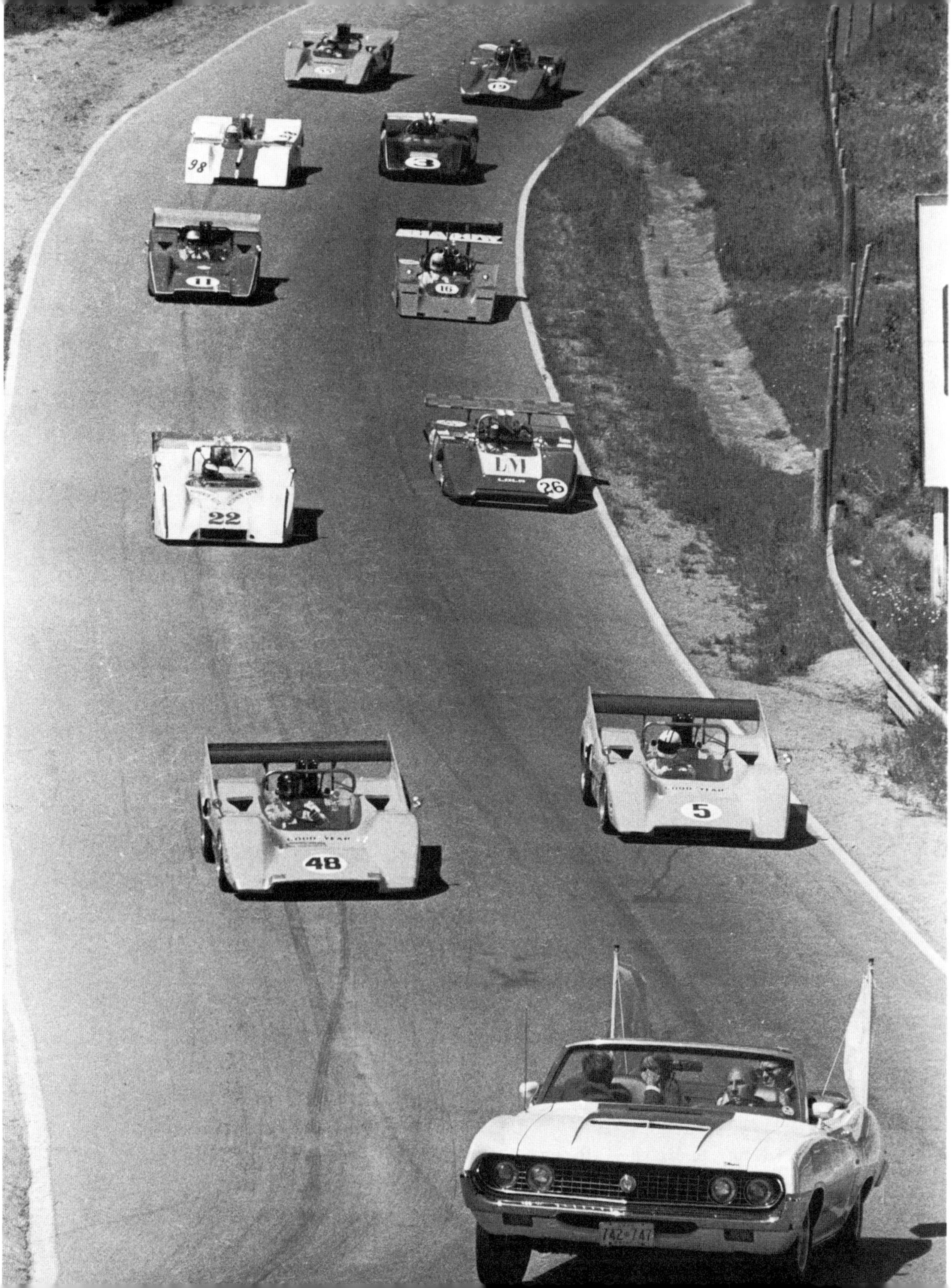
98
3
11
16
LM
26
22
GOOD YEAR
48
GOOD YEAR
5

not to worry, because it was probably just a bookkeeping snafu—the sort of thing that can happen to the best companies. She didn't sound convinced, and neither was I. Before going back to the table, I decided I needed a stiff drink to calm me down and stopped at the cocktail bar for a brandy. When I got back to the table, they were serving the desserts, but I wasn't feeling hungry any more.

I left the table again to call Melnick. He apologized and said he would be sending one of his people to the race and, not to worry, he would bring another check.

Next day we were all at the track for practice. I had a look at the latest McLaren M8D, and I was a bit flattered to see that, like the Ti22, it had fins along its sides. They ran them back past the rear wheel arches and used them as endplates for the rear wing, which was now mounted solid to the chassis behind the gearbox. I remembered that Bruce McLaren had told me the previous season that he thought I'd had a good idea, and he and Tyler Alexander had probably tested the fins long before they finalized the new bodywork.

Sadly, only 10 days before this opening race of the 1970 Can-Am, Bruce had been killed in a testing accident in England. The McLaren team was in shock but had the presence of mind to hire Dan Gurney to drive instead of Bruce. Like the previous year, he produced a really fast qualifying lap, more than 1 second quicker than anyone else. Dan always flew at Mosport. Denny Hulme, driving with bandaged hands after his car had caught fire at Indianapolis a couple of weeks before, qualified second, and Jackie Oliver was third in our Ti22, half a second slower. Peter Revson was fourth in the latest Lola T220, ahead of Lothar Motschenbacher in his ex-works McLaren M8B. The only other American-built car was the new AVS Shadow, designed by Trevor Harris, which George Follmer qualified sixth.

The Shadow was tiny. It was very radical in design, with small, 10-inch-diameter front wheels and 12-inch rears, allowing a very low body profile with minimal aerodynamic drag. It looked like a big kart with a huge engine. Follmer told me it handled like a kart, too. It was fast on the straights, but its brakes were too small. Trevor Harris was an old friend of mine, and everything he did was interesting and exciting. The car attracted a lot of attention, and the fans loved it. The Can-Am tech people were very upset because Trevor had built the radiators into the rear wing, and they were trying to say it was illegal. They made him relocate them before the next race. But I was really glad to see the car because, in the absence of the Chaparrals, it certainly brought some technical flavor to the Can-Am.

There was another new car, this one from the United Kingdom. It was the BRM P154, designed by Tony Southgate with the customary Chevy engine in the back. Driven by

Canadian George Eaton, it qualified seventh, but it was nearly 5 seconds slower than our car and didn't appear to handle very well. Our real competition was the McLaren team.

It was obvious that Barry Crowe had done a great job on our new engines, and we now had comparable power to the McLarens. Jackie told me he had trouble getting a clear lap in qualifying, and he thought we really did have a chance to win. The whole team was elated by that statement.

On race day, Deke laid out his press kits in his rented mobile home and filled plastic glasses with orange juice mixed with Mornin' Afta to be handed out to the press by Miss Mornin' Afta. Although a man who said he was from Bomac Industries turned up before the race, he said he didn't know anything about a check. But I decided to wait until Monday to sort out those things.

The car went very well in the warm-up, and Jackie said it felt really good on full tanks. We had over 100 bhp more than we'd had in 1969, and it made the car come out of the turns like a rocket. The Ti22 was getting a lot of attention and looked great. By the time they'd finished the pre-race show and paraded the drivers around the track, I was wound up like an eight-day clock. I was ready to go racing, and so was Jackie.

Hulme shot into the lead of the 80-lap race, with Gurney and Oliver hot on his heels. After about 10 laps, Jackie managed to squeeze past Dan, and at the halfway point, only about 3 seconds separated the first three cars. They were pulling away from the rest of the field at a fast clip. Then, on lap 40, Jackie got past Denny and took the lead. It was the first time since the Chaparral of Jim Hall in 1968 that an American car had led a Can-Am race. We all cheered him on as he went past the pits.

Dan also went past Denny and started swapping fastest laps with Jackie. Around lap 50, Dan squeezed past into the lead, but Jackie continued to try like crazy to get back again. It was really exciting—the best race anyone had seen since McLaren's domination had begun.

Dan and Jackie were going at it so hard that 16 laps from the end they had lapped all the rest including Denny, who was in great pain from his blistered hands and could hardly hang onto the wheel. The McLaren of Motschenbacher, in fourth place, was about to be lapped for a third time. He let Dan go by with no problem, but for some reason he decided to block Jackie. For more than three laps, he ignored the waved blue flags from the corner marshals, not to mention waved fists from Jackie. Dan went 12 seconds ahead, and Jackie had to make a kamikaze effort at the end of the curving Andretti Straight. In the process,

Motschenbacher was forced off the road and crashed heavily—near where a Canadian driver named Dick Brown had unfortunately been killed in practice in a modified McLaren M6B. Luckily Lothar was unhurt. I hate to see anyone crash, but at the time, I felt it was a just reward.

Jackie managed to make up about 3 seconds on Dan but just ran out of laps. They had both broken the lap record and lapped faster than the Formula One cars that had raced at Mosport the previous August. They both finished two laps ahead of Denny, and seven laps ahead of fourth-placed Tony Dean in a Porsche 908. Revson, Follmer, and Eaton all failed to finish.

After the slowdown lap, Jackie said to me, "There's going to be a problem! Motschenbacher wouldn't move over—I got mad and booted him off." I told him not to worry. I said I was going to file a protest against Motschenbacher's blocking behavior. So I paid my $100 protest fee. Lothar counter-protested Jackie for pushing him off the track. Jackie was fined $50 for violating the FIA Sporting Code, and Lothar was reprimanded for ignoring the marshals.

In the post-race press conference in the control tower, Dan Gurney said it was one of the hardest and most exciting races he'd had in his entire career, and praised the efforts of our team. Dan neither asked nor gave any quarter on the track, but he was always such a gentleman off it. That moment was a new high point in my racing life. We had all done our best to beat the dominant McLaren team, and had come closer than anyone had in a long time. The Ti22 was very competitive—and we had a new car in the works that no one knew about.

OPPOSITE: A Can-Am sight not seen since 1968: An American-built car, the Ti22 driven by Jackie Oliver, is leading the McLaren of Dan Gurney at Mosport Park in Canada. (Dale Von Treba)

The next day the mechanics, Mike Lowman and Al Willard, went back to the garage in Bowmanville to start getting the Ti22 ready for the next race two weeks later at St. Jovite, near Montreal. Jackie and I picked up Miss Mornin' Afta and took her with us to the bank in Toronto to cash the prize money check for $11,000, minus Canadian tax. I gave Jackie his 40 percent and paid Debbie her fee.

On the way to the airport, I finally told Jackie about the problems with the sponsor's check and that the Mosport prize money had saved our asses. He told me that if Motschenbacher hadn't gotten in his way, he would have won that race because the Ti22 was quicker than the McLaren with full tanks. He flew back to England, and I flew back to L.A., both looking forward to the next race with high expectations.

BELOW: Dan Gurney in the McLaren leads Denny Hulme and Jackie Oliver down the hill on the first lap at St. Jovite in 1970. Just a few minutes later the Ti22 flipped over backwards at 160 mph while cresting the hill on the back straight. (Dave Friedman)

CHAPTER 29

Strong Stuff, Titanium . . .

Comforted by being able to tell Ernie Kanzler that we had been in the money at Mosport—before I had to tell him about our other problems—I called him from Toronto Airport before flying back to L.A. He congratulated me and asked me to pass it on to the team. He said the race had been great to watch on TV, and everyone was excited about the car and Jackie doing so well. But he added that I should try to get this sponsorship business taken care of before the next race. I promised to do just that and got on the plane.

The Air Canada people at the gate recognized my name from the race publicity and kindly upgraded me to first class for the long flight to L.A. The Canadians are great racing fans, and any race in Canada is well supported. So I was feeling no pain when my secretary, Sharon, picked me up from the airport with her husband, Jack. She was really nervous about the sponsorship problem and needed me to reassure her that all would be well. In truth, I had no idea whether it would. When we got to my home in Santa Ana, Sally invited them in for a drink, and we all sat and talked about the race. The telephone kept busy with friends calling to say how much they'd enjoyed watching it on TV. My young son, Paul, was over the moon about it all. Nothing dampened my joy. I was totally confident about sorting out the sponsorship. Fortunately I had no idea what I was in for.

Early next morning, I went in to the office and called the head office of Mornin' Afta. I got their address from one of the sample packets I'd opened that morning. The stuff really worked—I was impressed. I was surprised to learn that the company claimed to know nothing about any sponsorship deal, suggesting that if I had one it was strictly with Bomac Industries, which had a deal to distribute their product in some states.

Next I called Melnick in Miami. He was unavailable, so I left word for him to call me. There wasn't much more I could do at that time, so I busied myself with the problems of preparing the Ti22 for the next race at St. Jovite on June 26.

I finally got a call from Melnick several days later. He said he was very sorry for the mess with the sponsorship check and suggested that the best thing for me to do was to fly to Miami on my way to St. Jovite the following week and pick up the money then. He had some people he wanted me to meet and he would supply a ticket from Los Angeles to Montreal via Miami. What day did I want to go? I told him, and he said a ticket would be waiting for me at the L.A. Airport and I would be booked in at the Miami Airport Inn. I agreed and hung up. I still had a very odd feeling about it all but decided that I should concentrate on getting the car ready for St. Jovite. After all, I now had enough money in the bank to meet the payroll expenses for a few weeks.

I talked with the guys in the back room about the new tooling they were making to build the new Ti22 car. I'd decided we could form and weld the titanium ourselves, so we were busy making fixtures and building some new purge chambers to use for the welding. The chambers allowed us to weld the metal in a totally inert atmosphere by passing argon gas into the chamber and slowly exhausting it out of a one-way valve on the top. The chamber was made from heavy, clear plastic sheets, welded at the corners and bolted to the sides of a box with handling gloves fastened inside it. It was crude, but it sure worked well. I even managed to get in a couple of days on the drawing board to work on the new suspension design before I had to leave for Miami.

All the racing magazines and papers wrote very nice things about the Ti22. Brock Yates put a full-page picture of the car in *Road & Track* and wrote a very complimentary article about it called "The Great White Hope." I sincerely hoped that the great publicity would help us to get a better sponsor. We had nine more races to run and could sure use some extra money.

There was some hope for new sponsorship from Texaco of Canada. The previous month, we'd helped Bob Bondurant make a TV commercial for them at Orange County Raceway in California. During a break in the filming, Bob had both scintillated and terrified the Texaco PR man by taking him round for a couple of quick laps in the Ti22. I had then managed to get him to agree to an exploratory sponsorship by providing us with gasoline and some contingency money. It wasn't much, but Texaco hadn't sponsored a Can-Am car before, and I was hopeful that something bigger would come of it.

The following Friday, I picked up the ticket and flew to Miami. Although I met with Melnick and was again promised a check, once again it failed to materialize. The next day

I received a message that he had been called out of town but would be in touch with my office. I left for the airport totally mystified. I figured that was the end of my relationship with Mornin' Afta. To this day, I am still not sure who Peter Melnick really was, and why he seemed to be interested in sponsoring a racing team.

When I arrived in Montreal, my pal Rick Holt, who did the PR for Gulf Oil and the McLaren team, met me at the airport. He had suggested I should come out early to meet up with a friend of his named Jean Legault, who was a French-Canadian motor racing journalist who might help me find a one-time sponsor for the race. At that point, I would have talked to Adolf Hitler if I thought he might sponsor the car. Jean immediately started to run around furiously trying to find us a Canadian sponsor, but it would all be to no avail.

Jean did help out in other ways. He put me up in his apartment, and arranged to interview me for the Canadian Broadcasting Corporation the Sunday before the race. I speak halting French, but it's not good enough to be on the air, so Jean promised to ask me a bunch of questions that could easily be answered with a simple "oui" or "non." The interview was a gas. When Jean was introduced, the moderator of the program said in French: "And now let me introduce Jean Legault, who is a renowned motor-racing journalist. Jean, there's a very well known priest at the Cathedral St. Jean Paul de Baptiste here in Montreal. His name is Father Legault, like yours. Is he a relative of yours?" Jean replied: "Yes, he's my father." Everyone in the studio laughed so hard they had to put on a commercial break.

On Wednesday, I collected Jackie Oliver from the airport, and after a meeting with some Labatt Breweries PR people to help publicize the race, we drove up to St. Jovite to meet up with the mechanics and check out how the car was progressing. Al and Mike had brought the car to the garage at the Grey Rocks Hotel in Mont Tremblant, very near the track, where we were staying. The car was ready, and we were excited about our chances of winning this one.

The practice and qualifying days were spent trying to stop the bottom of the monocoque tub of the Ti22 from wearing out on the many bumps on the St. Jovite circuit, while also trying to make quick laps with a driver who was learning the nuances of the track. I warned Jackie about the hill on the back straight. In races past, a couple of cars had done frightening back flips on the crest of this hill. One of them had been a Lola driven by a British Airways pilot, Hugh Dibley, who remarked that he never thought his first air crash would be in a racing car! The possibility of it happening again was very real. To minimize the risk, we set the gearing so that Jackie had to change gear just as he approached the apex. This tended to pitch the car forward at the apex and put the nose down a little. The important thing for the driver to remember was not to go up the hill close behind another car. He could lose the downforce on the nose and arrive at the apex with the nose up and ready for takeoff at 165 mph.

Dan Gurney again set the pace in his McLaren M8D with Denny Hulme three-tenths slower in the second works car, followed by Jackie in the Ti22, another half second down. But Jackie was very confident about his chances in the race, knowing from Mosport that his car was faster than the McLarens on full tanks. The works McLarens had 465 cid Chevy engines and they didn't know that we'd found a way to increase ours to a healthy 497 cid. The extra 30 cubic inches made about another 50 bhp and it really showed up with full tanks. Oliver's nemesis from the previous race, Lothar Motschenbacher, was alongside him on the grid, just under a second slower. Everyone was amazed that he'd been able to repair his car so quickly after the crash at Mosport. It was a smaller field at St. Jovite, with only 22 cars. The differential in qualifying times indicated there would be cars getting lapped within 12 laps. This would be a big factor, and Jackie was concerned about the traffic getting in his way again on such a narrow track. He was very determined to get past the McLarens as soon as he could, while they still had full tanks.

During the race morning warm-up session, the front left lower titanium suspension wishbone was broken by one of the bumps, and Jackie limped the car into the pits. We quickly changed it and hid it from those intrepid, nosy press guys, like Pete Lyons from *Competition Press & AutoWeek* magazine. We were still hoping to get some sponsorship from the Titanium Metal Corporation and didn't want any bad publicity about broken titanium parts to spoil our chances. Not that Pete ever wrote anything nasty about anyone—it wasn't in his nature.

A few cars came perilously close to lifting off at the top of the hill during the warm-up, and the track announcer talked on the PA system about the danger for competitors. Prompted by the race organizers, he even suggested that every team should make sure they had an adequate spoiler on the front of their car.

As the cars were called to the starting grid, and Jackie was putting on his helmet and gloves, Jerry Schmidt, a photographer who worked for *Competition Press & AutoWeek* with Pete Lyons, walked up and spoke to him. He said, "Jackie, I was watching you going over the top of that hill on the back straight in the warm-up, and your car looked nose-high. In fact, any car that was following others up the hill was going a bit airborne off the top. It looked real dangerous, so be extra careful on the first lap." Jackie smiled, said OK, and climbed into the car. I thought to myself, "Wow—he took the words right out of my mouth."

Jackie had the bit well and truly between his teeth. The Ti22 and the two orange McLarens ran away from all the others as soon as the flag dropped to signal the rolling start. They disappeared from the sight of the pits after the first right-hand turn, but you could hear the noise of all the engines echoing through those St. Jovite hills like a squadron of fighter planes from World War II. After what seemed like an eternity, the first McLaren reappeared around the last turn, closely followed by the second one. There was a big gap before Lothar appeared in his red McLaren. My heart dropped down into my shoes.

I ran to the race control center at the end of the pits. Burdie Martin, the chief steward, was standing in the doorway. "What happened to Oliver?" I yelled at him. Nobody in race control would tell me anything, so I waited for the track announcer to come over the PA with some kind of comment, but nobody said a word. In those days, when someone had a crash at a race and was hurt, they never announced anything until they knew the facts. So I figured Jackie had gotten into a wreck. There was nothing we could do about it. We just had to wait until someone told us what was going on. Meanwhile I counted the cars as they all went by, and there were four fewer than when the race had started. If the crash had been serious, they would have stopped the race to clean up the mess—so what the hell was going on?

About 15 minutes after the start, Jackie walked into the pits carrying his helmet. He looked at me with sadness in his eyes and said, "Peter, I'm sorry, but the car looks totaled!" I asked him if he was OK. He said he was, but the car wasn't. He explained that he'd gone up the hill close behind Denny Hulme and the Ti22 had just taken off and flipped over backwards at about 160 mph. He'd been so helpless that he just moved his hands to the bottom of the steering wheel, and closed his eyes as it flipped and cartwheeled several times before landing right side up, just off the road. Amazingly, Jackie had only a small scratch on his knee and a very slight whiplash to his neck, so he didn't need to go to the hospital.

I was in shock for a couple of minutes. Then I began to wonder why this had happened just as we were getting somewhere, and whether we could fix the car in time for the next race. I realized it would take us about five days to get the car back to the shop in California, and the race was less than two weeks away, back across North America at Watkins Glen in upper New York state. There was no way to do it. Besides, we had no idea how badly damaged the car was.

Jackie asked me to drive him back to the hotel for a soak in a hot tub, so I asked Al and Mike to collect the car on the transporter and bring it back to the hotel to find out the exact extent of the damage. Most of the suspension had been torn off in the crash, which was supposed to happen. Most of the bodywork had been destroyed in the cartwheels. The accident was a real test for the titanium chassis, and it had stood up impressively well. At first glance, the chassis looked pretty badly gronked and twisted a bit, but the cockpit and rollover bar were still intact, and that had saved Jackie's life. We all agreed that the car should be taken straight back to California and we would make the decisions about repairing it there. I phoned Ernie Kanzler and gave him the bad news. He took it pretty well.

Next day, I took Jackie to the airport and flew home. I took out my notepad on the flight and tried to analyze where we were and where we needed to go. I found myself trying to answer some pretty tricky questions. The Ti22 had finished second at Mosport and qualified third at St. Jovite. The way the car came out of the corners indicated that it had better acceleration than the McLaren. Was this due to better traction, lighter weight, or a more powerful engine?

Where did the driver figure into the equation? Jackie had passed Dan Gurney for the lead at Mosport, and that was a track where Dan had held the lap record. Was Jackie a better driver than Dan? Did I have the fastest car but not the fastest driver? Or did I have the fastest driver and not the fastest car? Or neither?

OPPOSITE: Mike Lowman photographs the wreckage while Ernie Kanzler climbs up for a closer look after the transporter got back from Canada. (Al Willard)

I had been taught at the Loyola University course on business management that a good way to solve choice problems was by doing a "trade study." You work out the most important features and qualities you need, and see how your various choices stack up against that list. I ended up giving Jackie Oliver the major slice of the credit for the success of the team and decided that if he was going to win a race, I needed to give him a better car. I also decided that if the Ti22 Mk 1 couldn't be repaired inside four weeks, I wouldn't even try to fix it with my limited resources. Instead, I would accelerate the build of the new car. After all, my goal was to win a Can-Am race—not chase after the McLaren team with a second-place car.

The battered Ti22 arrived back at the shop a few days later, and we tore it apart and checked the chassis. The titanium panels had been glue-bonded together as well as riveted for better strength. They proved to be very difficult to separate without distortion of the mating pieces. The chassis was twisted and seriously damaged. I estimated that it would require replacement of almost 80 percent of the tub members to regain its former strength and be good enough to race. That would mean fabrication of many new titanium parts, and this was not an easy thing to do. I'd made up my mind on the aircraft that I wanted to race a winner and not an also-ran, so we stripped it bare of all useful parts and pressed on with the new car.

BELOW: For the new Ti22's debut at Laguna Seca in 1970, we were assigned the pit next to McLaren. Mike Lowman is at the rear of the car, while I'm at the door. Al Willard is helping Jackie buckle in as Alex Groundsel watches. (Dale Von Treba)

CHAPTER 30

Ti22 Mk 2 Delivers

In designing the new Ti22 Mk 2, I took full advantage of everything we'd learned with the first car. Barry Crowe had managed to get even more horsepower from the 497 cid engine since the start of the season. We'd started out with 430 cid, so we'd had lots of horsepower before, but the first car had never reached terminal velocity at Riverside. The Mk 1 was still accelerating when Jackie had to brake at the end of the long back straight, even with the aerodynamic drag from the downforce it was generating. I decided to increase the wheelbase by 2 inches to 196 inches and make the car 4 inches wider, to use the extra horsepower to generate even more downforce.

I also decided to make the engine a fully stressed member again and to mount the rear suspension on the transmission housing. The suspension of the Mk 1 had been mounted to a subframe connected to the monocoque tub. The engine would be mounted to a plate on the front face of the cylinder block and reinforced by a subframe that connected to the block just ahead of the clutch bell housing. This was meant to result in slightly lower weight but slightly higher chassis torsional stiffness—a win-win situation.

ABOVE: Jackie Oliver takes the Ti22 Mk 2 down the hill straight at Laguna Seca. (Bob Tronolone)

I revised front wishbone suspension geometry and mounting arrangement to make for less "dive" at the front of the car under heavy braking. I decided to run the car one inch lower if possible and to use even stiffer springing, which would restrict the vertical travel even more. I didn't want any body roll at all if I could avoid it. I wanted as little disturbance as possible to the tire's contact patch area. I was hoping that all these improvements would add up to a car that could beat any McLaren with anyone driving it.

The crash at St. Jovite had a bad effect on our financial situation, simply because it screwed up the cash flow coming in from the racing. The $11,000 from Mosport had really helped, and Ernie Kanzler liked the idea of the car supporting itself. But now we were becoming a drain on his cash at a critical point in his business. He'd moved his boat-building operations into a bigger facility and was trying to make production boats, so his inventory costs were going up just as his overhead was. On top of that, he'd just gone through a costly divorce from his first wife. He'd become engaged to Annie, the former wife of a former neighbor, and was getting static from his trust fund administrator for spending too much.

Ernie called me into his office and told me I needed to get some sponsorship pretty soon, or he would be forced to stop making the rent and payroll payments. As I drove back to the office, I decided not to share that information with anyone because team morale needed to be as high as possible—and it would do no good, anyway.

I tried to think of any way I could possibly raise money to continue with the team. I still had Sports Headliners out chasing sponsors, and I made a call to Larry Truesdale at Goodyear in an attempt to get the rest of the money he'd agreed to send me. Larry said he didn't see how he could ask Goodyear to provide financial support for a car that was no longer in the races. I saw his point.

I called Jerry Willets, an old friend in Ridgefield, Connecticut, to ask for advice and even financial help. His full name was J. Macy Willets, and his grandmother was one of the same Macys who founded the world's largest department store. We'd met when I'd lived in Connecticut and worked for Motorsport Design Corporation, in which he'd been a partner. Jerry had owned a USAC Midget dirt car and loved racing. He was very sympathetic about my situation but couldn't help with sponsorship. However, he did tell me that in an emergency, he could be counted on for one month's payroll money if that would help. I thanked him, and in fact did borrow that money from him one time, repaying it later out of my own pocket.

As those options disappeared, I thought of another. At the penultimate 1969 Can-Am race at Riverside, our garage had been next to a team of amateur racers called Ecurie Vickie. They were a small band of enthusiasts with an old McLaren and a home-built engine, and they'd decided to enter a big race and see how they went. The car was a very old M1B and wasn't very well prepared, and they failed to qualify. It was all organized by Richard Callouette, a Los Angeles attorney who had named the team after his wife. They were very sincere in their efforts but seriously underfunded.

Callouette and I had had several friendly conversations about the Can-Am and he'd told me he was going to try and raise money to make a proper attempt at it the following year. During the Christmas holiday, he'd invited me to a party for potential investors in Ecurie Vickie in an Italian restaurant on Sunset Strip in Hollywood. There had been a lot of people, most of them professionals—doctors, lawyers, small business owners.

Now I wondered how Callouette's fundraising efforts were going, and I invited him to Costa Mesa to see what we were doing. Callouette listened to my tale of woe and thought he might be able to come up with a way for us to carry on. He asked me to set up an appointment for him to meet with Ernie. He said they'd already raised about $35,000 from supporters and could probably get more if they were involved with the Ti22 program.

My plate was very full with getting the new car built, so I was more than happy to turn the money stuff over to someone I thought could handle it right. Based on our first meetings, I felt I could trust Callouette. I figured this was the only option I had, and without his help, I would probably fail anyway.

As I understood it, Callouette's plan was to form a new partnership. Ernie would sign over his racing assets to the partnership, and Ecurie Vickie would take over the financial responsibilities. I would become a full partner with a 20 percent stake and still run the racing operations. The team's name would be changed to Titanium Racing Components (TRC), and we expected to use our titanium fabrication capabilities to generate cash flow in the off-season.

The deal would ultimately cost me dearly in terms of my career and finances. In retrospect, it's easy to think of things I might have done differently. But it all looked good at the time. I thought I'd saved everyone's job, and kept the team going so we would get the second car built. And I thought I'd gone from owning nothing to joining a partnership in which I had a 20 percent stake.

So I resumed the racing business at hand and went full-speed with the program to finish the new car. If we were going to get back to the Can-Am that season, I needed more staff. Alex Groundsel, an English mechanic who was an old friend of mine, joined the crew. Pretty soon, we were working day and night on the Mk 2 car.

When the new bodywork arrived, we took the twisted tub from the wrecked Ti22 Mk 1 and put it outside the back door of the shop to make room. Pretty soon everyone forgot it was out there, and one weekend, it disappeared. We figured the trash people had taken it and decided not to worry about it—after all, no one could use it for anything. Many years later, when vintage Can-Am car prices went through the ceiling, that twisted tub would probably have fetched around $200,000, because it was the key part to cloning the only Ti22 Mk 1 ever made. Isn't hindsight great?

One day, a very nice surprise came from Sports Headliners. They had persuaded Norris Industries, a large company in Los Angeles, to sponsor the car for the last two races of 1970. The president, Ken Norris, had agreed to pay $10,000 a race to get their name on the car. Norris Industries was in the automotive industry as one of the biggest wheel suppliers to the local GM plant, among others. In complete contrast, they also made porcelain toilet fixtures.

At our recommendation, Deke Houlgate was hired to do their PR. Deke went to meet Ken Norris and learned he was missing an eye. Ken was very self-conscious about it. He would often wear a patch over it in private, but on public occasions, he just had the glass eye. In those days, a famous shirt maker called Hathaway had a TV commercial and advertisements in magazines, using a man with a patch over one eye as the sophisticated executive-type buyer of their shirts. When Deke saw Ken's patch, he envisaged a good publicity angle. Somehow Ken was persuaded to wear the patch when he came down to the workshop for some publicity photographs with the car. I didn't know he'd lost an eye when he showed up with his patch on. After they'd taken the pictures, I was talking with him in my office and expressed my concern for what I thought was a temporary eye injury. I asked him how long he would have to wear the patch. He said, "I've lost an eye—didn't Deke tell you?" I managed to change the subject back to the car, and we parted friends. But I never saw him wear the patch again.

The *Los Angeles Times* liked to publicize their Riverside Can-Am race well in advance, and they ran a five-column picture spread of Ken Norris with the new Ti22—eye patch and all, in full view of millions of readers. When Norris saw it, he was very upset. That picture was Deke's undoing with Norris Industries. After the Riverside Can-Am, he wasn't used for PR again.

The car wasn't finished until the week before the Laguna race, so we didn't get any testing time on it. Jackie Oliver flew over. He usually stayed at my house in those days, and we drove to Laguna Seca together in his Porsche 911 he had sent over from England.

It was a seven-hour drive normally, but we did it in five. We went up Interstate 5 and then cut across to the Pacific Coast Highway, which was a straight and fast road with hardly any traffic. The Porsche got very light at the front at about 140mph. You could feel the front-end dance from side to side as it lifted. I'd never experienced "aero push" before.

There had been six Can-Am races since St. Jovite, and a McLaren had won all but one of them. Denny Hulme's hands had fully recovered and he'd won at Watkins Glen, Edmonton, Mid-Ohio, and Brainerd. Peter Gethin had replaced Dan Gurney, and had won at Road America. McLaren had failed only at Road Atlanta, where neither car had finished and Tony Dean's little Porsche 908 had won in the rain.

Laguna Seca was the penultimate race that year, and the track was extremely hard to pass on. We knew Jackie always went better in the race than in qualifying, but he would need to be on the front row of the grid to have any chance of beating Denny. But the opposition was getting stiffer, and a front row spot would be hard to get.

At the Glen, Jim Hall had shown his new secret weapon, the ground-effect, fully skirted Chaparral 2J fan-car, and Jackie Stewart had surprised everyone by taking third place on the grid. Hall had raced the highly controversial 2J again at Atlanta with Vic Elford driving, and he had grabbed pole position by over a second from Denny. Jim Hall and Chevrolet looked poised to take over from McLaren, but the reliability of the JLO engine that ran the big fans, sucking the car towards the track surface, was still a factor.

Other fast company for us at Laguna included Peter Revson, who was getting faster at every race in the new Lola T220. There was also Chuck Parsons in his works Lola, Chris Amon in the new March 707, a couple of BRMs for George Eaton and Pedro Rodriguez, a Ferrari 512 for Jim Adams, privately entered McLarens for Lothar Motschenbacher and David Hobbs, and the Ford G7A for John Cannon. All told, there were 33 cars entered for the race, and it promised to be a real battle.

The new Ti22 Mk 2 was quick right out of the box. Every time Jackie went on the track for practice, we were very careful to measure exactly how much fuel was used. Our fuel tank held about 76 gallons, but we wouldn't need all that capacity for this race. Every gallon that wasn't needed added more than 7 lbs. to the weight of the car, so it was important to know how much was in it at all times. I put one mechanic in charge of measuring and checking and refueling the gas tank.

The Chaparral 2J was almost a second quicker than anything else in practice, until the engine blew in a big way and ended Elford's weekend. That left Hulme and Gethin at the front of the grid in the works McLarens, Denny on 58.8 seconds, and Peter on 60.6. Then came Jackie and Revson with identical lap times of 61.2 seconds, and Amon in the March with a 61.8. With the fastest cars lapping at just over 60 seconds a lap and the slower cars at 70 seconds, the leaders should start lapping the slower cars within only seven laps.

The Can-Am Challenge Cup was the most important and prestigious international sports-racing series ever run in North America, and maybe even the world. To see a car of my own design so competitive certainly made me feel on top of the world. I figured we would either win that race or go down fighting to the last inch—depending on whether Jackie could get by both the McLarens. Either way, I figured I'd confirmed to Ernie Kanzler that his faith in me had not been wasted. I tried to call him with the news about our qualifying but couldn't reach him.

One important task for an auto-racing team manager is to sign up the various accessory and oil sponsors for contingency money—payments from suppliers if the car figures prominently in the results. There's a small contract that gives them the right to advertise the fact that the car won using their product. It's not a bad idea to wait until after qualifying to sign the contracts, because it can drive up the fee some if they think you have a good chance of winning. The biggest competition in those days was between the top racing oil suppliers, Valvoline and Castrol. I knew the reps for both companies, and after qualifying, they lost no time trying to get me to sign their contracts. I told them both that I would have to speak to the driver first.

Unlike the previous year at Laguna, we didn't have to work all night on the car. The crew had done a great job, and we even had time to get a real meal for dinner. By race morning, we were all ready for the warm-up and anticipating a successful race for the Ti22 Mk 2.

Ernie Kanzler didn't come to Laguna, but Ken Norris did, along with the principals of Ecurie Vickie. On race morning, we fueled up the car for the race distance, and Jackie drove it in the warm-up. He said the Mk 2 felt great, and we weren't to change anything at all. So we ran through our final preparation ritual, completed our pre-race checklists, and even polished the wheels.

At most tracks, the pits aren't the best place to watch a race, but the pits at Laguna were different. You could stand on the back of your truck and watch the cars almost all way round, except where they disappeared up the hill after the first sweeping turn. They were out of sight for only a few seconds until they reappeared at the famous left-hand Corkscrew turn, and then raced through the last downhill sweeps before the 90-degree right-hander

ABOVE: Taken from a tree near turn 6 at Laguna, this shot clearly shows the aerodynamic shape of the new Ti22. Note the air vents on the rear surfaces of the front fenders. (Bob Tronolone)

CHAPTER 30 · 287

ABOVE: Denny Hulme in his McLaren leads Jackie Oliver in the new Ti22 at Laguna Seca. The pair raced so hard that they lapped the rest of the field twice, and Jackie broke the track lap record. (Dave Friedman)

leading onto the start-finish straight. It was easy to see exactly what was happening the whole race, and that made it a wonderful spectator experience for everyone, not just the fans in the grandstands. I don't know anyone who dislikes going to the races at Laguna Seca.

All 32 starters got off safely. The cars on the first three rows stayed pretty much in qualifying order, and soon began lapping the backmarkers. By half-distance, Amon's big STP March and Revson's L&M Lola had been slowed by braking problems. We knew that Laguna was tough on brakes, so we'd enlarged the master cylinder capacity in an attempt to prevent the fluid from boiling, and it was working very well for us.

Getting past lapped cars was often a traumatic experience for the drivers, as was negotiating debris and oil as several cars blew up. When Gethin slid the second-placed McLaren off the track and stalled the engine, Jackie swept past into second place and soon caught up with Hulme in the leading car.

Jackie tried to get past Denny for nearly 40 laps. At one point, he almost lost it when he slid off the track in lapping a slower car. It cost him a couple of seconds, but he soon made it up and drove the fastest lap in the process in 62.4 seconds. Late in the race, the engine started to suffer a little from fuel-injection mixture control problems. We'd used a chamois leather as a filter when we put fuel in the car, but a miniscule speck of dirt was all that was needed to stick the fuel pressure control valve partially shut or open, and that caused some excessive richness of the mixture. Jackie paid no heed to the fuel gauge: it was better to have a rich mixture than none at all, and he pressed on. The problem cleared itself near the end, and he tried like crazy to find a way past Denny. When the checkered flag finally dropped, he was only a few feet behind. We all cheered like crazy and some of us wept with joy, me among them. I've always tended to be emotional, and that race had meant everything to me.

The crowd had seen the best Can-Am race since Mosport, when Jackie had raced Dan Gurney so hard. Attrition from mechanical problems and spins on dropped oil had taken half the cars out of the race. The pace had been so fierce that both Denny and Jackie had lapped the third-placed Lola of Revson once, and Amon, Rodriguez, and Parsons (fourth, fifth, and sixth) twice.

Jackie was thrilled about the performance of the Ti22 and gave me his Can-Am silver medal as a souvenir. Many people came along to congratulate us, and among them was my old pal, Chuck Parsons, who was still with Carl Haas and the works Lola team. He grinned, "Congratulations—you did it again!" Coming from him, it meant a lot.

Ken Norris was delighted and invited the whole team to the Mark Thomas Inn, his resort hotel, for a post-race celebration. When I said good evening to Mr. Norris, he told me it was OK to call him by his first name. I felt that was a good sign for some future sponsorship. He talked to Jackie and me for a long time. He said he would come to the Riverside race, and when I brought up the subject, promised to consider a Can-Am sponsorship for 1971. He asked me if we could bring the car to one of his factories after the Can-Am races were over for the employees to see, and I readily agreed.

At the party, Jackie told me he thought it was amazing how I seemed to rise to the occasion when difficulties arose. He'd been totally surprised that I'd held it all together somehow after the crash at St. Jovite. I said I'd put a really good team of people together. I also told him we had an excellent engine program and wanted to generate some added income from it. It was pretty obvious that BRM didn't have a very good engine, and I suggested that when he returned to the United Kingdom after the season, Jackie might ask BRM if they would like us to do their engines for them.

I found out something else important at the party. When Jackie described the fuel problem he'd experienced, most of the crew thought the Ti22 was running low on gas. I told them this wasn't the case, because I'd told the mechanics to put in an extra five gallons as a safety margin. Then Alex Groundsel said he'd been worried we would run out of gas, too, so he'd also put in an extra five gallons! That meant we'd had a whopping 75 lbs. of unnecessary weight in the car for the whole race.

Had we shot ourselves in the foot? I decided to have a team meeting before the next race and try to avoid stuff like that happening again.

There was a lot at stake for us in the *Times* Grand Prix at Riverside. It was the last Can-Am of 1970. If we could get another great result, it would mean better sponsorship money from Goodyear and the possibility of a full season of support from Norris Industries.

The racing magazines and the local Southern Californian newspapers gave us great coverage, and they made the Riverside race look like it was going to be a battle of titans. Jim Hall was obviously on the right track with his revolutionary ground-effect car. It was more than a breakthrough in roadholding technology. The SCCA had received several complaints from rival teams, including McLaren. It looked like they were planning to add another rule or two to the "no rules" Can-Am series. I hated to see that. My opinion was that if Jim Hall and GM had found a way to beat McLaren, then more power to them. It could only make the series more exciting and a better spectacle. The new Ti22 had done the fastest race lap at Laguna, but the Chaparral 2J was the fastest car. So I was going to have to design an entirely new car for 1971 because all I'd done was get even with McLaren—and you can't get ahead by getting even! I needed to start again with a blank sheet of paper. But first I decided to wait and see if the SCCA did anything with the rules.

Riverside was on my list as a "fast" track requiring a different approach relative to Laguna Seca. We had a high-downforce body design and not too many ways to lower the drag compared to cars with external wings. I was confident that we had at least as much horsepower as McLaren, but I asked Barry Crowe to try and get us a little more. He said he thought we could raise the swept volume of the engine to 510 cid, or 8366cc. But there was a downside. He thought that McLaren had already done the same thing, and believed that it could affect the engine's reliability. He thought we could possibly increase the rpm a bit, but with no time for testing it was dicey. I decided to stay with the engines we had. It was less than 10 days before we started practice, and we had a lot to do.

Riverside had a long, high-speed back straight followed by a left-hand kink and a 180-degree, slightly banked turn 9. The entry to turn 9 was a good passing place under braking, and if your car had good cornering capabilities, it would come out of it with good acceleration right through the fast first turn and into the esses on the front straight, all the way to the slow turn 6. In other words, the track was a good all-round test of straightaway speed and handling in both fast and slow turns. We would learn much about the new car. If you were near the entry end of the pits, you could check the cornering times of various cars in turn 9 and compare them with your own.

As raced at Laguna, the Ti22 was losing a little top-end speed on the straight to the McLarens, so we lowered the rear spoiler an inch, improving the maximum speed a fair amount. The Ti22 appeared to be as fast as the McLarens in turn 9. But the Chaparral 2J "vacuum cleaner" blew off all our doors by going more than 1 second faster than any of us in that one turn alone!

In qualifying, Elford turned the fastest lap with the Chaparral in 1:32.49. The rest of qualifying turned into a contest between everyone else to see how close we could get. Hulme won the contest with a lap in 1:34.69—more than two seconds slower, which was unheard of. Revson did 1:35.10 in the Lola T220, and Jackie managed 1:35.52 in our car, just ahead of Amon in the March at 1:35.92 and Gethin in the other works McLaren at 1:36.28. Gethin was more than two seconds quicker than Pedro Rodriguez in the evil-handling BRM. The rest of the 29-car field lagged far behind—some as much as 10 seconds a lap slower. If the

Chaparral lasted the distance it would be unbeatable, and would start lapping the tail-enders after only about five laps. The race would go more than 61 laps, so some cars would get lapped seven or eight times. That could prove to be dangerous.

The performance of the Chaparral caused a big stir in Can-Am circles, and all the major contestants were interviewed by the SCCA the evening before the race about its suction fans and skirts. Car owners Carl Haas and Roger Penske were both there, and I smelled a rule change in the offing. The SCCA officials—who had cleared Don Gates's 2J design before Jim Hall had even built the car—asked me for my views on the aerodynamic rules. I said I liked them as they were, because that was what the Can-Am was all about—fewer rules made for spectacular cars, which made for good racing for the spectators. I added that Chaparral still had big reliability problems and wouldn't solve them any time soon. I thought it was good to see new technology, and I had some of my own on the way. I asked the SCCA people if they would be considering a ban on the use of titanium if our car had produced the fastest lap in qualifying. They didn't answer but thanked me for my input, and I left. I went back to the track, and we ended up working nearly all night again in the garage, as did McLaren and Chaparral. There was never enough time to get a car ready for a race—you simply used all you had.

The rolling start of the *Times* Grand Prix was certainly exciting as the cars thundered over the start line and swept through the esses and out of sight.

The Chaparral 2J started to have problems with its auxiliary "vacuum" engine on the very first lap. Exiting turn 9, Hulme swept past to lead the race the second time into turn 1. Followed by Jackie in our car, the Chaparral disappeared into turn 2, but that was all she wrote. At the end of that lap, it was losing ground fast, and Elford was running in sixth place when he came into the pits to retire.

Meanwhile Jackie was losing ground to Denny, who was going away at an amazing rate of almost 1 second a lap. The race then turned into a bit of a parade. Jackie dropped to around 12 seconds behind, then started fighting his way back at about halfway, by which time Gethin had retired the other works McLaren with a blown engine. Denny had lost an engine in the warm-up, and this unreliability made me think they had done something to get more power. I found out later that Barry's suspicions had been correct—they were trying to run 510 cid engines.

Once again, the pace was too fast for everyone else, and both Hulme and Oliver lapped the entire rest of the field at least twice. That included Rodriguez, who finished third in his BRM after Amon had pitted for fuel, dropping the March to fourth position. Denny had sewn up the championship at the previous race at Laguna, but he added $50,000 to his winnings.

Ken Norris was again delighted with the result, and so were we. Jackie said the Ti22 hadn't handled as well as it had at Laguna, but had gone like a rocket down the straights. He said he was catching Denny and felt that if the race had gone another 10 laps, he might have won. But that doesn't count, so we settled for second place again.

We'd finished fifth in the 1970 championship after competing in only 4 races out of a possible 10. The press were very kind to us. At the prizegiving that evening in Riverside, Jackie was given a great hand of applause. Chris Economaki was the master of ceremonies, and he asked me to come up to the microphone and say something when they gave out the series prize money. I thanked the team and the sponsors and my wife for putting up with me while I'd been working all those hours. Then I did my impersonation of George C. Scott in the hit movie *Patton*: "No American ever won a Can-Am Series by blowing his engine or crashing his car! He won it by making the other poor bastards blow or crash theirs!" I promised to be back the next year to do just that. The audience loved it. We went home satisfied that we'd mounted the best American challenge to the McLaren team that year, and confident that we could get the sponsorship to do it again in 1971.

It looked like we would again have the best American-built race car. As I'd feared, the rules were changed before the 1971 Can-Am season. They banned "moveable aerodynamic devices," which included the Chaparral's suction fans. The Sports Car Club of America effectively excluded the fastest American-built car from their own series. Jim Hall and the Chaparrals were never seen again in the Can-Am.

CHAPTER 31

In and Out of a Bomb Hole

After the 1970 Can-Am finale at Riverside, Jackie and Lynn Oliver drove back to my house. We all planned to go to Palm Springs the following weekend with my wife and kids for some much-needed R & R. I'd given the team some time off, too.

We would have gone sooner, but the doctor who was one of the Ecurie Vickie board members had invited Jackie to play golf the following Wednesday. I'd thought it a bit unusual that Richard Callouette hadn't spoken with me after the race and asked Jackie if he'd had any contact with him. He had, just after the prize-giving ceremonies, when Callouette had paid out Jackie's prize money. I told Jackie that I felt a bit uneasy about the relationship with Ecurie Vickie. He said: "Peter, you worry too much. If there was anything wrong, I'm sure something would have been said before now."

Early the following Monday, Callouette called me at home and asked me to attend an Ecurie Vickie meeting at his law offices at 11:00 a.m. When I arrived, Callouette spoke first. He told me that he and the other principals had voted me out of the corporation. I was to go to the office, clean out my desk, and leave.

I asked why they were doing this but received no satisfactory answer. So I looked Callouette right in the eye and told him they would never race the Ti22 again, because they would never get any support for it. I said the agreements I had with sponsors like Goodyear were not corporate property—they were personal to me.

Still in total disbelief at what had just happened, I got up and left the room. A thousand things ran through my mind as I made my way to my office. I stopped off at a pay phone and called Larry Truesdale at Goodyear. I told him what had just occurred and asked for advice. He said, "Our agreement for racing tires and financial support is with you, Peter. They won't get a single tire from us as long as I'm in charge." I immediately felt a little better, but the true enormity of this new situation would take a while to sink in.

How had this happened to me? That was the question I kept asking myself. Why had they done it? The only reason that I could come up with was money. I was the highest paid guy on the team, thanks to Ernie Kanzler, and these were not multi-millionaires. If money was tight, they might cut expenses, reasoning that because they had the car, they no longer needed the designer.

I drove to Kanzler's office to speak with him but he was out, so I went home and told Sally what had happened. She was totally dumbfounded. I called a friend, and he suggested I speak to a lawyer but said I shouldn't expect too much to come of it.

A couple of weeks later, after some expensive but fruitless legal consulting, I called Ken Norris. I told him what had happened and he said the Ti22 Mk 2 would be on display at his factory until the following weekend. He said that possession was nine-tenths of the law, and he thought the car was mine, anyway. While I considered trying to take possession of the car, I decided against it, after lawyers told me I would need proof that I was the legal owner.

Of course, I didn't have anything, and I couldn't come up with an alternative. So I stopped all legal action. The reality that I'd lost control of "my" car drove me into a deep depression that I'd never before experienced. I couldn't come to grips with what had happened. I just went into a funk. My wife was worried and told me that feeling sorry for myself wasn't going to help. I had a family to support. If I wasn't going racing any more, I'd better find a regular job. That thought depressed me even more!

Next evening, just after dinner, Sally told me we needed to talk. Whenever a wife says that you'd better listen good. She said, "You have to remember that you had nothing before you met Ernie Kanzler. Now you have to start again, but you have one very big advantage that you didn't have before. You've designed and built two cars, and they've proven to be the fastest American-built cars in the Can-Am. You've got a reputation! So get off your ass and start designing your new car. I'm sure you'll find it much easier this time around to find another Ernie Kanzler to fund it all."

She was right. I couldn't argue with that logic. It was just what I needed to wake me up. I went to the unemployment office the very next day and signed up for benefits of $150 a week. I made a list of things to do and contacts to reach. It felt good to be back on track, so to speak.

Once again, I conducted a "trade study" to determine what it would take to have a winning car. I listed in one column the objectives that needed to be achieved, and in the second column the items that would be required. This time there were more than four.

One objective that had not been addressed before was the importance of having a car that was very highly adjustable aerodynamically. The Ti22 was designed like a wing, with spoilers and fins that could be modified to adjust the trade-off between downforce and drag, depending on the requirements of a "slow" track like Laguna or a "fast" track like Riverside. After Riverside, I'd realized that the Mk 2 car just didn't have enough aerodynamic adjustability.

There were two possible solutions. The first was to find a way to give the car downforce without any parasitic drag. This is what the fans built into the Chaparral 2J had done, however unreliably. The second was to make a very streamlined, low-drag car but to use wings to adjust the downforce when needed and still keep drag to a minimum. The SCCA had banned "moveable aerodynamic devices," so it didn't take me long to realize that the first solution would be virtually impossible to achieve.

One American designer had already tried the second solution—Trevor Harris, the innovative creator of the AVS Shadow. He'd built a very radical, low-profile car that actually pointed the way I concluded we needed to go. The only problem with his car was that he'd gone a little too far and inadvertently created as many problems as he solved. Although the AVS Shadow had shown promise during practice sessions, it suffered many mechanical failures that prevented it from finishing a single race. For example, he had gotten Firestone to make wide tires with a very low profile for 10-inch-diameter front wheels and 12-inch rears. It looked good but had caused two big problems—you couldn't get big enough brake disks inside those very small wheels, and you needed a unique gearbox to get the required gearing for them. It was tough enough to make an established, branded gearbox like the Hewland last an entire race. But to design and make a bespoke gearbox and test it properly would have taken about a year, and that wasn't acceptable in racing. Consequently Trevor had been forced to improvise the brakes and modify the existing gearbox, and his car had failed to finish a race. It basically suffered from inadequate braking and unreliable components. But it did show very good promise aerodynamically.

I called Goodyear and asked if they would support me with special, low-profile tires for a new Can-Am car I was going to design. To my surprise, they said they would be very interested in doing some R&D on low-profile tires with me, and asked what wheel diameters I was considering. I told them 12-inch or 13-inch at the front, and 15-inch at the rear. I wanted the tires to be as low-profile as possible—could they make a tire with only a 3-inch tread profile from the rim? They said they would look at it right away and get back to me. Later Goodyear assigned two design engineers, Dennis Crobacs and Ed Knight, to the project. Dennis had worked on the most demanding tire application ever—aircraft tires for carrier landings—so I felt confident that Goodyear could solve the problems.

I made my plans for designing the car and started thinking about who I could get to pay for it all. The list of potential benefactors was quite short, and the guy I put at the top of it was Don Nichols. He was the logical person, because he had formed a company called Advanced Vehicle Systems (AVS) to fund Trevor Harris's Shadow. The Shadow car had basically flopped, and then Firestone had dropped out of Can-Am racing, ending that tire development program. I'd met Nichols at several races, and after the Ti22 Mk 1 had crashed early the previous season, I'd let him have my room reservations for the races that we were going to miss. He'd given me his private telephone number and said that if he could ever be of assistance, I should give him a call. He was a very private person who lived with his family on the Palos Verdes Estates, an exclusive suburb of Los Angeles near the ocean. Nichols had been very successful as a Firestone race tire dealer in Japan, but I didn't know much else about him.

When I called and asked for a meeting he invited me to his house in Palos Verdes. We went into his sitting room, and I told him about the Ecurie Vickie situation. I asked if he would be interested in joining forces to build a new Shadow. He asked what I meant by "joining forces." I told him about my plans for a new Can-Am car but said I didn't want to do another car without some sort of ownership in it. I added that I had a personal contract for tire support with Goodyear and could bring them on board to make low-profile tires. I also had other sponsors who'd helped me build the Ti22, like Titanium Metal Corporation, who would provide product and maybe financial support. I would also help to get a major sponsor and had some people in mind. I was willing to work for minimum wages to keep the overhead down, and it wouldn't cost much for me to get started. I needed about $100 a week from him to help pay my bills. When we had some sponsorship on board, we could both draw some back pay to compensate for our out-of-pocket expenditures.

Don said he was interested in my proposition. He told me he had some things to check out but would give me an answer in a couple of days.

He called me back exactly as promised and told me he wanted to go forward. Once again, I was naïve about how to conduct business. Nevertheless, I went happily forward, content with the fact that I was once again living my dream. Very soon I would be designing another Can-Am car to challenge McLaren, and I reckoned I would be a 10 percent owner in the team.

BELOW: Vic Elford driving the radical AVS Shadow at the Mid-Ohio Can-Am race in August 1970. (Pete Lyons)

CHAPTER 32

Decisions, Decisions . . .

Don Nichols set up a company called Phoenix Racing Organizations to design, build, and operate the Shadow Mk 2 for the 1971 Canadian-American Challenge Cup. At the first meeting to discuss the new design, Don asked me if I could save money by using parts from the Mk 1 car, which had been drawn by Trevor Harris. I said I needed to see the car up close. At the end of the 1970 Can-Am season, it had been retired to a farm owned by Don's parents in Ohio.

So we flew together to Ohio, and Don rented a U-Haul truck to tow a trailer and the old race car back to California. If you want to get to know all about a person, try driving a couple of thousand miles non stop with them. You'll find out all kinds of stuff. On that particular drive, and in subsequent drives across America in Don's Cadillac to go racing, I discovered all kinds of interesting stuff about him, and I'm sure he found out a lot about me.

I soon discovered Don's enthusiasm for *Man of La Mancha*, the Broadway musical. He had brought along some tapes to keep us from getting bored. At first, I thought he was trying to imprint the phrase "To dream the impossible dream" on my mind as a way of spurring me on to greater creativity in race-car design. But later I decided that he saw himself as a kind of Don Quixote, tilting at windmills and trying to reach the unreachable stars. I know one thing. By the end of that drive, I not only knew all the words, but I'd heard much too much of them and wanted out of that vehicle in the worst way. But I didn't want to upset my new buddy, so I suffered in silence.

In between the music, we discussed his life. It was most enlightening and educational. He was definitely an entrepreneur in the true sense of the word, and I was glad he was.

It turned out Don had been in the Intelligence Corps of the army and had been sent to the army language school in Monterey to learn Japanese. He became fluent in the language and ultimately went with the army to Japan as a translator. After a while, he took his family to live with him in Tokyo. It wasn't long before he and his wife had started a school teaching English. He renewed his interest in motor racing and started distributing race-car components that were hard to get in Japan. Before long, he was the official Firestone race-tire dealer for Japan and started to make some real money. I guess at some point his family decided that they wanted to come back to the United States, so he liquidated his holdings and returned to California. Somehow he got involved with Trevor Harris, who designed the first Shadow for him.

After what seemed an eternity, we arrived back in Long Beach and unloaded that car into a small, rented industrial building. Next day, I started to take stock of what we had.

Trevor Harris was a really innovative engineer and extremely into exploring what made cars go fast. So he designed a car with the lowest frontal area of any sports-racing car ever made. It was calculated to be 13 square feet, against 19 square feet of the contemporary McLaren. The Shadow Mk 1 was designed with cooperation from the Firestone racing division, probably due to their previous relationship with Don. They made some radically low-profile, small-diameter tires to go under the low bodywork of the Mk 1. The rims were 10 inches in diameter at the front and 12 inches at the rear.

The front suspension was by rocker arms, and the front coil springs were so small they almost resembled valve springs. Because the rear rims were about 35 percent smaller than conventional Can-Am wheels, a special gearbox casing was needed to accommodate larger gears. Pete Weismann helped them out in this regard. The driver had to have his feet splayed out, so there was no space for a clutch pedal. He had to shift gears without a clutch.

The car went very fast in a straight line but only had 8-inch-diameter brake rotors on the front. Once they got hot, the braking performance was poor. On top of that, the engine overheated. The radiators for the Shadow's Big Block Chevy were initially positioned in the body, but then incorporated in the rear wing and mounted up above the rear wheels.

The Shadow Mk 1 was driven by George Follmer and Vic Elford in the 1970 Can-Am series, but couldn't finish a race. It was a sensational-looking race car, but not a real competitor to the McLaren team, which became obvious fairly quickly. After the 1970 Can-Am season, Don closed down his Advanced Vehicles Systems company and sold his plant and equipment.

In contrast, my titanium cars had made a big impact at the end of the 1970 season by getting the fastest lap and finishing second to Denny Hulme's McLaren in the last two races, lapping the entire field before the finish. It was obvious that I knew something about designing and building competitive cars, and that was why I had been able to get Don's attention.

I spent several days going over the little Shadow and Trevor's drawings, but the bottom line was that I found there was very little of this design I could carry over to a new car. It just wouldn't work for me. Finally I broke the news to Don that all I could salvage was the Weismann transmission and the spun half of the 12-inch rear wheels. I figured I could use the latter as the inner half of a new, two-piece front wheel with a new casting as the outer half. Later, I would regret even using that piece, because we had a hell of a time just trying to seal them and make them airtight when we bolted the two parts together.

Considering the trouble and expense he'd just had in bringing the car back to California from Ohio, Don took the news well. Thinking back on it, I could probably have done the evaluation in Ohio, but I figured Don wanted the car back in California anyway.

The next thing to decide was where to work on the design of the new car. Don liked secrecy, so it was decided that he would rent an office about halfway between our homes. That turned out to be in Long Beach. Don found a State Farm car insurance agent named Merl Dempsey on Atlantic Boulevard who had an empty room, and arranged to rent it by the month. I moved in my giant German drafting machine. The table was 52 inches high and a full eight feet wide, and could be adjusted so that it was flat or vertical—very exotic! The room was more like a broom closet, only 10 feet long by 8 feet wide, leaving space for the machine but little else. I managed to borrow a chair from Merl, but that was it. I started work on the new Shadow there in January 1971.

I had until June to get the car designed, built, and tested, so I knew I couldn't hang around. Goodyear had agreed to make some experimental tires that would fit 12-inch-diameter front wheels and 15-inch rears, but with a very low profile. I flew to Akron with Don and met Dennis Crobacs, the tire engineer heading up Goodyear's program. He was a very experienced engineer, and I was confident in his abilities. We fixed some target specifications for the tires and wheels. We planned to use 12-inch-diameter, 11-inch-wide fronts, and 15-inch-diameter, 16-inch-wide rears. Dennis gave me some sample tire profile drawings for reference, and we agreed on a target test date. I could now start to design the car in earnest.

The first order of business when designing a new car is to set the specifications according to the desired performance. I set the wheelbase at 98 inches, the front track at 60 inches, and the rear track at 57 inches, with an overall width of 76 inches and overall length of 147 inches. The dimension that would make the biggest difference in the performance was the overall height of the body over the rear wheels, which would reach just 24 inches. This was only attainable with the low-profile rear tires, and would make the airflow to the rear wing very effective in creating downforce. I put the radiator at the front, with a small wing just ahead and above the opening to help to trim the downforce. We would use a 497 cid Chevrolet engine with about 725 bhp and the five-speed Weismann-built transmission from the old Shadow.

I worked 16 or 18 hours a day in that little office. I had a telephone installed so I could communicate with suppliers, and I brought in a small radio for company. I was like a man possessed. Within a month, I had a packaging study done and an initial chassis proposal. Apart from occasional visits by Don, my only company was the radio. That got a bit boring when Los Angeles DJ Wink Martindale decided to hold a listeners' poll to decide the best song ever sung. Nat King Cole won pretty much every day with his big hit, "Mona Lisa." I got very tired of hearing it over and over again. After a while, I just switched the radio off. But then I found myself humming "Mona Lisa" to myself. I had to switch it back on to something else as background noise.

Don insisted on secrecy about the drawings that were going to be sent to our suppliers, so I had to change the name in the drawing title block from the official Phoenix Racing Organizations. I just couldn't resist a practical joke, so I changed it to Blivet Car Company. I don't think Don knew what the word meant. It was a very rude old cockney obscenity, and basically anyone who didn't know, didn't want to know!

By February, I'd finished the chassis and suspension packaging studies. Wow! Talk about putting a quart in a pint pot. I decided to use 12-inch-diameter Lockheed disc brakes all round. That meant the rears could be mounted outboard but the fronts had to be inboard because you can't get 12-inch brake rotors inside 12-inch rims. I used Porsche 914 driveshafts and constant-velocity joints to transmit the braking torque from the front wheels to the rotors. These driveshafts later proved to be among my problem children in terms of longevity. Getting enough braking power was tough enough without putting them inboard, but there was no other way except to increase the wheel diameter to allow outboard brakes, and I thought it was worth a try. Cooling them was actually easier than if they had been outboard. I simply put an air intake duct directly to an aluminum brake "hat" that fed the air directly to the center of each rotor, and it worked really well. When the car pulled into the pits, we simply blew air straight in from two small vacuum cleaners to stop the pads from "heat-checking" the rotors.

The problem with using those Rzepper-style CV universal joints outboard surfaced later in testing and at races. The torque that was generated under braking put small flat spots on the ball bearings in the CV joints, and they were soon brinelled (or flat-spotted) to a point that they didn't rotate anymore. During this process, a vibration would gradually creep into the front wheels, and the driver couldn't tell what was causing it. He often thought the wheels were out of balance.

Time was a big factor, so I decided on a semi-monocoque design with rectangular steel tube subframes at the front footbox and seatback member. Timet didn't make rectangular titanium tubes, so I used steel. I used titanium for all the suspension control arms and radius arms. I skinned the whole chassis in aluminum. It was pretty stiff at around 10,000 foot pounds per no part of a degree (that was my goal for torsional stiffness). I kept the chassis tub height to 10 inches and used the engine as a stressed member by running the titanium cantilever-type engine mount from the back of the gas tank side compartments of the tub out to the face of the bell-housing. The side gas tank sections of the tub extended past the rear bulkhead and ended in line with the back face of the engine cylinder block.

A U.S. gallon of gasoline weighs more than 7 lbs. I designed the Shadow Mk2 to hold 84 gallons in case we later turbocharged the engine. Imagine the handling transitions of a car that started out weighing 600 lbs. more than when it finishes. If the car weighed about 1450 lbs. empty, it weighed more than 2000 lbs. with full tanks. It always amazed me when cars with full tanks often lapped within a second or so of their qualifying times during race morning warm-up sessions.

Come March 1971, and I'd lofted out the body shape I wanted to use and found a fiberglass artisan to make the male plug and molds for our low-profile bodywork. The body would be low and flat to allow for the best airflow to the gearbox-mounted rear wing. I designed a small, adjustable front wing and mounted it just ahead of the radiator to help in trimming the aero balance of the car. We used quarter-inch Nomex honeycomb sheet to stiffen the large flat panels that made up the bodywork. We made the panels, then bonded the Nomex paper honeycomb material between them.

Incidentally, the Shadow Mk 2 was the first racing car to eliminate a vertical, plastic windshield. I turned up a small vertical lip on the bodywork edge just in front of the cockpit, and added another flat piece parallel to it underneath and about an inch away from the upper panel. Then I put a small NACA duct about a foot ahead of the opening to suck air into it, and allowed the air to escape vertically between the two panels just in front of the driver's face. We added a one-inch piece of Plexiglas to the trailing edge, so that technically it still had a windshield. It was the first "aero windshield." Even though it was in plain sight, the press boys totally overlooked it and no one asked me about it.

Meanwhile, Don Nichols found Charlie McHose, an artist who had been an instructor at the Pasadena Art Center College of Design. He engaged him to make some renderings of the finished car to use in a press release and to help raise sponsorship. Charlie did a wonderful job, and the car looked great in the artwork.

One day, Don came over and said he thought he'd lined up a sponsor—Universal Oil Products. UOP was heavily involved in research and design of the substrate that Chrysler would use in their automobile catalytic converters. The government had started to enforce emission standards, and the only way to use the platinum-based substrate in the converters was if the gasoline octane booster tetra-ethyl lead (TEL)was banned. The lead "poisoned" the platinum wash on the converter substrate and made it ineffective. The problem was that TEL was a very cheap way to boost the octane number of the basic gasoline from 84 to 90.

The chief of research for the catalyst program at UOP was Ted DePalma, who turned out to be the grandson of Ralph DePalma, the driver who had won the Indy 500 back in 1915. Ted was convinced that if the new Shadow was sponsored by UOP and ran on unleaded gasoline, it would go a long way to dispel the public perception that unleaded gasoline could burn the valves out of the cylinder head. The Detroit manufacturers were against adopting expensive catalytic converters and made no attempt to squash that belief. Ted DePalma found an ally at UOP in the form of Ben Williams, the corporate PR guy. Between them they persuaded John Logan, UOP's CEO, to consider sponsoring the Shadow.

It came down to one last thing: What guarantee could Don Nichols give that the car would be competitive and create the right kind of publicity? Don asked if I could help. I had a verbal contract with Goodyear for their tires at all Can-Am races. I told Don to tell Ben Williams to call Larry Truesdale at Goodyear and get an endorsement of my ability to design and build a competitive car. First I called Larry myself and explained what was happening. He said he would do his best to help us get the sponsorship, because Goodyear wanted to see a competitive American car in the Can-Am. Goodyear came through again. That did it, I guess. UOP agreed to sponsor us.

I don't know how much money was involved, but in those days it wasn't really that much. Even if it had been a generous amount, it would never have been enough. Racing-car programs eat money like candy. The more you have, the more you spend.

Don called up the PR guy, and they arranged a press conference in San Francisco to introduce the new car and show the world the McHose rendition of the UOP Shadow. We were off and running.

Shortly afterwards, Phoenix Racing Organizations moved into a workshop near Signal Hill, Long Beach, and the car began to take shape. After the first sponsorship check came in, as we had agreed, I asked Don Nichols to review my pay of $100 a week, and he increased it to about $400. He also gave me a check for about $1200 to help make up for some of the pay I'd missed out on. Sally said it was about time I got paid a bit more for working 16 hours a day, seven days a week!

There was a really good race-car fabrication shop in Santa Ana called Pro-Fab. We used them to make the chassis from my drawings, and they did it in record time. I don't remember them asking even one question as they did it. Pete Wilkins, the owner, had worked for Dan Gurney before starting his own business, making mostly off-road racing motorbikes, and he also liked to race dirt bikes himself. I'd once provided Pete with some titanium tube, and he'd made a bike frame for Husqvarna. It must have been very successful because the bike-racing organizers soon banned titanium frames. Pete was a great fabricator as well as a very smart man. He also made our suspension, our radiator, and lots of other bits. A real nice guy named Gerry Magnuson made our front suspension upright castings and the cast outer halves of the front wheels. The inner half was the spun aluminum piece of the old Shadow rear wheels that I'd reluctantly agreed to use in the new car. To save tooling costs as well as time and money, I bought the rear wheels and rear suspension uprights from Dan Gurney.

I'd decided to go all-out with the low-drag, "clean" air approach and wanted to buy the side-draft intake manifolds that I'd seen on the Chaparrals, because they cleaned up the airflow as it went over the engine cover. But there wasn't time to start our own engine build program. I couldn't do that as well as designing and building the car, so by May we'd negotiated a deal with Jim Hall to buy a couple of his old Can-Am Chevy engines with the special, side-facing intake horns. I didn't realize at that time that they no longer used those particular manifolds because they robbed the engine of power.

I needed to keep the engine cover as low as possible in order to make the rear wing work better. The Can-Am rules said that the bottom surface of any wing had to be no higher than 31 inches from the ground. In order for the rear wing to function well, it had to have good clearance between it and the rear bodywork.

The end result was that the Shadow Mk 2 looked very low and fast, and painted in black, even a little sinister. This made Don Nichols very happy. He liked that sort of image. And it made for great PR.

BELOW: With Oliver at the helm, the UOP Shadow Mk 2 leaves the pits for its maiden voyage at Canada's St. Jovite circuit in June 1971. (Peter Bryant)

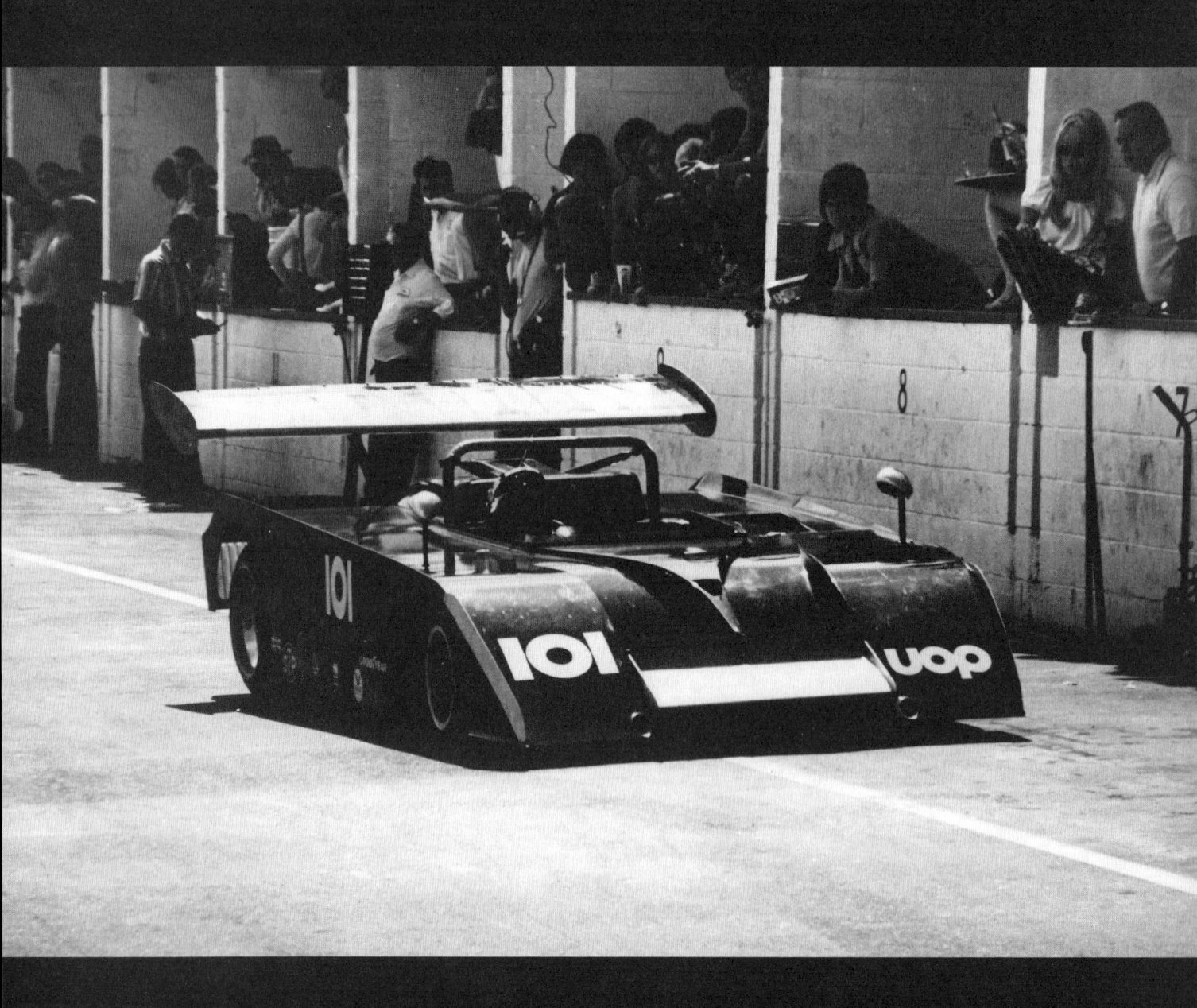

CHAPTER 33

A Fragile Piece

A few weeks before the first Can-Am race of 1971, Don Nichols persuaded Jim Hall to let us use his facilities and test track at Rattlesnake Raceway in Midland, Texas, to do our first testing with the Shadow Mk 2. Jackie Oliver had recently done a deal with Don to be our driver, and he flew there directly from England. Mike Lowman drove the transporter with the new car aboard, and Don and I went in Don's Cadillac limousine. It was black with tinted glass and a radio telephone, so we had our own sinister look to go with our new Shadow image.

Rattlesnake Raceway was an interesting experience. Beside the two-mile track, there was a large, flat area with a 200-foot diameter skidpan in the middle. Many people believed in testing on a skidpan to measure and optimize cornering G forces, but I didn't. A circular skidpan test may be good for comparing street-type cars, but not racing cars—unless all you want is a measure of how well they go around a skidpan. Making changes to the car so that it can go faster around a skidpan isn't the right way to go because it gets into a steady state of steering and acceleration, and to stop it understeering, you would disconnect the front anti-rollbar. You would never disconnect the front anti-rollbar on a race track. If the skidpan had a figure-eight configuration, with a little straight between loops, it would be more representative of what happens to race cars in slow corners, because the car would brake and accelerate in order to switch directions, more like a real cornering experience.

The first time we ran the Shadow, Jim advised us, "Go very slow at first and make lots

ABOVE: Jackie Oliver confers with team manager Ray Brimble (center) and me during practice at Road America. The front brake rotors are again being cooled by two vacuum cleaners. (Tom Schultz)

of noise to scare away the jackrabbits. They like to run across the track, and you don't want one of those in your face if you're going fast." Jackie made a slow lap, came back and told us there were several tortoises on the track, so could we please go and move them off it. Having been a city slicker all my life, I'd never picked up a tortoise. Boy, did I get a surprise—they pee like crazy when you pick them up and if you're not quick, it gets on you and makes you stink like a polecat.

Unfortunately, we had no comparable lap times, so the test was really just to make sure that the new car was safe to drive and to work out some bugs. Jim was very interested in the car design. He said it sure looked fast. His humor was so dry, I really couldn't tell whether that was a compliment or a ribbing!

Despite the warnings, our car hit a jackrabbit on the straight during the second day of testing. It was scooped up by the nose splitter at about 140 mph and it was nicely embedded sideways in the radiator, with no hope of being able to clean it out. So we removed the radiator and airfreighted it back to Pro-Fab in California to be fixed. When it didn't show up the next day, we asked United Airlines to find it. We didn't like the idea of being without a spare radiator at a race. It's an auto-racing rule—if you have a spare, you won't need it, but if you don't, you'll need it for sure. United said they'd lost it somewhere inside their freight transfer facility in Chicago. We told them they'd be sure to find it in a couple of days because, once that rabbit got ripe, they'd know exactly where to look. Sure enough, next day we got a call asking us what the hell was in that box? They hurriedly shipped it to Pro-Fab.

There was one other thing. On the last lap of the testing, I saw whitish smoke coming out the exhaust tailpipes when Jackie braked from speed at the end of the straight. I told Don I thought we might have a problem with the engine. Because we'd bought it from Jim, I thought we should ask him to have his engine builder look at it. Don asked Jackie how the engine had felt on that last lap and Jackie said he hadn't noticed any power loss, and it wasn't smoking when he came into the garage. Don said that perhaps it was dust or something that I'd seen.

We were going to miss the first Can-Am race at Mosport, because Jackie was under contract to the JW Gulf Porsche team to drive in the Le Mans 24 Hours the same weekend. We had still to decide whether to go to the second race, at St. Jovite. We sat around at Rattlesnake Raceway and had a meeting to talk it over. Jackie told us he had some other conflict with the St. Jovite date but could fly back to England the next morning and sort it out. He said he thought the Shadow Mk 2 had good potential and some great ideas, but he needed more testing to find out how good it was. We discussed what to do next. I had no doubt in my mind what we should do—we should go to St. Jovite and use it to find out how good the car was. After all, I said, I hadn't designed it to be a garage queen—I'd designed it to race in the Can-Am, so why were we dithering about? I guess that settled it. We headed back to the hotel. It was Miller Time.

I've always liked this American custom. It was a habit I'd gotten into in England. It wasn't unusual for us English racing "blokes" to have a beer after work—in fact, it may have been mandatory. Don Nichols didn't drink, so there never was a Miller Time with him. Come to think of it, I don't think I ever saw Don with his guard down, which is what happens when you drink beer—or so I've been told. I'm sure Don knew when mine was down. He was very astute. Letting my guard down is an inherent weakness of mine. I'm not saying I'm a pushover after a beer, but I do tend to take people at their word and talk a bit too much in my enthusiasm to share things with them. Even without a beer, now that I think of it . . .

Next day, the plan was that Don would take Jackie to the airport early, and I tried to get an extra forty winks. But no way was Don going to let that happen. He woke me up at 4 a.m. to ask if I wanted to go to the airport with Jackie. After all the late nights I'd recently worked, I didn't like being woken at 4:00 a.m., and I made no bones about letting Don know about it. It was Don who took Jackie to the airport. We would meet up with him again at St. Jovite.

Jackie and I were considered by the race promoters to have good publicity potential for the St. Jovite Can-Am. We had a brand-new, American-built car, but perhaps the main reason was that the previous year, the Ti22 had blown over and crashed at 160 mph on the crest of the hill on the back straight. The woman organizing the entry had contacted us right after our press conference, to be absolutely sure we were going to have our new car there. I guess Don had played a little game of hard-to-get with her, because she ended up offering to pay starting money if we showed up and raced. Later we learned that the promoters were so short of money, they'd nearly lost their rights to hold the race because they hadn't paid the sanction fee to the SCCA. So getting that starting money might require a little gamesmanship.

While we were en route to St. Jovite, Don called her from his radio phone in the Cadillac to make arrangements for collecting the money. Don told her that unless it was paid in cash at the border, we wouldn't go on to the race. It went right down to the wire, but eventually she made the arrangements to pay it. We collected it and drove on up to the Grey Rocks Inn at Mont Tremblant, where we were staying.

After the first practice session on the Thursday before the race, we took the suspension apart to check it all out, and found that the steel tubular lower rear suspension control arms had cracked at the welds. We had to reinforce and reweld them, and it took an all-night thrash in the hotel's garage. Luckily the Grey Rocks had excellent room service! When we got to the track the next morning, I must have looked like hell. Along with our mechanics, I hadn't slept at all.

Then, in the Friday practice, after we had a gotten a decent qualifying time, the exhaust system began to smoke in earnest. Closer examination showed that we'd burned a piston and needed to change the engine. That would have been OK—except we didn't have a spare. I contemplated fixing the engine myself, but we had a second engine at Chaparral, and Don said he would have them fly it out to Montreal in time for the race. I suspected that the engine was still at Chaparral because it hadn't been paid for yet. Don was a master at stretching out accounts payable in those days.

We hadn't seen the other cars before this race, and there were some new models from the factories in England. Jackie Stewart in Carl Haas's Lola T262 was out-qualified for pole position by Denny Hulme's McLaren M8F. It looked to me like the new Lola, with its strange-looking front end, was a real handful to drive. The nose was very rounded in the side profile, which suggested to me that it was intended for low drag—I figured that not much downforce would be generated on the front wheels. Then I noticed they'd made some holes in the forward downslope, three or four inches in diameter, and put a wire grate over each hole. I reckoned this was intended to cause drag, slowing the airflow as it went over the nose to generate downforce. I was willing to bet that this car had an aerodynamic problem, and they were attempting to put a Band-Aid on it. But Stewart was so good, he could have qualified the box it came in.

It hadn't taken the McLaren team long to catch on to the fact that the fences I'd run the previous year on the Ti22 really helped in creating more downforce. The new M8F sported fences that ran from front to rear. They say that imitation is the sincerest form of flattery, and I guess I should have been pleased to see that my ideas were catching on, but I wasn't. Now I was counting on the low profile of my car to make the rear wing work better for more total downforce and ultimate cornering speed. With an adjustable front wing and a low-drag profile to increase straightaway speeds, I was hoping for an advantage, especially on the "fast" tracks. One thing was certain. We definitely had the smallest frontal area of any car in the 1971 Can-Am.

All through practice, Jackie remembered only too well what had happened to the Ti22 the previous year on the back straight. Several drivers, including Stewart, had close calls when the nose started to come up at speed. This time, our own Jackie was lifting the throttle and taking care to shift gear just before the hump.

The whole McLaren team, including Denny Hulme, were under the weather with some kind of flu. Someone said it was caused by the little black flies that were all over the place. Even so, Peter Revson, who was now the second McLaren driver, qualified third fastest behind the Lola. Lothar Motschenbacher was fourth with his ex-works McLaren M8D, and Jackie was fifth with the UOP Shadow. That wasn't bad for the first race with a new car. It wasn't the fastest American-built car on the grid—it was the only one. There were two Porsches, a 917 for Milt Minter and a 908 for Steve Matchet. With 14 McLarens and 6 Lolas, we had 23 cars on the grid.

In those circumstances, and with a sick engine only two days of testing behind us, I considered our grid position to be very satisfactory. Ben Williams, our new sponsor's PR man, was delighted with our prospects for the race. Jackie told us the car was handling fairly well, and the tires seemed OK considering the bumpy and narrow track. He added that he could feel in the steering wheel that the front brakes were vibrating a little, so we replaced the inboard driveshafts before the race. The spare engine arrived, and we got the car finished after a second all-nighter.

On race day, when the cars came to the grid, Hulme looked very ill. Motschenbacher was also sick with the same thing and elected to start from the back of the grid. That put us up one place on the grid alongside Revson. It was pretty hot, and Stewart, who was wearing the latest in fire-resistant suits, looked like he was a good candidate to get overheated in the car.

But it wasn't Jackie Stewart who retired from the race—it was Jackie Oliver in our Shadow Mk 2, who was running in fourth place at the time. The Lucas fuel-injection system that we all used wasn't computer-controlled, like the systems today. The electric pump sent the fuel at about 90 psi to the metering valve, and the excess fuel was returned to the tank by a one-way pressure relief valve. The pressure relief valve encountered a tiny piece of debris from the fuel tank and started to stick open. This lowered the fuel pressure into the metering valve, causing misfires from fuel starvation. We'd taken precautions against this, including pouring the fuel through a chamois leather filter to keep dust out of the tanks. If Lucas fuel-injection had an Achilles' heel, it was that pressure relief valve. I couldn't believe our luck. Everyone was exposed to the same problem, because we all used Lucas fuel-injection. So why us, in our first race with our new car?

Stewart won the race. Hulme was so sick he threw up in his helmet (imagine how that went!) but he still managed to finish second, with Revson third. Denny was one tough bird! We were very disappointed but encouraged by our speed and vowed to do better in the next race in Atlanta the following month. But obviously we still had quite a few bugs to work out.

Next day, the race car went straight back to our shop in Long Beach, while we headed to Chicago to meet up with the UOP people on the way home. They asked us why we hadn't used unleaded gasoline at St. Jovite, as called for in our sponsorship contract. It was because I was refusing to do it until we had a gasoline that was equal to the best available at the track. I pointed out that we had high-compression engines and needed to use at least 104-octane gasoline to be competitive. UOP had 250 scientists who knew everything about gasoline refining and manufacture. They knew very well that the highest-rated unleaded gasoline you could buy at a street pump in those days was a 95-octane fuel made by Amoco. It was 55 percent the basic refined 84-octane gasoline and 45 percent BTX aromatic additives—including benzene, toluene, and xylene—that increased the octane rating. But the easiest way to raise the basic octane number was still to add a few grams per gallon of tetra-ethyl lead (TEL). This Amoco gasoline was obviously not good enough for us, but we agreed to test it on the dynamometer at Bill Stroppe's facility on Signal Hill and to share the data with UOP.

Back in California, we put an engine on the dyno and tried the 95-octane Amoco gasoline against 104-octane leaded fuel from Union Oil 76. Naturally, we lost a lot of power.

So UOP came up with their own exotic fuel for us to use. It was made from "isooctane" fuel with 45 percent acetone added. Isooctane, made by Phillips 66 in San Francisco, is a special unleaded gasoline that has gone through a second refining process, using a platinum catalyst and producing fuel that has an octane rating of precisely 100. It's used by all refineries to calibrate the "knock" engines use to rate the octane of their own types of gasoline. The second refining process makes Isooctane expensive to produce: at that time, it cost $1.50 a gallon, whereas premium pump cost about 38 cents. UOP took it and poured acetone into it—yes, the same acetone that cleans paint brushes—until it was 104-octane.

If you stood too close to a car's exhausts when it was running on this fuel, it would make you nauseous, and your eyes would water like crazy. It was nasty stuff, but by definition it was unleaded gasoline. Because of the high acetone content, I thought it might delaminate the safety fuel bladders in the race car, but UOP insisted it would not.

At least three races went by while all this was going on. To be honest, I fought putting this concoction into the Shadow as long as I dared. UOP told me that even though the fuel was devoid of TEL, it could still pick up some that had been deposited in the fuel bladders we'd previously used for leaded gasoline. This meant that it could get us disqualified if the octane of the gasoline in the car was tested. So I told the crew that if the SCCA wanted a sample of our gasoline to test, they should take it out of the drum, not the car.

We were running a 497 cid engine putting out about 735 bhp, and our fuel consumption was about 2.6 mpg. We needed 77 gallons for an average Can-Am race distance of 200 miles. That fuel weighed about 577 lbs. but we didn't want the car stopping for gas during the race. We weren't set up for fast refueling.

There was a vast difference in the performance and handling of a Can-Am car during the race-long transition from full to empty tanks. The key was how fast the car could go on full to half-full tanks. The idea was to try and run away at the start. Most drivers slowed down a bit after halfway to conserve the engine. So qualifying well on empty tanks didn't always mean you had a competitive car. Most of the time, we would use half-full tanks for practice and testing.

In those days, high-performance engine components were still hard to find, and the more horsepower and torque you had, the less reliability. So we changed the ring gear and pinion in the transaxle at 500 miles and the engine crankshaft at 500 miles, whether they looked like they needed changing or not. We tried to get two races on an engine, but often ended up nervously putting a new one in for the race, depending on how the first engine looked after practice. Each night after practice, we did an engine compression test and a valves-closed "leakdown" test to check if the pistons were still sealing. It was pretty expensive all around, especially if you blew an engine. Most engine problems were associated with camshaft or valve spring failures, or heat-related failures. Two hundred miles at full speed was very tough to do.

The meeting with UOP in Chicago was interesting on another level. John Logan, the CEO, explained that in order to sponsor us, he was going to have each of the UOP divisions give us $10,000. They would have their salespeople invite their best customers to each race, and would hold a cocktail party so they could meet "their" driver and some other members of "their" race team. UOP had quite a few divisions, including one that made and designed petroleum refineries, and another that made fragrances for perfumes like Avon cosmetics. Obviously UOP was very diversified, and that could work well for us in terms of their sponsorship.

The arrangement with the UOP divisions evolved and often gave us a place to work when we were on the road. Over the next couple of years, we would be on the road a whole lot, and we worked in the factory of UOP's Flexonics division at Bartlett, Illinois, and at the Mine Well-Screen division near Minneapolis, Minnesota. UOP was so nice to work with and a really great sponsor to have. The Bostrom division, which made aircraft seats in Milwaukee, even offered to make a custom race-car seat for Jackie, and did a great job.

Driving from Chicago back to Long Beach gave me plenty of time to analyze our progress. Three things were near the top of the list of problems to solve. First, we were going to need to hire a good engine builder—but who? My old engine builder at the Ti22 shop, Barry Crowe, had stayed on to work for the new owners and was unavailable. The guy I thought was the best was still former Chaparral engine builder Gary Knutson, but again he wouldn't leave McLaren. I'd a neighbor named Carroll Davis, nicknamed "Stump" because he was really stocky. I had known him since I worked for Shelby American in 1965. He'd been in Shelby's engine department and was part of a team that built dragster engines for Danny Ongais. He had a lot of experience and knowledge and had prepared Chevy engines for Lothar Motschenbacher, who had a pretty good record of finishing Can-Am races. We approached him, and he agreed to come on board.

The second problem was associated with the tires. We were having problems sealing the front two-piece rims to hold the air. On top of that, we weren't getting the kind of mechanical grip we needed from them, so I asked Goodyear to produce some softer compounds for a tire test at Riverside. I told them that Les Richter, the boss at Riverside Raceway, had complained that our tires were so hard that we were wearing out the track! I also wanted to change the profile a bit to stop them from heating up the edges of the tread at the sidewalls, or the "sipes," as Goodyear called them.

The third problem was the front vibration under heavy braking. The ball bearings in the front brake driveshaft CV joints were being flat-spotted by the high inertia loads and torque spikes being passed back and forth between the wheels and the inboard brake rotors. I talked to some guys I knew at Dana Corporation, and they suggested a new kind of bearing grease that had molybdenum disulphide as an ingredient. Until we had time to do something else, we also decided to change them for new before each race.

Back in Long Beach, a friend asked me if we had a place where we could work on the car when we got to Atlanta, and recommended a small race-car preparation shop owned by an Englishman named Ray Brimble. So I gave Ray a call, and we set up shop with him. Later Ray would become our team manager and look after the logistics for Don Nichols.

By the time we left to go to Atlanta, we'd picked up a handyman named Dan, who was also a car painter. We desperately needed someone to help our hardworking mechanics, Mike and Graham, with the maintenance of the bodywork and the various cleanup jobs that constantly needed to be done. Dan was also an excellent driver, which helped since we now had a white Ford Econoline van as well as the transporter.

The weather in Atlanta was extremely hot and very humid. We decided we could reduce the temperature for Jackie if we painted all the car's horizontal surfaces white, and jerry-rigged some ducts to cool him down. It wasn't a sinister, black Shadow anymore, but it worked—it was 30 degrees cooler in the car.

We were supposed to get some new, improved tires for the race at Road Atlanta, but they never arrived. In the meantime I had some new aerodynamic tricks to try. I put vertical fences on the front fenders and even alongside the raised area just ahead of the so-called windshield. Although they appeared to increase our downforce, the bottom line would be how well the tires gripped the road. Jackie did his best for us and wound up fourth on the grid, about 2 seconds slower then the man on pole position, Hulme in his McLaren. Revson was second in the other McLaren, and once again Stewart amazed us all with his efforts in the ill-handling Haas Lola.

Our tires wouldn't grip too well. I tried to improve the traction by changing the rear suspension geometry a little. It seemed to make no difference—the heat of the track surface was really killing our tires, and Jackie was sliding all the time. I began to think I might have bitten off more than we could chew with these low-profile tires. Designing race cars is a bit like pulling weeds—as soon as you think you've solved one problem, the solution causes another problem. The small tires had definitely given us an edge on top speed, but we were losing the mechanical grip that you need on slow corners where the downforce doesn't contribute very much.

But that wasn't what stopped us in the race. That fuel pressure relief valve played up again. Revson won the 82-lap race in a McLaren 1-2 with Hulme, and Motschenbacher finished third. We did 45 laps, and that was it.

I didn't like the way that things were shaping up for us. We had a great driver, but our car prep was suffering and our tire problems needed some urgent attention. I called Goodyear and tried to rattle their cage a little. But you can't get too aggressive when the only American race-tire manufacturer is supporting your efforts. By adding our "trick" tires to their Can-Am inventory, Goodyear had also created problems for themselves. Since there was no other tire manufacturer involved in the series, they had to supply enough tires for all the cars. If they made an improvement to the standard tire, it helped everyone but us. If they improved our tire, however, it would certainly cause problems for them with everyone else. I think they only agreed to make the "trick" stuff for us because they were really looking at other potential racing applications like Formula One. They apologized for not getting our new tires to Atlanta. I explained that UOP employees were going to be out in force at the next race in Watkins Glen, and we desperately needed to put on a good show for them there. They said they would try to ship the new tires to Los Angeles and hopefully we could test them before we left for the Glen.

Watkins Glen was almost a total disaster. The sponsor's management team arrived, and Ben Williams did his best to create a good relationship between them and the team by renting a box for them above our pits. Jackie Oliver went out of his way to keep John Logan interested in everything that was happening. Unfortunately, the new tires hadn't materialized and we had a lot of tire problems during Friday practice. We also encountered more engine problems, and never did get in a competitive lap. There wasn't much track time for us Saturday because the Glen had scheduled the famous six-hour GT race that day. In theory that meant we had a lot of time to go over the car and get it straightened out before our race on Sunday. Unfortunately, we ended up a dismal 18th on the grid after struggling to do a full lap without stopping to fix something.

To make things worse, the competition was heating up. The new Ferrari 712M showed up for Mario Andretti, and the 650 bhp Porsche 917/10 Spyder for Jo Siffert. Stewart grabbed pole position in the Haas Lola ahead of the McLarens of Revson and Hulme.

"Cheer up—things could be worse!" So goes the old joke, and we tried to cheer up. Sure enough, things did get worse! The UOP people probably didn't understand how dismal a showing we'd made. They were still very enthusiastic and sure we would put on a good show. The warm-up session on race morning ended about 45 minutes before the race was

BELOW: Mario Andretti in the latest Ferrari 712M dices with Jackie Oliver at the 1971 Watkins Glen race. Note the fences on the Ferrari, similar to those on the Ti22 and Shadow. I wonder where Ferrari got that idea? (Peter Bryant)

to start, so there wasn't much time to fix anything on the car if it went wrong. It did. Jackie complained that the engine seemed to have lost power. We pulled all the plugs and they looked OK, so we checked the compression, and that was fine too. Then we took off the valve covers to check the valve springs, and turning the engine over slowly, we discovered that a lobe had been wiped off the cam. Now we were in a real bind. It meant a serious loss in engine performance, and in trying to diagnose the problem, we'd eaten up the time we could have used to change the engine.

While all this was going on, Jackie was visiting with the sponsors and didn't know what was happening. Don and I discussed what to do. We knew we could still beat half the cars in the race, even with a down-on-power engine, so it was decided to change the oil to minimize the damage that the cam debris might do to the bearings, and race as we were. I was given the job of telling Jackie that he was about to race a car that had no chance of winning, because we needed to put on some kind of show for UOP. I took Jackie to one side and told him about our decision. His face dropped. He said, "Peter, I'm really not very happy about doing this. I hate the very idea of flogging round this track with an underpowered car." I apologized to him but replied, "Our sponsors want to see us race, so I've no option but to ask you to drive it until it melts." He walked away. I knew I'd just done the worst thing you could do to a racing driver. I've regretted doing it ever since. I should have let Don be the bad guy, because words are like bullets from a gun—once spoken, they can't be taken back.

Jackie followed his instructions to the letter. On about lap 60, three-quarter distance, the Shadow developed a vibration from a front brake driveshaft that started visibly shaking the right front wheel. I wanted Jackie to stop, but he carried on and, five laps later, he crashed into the barrier when the steering linkage finally broke. When he got out of the car, he was really upset and wouldn't speak to me. I didn't blame him. That race was an all-time low for me and I vowed I would make the car more competitive and reliable, no matter what it took.

That evening, after the car was loaded to go home, I discussed the whole reliability issue with Don. Jackie said we needed to do something, even if it meant missing the next race at Mid-Ohio. We decided to take the car back to Long Beach and hopefully do some tire testing and revamp our engine program. So I called Goodyear and they agreed to rent Riverside Raceway for a tire test three weeks later. Jackie felt better about it all and agreed to fly in for the testing. But I couldn't help feel that my relationship with Jackie had been damaged.

Stewart's Lola also suffered from tire problems and engine reliability. It had broken in two of the first three races, and at the Glen he had a puncture and lost a lap before the engine blew. In those days, reliability was king. Everyone knew that wiping lobes off camshafts and blowing big Chevy engines was a big contributor to race failures. Revson won for McLaren in another 1-2 with Hulme. Siffert was third in the underpowered but exciting 917 Porsche, two laps behind but proving that reliability pays. Andretti brought the big new Ferrari home fourth, also two laps off the pace. As far as I was concerned, they weren't any more competitive than our car, but they were sure beating us on reliability.

CHAPTER 34

Trouble with Rubber

The first tire test we did with Goodyear at Riverside, after our second race in the 1971 Can-Am, was almost a total disaster. After some exploratory laps, Jackie Oliver went for a fast lap with our UOP Shadow Mk 2 and at the kink near the end of the mile-long straight at about 200 mph—a speed we'd never seen before with this car—something really bad happened. Simultaneously, both front tires blew! It was amazing that Jackie didn't crash the car in the biggest possible way. He crawled back to the pits on the rims, and when he got back to us, his face was white.

The Goodyear guys worked out what had happened. The centrifugal forces in each of the small, wide, tubeless tires were enough to effectively increase the weight of the heaviest part of the tire, which was the tread. As the car went faster, the tread got so "heavy" that it pulled itself away from the wheel with enough force to detach the tire bead from the rim, causing the blowouts. This had never happened with 15-inch-diameter wheels, but the faster rotational speeds of our 12-inch wheels produced proportionately higher centrifugal forces. So we had a brand-new tire problem. That's the price you can pay for innovation!

There was no way to continue the test until we'd found a method of securing the front tires to the rims. Crashes due to sudden tire deflations were common in the 1960s and 1970s, and McLaren was now using bolts that pushed the tire bead against the edge of the rim, thus keeping the tire in place in the event of a puncture, and stopping the tire from pulling the car violently to one side. So we did the same. It solved the problem—but created another. Air leaked out around the bolts. I telephoned Tyler Alexander at McLaren, and he said they used flat washers with rubber O-rings in them. So we used them too. If safety was an issue, there were no secrets between the Can-Am teams.

The tires Goodyear provided for the test had shown a lot of promise as far as adhesion was concerned. Wear would be evaluated later. However, another problem that surfaced was unevenly distributed heat in the rear tires. I asked Goodyear to change the shape of the tire at the transition between the sidewall and the tread. They complained that every time they changed the tread design, they had to spend $10,000 to "Elox" the mold to include the tread configuration.

By then, dragster tires had no tread at all. I figured that if we also eliminated the tread, we could increase the rubber contact with the road surface and thus the traction, while saving expense for Goodyear. So I asked them to eliminate the tread. I also asked them to increase the front tire diameter to 13 inches for the Elkhart race and future test purposes. That would eventually allow me to put the front brakes outboard again and eliminate our problems with the brake driveshaft CV joints. Goodyear was happy, because they were already making 13-inch-diameter tires for Formula One development, and they were also keen to make us some new, low-profile, 15-inch rear tires without treads.

It was a real chore to find 13-inch-diameter wheels to test the new tires, but eventually we bought some modular wheels that were in two halves and bolted them together. Goodyear gave us time to test the new treadless tires before the next race at Elkhart Lake. The "slicks" worked great.

Pretty soon, all road-racing tires would be slicks, but it happened first in the Can-Am on the Shadow Mk 2 in 1971. The following year, Dennis Crobacs, the Goodyear tire engineer assigned to our project, was transferred to work in the Formula One program in England. The next thing was that all Goodyear's F1 teams switched to 13-inch wheels and slick tires. So once again a big development from the Can-Am had found its way onto the Grand Prix scene.

The Road America track at Elkhart Lake was one of my personal favorites, and the favorite American road course for many of the international drivers. About four miles round and with a couple of very fast straights as well as challenging turns, it's a great place for watching a motor race. One of the many viewing areas had been nicknamed "Thunder Alley" because it's narrow, with steep slopes on either side of the track, and the noise of all those Big Block Can-Am cars was just like continuous thunder. In the paddock, you can also get a pretty damn good Wisconsin *bratwurst* at the St. John the Baptist stand. A locally made *brat* sausage roll and a beer were standard lunch fare for most spectators and quite a few racers. I liked them because they reminded me of English sausages ("bangers," because if you didn't pierce the skins before frying them, they blew up!). The track is in Wisconsin's Tornado Alley, but although prone to storms, it's a beautiful resort area. It can get very hot and humid in the summer and this means that engine fuel mixtures needed to be watched closely to avoid burning out a piston.

When we'd finished the last tire test at Riverside, Goodyear had mounted up the best 13-inch and 15-inch tires and given us a spare set. We hung on to the 12-inch front wheels and tires and took everything to Road America. UOP had now supplied their own high-octane, unleaded gasoline potion, and we had six 55-gallon drums sitting in our paddock area to prove it. Our fuel feed problems appeared to have been solved. Everything seemed to be in place for a decent race experience.

We'd missed the fifth round of the Can-Am at Mid-Ohio. Stewart inherited the win with the Lola, and Siffert was second with the Porsche, after the McLarens of Revson and Hulme had succumbed to what were described as broken right-side driveshafts. The track was a very rough and bumpy experience for all, and Stewart, who had also broken some suspension stuff during practice, had just been lapped when Revson went out. My first reaction to the news of McLaren's driveshaft failures was that they must have found some amazing engine torque, but I realized they'd been caused by the inertial "spike" loads on the driveshafts when a track is bumpy and the rear wheels are constantly coming off the ground. In a way, I was glad we'd decided to swap that race for testing at Riverside. In contrast to what we were doing, both McLarens had inboard rear brakes at Mid-Ohio, but they switched Hulme's car to outboard rear brakes for Elkhart. We still had our inboard front brakes and outboard rears. After hitting 200 mph at Riverside, we knew we had excellent top speed capability.

In Friday practice, after wrestling with adjustable Koni shocks that seemed to want to readjust themselves, Jackie Oliver surprised us all with a flying lap that was only 0.004 second slower than the fastest man that day, Jackie Stewart in the Haas Lola T260. We'd started to call our driver "Ollie" when he did well, and that was a real morale booster for all of us. Ollie told us the car could be better in the slow corners, so it was an impressive performance. Ben Williams of UOP was as happy as a clam that he could report back to UOP that their new homemade gasoline was working so well.

True, the McLaren drivers weren't there on Friday. McLaren were again running a parallel Indycar program, and they were qualifying for an upcoming race in Ontario, California. On Saturday, Peter Revson opted to stay on in California, but Denny Hulme chose to fly to Wisconsin in time for Can-Am qualifying. "The Bear" shook everybody with a pole position almost 2.5 seconds faster than Stewart had gone on Friday. Ollie got it all right and knocked another 1 second off his Friday time to qualify alongside Denny and in front of Stewart. But our ecstasy was short-lived.

A close inspection of the tires by our Goodyear guys revealed that the wear was very bad on the rears. They advised us to revert to the old tires if we wanted to finish the race. It was a bitter pill to swallow, and I asked Jackie what he wanted to do—run the new stuff or revert to the old, which wasn't as competitive. I'd vowed I would never again ask Jackie to race a defective car, as I'd had to do at Watkins Glen. He said I was the one who had to decide, and he would do his best with whatever tires I chose. So I picked the best of the new tires, and we went with them for the race.

On race morning, John Timanus, the SCCA's technical inspector for the Can-Am, asked me to supply a sample of the fuel we were using. My mind started imagining all kinds of scenarios, but I figured what the heck, they wouldn't have time to analyze it before Monday, so why worry? So I found an empty Gatorade bottle and filled it from one of our fuel drums. Then I realized our fuel was pale green, like the Gatorade drink. So I put a label on it and wrote, "Highly Flammable Toxic Poison—Do Not Ingest" with a big red triangle around it. I walked over to the SCCA motor home in the paddock. Four SCCA officials were inside, having a quiet conversation and a smoke, and I said, "This is a fuel sample for John Timanus. Whatever you do, don't let anyone drink it—it's a deadly poison." At that very moment, the door opened and Timanus came in, very hot and red-faced. He went right up to the dinette table, and before anyone could stop him, picked up the bottle, took off the lid and took a giant gulp of our fuel. We all looked in amazement as his face turned into a horror-stricken mask. He immediately puked noisily straight across the table, and the fuel caught fire from someone's cigarette on its way towards the window drapes. I nearly fell down, I laughed so hard. I almost peed myself. The drapes were fire-resistant and they self-extinguished, but John was coughing, and his eyes were watering. I grabbed the bottle from him and replaced the lid. I said, "That was the fuel sample you asked me for. I've heard of the taste test, but don't you think you took it a bit too far?" As I left, the other guys were giving John some water to gargle to get rid of the taste. I never did get any test result, and the SCCA never asked to test our fuel again.

The ambient temperature for the warm-up session was over 90 degrees, with high humidity. Jackie reported that the slick tires had lost all the stickiness they'd had before. When the race started, Hulme's McLaren leapt into the lead and started to pull away from Jackie's Shadow. Very soon, Jackie's tires had basically changed characteristics and were now just carcasses on the rims. It must have been totally frustrating for him to be struggling to stay in front of drivers he'd out-qualified so well. It didn't take Stewart long to get past him, and Revson—incredibly, up from the back of the grid—also zoomed into third place. Stewart was out with a blown engine only two laps later, but our Jackie was gradually slipping back into the clutches of the field.

On lap 15, a tire went flat on the Shadow at the end of the front straightaway. Jackie carefully drove the three miles back to the pits, and we changed the tire. He came out of the pits in 11th place but had another puncture a few laps later and finished 12th. Hulme's engine broke its crankshaft, and Revson won again from Siffert in the reliable Porsche.

Our Shadow Mk 2 had finally finished a race, but it was the last car still running. I have to give Ollie a lot of credit for doing that. Some of the top drivers would have dropped out after the second flat tire, but he'd spent a lot of time with the big UOP contingent that had shown up, and I think he really wanted to finish for them.

Afterwards, the team's spirits were decidedly positive about the future. The engine was still running, and the front brake driveshafts were OK—it looked like the special grease from Dana was doing the trick. All we had to do now was get tires that were both fast and could live the entire race. I went and found my buddy Lee Gaug, who was now Goodyear's racing manager for the Can-Am. He said he would have some good tires for us at the next race. He'd been very impressed by the Shadow's qualifying pace and was 100 percent behind our efforts with the new tire format.

Next day, we set off to set up shop at UOP's Flexonics division in Bartlett, Illinois, which would be our base until we left for the next race at Donnybrooke in Minnesota in a couple of weeks. Flexonics made flexible bellow-type expansion joints for use in connecting pipes that carried steam or hot chemicals. They had great R&D facilities, and I soon discovered that equipment for testing and analyzing bellows and springs was available.

This was a happy coincidence. I'd been trying to make stronger suspension coil springs to handle the load changes due to aerodynamic downforce at speed. I'd designed what I thought were "progressive" springs and asked Jackie to get some made for me in England. In those days, most race cars used double wishbone independent suspension. The coil spring was around the shock absorber, mounted from the frame to the outer end of the lower wishbone. As the wheel jounced up, of course, the shock was compressed. But the shock had to be mounted at an angle of about 40 degrees, so if the wheel compressed an inch, the spring and shock only compressed a little more than half an inch. Because of the angularity of the "coilover" unit, the ratio of shock travel to wheel travel became worse by a small amount, which in effect meant the spring had a regressive rate instead of a constant rate. That's not good. To fix it, we designed springs that had coils near the end that would close down on each other. In theory, this should have resulted in an increase in the overall spring rate as it was compressed. In practice, it didn't seem to work like that. The new "progressive-rate" springs had been sitting in the transporter waiting for me to find time to evaluate them—and Flexonics was the place to do it.

While Goodyear worked on our new tires, and our mechanics (now led by Ray Brimble) sweated over preparing the car, I went into the air-conditioned test laboratory at Flexonics and played with my springs. It was about 100 degrees and very humid that summer in Illinois, so that was what the mechanics said I was doing! It was very interesting. I found that even if I changed the pitch of the coils in the springs so that they got closer together and even bottomed out against each other when compressed, the rate was still linear, albeit higher. My conclusion was that if I wanted to have a progressive-rate coil spring, it had to have tapered wire. But much later, I discovered that was wrong, too.

It wasn't until 2004 that I found a way to make a progressive-rate spring setup that worked. At the time, I was making rebound-control shocks for Amtech Corporation in Las Vegas to help in stopping high CG (center of gravity) vehicles, such as SUVs, from rolling over. It took two springs to do it—one to control the jounce (bump) and one to control the droop (rebound). My patents on this technology are on the United Stated Patent and Trademark website, www.uspto.gov.

The people at UOP Flexonics were fantastic to us and gave us lots of help in many ways. We decided that if we were still with UOP in 1972, we would ask them if we could make the Flexonics factory our base of operations for the Midwest and East Coast Can-Am races.

We arrived at the Donnybrooke track a day early so that Jackie and I could check it out, having never raced there before. The first thing we noticed was that we would have a big tire problem. The entire track was twisty, and we wouldn't see much speed until the start-finish straight. This was a very long straight (long enough to be used part-time as a drag strip), and it ended with a banked right-hander that could possibly be taken at full speed. However, we'd discovered in testing that the high-speed banked turn at Riverside would really heat up the outside tires and small pieces of tread would be torn right off. If you stood on the outside of the turn as the car went by, you could feel the rubber pieces hitting you. So what you really needed was a hard tire compound for that turn, and a soft compound for the rest of the track.

We still had the original tire from Elkhart and knew that it would quickly deteriorate in this place. Frantic calls to Goodyear did no good, and we reluctantly decided that Jackie would have to back off a little in turn 1 to make the tires last the whole race. Once again a whole division of UOP, based in St. Paul, Minnesota, sent their people to the race, and they invited us to use their facilities to prepare the car before the next race, at Edmonton in Canada.

Out of 22 cars on the grid, Ollie was fifth behind Revson, Hulme, Stewart, and Lothar Motschenbacher with his McLaren M8D. Ollie got off to a great start and, in the first right-hander, as Stewart nipped by Hulme to take the lead, he almost followed him through into second place, but Denny held him off. Then the Shadow began to fall back as the tires gradually deteriorated. But that wasn't what put us out of the race. It was our old enemy—a front CV joint lost a grease seal. The vibration through the front axles forced Jackie to stop after 28 laps. When I examined the CV joint boot later, I found it had split on a seam. It was just a bad part.

The team were disappointed but still optimistic that soon our luck would change. It had to: of the seven races so far, we had competed in five and had yet to finish in a decent position. The car had shown enough promise to get a podium spot and keep UOP happy. But quietly I decided that after the season ended, I was going to revert to the conventional tires. I'd concluded that trying to prove a point with experimental tires while actually racing was the wrong way to go. Our results didn't seem to hurt us publicity-wise. All the world loves an underdog, and as such, we had nothing to lose. I just yearned to get a good finish to clinch the UOP sponsorship for another season.

We set up shop in the Mine Well Screen Division of UOP in St. Paul, and prepped the car for the next race at Edmonton, the last in Canada before the traditional series finales at Laguna and Riverside. I'd never been to Edmonton before, but I'd heard that even at that time of the year, it was cold and wet. If it was cold, we had a better chance to finish with our temperamental tires because they would be less likely to overheat. We had two weeks to get the car ready and get it the 1300 miles to Edmonton. It would be a real push, so the mechanics worked hard on the car while I spent many hours on the telephone to Goodyear and our other suppliers, trying to get tires and parts sorted out. The UOP guys had a nice spray booth, so we repainted the whole car white. Once again, Ben Williams was lining up his UOP contacts in the area. The group's Mine Well Screen division made special filters for all kinds of mining operations, and they had a big presence in Alberta.

By the time we were ready to leave, we'd cut it real fine, and that meant a nonstop thrash to get up to Edmonton in time for practice. Our two-vehicle convoy was the Chevy pickup, which had a sleeper compartment, a ramp for the car, and some cupboards for spares, and the Econoline van. Ray Brimble put a big sheet of plywood over the top of the van's cargo compartment to make a makeshift bed. He also tweaked the van's engine, so the convoy could charge across Canada at up to 100 mph. The only time we stopped was to pee and gas up the vehicles. The transporter was very fast, and we used to put the van in its draft, about 10 feet behind. It was scary! Luckily the Trans-Canada Highway was almost deserted, but I was mighty glad when we finally pulled into the hotel in Edmonton the night before first practice.

Next day, we got to the track, and it rained straight away. It was so cold that Ray stopped on the way and bought some hand warmers for everyone. We were still in tire trouble, but the cold weather and the rain were big equalizers, and Ollie excelled in bad conditions. The track owners had used old tires, buried halfway into the ground, to mark the edge of the track in some really fast corners. Several cars clipped them, and it usually did its best to rip the nose right off. The track surface was rough and varied, and Ollie said it was difficult to get a fast lap without hitting one of those tires, so we kept his practice to a minimum. We ended up fifth on the grid behind Revson, Hulme, Stewart, and Motschenbacher.

Eric Broadley, the owner of Lola Cars, was visiting to check on the development of the latest Can-Am T260 that Stewart was driving when he wasn't busy winning the Formula One title for Ken Tyrrell. They'd made some radical changes to the front bodywork and moved the rear wing to help balance the car. I knew how that went, because I was doing the same thing at every race we did. Bob Marston had designed the T260, but Eric was taking a personal interest in its development. In 1961–62, I'd worked many hours with Eric on the first Lola Formula One car. In a quiet moment at Edmonton, I was chatting with him and I mentioned that when we'd taken the first Ti22 to Laguna for the first time, I'd felt the worst of all trepidation. I was really afraid I might have totally missed the mark in designing the car and would get laughed out of the place. He smiled and said, "Peter, don't worry, I get that feeling whenever we make a new car. It doesn't mean anything—it's natural." After that, I never had bad new-car jitters ever again.

The 1971 Edmonton Can-Am turned out to be a test of survival for everyone. It was very cold and it rained on and off all day. Stewart persuaded the organizers to move some concrete barriers that were in a dangerous location, but he couldn't get them to dig out those damn half-buried tires. During practice, Jackie finally clipped one, and it broke off a piece of the front fender. We had to do a hasty fiberglass repair. The rules said that if the bodywork got damaged, the driver had to stop to get it repaired or replaced. We didn't have a spare nose, so we got ready some aluminum, some rivets, and a drill in case we ripped off another fender in the race and got ourselves black-flagged.

Before the start, the McLaren mechanics found a bolt in the intake manifold of Revson's engine and had to tear off the manifold to get it out. This meant that everybody moved up a grid place, and Revson didn't get on track for several laps, which he had no hope of making up. Hulme never did like driving in the wet, and it was drizzling when the race started. He dropped to third behind Stewart and Ollie. After 24 laps, Hulme was able to squeeze by, but Ollie kept him honest, and we were elated to be in the top three at last.

Stewart had a big lead but had to take to the grass in lapping Motschenbacher, so Denny and Ollie closed him down. Then the Lola was hampered by a problem in the rear suspension and slowed. Denny took the lead—but Oliver caught one of those pesky buried tires and ripped the whole of the right front fender off the nose. The officials black-flagged him. As the first three cars had lapped the field a couple of times, we had time to rivet on our makeshift aluminum and still finish third, albeit a lap or so behind the Lola.

We'd done it—a top-three finish! OK, there were only 14 cars running at the end, but we'd lapped them all except Jo Siffert's Porsche in fourth place. Still, I wasn't about to consider the Shadow Mk 2 to be fully competitive with the McLarens and the new Lola, because the track conditions had been so much in our favor. It had basically taken tire traction out of the equation and Ollie's mastery of the rain had made our third place possible. Once again, I talked to Goodyear and begged them for some new tires for Laguna Seca, which was next on the agenda.

That night, we all went back to the hotel and had a much-needed celebration party—except Jackie and Don Nichols, who were invited to dinner with the UOP people. Their PR guy, Ben Williams, was so thrilled by our result that he'd retrieved the broken piece of fender, which had the UOP logo on it, so he could hang it on the wall in his office. It was the wee hours before we all finally went to bed, dreaming of even greater things in California.

CHAPTER 35

Peter Bryant, B.I.S.I.A.

Just after the Elkhart Lake race, where we'd run UOP's new fuel potion, I was asked by Ben Williams if I would make a presentation to the Milwaukee Section of the Society of Automotive Engineers (SAE) about the use of high-octane unleaded gasoline in the Can-Am. The presentation was to be called, "The UOP Shadow: An Exciting Laboratory," and it was scheduled two days after the Edmonton race. Ben told me the Bostrom aircraft seat division of UOP would be sponsoring the whole thing and would pay my expenses.

This was an opportunity to fly home! I would have done anything to avoid that long drive from Canada to California, so I agreed to fly to Milwaukee the Monday after the race and speak to the SAE on Tuesday evening. When I got on the plane it was full of racers, and I sat next to Eoin Young, the secretary of the McLaren team, and Stirling Moss. A lot of the other guys from McLaren were also on the plane, and Denny Hulme was in good form. It was a fun flight, and Ben Williams took a bunch of pictures of it all. I admit that I was a bit hungover. In that condition, I always have a very light sense of humor, so I told a lot of jokes, and we all laughed a lot. It was a welcome change from the usual post-race depression I'd been through most of that year.

ABOVE: My new business card, which stressed my unusual academic degree. (Peter Bryant)

I was met at Milwaukee Airport and taken to my hotel by Bob Ulichny, who was going to be the SAE's moderator at the presentation. He happened to be the plant supervisor of a big metal fabricating company called Ladish Co. in Cudahy, Wisconsin. He told me they made titanium forgings for aerospace applications and nuclear submarines and asked me if I would like a tour of the plant. Naturally, I did. So next morning he picked me up and took me to Ladish. They were heating giant ingots of titanium to red-hot temperature and then forging them into all kinds of things, from components for the Boeing 747 landing gear to giant rings of titanium for Minuteman missiles. It was amazing to see them take a glowing-hot titanium ingot out of an oven with a special fork-lift truck, with long forks that gripped it by the sides. They then positioned it under a four million horsepower hydraulic forge that came down and punched a hole right through the middle. That's right—four million horsepower! When the forge came down to punch the hole, it felt like the whole town of Cudahy jumped into the air. Then they took the ingot and put it in a roller that rolled it from 4 feet in diameter to over 10 feet. I was really impressed by this example of good old Yankee ingenuity.

The SAE had advertised my presentation in their national publication, *Automotive Engineering*, and they had the best-ever attendance at a Milwaukee Section meeting. Engineers from Ford, GM, and even Porsche came from far and wide to hear me say something about the problems associated with using unleaded fuel in a race car. I hadn't realized this was such a controversial subject. The automobile manufacturers were still resisting the EPA over emission controls. I'd never done anything like this before, and I'd assumed it would be like a pleasant conversation with a bunch of friends. Was I ever wrong!

During the pre-dinner cocktail hour, many people came up to me to say how much they were looking forward to hearing about our problems with the racing engines and unleaded gas. I realized that in the question and answer period following my presentation, there would be some tricky questions to answer. I decided that in deference to my sponsors, I would short-circuit that whole situation.

After the dinner, Bob introduced me to the audience, and I said, "Thanks for the nice introduction, Bob, and thanks for the tour of your Ladish plant today. Now I understand why America is winning the space race! Ladish sure does amazing things with titanium, so perhaps they would make some bits for my next race car?" Then I added, "I know high-octane unleaded gasoline is a controversial subject and that many of you will have questions for me when I'm finished. I'm going to put those questions into two categories. First, good questions that I'll answer right away. Second, tricky questions that are designed to get me to say something that a person could wave in front of the EPA and say, 'See, I told you so!' Like I said, I'll answer all the good questions. But if you ask me a tricky question, I'll come right down there and punch you on the nose!"

That did it—they all laughed. When question time came, one man asked me what material we used for the valve seats. I gave him a look and told him the question bordered on tricky, but it so happened that GM supplied us with valve seats made of Stellitte, which was a very hard material, so he was out of the woods. He laughed. The last questioner asked me what college degree I had. Well, I don't have a formal degree of any kind, so I gave him the same answer Ernie Kanzler had given me some years before, when I'd asked him if he had a degree. I said, "I have a B.I.S.I.A.," and I sat down.

They gave me some rousing applause, and Bob presented me with a handsome SAE gift of engraved drafting scissors. I still have them. As the hall emptied out, a couple of people came by with follow-up questions, and one of them was the guy who'd asked about my degree. He said, "I've been trying to figure out what a B.I.S.I.A. is." I told him, "It means I'm a race-car designer Because I Say I Am."

He laughed and asked me for my card. I gave him one with my name and home address on it. I thought no more about it until the following Christmas when a box of business cards arrived at home. They said, "Peter E. Bryant, B.I.S.I.A., Race Car Designer." It was real nice gift from him, and I thought it was great fun.

Bob Ulichny later nominated me to be an SAE member, and I've now been a member over 34 years. It's a great organization.

BELOW: Mixed emotions. Imagine how I felt seeing my first design doing so well against my latest creation. David Hobbs in the Ti22 harries Jackie Oliver in the Mk 2 Shadow at Laguna Seca in October 1971. (Peter Bryant)

CHAPTER 36

Mixed Emotions

A comedian once described mixed emotions this way: "Watching your mother-in-law going over a cliff in your new car." When we got to Laguna Seca, I suffered a bad case of mixed emotions because on the list of entries was the Ti22 Mk 2, my second titanium car, which was to be raced by David Hobbs.

When Ecurie Vickie went bankrupt, and the car and parts were sold in an auction by the IRS, it was apparently purchased by a new team I hadn't heard much about before. I think that one of the principals was Jerry Titus, the Trans-Am star. It was entered by T-G Racing, which had run a McLaren M12 in the 1970 Can-Am for Jerry Titus, and was sponsored by Delta Tire, a U.S. retail chain. Its specification looked much the same as it had in 1970, except for bigger brakes.

It was going to be tough enough to beat the Gulf McLarens and Stewart's L&M Lola. Now we were also going up against the car that had broken the Laguna lap record the previous year on the way to finishing second. We'd never raced our Shadow Mk 2 here—nor even tested it. This was a track that required lots of downforce and great brakes, so it was going to be very tough weekend. Goodyear had brought some new tires for us that were intended for Formula One, and we eagerly put them on the car straight away.

ABOVE: David Hobbs at speed in the Ti22 Mk 2 at Riverside. (Mike and Pat Smith)

In the very first practice, Hobbs did exactly as I'd feared he might in my old car—he beat the previous best lap time by the Ti22 Mk 2 by nearly 2 seconds with a lap under 60 seconds. It took all the skill of the McLaren drivers to get the pole away from him, and Hobbs ended up third—ahead of Stewart's Lola. The Lola had now been fitted with a really enormous, outrigged front wing—one journalist called it a cow catcher—to improve the front-end downforce and allow them to crank up the rear wing a bit more. Stewart also bettered the previous year's pole time by getting round in under 60 seconds. Meantime, Jackie Oliver complained that the UOP Shadow was sliding all over the track, so we added some more air dams and cranked up the rear wing. Jackie had always been able to control an oversteering car, and he looked spectacular as he threw it round the track. He finally got in a lap under the old record for fifth place on the grid, which was a superhuman effort.

Laguna Seca always brought out new cars, and this year it boasted a bigger grid: 30 cars instead of the usual 22. Among them was the BRM P167, driven by Brian Redman. It was the P154 that had previously been uncompetitive, but they'd made a bunch of improvements, and the modified car was quite a bit faster. Redman wound up alongside our UOP Shadow in sixth place on the grid. Redman was a great driver and a force to be reckoned with. Another addition to the competition was Vic Elford in a McLaren M8D. Roy Woods bought this car from Tony Dean on the Thursday evening after Elford wrecked his rebodied M8E. Elford was no slouch either, and knew the track from driving for Jim Hall the previous year. This wasn't going to be an easy race at all.

An additional problem for us was that Goodyear had improved the conventional tires used by all the other teams so that they no longer suffered from the vibration or "chatter" that had plagued them in the past. Revson told me they made an incredible difference to the works McLaren. That made me think I was really on the wrong track with our small tires. In fact, I had no more doubts about the small tires. I made up my mind that if I still had a job next year, they would go the way of the dodo bird! Meanwhile we had to get past this race first.

Hobbs's crew were having fits trying to keep the titanium car together, and in the warm-up they almost lost their grid position when the rear suspension broke. At the start of the race, Ollie got away great and went past "Hobbo" into fourth place—phew! That was a relief, because my new car was faster than my old one for a minute! But the Shadow only lasted 24 laps before Jackie pulled into the pits with a broken throttle cable and overheating brake fluid. Hobbs also ran into problems when he clashed with Dave Causey's Lola T222 and had to pit for a new rear wheel. The Ti22 wouldn't restart and so it was out of the race. Funnily enough, that wasn't good for my morale, either.

The new F1 tires weren't doing the trick, and once again we'd failed in our role as a

ABOVE: Jackie Oliver races the Shadow Mk 2 at Riverside. The rear wing has been moved forward to change the aerodynamic balance. (Mike and Pat Smith)

Can-Am challenger. Revson was declared the winner despite being black-flagged for dropping oil as he started his last lap. Stewart was second, followed by Hulme on the same lap. Redman was fourth, a lap down but still a lap up on Siffert and everybody else. When the leaders lap everybody twice, it says to me that if you're going to beat them, you need to get your act together real quick. I was already worrying whether our tires would behave themselves at the last Riverside race, two weeks later. Riverside was a fast track, which suited our aero package, but we would need a miracle to get past the McLarens and that Lola.

While we struggled to get some decent tires, the competition from McLaren heated up even more. They showed up at Riverside with new engines that were now out to 510 cid, and stronger than 40 acres of wild garlic. The fight to be Can-Am champion was going down to the wire. Revson was leading Hulme by enough points that he would be champion if he finished no lower than sixth—even if "The Bear" won the race. Of course, we were way down in the standings and no threat to anyone.

After the throttle had stuck and broken the cable at Laguna, we'd finally changed our intake manifold from the side draft configuration to the downdraught setup that everyone else used, and had gotten some extra power for our efforts. We now had 13-inch rims on the front and 15-inch rims on the rear, but we'd never run them on a track with a straight as long as Riverside. When we'd run the 12-inch tires in our testing there, they'd jumped off the rims going into turn 9 at the end of the straight at nearly 200 mph. In the first practice for the *Times* Grand Prix, the 13-inch tires did pretty much the same thing, but luckily Jackie again got the Shadow back to the pits without damage. Now we had a really big problem. The 13-inch rims had a different rim design than the 12-inch ones, making it almost impossible to install the bolts to hold the tires on. The angle between the bolt and the tire bead was too big, and once again the bead of the tire came away from the rim, and each tire deflated. But we persevered with the bolts, and Ollie managed to get fifth place on the grid before it happened again.

His lap time would have put him on the pole the previous year, so it wasn't for lack of trying. Hulme and Revson qualified on the front row ahead of Stewart and George Follmer in Roy Woods's McLaren.

We decided to use epoxy on the bolts to help seal them and let it cure overnight. Meanwhile we considered our options if they still didn't seal. The only one we had was to go back to the 12-inch front wheels. The 13-inch rims were so hard to seal that in the race morning warm-up session, they leaked the air and deflated again. We decided to put a set of 12-inch rims and tires back on for the race. But we still had to find the bolts and try to secure and seal them. Tyler Alexander lent us some sealer O-ring washers. By the time we got the last wheel done and back on the car, the grid had left, and Jackie had to start from the pits. He tried as hard as he could and even passed some cars, but after about 12 laps, he felt the tires deflating again and pulled into the pits.

And that was it for the 1971 Can-Am season. Hulme and Revson finished 1-2 for McLaren, and Revson was the champion. Jackie was 12th in the points table. The extra speed we'd gotten by making the car low-profile had hurt us instead of helped us. Our car was very fast at the end of the straights, but that was our downfall at Riverside because it forced the tires to jump off the front rims.

We certainly hadn't done as well in the 1971 Can-Am as we would have liked, but we had nothing to be ashamed of. We were the only American team to build and race a new car that year. We'd even put the UOP Shadow on the front of the grid and finished a race in the top three. We were the first car to prove that high-octane unleaded gasoline works in race engines, and we'd found out a lot more about the aerodynamics of Can-Am cars. So where to next?

At Laguna, I'd already asked Ben Williams if UOP was happy about sponsoring the Shadow team. He answered, "Absolutely!" He told me that all the UOP people who had come to a race with customers wanted more. He'd been told by one top UOP sales executive that he'd clinched a multi million dollar deal simply by bringing the client to see the car race. So I asked if UOP would be sponsoring us the following year. He said, "Without a doubt!" Boy, was I relieved to hear that.

I'd never liked the game that happened at the end of the season when the teams renegotiate their deals with sponsors, drivers, and mechanics. But Don Nichols had once told me that he would never fire me, so I figured I would get to do another version of the Shadow for the 1972 Can-Am. I continued to analyze our situation and make plans.

Once again, Don gave me his speech about keeping as much of the old car as possible to save money. When I looked it all over and examined the options, actually it didn't make sense to make a new chassis from scratch. Don said that he was thinking of having an engine turbocharged, and I knew that would mean the car would need to carry a lot of fuel. The Shadow Mk 2 held 84 gallons and averaged about 2.5 mpg with about 750 bhp. I figured that a 1000 bhp turbo engine would only get about 2 mpg. At that consumption rate, a nonstop, 200-mile Can-Am race would take about 100 gallons. You can imagine how much the handling characteristics would alter while the engine used up more than 750 lbs. of gasoline over the course of a race. But that wasn't the problem, because there was no way I could get all that extra fuel in the car. I'd already run 10-inch-high gas tanks past the back of the seat, and making even bigger fuel capacity wasn't in my book at all. If Don wanted a turbo, then we would have to refuel during the race. I'd noticed that as the Chevy engines were getting bigger, some of the cars were already running out of fuel before the race was over, like George Follmer at Riverside. I decided that the size of the fuel tanks we had was optimum.

The other big change was going to be aerodynamic. I'd decided to run the standard Can-Am rims and tires in 1972, so I would have to redesign the bodywork. And that meant new thinking about downforce.

So I told Don that I wanted to go to 15-inch wheels and reconfigure the bodywork, but to keep the same chassis, which was now proven and had been reliable for us. The 10-inch-high gas tanks gave us lots of options for radiator ducting, too. I also decided that I would try outboard front brakes as soon as I could get some new front uprights made to locate them.

We'd been using a Weismann transmission, and it was showing signs of age. We talked to Pete Weismann, and it turned out he was working on a new transmission for Indycars with a better ring gear and pinion location for eliminating driveshaft angularity problems. We ordered one to test. Don wanted to keep the car as American as possible, and Pete was a pretty smart American engineer. He later went on to build the first semi-automatic transverse gearbox for the McLaren Formula One car.

The rim/tire assemblies on the Shadow Mk 3 were going from only 18 inches in diameter at the front to the standard 23.5 inches, and the rears were going from 23.5 to 26.8. In my suspension geometry, I permitted the wheels to jounce a maximum of 1.5 inches, and that determined the height of the bodywork over the wheels. I decided to try at least two different body aero configurations when we next went testing. My primary choice was one that had deep air channels running from the nose inside the wheel arch area and continuing on either side of the cockpit and through the radiators, which were to be mounted on the top of the gas tanks on either side of the seat back. My secondary configuration meant closing in the tops of the channels in front of the radiator and then opening them up to reduce drag. The back tip of the rear deck lid area would curve downwards behind the tops of the wheels to help the rear wing to work better. I would make provision to mount a smaller front wing between the front fenders for balance adjustments.

Some other big changes were happening at the Shadow race team that would also be sure to impact the results in 1972. I guess UOP upped the sponsorship money quite a bit, because we moved the team into a bigger, 10,000-square-foot facility in Signal Hill near Long Beach. Things started humming.

I kept my little office on Atlantic Avenue. I was now the team engineer and didn't work on the cars anymore. We tried to keep our own game of "musical mechanics" to a minimum, but one guy played the game real fast. At Pete Weismann's suggestion, we hired a crew chief who had worked with Pete on an Indycar team. I guess he wasn't used to the freewheeling style of the crew and the purse-string control of Don Nichols, because suddenly he was gone. Ray Brimble renewed as our logistics guy and team leader, ordering the parts and interfacing between the team and Don. We had Dan, the parts chaser and general factotum. There was Graham, a long-haired English hippy mechanic from Peter Gregg's Florida-based Porsche team, who now wanted to live in California. We got another mechanic/helper named Bill who doubled as our truck driver. I was very happy when Ronnie Spellman, a first-class mechanic who'd worked with me before, also joined us. And I was sad when Mike Lowman, who'd come with me to Shadow after working for me on the Ti22, decided to go back to England with his wife.

After unsuccessfully—again—trying to recruit Gary Knutson from McLaren to build our engines, we did what we considered the next best thing and hired their best engine builder, Lee Muir, to run our engine program.

Don persuaded UOP to supply an 18-wheel tractor/trailer rig and a new motorhome to use for hospitality at the races. The UOP Shadow team were certainly upping the effort for 1972, and it was going to be very visible to anyone who attended a race that UOP was deadly serious about the Can-Am. But the series was obviously going to be even tougher.

A couple of weeks after the 1971 finale at Riverside, Roger Penske confirmed rumors that he would be running works-supported, turbocharged Porsches the following season. The reaction of Teddy Mayer at McLaren was to order his own turbo program and sign Jackie Stewart, the new Formula One World Champion, to replace Peter Revson, who was going to race Formula One McLarens instead. And there were tales of a radical, superlowline new Lola.

The 1972 Can-Am was going to be very exciting.

BELOW: With the team motorhome in the background, Jackie Oliver poses with the new Shadow Mk 3 at Laguna Seca in 1972. (Peter Bryant)

CHAPTER 37

Aero Advances

In February 1972, we took the Shadow to Orange County Raceway in Southern California to do some aerodynamic evaluation testing of the new body shapes. In those days, the computer was far in the future, and we were still using a handmade height-recorder to evaluate our aero downforce. We did the tests by running the car down the drag strip and recording suspension height changes at 120 mph. If we cranked up the angle of attack of the rear wing from a chord angle of 6 degrees to 8 degrees, we actually lost 70 lbs. of rear downforce because the wing stalled. So we left the wing at 6 degrees and installed a rear flap about three inches long at the trailing edge at an angle of 30 degrees. The stall was eliminated, and we picked up 80 lbs. of downforce. It was difficult, painstaking work because, as soon as you found an improvement, you had to change the static ride-height to compensate for the changes that the extra downforce would make to the attitude of the car. I started looking at the design of slotted wing flaps as a potential method to increase the downforce but decrease the drag.

We chose Laguna Seca for our first proper track test with Jackie Oliver. We'd raced the Shadow Mk 2 there, of course, so we had comparative lap times on file. In addition, it was a great place to test the effects of aero changes because you could see almost all the way round from the pits, so you could easily check and compare sector times for each body configuration tried. And the track manager, Bob Hugill, was looking for publicity to help generate income, so he gave us a sweet deal.

The aero testing went well, and we had some new 15-inch Goodyear tires that also worked very well. The body shape with the deep troughs turned out to generate the most downforce, and it was fairly easy at Laguna to trim the aero balance. Apparently we'd also picked up a bit more power, and before the test was over Jackie smashed the lap record. He could lap in qualifying trim in around 48 seconds. That was fantastic news.

Bob Hugill came down to the pits to see for himself, and the newly appointed Shadow PR man, Brad Niemcek (formerly with series sponsor Johnson Wax) was in orbit. I was glad to see that Don had hired a real pro to do our PR work. It would help Ben Williams of UOP to maximize the PR value of the sponsorship, and Brad was a fun guy to have around. He was one of the founders of the Polish Racing Drivers Club of America (PRDA), along with Tony Adamowicz (known as "Tony A-to-Z") and Oscar Kovaleski. The PRDA was a tongue-in-cheek pseudo organization, and the qualifications for membership included, "Must be of Polish origin," "Need not be of Polish origin," "Must be a driver," and "Need not be a driver."

With his great sense of fun, Oscar was a very popular member of the traveling Can-Am community at that time. On one occasion, the CEO of Johnson Wax was going to visit a race, and one of the SCCA marketing people handed members of the team one of those flat tins of the popular wax polish. He asked us all to make sure that when the VIP was being shown around pit lane, we were busy polishing our race cars with the stuff. Well, Oscar and his wife polished their car straight away, emptied the tin, and filled it with some caramel-flavored ice cream that happened to be the same color as the wax. As the Johnson executive walked past, they were sitting on their pit counter, eating the ice cream with plastic spoons. It stopped the guy in his tracks. He did an absolute classic double-take. He stood open-mouthed in front of Oscar, looked at the tin, looked at Oscar, looked back at the tin. Oscar finished his mouthful, scooped up another helping, opened his eyes wide, licked his lips, grinned broadly, offered the spoon to the guy, and said, "Mmmmm! Want some?"

That winter, along with Tony and Oscar, Brad had finished second in the famous Cannonball Run. They had a unique strategy because they tried to do the coast-to-coast marathon without stopping in a Ford van loaded with a bunch of 55-gallon gasoline drums, a Porta-Potti, and a supply of food and water—probably of the Polish variety. They completed the course from Manhattan island in New York to Manhattan Beach, California, at an amazing pace and were only beaten by Dan Gurney and Brock Yates in a Ferrari. They would have won it but they made a wrong turn at Indianapolis. Can you imagine how dangerous it was to drive a van loaded with 55-gallon drums of gas at breakneck speed across America? Let alone living in a closed vehicle with a Porta-Potti fueled by Polish sausages and knishes. I bet that was fun!

The off-season was a dead time for racing news, and it wouldn't take long for the press to learn about the testing performance of the new Shadow. So publicity photos were taken, and

Jackie Oliver,
driver, UOP Shadow

Peter Bryant,
designer, UOP Shadow

UOP Racing Team

ABOVE: The official 1972 Shadow racing team photo, taken after Jackie broke the Laguna Seca track record. Don Nichols is at the far left; I'm kneeling beside the car. (Shadow Publicity)

CHAPTER 37 · 343

we all went happily back to Long Beach to get ready for the first race. What a relief it was for me that Jackie and Don Nichols were so happy with the car! I slept well after that test.

It's amazing how the development of the most subtle aerodynamic features of a race-car body can make such huge differences in how the car grips the track. The big difference between then and now is simply that the analysis tools today are so much better, thanks to the invention and development of the microprocessor. The weirdest thing is that much of the aero development we're doing now is based on a technological breakthrough from the nineteenth century. Computational fluid dynamics (CFD), a very common 3D analysis technique for flow visualization, is all based on some "balance equations" developed in 1822 by Claude-Louis Navier at the Sorbonne in Paris, France, and Sir Bernard Stokes at Cambridge University in England. They were trying to make more efficient sails for ships going to the New World. Part of their Navier-Stokes equations was based on a calculation so complex that it couldn't be resolved properly until the computer was invented in the twentieth century. Now CFD is used by all race-car designers for flow analysis.

When I was designing the Shadow Mk 3, I tried to buy a surplus computer with computer-aided design software in it from the McDonnell-Douglas surplus store just around the corner from my office. They wanted $80,000 for it. It was seven feet tall and weighed about 200 lbs. The 8-lb. laptop I use now has a very good CAD program that can do a mass properties analysis of a 3D shape with two clicks of the mouse. I can solid-model a shape and have it CFD-analyzed for under $300. The computer and software cost me about $7000.

Back in the good old days, I spent many hours reading books about airfoil shapes, trying to educate myself, because all I had was a B.I.S.I.A. By the time I finally quit auto racing, I was really getting into slotted wings, and I'm kind of sorry I didn't pursue that.

On May 11, 1974, I was invited by Bernard Pershing of the American Institute of Aeronautics & Astronautics to present the first definitive paper on "Can-Am Cars & Ground-Effects" at the AIAA's Second Symposium on Aerodynamics & Racing Cars in Los Angeles. It was later published by Motorbooks International.

By the time we got the Shadow Mk 3 to Mosport for the first race of the 1972 Can-Am, we'd managed to tune the total downforce at 100 mph to over 900 lbs. At full speed, it could push the car down to within a half-inch of the track surface, generating more than 1G of force. If the track had twisted and gone upside down, the car would have still clung to it. As a result, our suspension springing got stiffer and stiffer, and our car went faster and faster.

BELOW: This picture of the rear bodywork of the Mk 3 shows all the air exit ducts. The rectangular housing goes over the oil cooler. (Peter Bryant)

CHAPTER 38

Porsche Spoils the Party

We didn't know it at the time, but the first race of 1972 at Mosport Park, which was the 50th round of the Canadian-American Challenge Cup, marked the beginning of the end for the series. Roger Penske's team showed up with the turbocharged Porsche 917/10K, with Mark Donohue driving. We'd raced before against a naturally aspirated Porsche 917 and beaten it, but this car was something else entirely. It raised the bar so far above our heads that we knew we would never be able to touch it again.

Jackie Oliver and I took one look at the new Porsche and almost blanched. Trying to find something comforting to say to him, I remarked that anything that complex had to break down pretty often, and told him not to worry. One journalist said they had 1000 horsepower. I couldn't figure how they had enough gasoline to finish a race without refueling but found out they had an auxiliary tank mounted in the rear wheel arch area. The twin-turbo 5.7-liter V12 reputedly weighed about 650 lbs., whereas a Big Block Chevrolet V8 weighed about 500 lbs. But the turbos almost doubled the horsepower—a pretty good trade-off, I thought. Porsche said that for the sake of the competition, they would sell a small number of 917/10K cars to private teams for about $175,000. Or you could buy the engine for $66,000 and put it in any car you liked.

After our well-publicized test at Laguna, Roger Penske had told the press he was worried about the new Shadow. Looking in awe at his new car, I doubted that. I don't think Roger was really going to worry about anything anymore as far as the Can-Am was concerned. His strategy was to make the rest of us worry, and it was working. Before practice at Mosport, Tyler Alexander of McLaren must have spent at least an hour looking over every aspect of this new threat. I asked him what he thought, and he replied, "I think we've all got trouble!" At one point, I thought McLaren would buy a Porsche engine, but they didn't.

The first practice turned out to be a frustrating experience for the UOP Shadow team, because we ran into fuel-feed problems, and our new Weismann gearbox acted up and broke the second-gear teeth right off. I got on the telephone and tried to persuade Pete Weismann to come to the race and help us out with the gearbox. He said he was too involved with his Indycar project and couldn't get away. So we soldiered on with it.

The track was really bumpy, and everyone complained about traction out of the slow turns—except Donohue. He put the Porsche on the pole with a lap in 1:4.2, ahead of the all-new McLaren M20s of Peter Revson on 1:15.0 and Denny Hulme on 1:15.2, with Jackie fourth on 1:15.6. The next fastest car was 3 seconds slower! Jackie said he had a real flyer going until the engine spluttered with another fuel-feed problem, so he thought he could get past the McLarens based on the car's handling, which he really liked.

At the start, Donohue took off like a rocket. Ollie overtook Denny into third place, but it was all to no avail, because the gearbox overheated and put us out after only six laps. A seized throttle linkage delayed the new Porsche, and Hulme was the winner, with Donohue second and Revson classified third after a late-race engine failure.

I found out later that the plumbing of our exterior-mounted oil pump had been installed back to front, which was why it had overheated. It wasn't fair! The previous year, we'd run an older Weismann gearbox, and it had been the one bullet-proof component we could trust. All I'd done was trade it in for a newer, better model—and this was happening. I spent a lot of time talking with Pete Weismann about it. When I asked him why a gear had broken, he said it was from a new supplier he was trying, and that made me really nervous. I began to make contingency plans and told Don Nichols I wanted to buy a new Hewland gearbox in case the Weismann transaxle turned out to be a lemon.

So we had a few problems to solve before we went to Road Atlanta. I got back to my little office and immediately started drawing up the major modifications we would need to the chassis to enable us to change over to a Hewland LG transmission. I couldn't wait until I had a gearbox in my hand to start, so I called Carl Haas, who was the Hewland distributor for the United States, and he sent me all the Hewland data I needed. I had to design a completely new rear suspension crossmember and mounting method, and get the parts made. It also meant changing the mountings of the engine oil cooler and the rear wing.

I then asked Ray Brimble what was happening about the new front uprights I'd designed to put the front brakes outboard. The McLaren team had switched their rear brakes to inboard from outboard, but I wasn't ready to do that. Our problems with the front brake driveshafts had been ameliorated somewhat by the new grease, and I knew they were being created by the torque inertia. I wasn't ready to have that problem at the rear, too! Ray promised to contact Gerry Magnuson and find out what was happening. When you need something in a hurry in auto racing, you often have to pay a premium or even in advance, so I told Ray to keep after Don, as well as Gerry.

I was beginning to dislike the problems that can arise from having many people working on a car. We kept lists of tasks and who did what, but mistakes still happened occasionally. The Can-Am cars were getting very complex, and it wasn't like my good old Formula One days when you could do a race with only one or two mechanics per car. I'd also realized that as the engineer, I simply had to trust the mechanics, much like the driver has to. I remember someone from the press asking Stirling Moss if he ever worried about the wheels being properly done up. He replied that if he ever felt the need to get the wheel wrench and check that they were tight, he might as well take off his driving suit, get rid of the mechanics, and take the car apart himself. It was a matter of trusting the mechanics to do their job properly. But I was a mechanic first and a designer second, so I constantly worried about things that could put the car at risk of a DNF. Although I'd moved from being a race mechanic to a race engineer, it was sometimes a very frustrating experience for me.

Specifically, I started worrying about the effect of more horsepower on our reliability. It's great to have a lot of power, but if you lose your engine durability, you have to consider taking a step back and looking at how best to run qualifying versus the race itself. McLaren were now using special engines for qualifying. Maybe we should follow their example: as the old saying goes, "To finish first, first you have to finish!"

We decided to go to Atlanta a couple of weeks before the race to do some testing. A couple of the other teams did the same, but got there after us. It was another of those hot, humid summers in Georgia and overheating was again a big concern. The first disaster happened when Jackie had the throttle stick wide open as he was going up the hill from the first turn. There's a left-hand swerve, and it was very scary to see the front tires locked and skidding at 165 mph, making lots of smoke as the rears pushed the car as fast as they could into the barrier. The Shadow went into the barrier hard enough to bend the right side of the tub very badly. Luckily Jackie wasn't badly hurt, but he had a few bruised ribs.

We were camped in Ray Brimble's old race shop and decided that the fastest thing to do was to strip the chassis down to its bare bones and fly it back to Pro-Fab in California to get it repaired. If we'd driven straight back, we would have lost at least two days each way, so it made good sense. We had some spare body parts with us. We left the pedals and seat divider in place but took off all the suspension and other parts. I flew back to work with Pro-Fab, and they performed some kind of miracle by repairing the tub in two days. We got the chassis back to Atlanta in plenty of time to rebuild the car before the race.

As we were working in the shop the Monday before the race, Mark Donohue also had a big accident when his Porsche lost the back part of its bodywork on the return straight. The car was destroyed, leaving him just about strapped to the engine. Luckily he wasn't seriously injured, but he did require knee surgery, so Roger Penske brought in George Follmer to drive.

It didn't look good for us. We had another gear break off all its teeth in the Weismann transaxle, and the engine was getting very hot, causing fuel vaporization. Everyone had a theory about why the engine was overheating, but I wasn't happy with any of the explanations. The design of any engine cooling system is based on simple heat rejection calculations. It's a matter of getting the air through the radiators efficiently and ensuring you have sufficient radiator capacity. I was concerned that the airflow wasn't going through the radiator properly. Should I put on some more entry ducting? Or did I need more efficient exhaust ducting? Or perhaps I needed to look at the efficiency of the engine water pump? Or did we have a blown head gasket? Lee Muir, our engine guy, checked that out and the gaskets were OK. Lee said that because we now had more power, we were making more water jacket heat for the radiators to cool. It was now the Saturday before the race, and I couldn't do anything about the water pump, so I changed the ducting to make the air go through the radiators better. Jackie went onto the track to check it out and almost immediately broke a driveshaft. I was beginning to think that Atlanta was not a good place for us.

There were other disasters that Saturday, too. David Hobbs had a rear suspension failure in his brand-new Lola T310 and did a nice set of 360 degree spins at about 180 mph. Luckily he didn't hit anything. Then a conrod broke in Revson's engine, which oiled up the track. Follmer got the pole in the Porsche with Hulme beside him, and Revson shared the second row with a very fast newcomer, François Cevert in the ex-Revson McLaren M8F. Oliver never got in a good flying lap and ended up on the seventh row of the grid—our worst-ever starting position. On race morning, Jackie did get to put in a much faster time in the warm-up than he had in qualifying, but then the gearbox shucked the teeth off yet another gear. I felt totally frustrated about it all. The worst part was that UOP had invited a whole bunch of important guests, and Jackie had to entertain them. I bet that was tough going.

The only people who didn't think the Atlanta race was a disaster were the Penske Porsche team, because Follmer won it for them. It was so hot that drivers were stopping at the pits to get buckets of water thrown over them. Jackie had the throttle stick wide open again, but he didn't crash this time, and got back to the pits by switching the engine on and off. We discovered that a small tube carrying fire extinguisher gas into the footbox had come loose from its riveted clip and was holding the throttle pedal full open after it was pushed past it. It was obvious that this is what had caused the throttle to stick the first time, and Jackie was justifiably furious. I didn't know where to put my face and promised Jackie it would never happen again. We got him back into the race, but when the engine blew at 20 laps, I was almost glad it was over for us. Hulme was unhurt when his McLaren blew over backwards on the return straight, landing upside down. Revson's M20 went out with a magneto problem, and Cevert's engine broke its camshaft.

Next day, Don and I flew back to Long Beach, and the crew went back to Ray's shop to get the car ready for Watkins Glen. I didn't like what was happening with the car. I knew it would be hot at the Glen, too—but what to do about it?

We asked Pro-Fab to make us a second chassis and a second set of suspension parts. It wouldn't hurt to have a second car to fall back on if the Atlanta scene ever happened again. Don agreed because he said that things were looking good with UOP for the following year, so he was thinking of running two cars in some of the six Can-Am races that were left. We were going to be on the road for quite a spell, because we'd planned to do the Glen, Mid-Ohio, Elkhart Lake, and Donnybrooke without returning to our HQ, and had arranged to base ourselves after the Glen in UOP's Flexonics plant in Illinois. Don had decided to rent a couple of apartments in Bartlett, Illinois, for the team during that period. I asked him if we could do some aero testing to solve the cooling problems, and he agreed but not until after Watkins Glen.

It turned out the Atlanta engine had suffered a broken valve spring and had then "dropped a valve." This expression means that after a valve spring has broken or the engine has been over-revved, a valve sticks open a little and the piston hits it and bends it. Then the other valve opens and chops off the bent one, and that usually means the piston will break, and the engine will blow. It's very nasty sequence of events. I hoped this didn't mean we were going to have a spate of engine failures to deal with on top of everything else. I wondered what the hell was happening. We had hired McLaren's best engine builder, so what else should we do? I telephoned Lee, and he said it wasn't unusual to get a batch of faulty parts, and he would do his best to see it wasn't a trend. He asked me what I was doing about the engine cooling problem. I told him there wasn't time before Watkins Glen for any aero testing, but I would be making some changes to the body to make the radiators cool better, and I was having a special radiator made at Pro-Fab that would increase the cooling capacity. It was another case of using a Harris Tweed jacket to cure dandruff, but I had no time to do anything else.

When I thought a bit more about the whole picture, I realized that when Penske had upped the ante with the turbocharged Porsche V12, the rest of the competitors had all gone balls-out to get more power from our stock block Chevrolet V8s. We weren't the only team having engine-related problems. McLaren was having engine and drivetrain failures, as was the Haas team with the new Lola. I was willing to bet there was more to come.

I really hated to redesign the bodywork, because it had given the UOP Shadow great handling characteristics. Whatever I did with the shape to improve cooling efficiency, we would lose downforce or pick up some drag. Years later, when vintage racer Bud Bennett raced the Shadow Mk 3 body shape with a turbo engine, he had no cooling system problems at all. He said the water pumps we used in the 1970s were crap compared with those available now.

The team was already at the Glen and Jackie had run a few laps when I arrived with my ugly L-shaped radiator under my arm. It was hot again, and already the cooling system was showing signs of trouble. The mechanics didn't seem glad to see me, and when they saw the radiator, they all laughed. "Anyone got a better idea?" I challenged. They mounted it, and it seemed to help the system cool a bit better. It took air from the front right intake duct channel and not only passed it through the main radiator body on the right side, but through another duct that also vented through the side of the car. It added another couple of quarts of water, too, and that didn't hurt. I was beginning to feel like a nuisance to the crew because I was so edgy. I stayed late to work on the car myself to make sure everything we needed to do was covered. I asked Lee if we should buy a water pump from the McLaren supplier, but he said ours was the same kind of pump, so it must be that our cooling system was inadequate. That did it for me. I decided to change the radiator intake duct system right after that race.

The other teams complained about "chatter" from the latest Goodyear rear tires when exiting corners, but we never experienced it. Even so, Jackie was out-qualified by Revson, Hulme, Follmer, Cevert, and Hobbs, the Lola only 0.035 seconds faster than the Shadow.

The only guy to get relief in our garage was a prisoner some state troopers brought in to get his handcuffs cut off. They'd arrested him for being drunk and disorderly. He had gigantic wrists, and when they cuffed him, his hands went blue and got very swollen. They couldn't turn the key, so they asked us to cut off the cuffs. Boy, was he ever thankful. I think that incident must have distracted one of our mechanics because, in the race, Jackie had to stop to replace a brake pad that had been installed back to front and was causing all kinds of problems. After he went back out, he crashed into the guardrail when the brakes failed completely after only 18 of the 60 laps. Hulme and Revson finished 1-2, kicking everyone's butt including the Penske team, who proved to be just as fallible as anyone else in the heat. Hobbs gave up third place to Cevert to get a bucket of water in the face in the pits. It had been a killer weekend, and I was glad it was over.

Our record was now zero finishes from three starts. I was determined that we would finish the next race, or someone would be leaving the UOP Shadow team. There was something very wrong. Jackie knew it, too, and at one point he asked me if it was true that some of our mechanics smoked pot. This was the 1970s, and lots of young people smoked weed. I knew a couple of the mechanics did but had never worried that they would when they were working. I told Jackie I had no control over what they did in their own time, but I wouldn't hesitate to ask Don to fire anyone I caught doing it in working hours. He said, "Well, something's very wrong, and it has to be fixed. If we're going to have a sponsor next year, I need to finish a race!"

In front of Ben Williams of UOP, I promised that if he didn't finish at Mid-Ohio, I would resign in favor of any engineer he cared to name. No pressure on me, then.

BELOW: A front view of the revised radiator ducting on the Mk 3. (Pete Lyons)

CHAPTER 39

A Job on the Line

I got down to business just as soon as we'd set up shop in UOP's Flexonics plant in Bartlett, our temporary base for the next four races. I hired Bill Petrie, an English mechanic who had some drafting layout experience, to help me out with reworking the bodywork of the Shadow Mk 3. I'd drawn up a NACA-type duct full-size in Long Beach, and I gave him the drawing to lay up the new ducts on the fenders of the car. We made a mockup of the actual duct and had some fabricated in fiberglass. I closed off the deep troughs that went around the cockpit, and with help from my old friend Bob McKee in Palatine, found a fiberglass shop to do all the body modifications and make some new molds and body parts. We needed spares as well as a body for the second car.

The Glen crash didn't really do much damage to the chassis. The body was damaged, but it wasn't a problem because I was going to change the nose section of the car anyway. Meanwhile, the second chassis was finished and was sent up to Bartlett. Don Nichols had put in Lee Muir as the liaison man with Danny Jones, who was doing the turbo engine development for us in Detroit. Lee liked that because his family lived near Detroit, and it gave him a chance to visit home. He'd also recruited a mechanic from McLaren to assist him with the engine chores, so now we had nine people on the road.

ABOVE: With the side channels gone and the new "duck bill" nose tips, we found we didn't need the Mk 3's front wing on fast tracks. (Peter Bryant)

The body modifications went well. We put the radiators back into the original configuration and used the same exit ducts in the rear body to get the air out. I changed the chisel-point nose tips of the fenders to more of a "scoop" configuration and figured it might even increase our front-end downforce. I'd tried various wings on the nose, and the original one located between the fenders seemed to work best if we found we needed a wing.

Meanwhile Lee checked out the engine from Watkins Glen and found it had a couple of broken valve springs again. He ordered some from a different supplier. Looking back over our data, it looked like the valve springs broke after about 150 miles of racing. That wasn't good, since most of the races were 200 miles! I told Lee that until he solved the failure problem, he should be prepared to change valve springs on every engine after the last practice and maybe even just before the race started. I had Pro-Fab send me all the parts I would need to convert the car to a Hewland transmission, and Ray picked up two transmissions from Carl Haas. There wasn't time to install the Hewland before leaving for Ohio, so we put all the stuff in the truck.

We took along the second chassis and its bodywork to assemble at the Mid-Ohio circuit. That went well, so we decided to use the newer Shadow for this event, and the older car as a spare. Don wanted to install his turbo engine in the older car, but the turbo was still a work in progress.

Practice and qualifying turned into another frustrating experience. Twice we had to overhaul the Weismann transaxle because it stripped the teeth off gears. We finally managed to get in a couple of flying laps, and Jackie qualified fourth fastest. George Follmer was over 1 second faster than the Shadow in the Porsche (which the rest of us had taken to calling the Panzer, after the fearsome World War II German tanks), and the McLarens lined up between them. We had some satisfaction by out-qualifying David Hobbs in the works Lola and a couple more Porsches, including one 917/10K turbo driven by Peter Gregg.

I remembered what I'd said to Jackie about replacing me if we didn't finish this one. When we got back to our base for this race, which was a garage that maintained ambulances, I called the whole crew together and told them I'd had enough of the gearbox failures and that we were going to switch over to a Hewland transaxle there and then. And by the way, we would also switch the engine for a fresh one, so it would be an all-night thrash. I split the crew into two groups and told them that half could go back to the hotel, and then come back to the garage at 2:00 a.m. and trade places with the others. I would personally supervise the Hewland transaxle installation and take the Weismann Locker out of the old transmission, install it in the Hewland, and reset the ring gear and pinion. Everyone agreed to this plan, and I think it helped because I would be the only guy working all night. The

McLaren team was in the same building as us, and they worked all night, too. The second crew came back on time, but we still ran late getting all the modifications done. The last things we had to do were to check the suspension setup and fabricate the revised gearshift linkage. By the time we got those done, there wasn't even time to load the car onto the transporter. I asked one of the ambulance guys if he would lead the way with his siren on, but he said it wasn't legal, so Ray drove the race car to the track with us following closely in our station wagon, with a towrope handy in case something happened. We just got into the paddock in time for the warm-up session.

I'd hit the gear ratio selection right on the money, and Jackie had a good session until the car sprang a gasoline leak around one of the tank connections. By then, I was so tired that I just told Ray that I needed him to take charge and get the car sorted out for the start. When the race did finally start, everyone in our pit knew that my job was on the line and that I was personally going to handle any situation that arose.

Follmer took off like a rocket in the Porsche, followed by Peter Revson and Denny Hulme. Ollie had a bit of a dice with Hobbs in the Lola, and then it started to rain. Follmer spun twice without losing his lead. The first car into the pits for rain tires was Hulme's McLaren. McLaren was still using four lug nuts to hold the wheels on, and it seemed to take forever to change them. Revson, Hobbs, and others came in to switch tires too, but I decided to keep Jackie out as long as possible on his slicks. I figured that changing over to wets was the driver's decision to make, anyway. Jackie was soon making all kinds of headway, and he was able to unlap himself on Follmer and push even harder. Pretty soon he was in second place and catching up to the Porsche in leaps and bounds. At the finish, Jackie was only a few seconds behind George, and they were both three laps up on the third-placed car, Milt Minter's naturally aspirated Porsche 917/10. Revson retired with a gearbox failure, and Hulme finished another lap behind, with Hobbs a lap behind him. We were the first "atmo" car to finish the race, so I told Ben Williams that when he called in the result to UOP, he should tell them we were first in class! He was beside himself with joy, and so was I. We'd finally finished a race—and nearly won it.

When Jackie asked me why the car had handled so well in the wet, I was a bit reluctant to admit to him that the rear anti-rollbar mounting bracket had broken on one side, and the bar hadn't been working at all. What a strange thing—something had broken that actually helped make the car go faster in wet conditions! But I told Ollie that it had been his fantastic driving that had made all the difference. Actually there was a lot of truth in this. If I had to race a car in the rain and a choice of any driver in the world, the only one I would have considered was Jackie Oliver. He was truly magnificent that day in Mid-Ohio.

Jackie later gave me a bonus check for $500 he had gotten from a previous race as an oil company endorsement. I really appreciated that token of thanks for my efforts. It made working all night even more worthwhile. Ben Williams told me he was glad because the result meant I would be staying on with the team. Boy, so was I!

We all hurried back to Bartlett to get ready for the next race at Elkhart Lake two weeks later. Don had persuaded Carlos Pace, the up-and-coming Brazilian driver, to drive for us at Elkhart, so now we had two cars to get race-ready.

When Lee examined the engine that had finished the Ohio race, he found it had two broken valve springs. That race was 172 miles long, and it was obvious that we had an ongoing problem making an engine last a 200-mile race distance. If we had difficulty getting only one car to finish a race, what were we in for with two? By then, Lee was spending time between the turbo development and the current engine program and relied heavily on Stump Davis to rebuild engines back in Long Beach. I expressed my concern to them both. Broken valve springs are one of those problems that can get blamed on the driver over-revving the engine by accident, and I wasn't totally convinced they believed we had a real problem. But Lee and Stump promised to make a concentrated effort.

I'd just about run myself out of gas at Mid-Ohio by working all night, and had come down with some kind of flu, but I loved to race at Elkhart Lake and was looking forward to it. When we got there, it turned into a nightmare with the two cars. I wanted to try some different aero tweaks to see if I could make the car faster on the straights, but the rain wouldn't cooperate, and it was hard to get two laps in a row. Jackie's car suffered shock absorber problems, and we went through every shock we had, trying to find some that would be consistent. They seemed to be undoing the rebound control adjustment, and we ended up trying to epoxy them at one setting. Road America is very critical for shock rebound control because of the high speeds and the need to prevent the car from pitching too far forward under heavy braking. The second Shadow had all kinds of rain-induced electrical problems, and Carlos complained about a vibration from the inboard front brakes. Carlos was very patient with us and very complimentary about the car's handling, but he really hated that vibration. He told me that with regular outboard brakes, he felt that the car would be much better and probably faster. He didn't like driving in the rain, and it rained on and off all through the first day of practice.

Pole position was easily taken by Hulme with a lap over 2 seconds faster than anyone else. Like the previous year, there was a conflicting Indycar race, and Revson was one of the drivers affected, so he lined up the second works McLaren way down the grid. Follmer had problems in qualifying and ended up in 13th place in the Panzer, but François Cevert also managed to find a dry lap and stole second place on the grid in his older McLaren M8F. The fast long straights of Road America suited the V12 Porsches to a tee, and both Milt Minter and Gregg got ahead of Jackie on the grid. Jackie finally got in a decent lap between the showers and qualified fifth, ahead of Hobbs in the Lola. Carlos was way down the grid, the 29th of the 34 cars that qualified.

The NART team appeared at this race with their Ferrari 712M, which had also copied the high side fences from my Ti22. Jean-Pierre Jarier qualified the car in 10th place, and their presence certainly made the Can-Am scene even more international and interesting. Although it was a constant struggle to get near the front of the grid, nobody on my team was complaining. UOP was being very supportive and was very happy to see us run a second car. Ben Williams said that John Logan, the CEO, was extremely happy with the results that they were getting from their involvement with us in the Can-Am. The people at the Bartlett UOP Flexonics plant came in droves to watch us at Elkhart.

Once again the race turned into a reliability derby. Jackie made a great start and was in third place by the third lap, behind Hulme and Cevert, but it only took George seven laps to catch them. The Porsche went into the lead on the seventh lap when Denny's McLaren was stopped by electrical problems. Revson retired with a broken clutch, so the McLaren boys were finally seeing what it was like to find themselves up against a dominant force. Jackie held down third place past the halfway mark, but just as it looked like we would get another podium, he came into the pits, and retired. We told the press that the problem was a broken exhaust system, but actually it went a bit deeper than that. Pace had no luck at all and went out after only four laps with electrical problems. He didn't have a very happy first Shadow experience!

Follmer's Porsche was the only car to go the full 200 miles, finishing a lap in front of Cevert's McLaren. Gregg inherited third place with his Porsche, and Jarier fourth in the Ferrari. One or two cars ran out of gas, and that revived my thoughts about turbo engines being gas-guzzlers, especially when it was rumored that Porsche were now getting 1200 bhp out of the 917/10K. By my calculations, Follmer was running on fumes at the end of that race.

Carlos Pace's comments had made inboard front brakes an issue again, although Jackie wasn't complaining about them. We were renewing the CV joints before the practice sessions and before the races, and it had been paying off. But I couldn't see the point in making new front uprights if we weren't going to try the outboard setup. I asked Ray to find out when the uprights would be ready. He said they only needed some machining on the castings. I wanted at least to put them on for Carlos's car. We also decided we needed to do an engine test to confirm whether the valve spring problem persisted, so we scheduled a test at Donnybrooke prior to the race weekend. We needed to test there anyway because we had to check how our tires would hold up for the race. The problem we'd had the previous year with tire heat generated in the first turn was still a factor, and it would help if we had a strategy to use for the race.

We started our engine evaluation test with a brand-new engine, using the laps to set up Jackie's car and test the tires. It was soon obvious we had the same tire problem as before. Lumps of rubber could be seen flying off in the first turn and Jackie told me that if he really stood on it there, the tires would overheat and he would be struggling through most of the other turns until they cooled. In spite of that, Jackie was going round close to the Can-Am lap record. We did about 157 miles, and then some valve springs started breaking in the engine. We had no engine builder on hand so we changed the springs ourselves and carried on testing.

OPPOSITE: The two Porsches lead Denny Hulme's McLaren and Jackie Oliver in the Shadow at the start of the 1972 Laguna Seca race. (Pete Lyons)

Don and I weren't communicating much now that Ray was handling logistical stuff such as petty cash expenses and so on. I called my wife from Donnybrooke, and she told me something that simply stunned me. Sally had looked through my copy of *Competition Press & AutoWeek* to see if there was any news that might interest me. Lo and behold, there was a story that UOP was going to sponsor the Shadow team to race in Formula One the following season. It went on to say that Don Nichols had retained Tony Southgate to design the car. I couldn't believe this had happened without Don telling me. Sure, it made good sense to go to Formula One, and it was great he had convinced UOP to do it—but why hire Southgate?

I'd met Southgate as a Formula One mechanic for Reg Parnell in the early 1960s. He was a draughtsman at Lola Cars when Eric Broadley designed his first F1 car in 1962. Tony subsequently designed the BRM Formula One car that Jackie Oliver raced in 1970 before going Can-Am full-time with me, and that probably influenced the decision. It was someone Jackie knew who had recent F1 design experience—but nobody had been remotely impressed by

Southgate's Can-Am designs for BRM, and that was what really bugged me.

Over the previous two years, I'd worked long and hard for UOP and Shadow—very hard. My cars had proven to be competitive. It was very tough to make a car last 200 miles. I felt I'd demonstrated my dedication and had earned a chance to design a UOP Shadow Formula One car. I called Don to confront him about it, and he asked me to meet him in the parking lot of the motel. He had Jackie with him. He told me he'd intended to tell me after the Donnybrooke race, but somehow *Competition Press & AutoWeek* had gotten the news from UOP. He reiterated that he had no intention of asking me to leave the team. I won't go into what else was said at that meeting. Suffice to say that I walked back to my room feeling terrible. It was happening again! It was just like the situation with the Ti22 team at the end of the 1970 season. I was very, very depressed.

BELOW: Jackie Oliver drives my Shadow for the last time at Riverside on October 29, 1972. He finished fourth behind the Porsches and McLarens. (Pete Lyons)

CHAPTER 40

The End Game

I hardly slept a wink the night after I'd learned that Don Nichols, UOP, and Jackie Oliver were going into Formula One together in 1973, and that I'd been passed over as their designer. The news had devastated me. And yet, next morning, I woke up and decided that I was going to make the most of what remained of the 1972 Can-Am season—whatever happened.

We returned to the Donnybrooke track and practice began. The aero changes I'd made to the Shadow Mk 3 had corrected the cooling problems, but the reduced downforce was hurting our cornering in the mid-speed range. I knew we had pretty good horsepower compared with the previous year, because we were 2 seconds a lap faster. But we were still struggling to be as fast as McLaren.

Jackie was more than 1 second slower than Denny Hulme and Peter Revson in qualifying, but I knew that McLaren were building high-power qualifying engines to try and beat the Porsches out of pole position. In the middle of the final session, Revson blew his engine in a big way near the fastest part of the front straight. He must have been doing nearly 200 mph when it went off like a bomb and oiled up the track, sending him into turn 1 at a frightening speed with a dead engine. So those qualifying engines were unreliable, and McLaren would probably not race with them. But Porsche was in the catbird seat with regard to engines. They could simply turn a screw that changed the boost pressure of their turbochargers, and dial in just as much power as it took to blow us all away in qualifying. On top of that, they'd found room for about six more gallons of gasoline in the 917/10K, and that meant they could use as much power as they needed to beat us all in the race, as well.

Mark Donohue was back in action, and he took the pole position with teammate George Follmer alongside him. It looked like the makings of another Porsche runaway. The works McLaren M20s were on the second row, leading the rest of our underpowered, naturally aspirated "class" by about 1 second. François Cevert's ex-works McLaren M8F and Milt Minter's Porsche 917/10 both qualified faster than Jackie's Shadow and David Hobbs's works Lola T310 in eighth place. Because our own turbo engine wasn't ready yet, the second Shadow was again given to Carlos Pace to drive. Carlos managed to qualify 10th, just behind Greg Young in the McLaren M8F that had won this race the previous season in Hulme's capable hands.

We immediately had another big Shadow disappointment when Carlos stopped on the third lap with electrical problems. It turned out that the "bullet-proof" Scintilla Vertex Bosch magnetos that we all used weren't bullet-proof after all. Even though we'd lost half our team, the race was exciting to watch for a while. Hulme managed to get past Follmer into second place, and a few laps later, right in front of us on the main straight, he made a stab at getting past Donohue for the lead going into the banked first turn. But he couldn't pull it off and the race turned into a procession when Denny's engine let go, leaving Revson as McLaren's only challenger. That challenge ended with a dropped valve when he was about 3 seconds behind the two Panzers. Well, that was a surprise—both McLarens out with blown engines. They had wrung them out to 509 cid and were revving them over 7000, so maybe that was too much for a pushrod engine in those days. Of course, nowadays the same type of engines in NASCAR are revving to 9000 and producing well over 800 horsepower.

Mark and George put on a "Bruce and Denny Show" of their own, playing swap-the-lead until halfway, when one of Donohue's gigantic, 19-inch-wide rear Goodyears blew as he came out of the banked first turn at full speed, spinning his Porsche off the track. It happened right out of the blue and he was lucky to escape injury. That incident put a whole new perspective on the possibilities for us. It left Follmer in the lead with Cevert second, Milt Minter third in the Vasek Polak Porsche, and Ollie fourth, not far behind. We started giving Jackie pit signals, showing him the gap to Minter and urging him to hurry.

Follmer had lapped everyone and was coming up to lap Minter and Oliver again with one lap to go when he suddenly ran out of gas and couldn't reach the pits. When he didn't come by, we showed Ollie a pit board saying there was one lap to go—which was wrong! Follmer had been a lap ahead of Cevert, the new leader, so there were actually two laps left. Ollie tried frantically to pass Minter but couldn't quite make it and finished third. Donohue was initially credited with the fastest lap, but I'd thought Ollie had beaten it in his last-ditch effort to catch Minter. When I ran into journalist Pete Lyons the next morning, I asked him if he knew who was finally credited with fastest lap. He told me it was Follmer at 1:28.308. I checked our own lap times and found that Ollie had gone quicker than that on the penultimate lap. Somehow the timekeepers had missed it, which was a bit galling. Interestingly enough, the official fastest lap would have put Follmer ninth on the starting grid, which speaks volumes about the qualifying and race strategies of the top teams.

I was interested in one particular aspect of the race. It was 212 miles long instead of the usual 200, and those extra 12 miles had run Follmer's Panzer out of gasoline with a 92-gallon tank. The Porsches had started with 690 lbs. of gas in the tanks. Leaving aside the size of the fire that much gas could cause in the event of a big crash, the difference in performance and handling during the transition from full to empty was very significant. These fuel tank volumes were ridiculous. I thought they should shorten the races to 160 miles, which would also have produced better racing. But my views wouldn't amount to a hill of beans pretty soon, anyway, so I didn't bother talking to anyone at the SCCA about it. In the future, gas mileage would be a big part of strategy in all track-racing categories. The following season, the SCCA turned its Can-Am races into split events, with two heats. The turbos were certainly changing the Can-Am.

Once again, Ben Williams, UOP's media guy, was ecstatic and so apparently was everyone else at UOP. I was very happy for a while, too, but I could see the end in sight after the *Competition Press* article, and I didn't like the look of it. I still couldn't understand why Don Nichols hadn't talked with me about his Formula One plans. I thought I was supposed to be a 10 percent stockholder in the team.

There were 10 cars fewer at the Edmonton race, and once again, it was cold and a bit wet. They still had those damn half-buried tires on the corners and the Panzers, which hadn't been there before, found them first, tearing up their pristine noses quite nicely. But the Penske Porsches then replayed Donnybrooke, and had no visible trouble dominating the qualifying times. Hulme and Revson did their thing to fill the second row, and Minter and Cevert had the third row again. But this time it was a different story for our UOP Shadow team. Instead of Oliver lining up next, Pace found his groove in the second Shadow and went 0.025 second quicker than Jackie. It wasn't much, but it was enough for Hobbs to sneak into eighth spot and relegate Oliver to ninth.

Jackie was a bit surprised to be behind Carlos and Hobbo. But he reckoned he always did better in the race than in qualifying. He was wrong about it this time, because it was Carlos's turn to get the spotlight on him. He was very happy to finish the race in fourth place behind Donohue, Hulme, and Follmer, with Hobbs and Revson behind him. Jackie went out early with a broken driveshaft. The first three lapped everyone at least once and a lot of cars were lapped several times. Carlos told me afterwards that he'd finally got the hang of these Can-Am cars. He liked driving the Shadow, and if he had felt more comfortable with the front brakes, he could have done better. I asked him what it was that made him feel uncomfortable, and he told me he could feel that disconcerting vibration whenever he applied them. I figured those inboard front brakes were spooking him a bit. It was funny, because unless Oliver had a real problem, he didn't ever complain about the brakes. What bugged him the most was our power shortage.

We had now scored three top-four finishes in the last four races. Going into the final two races of the season in California, I was hoping we had a trend started. The whole Shadow crew were looking forward to the next race at Laguna Seca. In testing there before the season, Ollie had smashed the lap record.

Right after Edmonton, Lee Muir loaded Jackie's newer Shadow on our single-car transporter and headed home to Livonia, Michigan. He and Rayburn, his trusty assistant, were going to put the turbo engine in it and prepare it for racing. The rest of us finally went back to Long Beach. It had been a long time since I'd been home and seen my wife and kids.

When he got back, Ray Brimble decided to take a day off on the weekend between races and do a bit of trail biking near Griffith Park. It turned out to be a bad idea, because he crashed coming down a fire road and broke his leg in three places. They took him to a hospital and did some surgery, but something went wrong and he developed blood poisoning. It was touch-and-go for him and he nearly died. I went to the hospital to visit him and told him he wasn't going to get away with this because he was needed in Long Beach, so he should just stop lollygagging around and get back to work. Amazingly, he limped back to work before we left for Riverside. We were very good friends and there weren't any secrets between us.

Ray was an amazing guy who'd apparently led a charmed life. Not only had he had some horrendous crashes in racing cars, but he'd survived a fall while working on the television and GPO telephone tower in the center of London. He was an "iron fighter" installing girders in buildings. He was working at the top of a high crane, winding out the counterweight to enable it to pick up a heavy load at the opposite end of the boom. The cable broke and the counterweight ran out to the end of the boom, causing the crane's main structure to break. The boom started to fall to the ground with Ray on it. He was 275 feet in the air when it started to come down. He rode it down to about 90 feet from the ground, and then jumped clear. He landed on his back in the middle of some steel reinforcing rods on the site below. He was taken to the hospital unconscious, a mass of bruises, but otherwise he only suffered a concussion. No bones were broken and he was back at work a week later. One of the newspapers published a photograph of him falling that a passerby had taken. He kept it in his wallet and showed it whenever the story was told. Mind you, it took a couple of beers for the story to come out, because he really didn't care to discuss it much.

He told me after the trail bike accident that he'd had a near-death experience and had been visited by the devil. It had genuinely scared him. He'd seen the error of his ways and was going to set things right in his life. It was amazing to see such a change in a guy, and he kept his word. Ray and his wife had separated, but he got back together with her after the Can-Am season had finished, and then took his family back to England to start afresh.

He got a job as the team manager of Graham Hill's new, independent Formula One team, which ran a "customer" Shadow DN1 in 1973. Sadly, Ray was killed at the end of 1975 when Graham crashed his private plane while trying to land in the fog at an airfield near London. I guess his luck had finally run out. I lost a couple of good friends in that crash, because I had also been a mechanic for Graham Hill.

I was still using the little office in Long Beach and there wasn't a lot for me to do, so I laid out an Indianapolis single-seater with an Offy engine in quarter-scale. I went over to the race shop one day at the request of Don and Jackie, who had stayed over in the States for the last two Can-Am races. Don announced that now that the team was to be more closely linked with UOP, he planned to relocate everything to Illinois. He told me I was welcome to go with them or leave and do something else. I asked him if he was going to issue any stock to me in Phoenix, and he said I had no stock. Apparently I was just another employee—and not a very well paid employee compared with the money Ernie Kanzler had been paying me.

I didn't put up much of a struggle. At that moment I just wanted to get out of there as fast as I could. I left and went home. I talked things over with Sally and we agreed that we didn't want to move to Illinois under any circumstances—we'd tried living in Connecticut and there was no way we were going to live anywhere where it gets below zero in winter. I decided to say no more to Don Nichols about anything until after the last race at Riverside, thus giving myself nearly a month to check things out and see what other jobs might be available. I could have asked Nichols if he wanted me to design a new Can-Am car for 1973, but do it in California, but somehow I couldn't bring myself to ask him for anything.

So it was with mixed feelings that I set out for Laguna Seca. I'd loved this circuit ever since first setting foot in the place as a race mechanic for the Shelby Cobra team in 1964, partly because it reminded me of the Brands Hatch short circuit in England. A successful race at Laguna Seca was (and still is) really a matter of getting two things right, besides the given power requirements. The car needed lots of downforce to enhance its cornering, and good brakes that could cool quickly and didn't fade. We always took special precautions to increase the capacity of the brake fluid reservoir and to open up the cooling ducts, but there just wasn't enough straightaway between the bends to get the brakes properly cooled. Can-Am cars generally didn't have long enough straights to reach terminal velocity, so we basically used the untapped horsepower to power aero devices that increased the downforce, almost regardless of the drag they caused. It also didn't hurt to tighten up the shocks to limit the pitching forward and backward under heavy braking and acceleration. We used the biggest anti-rollbars we could, and that was pretty much the secret for the setup. Because of our test data from earlier in the year, I was confident that we had the best aero configuration of any car running there. We didn't have the power to haul the Shadow round the little road course as fast as McLaren or Porsche, but Jackie Oliver always did well there and even held the unofficial lap record.

Laguna always attracted a big field, most of them amateurs who were there to have a go with the big boys. It was a great race for action, and your grid position was very important. There would be a difference of about 10 seconds a lap between the fastest and the slowest, but it was hard to pass slower cars on the twisty track. The fastest would be lapping in less than 60 seconds and would start to lap the slowest within five or six laps. Two years before, Jackie and Denny Hulme had lapped the entire field at least twice and some cars eight times. So to win this race a car would need to complete somewhere around 300 overtaking maneuvers, creating plenty of opportunities for accidents.

When qualifying was over, people were coming over to take another look at the Shadow Mk 3. The only cars faster were the two Panzers of Donohue and Follmer and Revson's M20 McLaren. Jackie managed to out-qualify Hulme by nearly half a second to get on the second row of the grid. I was a bit disappointed that we hadn't equaled our pre-season testing times, but several factors prevented that. We'd had a different body configuration with even more total downforce, and we'd had a pristine track to ourselves. Now the track was quite oily and hot, and nobody got a clear lap without having to pass someone else. In fact, nobody beat the best lap times that had been set the previous two years.

When the race got under way, the Penske Porsches took off and ran away from everyone. Ollie valiantly held onto third place, but the engine started blowing out oil and he retired after only 22 laps. Both the works McLarens retired, Hulme with an engine problem and Revson with a gearbox failure. Follmer and Donohue staged a 1-2 while Cevert was third in Denny's old car, two laps down and two laps ahead of Minter.

The final Can-Am of 1972 at Riverside promised to be a very interesting event. It was to be run over 201 miles, within the range of the turbo Porsches. Our twin-turbo car was delivered on Friday afternoon by Lee Muir. The turbochargers were enormous and had to be packaged at the back of the car, hanging off the gearbox. The exhaust plumbing was so complex, it looked like a big bunch of snakes. But that's one of the beauties of turbocharging—the complexity doesn't matter because the exhaust system doesn't need to be "tuned" to make power.

I wasn't sure about our fuel economy. The maximum amount of gas we could carry in that car was 84 gallons. When you added a few miles for parade laps or wave-off starts, and allowed for something left in the tank, this meant that it would have to get 2.5 mpg. I calculated it would probably do about 2.1 mpg, so we might need to screw down the boost pressure after qualifying to go the race distance. That was another great thing about turbos—it was so easy to detune them a bit after qualifying was over. The report I had from Lee on the dyno test of the turbo engine said it had an estimated torque of 1250 ft. lb. at 4800 rpm. I'd already been seeing driveshaft failures on the McLarens as well as our car, so I upsized the universal joints in the driveshafts to the biggest possible and ordered some solid "spider cross" centers for them that had solid bronze bearings, instead of the usual needle roller bearings. We put all-new gears in the Hewland transmission and hoped nothing else would break. The car we had run at Laguna was renumbered 102 and the turbo already had 101 on it.

The turbo car arrived completely untested, so we decided to run some private exploratory laps at the Ontario Motor Speedway, which had opened two years before only a few miles northwest of the Riverside road course. The transporter got stuck in the tunnel onto the infield, and by the time we freed it and got the car unloaded, it was nearly dark. We were undeterred because that part of California has a lot of ambient light and the Speedway's barrier wall was painted white, and it was decided to go ahead and have Jackie put some laps on the car.

In no time at all, Jackie started lapping at about 150 mph. The exhaust pipes were glowing cherry red from the cylinder head all the way to the turbocharger wastegates and even beyond. It was eerie to watch the Shadow going round the banked track because of the low, loud drone of the exhaust and the whistling turbos. I quietly figured that even though Lee had wrapped everything he could in insulated foil, the immense heat would cause all kinds of problems. The way it was all plumbed together, I didn't see any way that this heat-generating monster could be reliable. But it was early days for this package and you have to start somewhere. We loaded up the car and headed back to Riverside to unveil it on Saturday.

NASCAR racer Bobby Allison was going to drive the 102 car pending Jackie's decision on the turbo project. So after Jackie had posted a token qualifying time in it, he was fitted in the naturally aspirated car and went out for some practice. Bobby had to be one of the friendliest people I'd ever met. The only time he wasn't smiling was when he was talking in his quiet way, or listening intently. Unfortunately, his ride disappeared when Oliver had to park the turbo car.

When we unloaded the turbo, the press swarmed all over it. They asked me questions I couldn't answer and got short with me when I told them I couldn't comment. Pete Lyons reported later that Bobby said the exhaust plumbing looked like someone had tried to put antlers on a canary. I thought it looked more like a bunch of snakes fighting. Frankly, the whole mess looked very amateurish and I saw no reason to show something that bad in public. I knew we had no provision for fast refueling, so it was a bit strange to show up with an untested turbo project. The only conclusion I could come to was that Don Nichols needed to show UOP where their money was being spent. When Jackie came into the pits, he kind of grinned a bit and said it felt like he was spinning the wheels every time he applied the throttle after shifting gear. But after a few exploratory laps, the turbocharged car was parked after it burned out a piston or two. Apparently there were fuel-feed issues still to resolve. I figured the standard Lucas fuel-injectors were having trouble passing enough gas at the higher rpm, but as it wasn't going to be my concern anymore, I kept that to myself. When anyone asked me what went wrong with the turbo, I told them it was having trouble passing gas, which usually elicited a smile.

I'd never thought that you could have too much power in a Can-Am car, but the trade-off of full tank weight against engine output must have been getting close to critical. I thought that if I ever had an opportunity to design another Can-Am car, I would go for a smaller car with Formula One wheels and less overall weight, with a power-to-weight ratio similar to the Porsche 917/10K. That car had more than 1000 bhp and weighed over 1650 lbs. empty, or more than 2300 lbs. when full of gas. So if you built a car weighing 1200 lbs. empty and just over 1800 lbs. when fuelled up, you could get similar performance with less than 750 bhp. That would easily be attainable by supercharging a decent four- or six-cylinder racing engine. I figured a lighter, smaller car would have a decided advantage in cornering, and so 600 bhp might even be enough. I preferred supercharging to turbocharging because it didn't cause such horrendous heat problems.

But this was all academic. I knew my time in racing was coming to an end.

Our engine builders may have given up trying to extract more power from the 495 cid Chevy, but McLaren hadn't. Gary Knutson had pushed a couple out to 562 cid for them by stroking the crank and boring it out to the maximum. Hulme hit over 205 mph at the end of the straight and told me the new engine was putting out more than 800 bhp. This sounded about right, since the 1000 bhp Porsches were going 212 mph. With this power struggle going on between McLaren and Porsche, I felt that reliability alone might win the race for us, even with our lowly 775 bhp. I speculated that the Panzers could run out of gas before the end and the McLarens could blow up.

Although this was to be my last race with Shadow, I hadn't talked to anyone about it except my wife and my old friend Deke Houlgate. Deke had called me to have a beer together because he was covering the race for the *Los Angeles Herald Examiner*. He was always looking for an inside scoop, and I told him about the turbo. I explained that I might be leaving Shadow, but it hadn't been announced officially. On Saturday morning, Deke walked up and handed me a copy of his newspaper. In it was a very nice article about my Can-Am endeavors that read like an epitaph. I told Deke I wasn't dying—just moving on. But I was touched by it.

Jackie qualified the atmo car in a respectable sixth position behind three turbo Porsches and the two works McLarens, qualified respectively by Follmer, Hulme, Donohue, Revson, and Minter. I was real pleased that Ollie was over 1 second faster than both Cevert and Hobbs. The race confirmed that the McLaren dynasty was over in the Can-Am. Follmer won it after following team orders to let Donohue go by. Then Donohue had to stop for a rear wheel change and ran out of gas on the last lap, dropping him into third place behind Revson. The Shadow had a gearbox problem that forced Ollie into the pits two laps from the end, but he was far enough ahead of Hobbs to get fourth place. The low-line Lola was fifth, also two laps behind the winner.

The Can-Am would never be the same again. McLaren pulled out after that race, leaving the Porsches to dominate in their place.

For me, Riverside 1972 was kind of a double farewell. The two-year-old Ti22 Mk 2 car, which I considered the best I'd designed, showed up in the hands of its new owner, an amateur driver named Nick Dioguardi. He qualified it 22nd on the grid with a fairly respectable time, but was delayed in the race by a flat tire and was classified in 13th place. The very first car I'd designed, the Ti22 Mk 1, had finished 13th in its first Can-Am race at Laguna in 1969. Unfortunately I would never see the Ti22 Mk 2 again, because the next time Nick raced it at Riverside in a club event, he crashed and it burned to the ground, a total wreck.

In the final Can-Am points standings of 1972, George Follmer was crowned as the new champion, and Jackie Oliver ended up eighth. In front of him were three Porsche drivers, three McLaren drivers, and one Lola driver—Hobbs, who beat Jackie by just two points. The UOP Shadows were the only American-built race cars in the series that year, and no American-built car would ever run in the series again.

Guys like me are never totally satisfied, but looking back over those 1971–72 seasons with Shadow, I did feel I'd done my best to produce a competitive Can-Am car. I just wished our reliability had been better. My cars had qualified in the top six on 11 occasions and had been in a position to win a couple of times. The Shadows hadn't been quite as competitive as the titanium cars in 1969 and 1970, but Porsche hadn't been in the series then. It had been an intense four years for me as a race-car designer, and I was about ready to do something else and spend some time with my wife and kids. I needed a break to think about my future.

Just after the Riverside race, Ben Williams of UOP had a proposition for me. UOP had been invited to exhibit the Shadow at the San Francisco International Auto Show, which would begin the second weekend after the race. Ben said that Jerry Diamond, who was running the show, had asked if Jackie Oliver or I could attend and serve on a public forum twice a day to answer questions from the show crowd. It was an eight-day show. Stirling Moss and George Follmer would also be answering questions about the Can-Am cars. Ben said UOP would pay me $500 to do it, and my hotel and out-of-pocket expenses would be paid by the show organizer. UOP had been a great sponsor, so I was glad to be offered one last involvement with them.

Besides the show, I had one more thing to do with Shadow. A few days later, I went to my office with Jackie, who was taking a more active role now that UOP were going to Formula

One. He looked over my drawing files and picked some out to keep at the factory, leaving all the Shadow Mk 2 stuff and only taking part of my work on the Mk 3 body. I took the rest of the drawings and my drawing board home, and took out an advertisement in the "Positions Wanted" section of the *Competition Press & AutoWeek* classifieds.

A week later, I picked up the single-car transporter with the 102 car on it and headed up to San Francisco. The show was a lot of fun for a change. I discovered I had a natural flair for public speaking, and I now enjoy doing it for the Society of Automotive Engineers (SAE), mostly in American colleges.

My advertisement bore no fruit, and I faced the reality that I was now at the end of my racing career and needed to find something else to do. That was a bit hard to swallow. It seemed amazing to me that in a country as big as America, there was so little real race-car development happening. I had to face the fact that there were no race-car manufacturers really active except Dan Gurney and Parnelli Jones, and they already had designers. If I wanted to stay in racing, I would need to go back to England—but that idea was quickly dismissed. I reluctantly signed up for unemployment benefits and started looking for a job.

After driving Shadow's small transporter back from San Francisco, I took it home to Santa Ana with the race car on it so our kids could get one last look. I unloaded it outside our house and let our kids and my neighbors' kids sit in it for pictures. Then, with the neighbors' help, I loaded it up again. I contemplated running it down to the Department of Motor Vehicles to register it in my name, and then informing Don Nichols that I was keeping it to compensate for the stock I believed he owed me in the team. But Sally talked me out of it, pointing out that I was looking for another design position, and it wouldn't go down well for me to be in a legal mess with Nichols. So I took it back. I asked Nichols for the $500 that Ben Williams said he had for me for doing the show. Nichols had one more bullet in his gun, and he fired it. He told me he would give me the $500 when I returned the drawing board from my office. I'd signed up for unemployment, money was tight, and I was looking for work. I knew the board was worth more than $500 and I should tell him to go to hell, but then I remembered that you couldn't eat a drawing board.

Any bloke knows that!

Epilogue

I had 15 fantastic years in auto racing. I'm proud that I was responsible for some of the very few Can-Am cars that were designed and built in America. Only four such cars scored points in the series between 1966 and 1972: Jim Hall's Chaparrals accrued a total of 74 points, my Ti22s and Shadows scored 97 points, and Bob McKee's cars scored 4 points. After 1972, no American cars ran in the series. I sleep well in the knowledge that the people who own and drive the cars I designed (and maybe replicas of them) in vintage racing will have the same non-erasable smile that I have.

I am happy to say that the two Ti22 cars I built, which had been destroyed in crashes, are being re-created from my original blueprints at the time of writing, and should be seen on the vintage racing scene some time soon. The two original Shadow Mk 3 cars are still racing in vintage races and are usually pretty competitive. The dedication of enthusiastic car people like Fred Ciska to preserving the Shadow Mk 3 is priceless.

I didn't continue in auto racing after the 1972 Can-Am. In 1973, I started work as a consultant in the recreation vehicle engineering business. Within six months, I became the VP of engineering for Majestic Motor Homes,

LEFT: The first RV I designed from top to bottom was in 1975, not long after the Arab oil embargo hit. The Majestic SL-18 was the first American minivan with a pop-up roof. The company was owned by a very nice gentleman named James Bond. (Peter Bryant)

ABOVE: In 1980 I designed a special lightweight bus structure for Continental that we put on a GM chassis and called "the world bus." Because it was made from lightweight interlocking aluminum extrusions, it had enough room for 113 passengers. It was sold in Peru, where they often crammed that many people into it. (Peter Bryant)

and designed their new product, the Majestic SL18—the first American minivan-type of RV. That launched my new career in what I called "civilian life," and within a year I became the vice president of engineering for Revcon Motor Homes, working a half-mile from my house in Fountain Valley, California. My kids loved that because we got to take a RV anywhere, any weekend we wanted.

I went on to become a co-owner of Continental Motor Corporation, making buses for sale in developing countries. Finally I had a third very successful career, lasting over 20 years, in the engineering consulting business. I hold eight patents in the United States, and the most recent deals with a new technology to help stabilize vehicles and prevent rollovers (see www.amtechspring.com and www.sae.org/technical/papers/2004-01-3534).

In 1995, after meeting Carroll Shelby at Sears Point during the 30th anniversary celebration of Cobra's victory in the FIA International Championship of Makes, I went to Las Vegas and designed and built the concept Shelby Series One car—but that could be a whole new book!

At age 70, I am still working full-time as an automotive engineering design consultant to pay my bills, and live with my second wife, Lois, in sunny Las Vegas. I want to say a very special thank you to Lois. Without her urging, encouragement, and support, I could never have written this book.

If you're looking for me, you can find me at members.aol.com/pebryant.

ABOVE: In 1996 I designed and built a concept sports car for Carroll Shelby. The Shelby Series One was powered by a front-mounted Oldsmobile Northstar engine. (Peter Bryant)

Index

Page numbers in italics refer to photographs and captions

A

Abernathy, Bruce, 119–20
Adamowicz, Tony, 342
Adams, Jim, 285
Advanced Vehicle Systems (AVS), 197, 297, 300
  See also Shadow Mk1 AVS
Aerodynamics
  airflow, 202, 203–4
  computer analysis, 344
  downforce, 180, 202–3, 259–61, 344
  testing, 341
Agajanian, J.C., 158
Agapiou, Charlie, 176, 177, 178, 186, 252
Agapiou, Kerry, 176, 178, 252
Aintree, 31, 87, 98–99, 104, 126
Alan Mann racing, 245–46
Alexander, Jesse, 58
Alexander, Tyler, 221, 225–26, 268, 320, 337, 347
All American Racers, 185–86, 187
Allen, Buck, 175, 176, 177
Allison, Bobby, 370
Allison, Cliff, 28, 32, 40, 50, 56, 59, 87
Amon, Chris
  Aintree, 126
  Argentine Grand Prix, 135
  Belgian Grand Prix, Spa, 128
  Ferrari team, 135
  fitness, 128, 133
  French Grand Prix, Reims, 125, 131–32
  Goodwood, 124, 126
  Italian Grand Prix, Monza, 134–35, 135
  Laguna Seca, 19, 226, 285–86, 289
  Lakeside circuit, 122
  Los Angeles Times Grand Prix, Riverside, 15, 235, 236, 238, 239, 291–93
  Matra team, 135
  Monaco Grand Prix, 127
  New Zealand Grand Prix, 117, 119, 120
  Nürburgring, 133–34
  Reg Parnell Racing, 124, 125, 125–26
  Sandown Park, 123
  Silverstone, 126, 132–33
  Solitude, 133
  South Pacific Trophy, 122–23
  Texas Speedway, 245
  Zandvoort, 129
  Zeltweg, 134
Anderton, Piers, 261
Andretti, Mario
  Laguna Seca, 226, 227
  looking at Ti22, 227
  Riverside, 182, 235, 236, 238–40, 239
  Texas Speedway, 245
  Watkins Glen, 316, 317, 319
Ardmore circuit, 79, 80–81
Armstrong Rubber Company, 157
Ashmore, Gerry, 88, 89
Aston Martin cars, 25, 43, 56
Atkins, Cyril, 130
Atkins, Tommy, 87
ATS team, 129
Australian Grand Prix, 121
Autocoast team
  See also Ti22
  inception, 196–98
  Laguna Seca, 230
  publicity, 221
  sponsorship, 201, 221, 254, 258, 261–63

B

Baghetti, Giancarlo, 88, 89
Balch, Jack, 175–76
Bandini, Lorenzo, 89, 100, 141
Barnes, Chuck, 236, 241
Barnes, Jack, 258, 273
Barnes, Sharon, 258, 266, 268, 273
Barth, Edgar, 68, 71
Bartz, Al, 190, 191, 197
Beatles, 99
Belgian Grand Prix, 61–63, 102–3, 128–29
Bennett, Bud, 352
Beresford, Don, 86, 102
Bianchi, Lucien, 68, 72, 128–29
Bignotti, George, 193
Bill Thomas Race Cars, 181
Biro, Pete, 217
Blivet Car Company, 302
Blocker, Dan, 143, 172, 178, 183, 186
Bolster, John, 31, 45
Bomac Industries, 262–63, 265–66, 269, 273–74
Bond, James, 374
Bondurant, Bob
  King Cobra testing, 177
  Texaco commercial, 274
  Ti22 testing, 210, 221, 260, 265
Bonneville Salt Flats, 149, 153, 172
Bonnier, Jo
  Goodwood, 50
  New Zealand races, 77, 81
  Nürburgring, 59, 68, 71
  Silverstone, 126
  Yeoman Credit team, 77, 77
  Zeltweg, 134
Bowmaker Finance team, 6, 93, 94, 103–4
Boyd, Walt, 178, 184
Brabham, Jack
  Aintree, 87
  Australian Grand Prix, 121
  Belgian Grand Prix, 62, 103
  Cooper car, 62
  German Grand Prix, 68, 71, 105
  Indianapolis 500, 153, 159, 167
  Lombank Trophy, 87
  Los Angeles Times Grand Prix, Riverside, 238
  New Zealand races, 80–81, 111, 112, 117, 119, 120
  Nürburgring, 68, 71, 105
  Pau, 69
  Sandown Park, 123
  Silverstone, 50
  Snetterton, 87
  Solitude, 133
  South Pacific Trophy, 122
  Spa, 62
  Texas Speedway, 245–46
  World Championship, 74
  Zeltweg, 134
Brabham cars
  BT3, 117
  engines, 47
  Formula B Brabham, 203
  Indianapolis 500, 153, 167
  Lakeside circuit, 122
  New Zealand Grand Prix, 117
  Nürburgring, 133
  Solitude, 133
Brainerd, 285
Braking systems
  cooling, 18
  Dunlop "Maxaset," 122
Brands Hatch, 42–43, 44–45, 75
BRDC International Trophy, 126
Bridgehampton, 180, 186, 191
Brightman, Ron, 36, 38, 39
Brimble, Ray
  accidents, 366–67
  Edmonton, 327
  Mid-Ohio, 357
  Road America, 307
  Road Atlanta, 315
  Shadow Mk2 team, 325
  Shadow Mk3 team, 339, 348–49, 351, 360
Bristow, Chris, 50, 62–63
British Grand Prix, 32, 98, 104
British Racing Mechanics Club, 137–38
British Racing Partnership, 62, 77, 126, 132, 164
BRM cars
  Aintree, 87
  Belgian Grand Prix, 103
  BRM P57, 99
  BRM P61, 132
  BRM P154, 268, 334
  BRM P167, 334
  designers, 360–61
  drivers, 209
  engines, 24, 290
  French Grand Prix, Reims, 130–31, 132
  German Grand Prix, Nürburgring, 105
  Goodwood, 20, 24, 25, 50, 87, 98
  Italian Grand Prix, Monza, 106
  Laguna Seca, 285, 334
  Los Angeles Times Grand Prix, Riverside, 291–93
  Mosport Park, 268–69
  New Zealand Grand Prix, 80
  patron, 114
  Silverstone, 50, 99, 132
  U.S. Grand Prix, 222
Broadley, Eric
  Aintree, 98
  Bowmaker publicity shot, 4–5
  car design, 95–96, 97, 103, 149, 327, 360
  Dutch Grand Prix, Zandvoort, 100
  Edmonton, 327
  Nürburgring, 56
Brooks, Tony, 50
Brown, Dick, 270
Brown, Louise Blyden, 68
Brown, Orin, 142
Brussels Grand Prix, 98
Bryant, Allan, 21
Bryant, Bob, 115, 116, 120, 121
Bryant, David, 21
Bryant, Elizabeth, 181, 228, 230, 375
Bryant, Eunice, 21
Bryant, George, 164
Bryant, John, 21
Bryant, Lois, 375
Bryant, Paul
  birth and childhood, 106, 123, 197, 228, 230, 273, 375
  move to America, 146, 178
Bryant, Peter
  See also specific cars, people, races, and teams
  with Borg Warner Trophy, 161
  Bowmaker publicity photo, 4–5, 94
  bus design, 375
  business card, 329
  early life and family, 21, 44–45
  and Ecurie Vickie, 237, 283, 294–95
  education, 258, 344
  first airplane flight, 76, 78
  heroism, 183, 184–85

376 · CAN-AM CHALLENGER

H&L Motors F2 team, 64, 65
with Lister Corvette, 30, 31, 37
with Lola cars, 6, 94, 111, 189, 195
Lotus production team, 26, 32
marriage and family life, 106, 181, 216, 228, 230, 254, 375
move to America, 146
musical talents, 217
New Zealand Grand Prix banquet, 110
patents, 325, 375
personal cars, 164, 175
presentations, 329–31, 344, 372–73
RV design, 374, 374–75
salary, 21, 75, 146, 197, 230, 305, 367
with Shadow Mk2, 18, 307
Shadow UOP team, 343, 353, 356–58, 367, 371, 373
Shelby American team, 173, 174
Taylor & Crawley Racing Team, 41–51, 52, 53
Texaco commercial, 256
with Ti22, 205, 220
with Tyler Alexander, 221
Yeoman Credit team, 74–75, 76, 77–82, 85–93

Bryant, Sally
home, 75, 146, 181, 367
hospitality, 273
move to America, 146, 178
Peter's career, 43–44, 78, 123, 137, 228, 230, 254, 262, 295, 305, 360
pregnancies, 82, 102, 181

Butler, Ron, 178

C

Cabianca, Giulio, 56, 58
Callouette, Richard, 283, 294
Callouette, Vickie, 283
Camoradi team, 56
Campbell, Colleen, 149, 173
Campbell, Gary, 149, 173
Can-Am Challenge Cup, 17, 19, 183, 190
Cannon, John
death, 178, 180
Laguna Seca, 178, 285
Mount Fuji Nippon Grand Prix, 252, 253, 254
test driving Ti22 Mk1, 260
Cannonball Run, 342
Cantwell, Chuck, 176
Cardew, Basil, 126
Carter, Duane, 145, 165
Causey, Dave, 334
Cevert, François
Donnybrooke, 364
Edmonton, 365
Elkhart Lake Road America, 359
Laguna Seca, 369
Riverside, 371
Road Atlanta, 350–51
Watkins Glen, 352–53
Challenger car, 149

Champion (spark plug company), 243
Chaparral cars
Can-Am series points, 374
Chaparral 2E, 180
Chaparral 2G, 186
Chaparral 2H, 226, 238, 245
Chaparral 2J, 285, 291–92
Chevrolet engines, 142
Elkhart Lake, 186
Laguna Seca, 180, 226, 228–29, 285, 291
Los Angeles Times Grand Prix, Riverside, 142, 235, 238, 291–92
Road Atlanta, 285
Texas Speedway, 245
Watkins Glen, 285
wings, 202
withdrawal from Can-Am racing, 293
Chapman, Colin
being impressed with titanium Ti22, 224, 227
car design, 47, 50, 62, 63
Italian Grand Prix, Monza, 90, 93
Lotus team, 13, 26, 27, 28, 29, 95, 207
Reims, 103
Silverstone, 40
Watkins Glen, 224
Chevrolet engines, 217–18, 242–43
Chinetti, Coco, 140
Chinetti, Luigi, 139–41
Chiti, Carlo, 129
Ciska, Fred, 374
Clark, Derek "Nobby," 26, 27
Clark, Jimmy
Aintree, 99, 104, 126
Belgian Grand Prix, Spa, 103, 128
British Grand Prix, 104
Dutch Grand Prix, Zandvoort, 99
French Grand Prix, Reims, 131–32
German Grand Prix, 68, 105
Indianapolis 500, 153, 158, 167
Italian Grand Prix, Monza, 90, 93, 134
Los Angeles Times Grand Prix, Riverside, 142–43
Lotus team, 29, 125
New Zealand races, 80, 81
Nürburgring, 56, 68, 105, 134
Silverstone, 99, 126, 132
South African races, 108, 109
Zeltweg, 134
Coad, Dennis, 141
Cobra cars
chassis, 175
Cobra 427, 175, 177
Cobra Daytona Coupe, 177
Cobra GT40, 179
King Cobra, 142–43, 177
Laguna Seca, 179
Riverside, 142–43, 177
Shelby American team, 178
Willow Springs, 177
Collins, John, 176

Colotti, Valerio, 96, 138
Computational Fluid dynamics (CFD), 344
Connaught cars, 24, 25
Continental Motor Corporation, 375, 375
Convair Aviation, 259
Cooper, John, 103
Cooper cars
Aintree, 87, 104
Belgian Grand Prix, Spa, 62
Brands Hatch, 45
British Empire Trophy race, 85, 91
British Grand Prix, 104
Cooper-Alta cars, 24, 25
Cooper-Bristol cars, 24
Cooper-Climax, 50, 62, 64, 68
Cooper-Maserati, 50, 89
Cooper Monaco, 62, 175
Cooper T47, 62
Cooper T51, 77, 81, 91
Cooper T53, 77–78, 80, 85, 85, 117
Cooper T60, 104
Cooper T66, 134
Coventry Climax engines, 66
Ford engines, 134, 142
Formula 2 Cooper, 65
Formula 500cc, 62
Formula Junior Cooper, 45, 184
French Grand Prix, Reims, 132
German Grand Prix, 68, 71
Goodwood, 24, 25, 46, 50, 84, 98, 126
Gran Premio de Napoli, 89
Holbay engines, 184
International Cooper, 87
Lakeside circuit, 122
Lavant Cup, 98
Lombank Trophy, 87
Los Angeles Times Grand Prix, Riverside, 142
Monaco Grand Prix, 100
New Zealand Grand Prix, 80–81, 117, 119
Nürburgring, 68, 71, 134
Paris Salon race, Montléry, 72
Pau, 65
Sandown Park, 123
Silverstone, 50, 85, 91
Snetterton, 64, 87
South Pacific Trophy, 122
Yeoman Credit team, 77
Zeltweg, 134
Cordts, John, 252
Corvette cars, 30, 31, 31–36, 34, 37, 151
Costin, Frank, 31
Costin, Mike, 26, 28, 31, 137
Coventry Climax engines
Climax FPF engine, 98
displacement, 47
distributor settings, 73
rebuilding, 42, 65–66, 68, 74, 77, 102
V8 engine, 95, 96, 104
Cramer, Peyton A., 181, 183, 186, 187

Crobacs, Dennis, 296–97, 301, 321
Crombac, Gérard "Jabby," 27, 72–73
Crosthwaite, John, 148
Crowe, Barry, 257, 258, 269, 281, 291, 292, 314
Crystal Palace circuit, 37, 102

D

Daigh, Chuck, 145, 233
Damone, Vic, 169
Dana Chevrolet, 181, 182, 183, 183
Davis, Carroll, 314
Davis, David E., Jr., 246
Davis, Glenn, 222, 233
Davis, Stump, 358
De Beaufort, Count Carel Godin, 66, 71, 105, 134
Dean, Tony, 270, 285, 334
Dempsey, Merl, 301
DePalma, Ralph, 304
DePalma, Ted, 304
DeSoto cars, 164, 175
Devine, Don, 141
Diamond, Jerry, 372
Dibley, Hugh, 275
Dioguardi, Nick, 372
Donnybrooke, 324, 325–26, 360, 363–65
Donohue, Mark
Bridgehampton, 191
Donnybrooke, 363–64
Edmonton, 365–66
Elkhart Lake, 186
Laguna Seca, 368–69
Mid-Ohio, 194
Mosport Park, 347–48
Penske team, 191
Riverside, 188, 371
Road America, 193, 194
Road Atlanta, 350
Dowd, Al, 175
Downforce, 180, 202–3, 259–61, 344
Drag racing, 149, 151
Duckworth, Keith
and Ford engines, 235
founding Cosworth Engineering, 31
Los Angeles Times Grand Prix, Riverside, 238
Lotus production team, 26, 28
Monaco Grand Prix, 100, 102
Dutch Grand Prix, 99–100
Dutton, Tom, 245

E

Eagle cars, 197
Eaton, Bill, 176

Eaton, George, 245, 269, 270, 285
Economaki, Chris, 209, 236, 240, 293
Ecurie Vickie
 bankruptcy, 333
 firing Peter Bryant, 294–95
 Laguna Seca, 286
 Riverside, 237, 282–83
 Ti22 financing, 282–83, 294
Edmonton, 285, 326–28, 365–66
Elford, Vic, 285, 291–92, 298, 334
Elkhart Lake, 183, 184–86, 192, 321–24, 358–59
Emery Paul, 24
Emeryson cars, 24
Endruit, Jim, 29, 98
ERA cars, 24
Ewer, John
 Crystal Palace circuit, 37
 Lister Corvette, 30, 31, 32–33, 35–36, 37, 38, 39
 Silverstone, 35, 36, 38, 39
 Snetterton, 30, 32

F

Fairman, Jack, 145
Fangio, Juan Manuel, 20, 22, 24, 25
Ferguson, Harry, 122
Ferguson cars, 117, 119, 120, 122, 163
Ferrari cars
 Belgian Grand Prix, 62, 103
 Cannonball Run, 342
 clutch, 138, 141
 design, 317
 Dino 196S, 56, 58
 Dino 246S, 56, 58
 Elkhart Lake Road America, 359
 Ferrari 156, 88, 89, 132, 134
 Ferrari 250P, 136, 138, 139, 140–41, 142, 233
 Ferrari 512, 285
 Ferrari 612P, 226
 Ferrari 712M, 316, 317, 319, 359
 Ferrari Dino, 138
 Ferrari Dino 156, 71
 Ferrari Dino 196S, 52
 Ferrari P4, 187
 Ferrari Super Squalo, 118
 Ferrari Testa Rossa, 56, 59
 Ferrari Thinwall Special, 22, 23, 24
 German Grand Prix, 105
 Goodwood, 23, 24
 Gran Premio de Napoli, 88, 89
 Italian Grand Prix, Monza, 90
 Laguna Seca, 19, 226, 285
 Los Angeles Times Grand Prix, 142, 233, 235, 236, 238, 239
 Monaco Grand Prix, 90, 100
 Mosport Park, 140–41
 New Zealand Grand Prix, 118
 Nürburgring, 52, 56, 58, 59, 105, 134
 Pepsi Cola Canadian Grand Prix, 141
 Riverside, 15, 136, 142, 233, 235, 236, 238, 239

 Silverstone, 22, 50, 132
 Solitude, 71
 Texas Speedway, 245
 Watkins Glen, 316, 317, 319
 World Championship, 93
 Zandvoort, 129
Ferrari team, 135, 138–40, 209
Firestone
 AVS Shadow tires, 296
 racing division, 240
 withdrawal from Can-Am racing, 297
Flockhart, Ron, 24
Follmer, George
 championship, 372
 Donnybrooke, 363–65
 Edmonton, 365–66
 Elkhart Lake Road America, 359
 Laguna Seca, 368–69
 Mid-Ohio, 356–57
 Mosport Park, 267, 268, 270
 Riverside, 336, 338, 371
 Road Atlanta, 350–51
 San Francisco International Auto Show, 372
 Watkins Glen, 352
Ford, Henry, Sr., 196, 207
Ford cars
 See also Cobra cars; Lola cars
 design, 147–49
 Ford G7A, 285
 Ford GT "J-car," 177
 Ford GT40, 177, 209
 Ford Mustang GT340, 175
 Ford Mustang GT350, 174, 176, 177
 Ford Special, 239
 Ford X1, 177
 Indianapolis 500, 148, 149
 Laguna Seca, 285
 Le Mans, 175, 177
 Los Angeles Times Grand Prix, Riverside, 239
 Sebring, 177, 209
 suspension, 176
 Texas Speedway, 245–46
Forghieri, Mauro, 130, 138
Formula 2 series
 engine displacement, 24
 push starts, 22–23
Formula 5000 series, 196, 197–98
Formula One series
 engine displacement, 24
 push starts, 22–23
 safety, 156
 sponsorship, 156
Foyt, A.J., 142, 153, 158, 160, 167
Francis, Alf, 24
Frankel, Bobby, 262
French Grand Prix, 125, 129, 130–32
Fuji International Speedway, 249–54

G

Gail, Dick, 194
Galloway, Barry, 241
Gardner, Frank, 239
Garner, James, 209, 238
Gasoline, 167–68
 unleaded, 312, 329–31
Gates, Don, 292
Gaug, Lee, 324
Gavin, Bill, 238
Gendebien, Olivier, 59, 68, 69
Genie cars, 141, 142–43
Gerard, Bob, 24
German Grand Prix, 67, 68–71, 104–5
Gethin, Peter
 Laguna Seca, 285–86, 289
 Los Angeles Times Grand Prix, Riverside, 291–92
 McLaren team, 18
 Road America, 285
Ginther, Richie, 56, 103, 106, 128, 142
Glick, Shav, 221–22, 234
Glover Trophy, 50, 87, 98, 126
Goodwin, Mike, 173
Goodwood
 1953 season, 20, 21–22, 23
 1960 season, 46, 50
 1961 season, 86, 87
 1962 season, 95, 98
 1963 season, 124, 126
 trophies, 42
Goodyear
 fuel cells, 216
 photographer, 217
 Shadow Mk2 tires, 296–97, 301, 304, 314, 316, 318, 320–24, 328
 spiked tires, 172
 Ti22 sponsorship, 237–38, 240, 241, 254, 261, 282, 290, 294
 Ti22 tires, 203, 237–38, 244, 249, 264
 tire chatter, 334, 352
Goth, Mike, 180, 203
Gould, Harry, 24
Graham, Doug
 Brands Hatch, 42–43, 44, 45
 Nürburgring, 55, 56, 57, 58, 59
 travel to New Zealand, 115
Gran Premio de Napoli, 87–90
Gran Premio Siracusa, 92
Granatelli, Andy, 163
Grant, Gregor, 100
Grant, Jerry, 142
Greene, Keith, 50, 55, 56, 58, 59, 99
Gregg, Peter, 356, 359
Gregory, Ken, 77
Gregory, Masten

French Grand Prix, Reims, 131, 132
German Grand Prix, 68
Indianapolis 500, 131, 144, 145, 150, 151–52, 157, 158, 159, 164, 166
Karlskoga, 105–6
Nürburgring, 56, 68
practice at jumping out of cars, 90
quitting Thompson's team, 159, 160
Roskilde, 105–6
Sandown Park, 123
Griffith, Willy, 29
Griggs, Peter, 339
Grouby, Barry, 116, 120
Ground-effect, 203–4, 215, 344
Groundsel, Alex, 234, 244, 280, 283, 290
Gurney, Dan
 Cannonball Run, 342
 car design, 187, 305, 373
 Dutch Grand Prix, Zandvoort, 99
 Elkhart Lake, 185–86
 German Grand Prix, 68–69, 71, 105
 Goodwood, 50
 Indianapolis 500, 145, 148, 153, 167
 Laguna Seca, 226, 229
 Los Angeles Times Grand Prix, Riverside, 142, 235, 236, 238–40, 239
 McLaren team, 18
 mechanics, 244
 Mosport Park, 267, 268–70, 270, 271
 New Zealand Grand Prix, 80
 Nürburgring, 53, 56, 59, 68–69, 71, 105, 133
 St. Jovite, 272, 276

H

Haas, Bernie, 189
Haas, Carl
 drivers, 19, 289, 310, 315, 316, 322
 Elkhart Lake, 192
 Hewland distributorship, 348, 356
 Lola cars, 235, 352
 Los Angeles Times Grand Prix, Riverside, 292
 Paul Newman's sponsorship, 265
 Road America, 193
 Simoniz team, 189–90, 194, 235
 team, 130, 194–95, 352
 Texas Speedway, 245–46
Hailwood, Mike, 125, 132, 133, 135
Halibrand cars, 167
Hall, James, 24
Hall, Jim
 Belgian Grand Prix, Spa, 128
 Bridgehampton, 191
 British Racing Partnership team, 126
 car design, 202–3, 290, 292, 293
 Chaparral cars, 187, 217, 285, 292, 374
 drivers, 334
 Elkhart Lake, 186
 engines, 305
 Goodwood, 126

Laguna Seca, 180
Los Angeles Times Grand Prix, Riverside, 142
Rattlesnake Raceway, 18, 307–8
Road Atlanta, 285
Silverstone, 126, 132
Texas Speedway, 245
Watkins Glen, 285
Zeltweg, 134
Hamill, Ed, 180
Hamilton, Duncan, 24, 25
Hansen, Jerry, 194
Hansgen, Walt, 168, 169
Harris, Gillian, 75, 100, 104, 109
Harris, Trevor
car design, 197, 296, 300–301
Mosport Park, 268
sponsorship, 297
Harrison, George, 99
Hartman, Wayne, 215
Harvey Aluminum, 211
Haskell, Isabelle, 139
Hawthorn, Mike, 22, 23, 24, 25, 41
Hays, Charlie, 180
Healey, Donald, 21
Henry, Jason, 24
Herrmann, Hans, 59, 68, 71
Hewland, Mike, 238
Hewland transmissions, 348, 356
Hi-Shear Corporation, 214
Hill, Graham
Aintree, 87, 126
Belgian Grand Prix, 103
BRM team, 125
BRMC dinner, 137
death, 367
Dutch Grand Prix, Zandvoort, 99
French Grand Prix, Reims, 132
German Grand Prix, Nürburgring, 68, 71, 105
Glover Trophy, 87, 98
Goodwood, 50, 87, 98
Italian Grand Prix, Monza, 106
Lakeside circuit, 122
Lavant Cup, 87
Los Angeles Times Grand Prix, Riverside, 142
Lotus team, 13, 32
Monaco Grand Prix, 128
Mosport Park, 141
New Zealand Grand Prix, 80, 111, 112, 114, 117, 119
Silverstone, 50, 99, 132
South African Grand Prix, 109
Watkins Glen, 141
Hill, Phil
Belgian Grand Prix, 103
French Grand Prix, Reims, 130
Monaco Grand Prix, 100
Nürburgring, 56, 59
Sebring, 209
Silverstone, 50

World Championships, 93
Zandvoort, 129
Hinstead, John, 119
H&L Motors F2 team, 64, 65, 68, 74
Hoare, Jack, 175, 177, 178
Hobbs, David
Can-Am points standings, 372
Donnybrooke, 364
Edmonton, 365
Elkhart Lake Road America, 359
Laguna Seca, 285, 332, 333
Mid-Ohio, 356–57
Riverside, 371
Road Atlanta, 350
Watkins Glen, 352–53
Hocking, Gary, 108
Holbert, Bob, 43, 142
Holman, John, 230, 254
Holman & Moody team, 226, 230, 245
Holt, Rick, 262, 275
Holt, Tim, 262
Honker cars, 182
Hooker, Tom, 143
Houlgate, Deke, 221, 236, 258, 266, 269, 284, 371
Howes, Bobby, 44
Hudson, Skip, 142, 172
Huffaker, Joe, 141, 168
Hugill, Bob, 341–42
Hulme, Denny
Brainerd, 285
Can-Am dominance, 225
Donnybrooke, 326, 363–64
Edmonton, 285, 327–28, 329, 365–66
Elkhart Lake, 185–86, 322–24, 359
Laguna Seca (1969), 19, 226, 229, 230, 231
Laguna Seca (1970), 285–86, 288, 289
Laguna Seca (1971), 336
Laguna Seca (1972), 361, 368–69
Los Angeles Times Grand Prix, 235, 238–40, 291–93
McLaren team, 18, 19, 218
Mexican Grand Prix, 238
Mid-Ohio, 285, 322, 357
Mosport Park, 267, 268–70, 348
New Zealand races, 77, 81
NZ Gold Star, 82
Riverside, 182, 187, 235, 238–40, 336–37, 371
Road America, 322–24, 359
Road Atlanta, 285, 315, 350–51
St. Jovite, 272, 276, 277, 310–12
Texas Speedway, 245
USRRC racing, 184
Watkins Glen, 285, 316, 319, 352–53
Hurtubise, Jim, 159–60
HWM cars, 24
Hyslop, Angus, 119

I
Ickx, Jacky, 209
Indianapolis 500
1915 race, 304
1961 race, 167
1962 race, 145, 148
1963 race, 145
1964 race, 131, 144, 145, 145, 147, 149–60, 150, 154, 155, 161, 166, 167–70
Borg Warner Trophy, 161
economics, 155–56
fans, 156, 168
race strategy, 167–68
Indianapolis Motor Speedway
Gasoline Alley, 155
track design, 170
wall, 159–60, 170
International 2000 Guineas at Mallory Park, 102
Ireland, Innes
Aintree, 126
BRDC International Trophy race, 126
British Racing Partnership team, 126
BRMC dinner, 137
French Grand Prix, Reims, 132
friendship with Peter Bryant, 112
German Grand Prix, Nürburgring, 68, 71
Glover Trophy, 98, 126
Goodwood, 50, 98, 126
London Grand Prix at Crystal Palace, 102
mechanic, 41, 62
Naples, 90
New Zealand races, 111, 112, 114, 115, 119, 120
salary, 75, 146
Silverstone, 50, 126
Team Lotus, 75
Zeltweg, 134
Italian Grand Prix, 88, 90, 93, 106, 134–35

J
Jackson, Charlie, 147
Jackson, Peter, 96
Jaguar cars, 25, 45, 181
Jarier, Jean-Pierre, 359
Johns, Bobby, 165
Johnson, Eddie, 155, 163, 164, 167, 169, 170
Jones, Danny, 355
Jones, Parnelli, 153, 158, 167, 373
Junor, Bruce, 258

K
Kagel, Clarence, 163–64
Kanzler, Annie, 282
Kanzler, Ernest, 196, 207

Kanzler, Ernest, Jr.
Autocoast team management, 254, 257
Autocoast team sponsors, 203, 241, 261, 266, 273, 282, 283
Autocoast team sponsorship, 197, 198, 201, 230, 282
Formula 5000 series, 197–98
Laguna Seca, 223, 228, 230, 286
Los Angeles Times Grand Prix, Riverside, 237
Mount Fuji Nippon Grand Prix, 254
personal background, 196–97, 207–9, 228, 230, 282
publicity, 258
relationship with Peter Bryant, 197, 230, 240, 295, 331
St. Jovite, 278, 279
Sebring, 207–9
yacht, 197, 208, 262
Kawai, Minoru, 254
Kennedy, John F., 137–38
Kent, Washington, 189, 191
King, John, 78
Knight, Ed, 296–97
Knutson, Gary, 225, 240, 243, 257, 314, 339, 371
Koufax, Sandy, 141
Kovaleski, Oscar, 342

L
Ladish Co., 329–30
Lady Wigram Trophy race, 81, 113, 120
Laguna Seca
1964 season, 179
1967 season, 186
1968 season, 19, 178
1969 season, 19, 220, 223–25, 228–30, 229, 231
1970 season, 280, 281, 284–86, 287, 288, 289–91
1971 season, 332
1972 season, 340, 361, 368–69
car testing, 177, 341–42
pits, 286, 289
track configuration, 213
track record, 341, 343
Lakeside circuit, 122
Lamar, Paul, 214, 220, 232, 234, 235, 260
Lane, Ray
Belgian Grand Prix, Spa, 128
French Grand Prix, Reims, 131
Nürburgring, 133
South African races, 106–9, 111
Lantz, Walter, 196
Las Vegas circuit, 180, 186–87
Lavant Cup, 87, 98
Lawton, George, 68
Le Mans, 27, 96, 175, 177–78
Lee, Gordon, 45

Legault, Jean, 275
Levegh, Pierre, 96
Levin, New Zealand, 81, 119–20
Levy, Maurice "Mo," 50, 51, 53–54, 59
Lewis, Jackie
    father, 65, 72, 73, 74, 75
    German Grand Prix, Nürburgring, 68–70
    Paris Salon race, Montléry, 72
    Pau, 65, 69
    Snetterton, 64
    Solitude, 72
    Stuart Lewis-Evans Trophy race, 74, 75
    World Championship, 74, 75
Lister, Brian, 31
Lister Corvette, 30, 31, 31–36, 34, 37
Lister Jaguar, 45
Lobinger, Teddy, 203
Logan, John, 304, 313–14, 316, 359
Lola cars
    Aintree, 98, 104
    Australia races, 6
    Belgian Grand Prix, 103
    Bowmaker publicity shot, 4–5
    Brands Hatch, 45
    British Grand Prix, 104
    design, 360
    Donnybrooke, 364
    drivers, 289
    Edmonton, 327–28
    Elkhart Lake, 185–86, 322, 359
    engines, 95, 96, 98, 132, 135, 352
    French Grand Prix, 125, 131
    fuel bladder, 149, 204–5
    German Grand Prix, 105
    Glover Trophy, 98, 126
    Goodwood, 95, 98, 126
    Italian Grand Prix, Monza, 135, 135
    Lady Wigram Trophy race, 120
    Laguna Seca, 226, 285, 289, 333–34
    Las Vegas, 194
    Lola F1, 4–5, 6, 94
    Lola Mk1, 56
    Lola Mk2, 119
    Lola Mk4, 95, 95–96, 97, 98, 103, 105, 119, 125, 135
    Lola Mk4A, 131
    Lola T70, 181, 183, 184, 185–86, 189, 193
    Lola T70 Mk 3B, 190
    Lola T160, 190, 194
    Lola T163, 226, 235, 245
    Lola T220, 268, 285, 291
    Lola T222, 334
    Lola T260, 322, 327–28
    Lola T262, 310
    Lola T310, 350, 364
    Los Angeles Times Grand Prix, 235, 238, 291
    MG gearbox, 56
    Mid-Ohio, 322, 356–57
    Monaco Grand Prix, 127
    Mosport Park, 267, 268
    Mount Fuji Nippon Grand Prix, 252
    New Zealand Grand Prix, 117, 119
    Nürburgring, 56, 105, 134
    Rand Grand Prix, 108
    Reims, 125, 131
    Riverside, 182, 235, 238, 291, 371
    Road America, 193, 322, 359
    Road Atlanta, 315, 350
    St. Jovite, 275, 310
    Sandown Park, 123
    Silverstone, 132
    South African races, 106
    South Pacific Trophy, 122
    Texas Speedway, 245–46
    USRRC racing, 190
    Watkins Glen, 316, 319, 352
    Zandvoort, 129
    Zeltweg, 134
Lombank Trophy, 86–87, 98
London Grand Prix, 102
Longford, Australia, 122
Los Angeles Times Grand Prix
    1958 race, 233
    1963 race, 141–43, 233
    1964 race, 175
    1969 race, 221–22, 233, 234–40, 239
    1970 race, 284, 290–93
Lotus cars
    See also Team Lotus
    Aintree, 99, 104
    Belgian Grand Prix, 61–62, 103
    Brands Hatch, 44, 45, 75
    British Grand Prix, 32, 104
    drivers, 28, 29
    driveshaft, 48
    engines, 27, 42, 47, 132
    exhaust system, 27
    fabrication, 26
    factory, 26
    factory rockets, 27–29
    Formula Junior Lotus 20, 118
    French Grand Prix, Reims, 130, 131, 132
    gearbox, 48
    German Grand Prix, 68–69, 71, 105
    Glover Trophy, 98, 126
    Goodwood, 46, 50, 87, 98, 126
    Gran Premio de Napoli, 88, 89
    Indianapolis 500, 153, 167
    Intercontinental Lotus, 87
    Lavant Cup, 87
    Levin, New Zealand, 81
    Lombank Trophy, 87
    London Grand Prix at Crystal Palace, 102
    Los Angeles Times Grand Prix, 142
    Lotus 7, 26
    Lotus 11, 26, 32, 62
    Lotus 15, 41, 42, 44, 45, 51, 55, 57, 59
    Lotus 16, 29, 40, 47–48, 50
    Lotus 18, 46, 48, 49, 50, 51, 61–62, 68–69, 77, 79, 80, 88, 89, 90
    Lotus 19, 141
    Lotus 23, 141, 142
    Lotus 24, 99, 103, 106, 108, 126, 131, 132
    Lotus 24 BRM V8, 132
    Lotus 25, 29, 103, 104, 105, 108, 132, 133, 135
    Lotus-BRM, 102, 126, 130, 134
    Lotus-Climax, 99, 134
    Lotus De Dion, 26
    Monaco Grand Prix, 51, 59, 90
    Mosport Park, 141
    Nassau Speed Week, 42
    New Zealand Grand Prix, 80, 118
    Nürburgring, 51, 55, 57, 59, 68–69, 71, 105, 133, 134
    Pepsi Cola Canadian Grand Prix, 141
    Riverside, 142
    Roskilde, 105–6
    Silverstone, 32, 40, 49, 50, 99, 132
    Snetterton, 87
    South African races, 106, 108
    Spa, 61–62
    Stuart Lewis-Evans Trophy race, 75
    transaxle, 48
    UDT Lotus, 105–6
    Yeoman Credit team, 77
    Zeltweg, 134
Lowman, Mike
    Laguna Seca, 280
    Mosport Park, 264
    Rattlesnake Raceway, 18, 307
    St. Jovite, 275, 278, 278
    Shadow team, 307, 339
    Texas Speedway, 244
    Ti22 team, 271
Lowther, Ed, 194
Lyons, Pete, 194, 276, 364, 370

M

MacDonald, Dave
    funeral, 172
    Indianapolis 500, 145, 149, 151, 154, 157, 159, 162–64, 167–72, 171
    Los Angeles Times Grand Prix, Riverside, 142–43
Macklin, Lance, 24
Maggs, Tony
    Australian Grand Prix, 121
    French Grand Prix, Reims, 132
    Glover Trophy race, 126
    Goodwood, 126
    Italian Grand Prix, Monza, 134
    Lady Wigram Trophy race, 113, 120
    Lakeside circuit, 122
    Levin, New Zealand, 119
    New Zealand races, 110, 111, 112, 117, 118–19, 120
    Reg Parnell Racing, 125
    Sandown Park, 123
    South Pacific Trophy, 122
Magnuson, Gerry, 305, 349
Mairesse, Willy, 56, 59, 62, 134
Majestic Motor Homes, 374, 374–75
Mallory Park, 102
Malone, "Mahogany Boots," 53, 59–61
Mann, Alan, 239
Marcel, Bill
    See Rosokovsky, Bill
March cars, 285–86, 289, 291–93

Marr, Len, 24
Marsh, Tony, 68, 75
Marshman, Bobby, 158, 167
Marston, Bob, 327
Martin, Burdette, 249, 251–54, 277
Martin, Gordon, 172
Martindale, Wink, 302
Martyn, Christopher, 55, 59
Maserati cars, 25, 56, 118
Matchet, Steve, 311
Mayer, Teddy, 339
Mayer, Tim, 142
Mays, Raymond, 20, 22
McCrary, Bill, 240
McGurk, Bill "Stroker," 32, 33
McHose, Charlie, 303–4
McKee, Bob, 355, 374
McKee cars, 194, 374
McLaren, Bruce
    Aintree, 87, 104
    Australian Grand Prix, 121
    Belgian Grand Prix, Spa, 62
    BRDC International Trophy race, 126
    British Grand Prix, 104
    Can-Am championship, 246
    Can-Am dominance, 225
    car design, 237, 268
    death, 268
    Elkhart Lake, 185–86
    Glover Trophy race, 126
    Goodwood, 50, 87, 98, 126
    Lady Wigram Trophy race, 113, 120
    Laguna Seca, 19, 225, 226, 228, 229, 230, 231
    Lakeside circuit, 122
    Lavant Cup, 87, 98
    Los Angeles Times Grand Prix, 235, 238–39
    McLaren team, 18, 19
    mechanics, 225–26
    Mexican Grand Prix, 238
    Monaco Grand Prix, 100
    New Zealand races, 80–81, 111, 117, 118, 120
    Nürburgring, 68, 134
    Riverside, 187, 235, 238–39
    Sandown Park, 123
    secretary, 120
    Silverstone, 126
    South Pacific Trophy, 122
    sportsmanship, 225–26, 228, 230
    Texas Speedway, 245
    USRRC racing, 184
McLaren cars
    See also Team McLaren
    aerodynamics, 180
    brakes, 322, 348
    Bridgehampton, 191
    Can-Am dominance, 285, 290
    design, 259
    Donnybrooke, 326, 363, 364

Edmonton, 328
Elkhart Lake, 185–86, 322–24, 359
engines, 292, 336, 339, 349, 352, 363, 364, 371
fuel bladder, 204–5
German Grand Prix, 68
Glover Trophy, 98
Laguna Seca, 226, 229, 285–86, 288, 289, 333–34, 361, 368–69
Los Angeles Times Grand Prix, 235–38, 239, 291–92
McLaren M1A, 180
McLaren M1B, 178
McLaren M6A, 185–86
McLaren M6B, 191, 226, 235, 270
McLaren M8A, 194
McLaren M8B, 225, 226, 235, 268–70
McLaren M8D, 268, 276, 311, 326, 334
McLaren M8E, 334
McLaren M8F, 310, 350, 359, 364
McLaren M12, 245, 246, 333
McLaren M20, 348, 351, 363–64, 368
McLeagle, 226, 229, 235, 238
mechanics, 221
Mid-Ohio, 194, 322, 356–57
Mosport Park, 267, 268–70, 270, 347–48
Mount Fuji Nippon Grand Prix, 252
Riverside, 15, 182, 235–38, 239, 336–37, 362, 371
Road America, 193, 322–24, 359
Road Atlanta, 315, 350, 351
St. Jovite, 272, 276, 277, 310, 311
Sebring, 177
Texas Speedway, 245, 246
tires, 320, 334
USRRC racing, 184
Watkins Glen, 316, 319
Weismann Locker differential, 218
McNab, David, 56
Melnick, Peter, 262–63, 265–66, 268, 274–75
Mercedes-Benz cars, 96, 98
Methanol fuel, 117–18, 167–68
Mexican Grand Prix, 142, 238
Mexico City USRRC race, 189–90
Meyer, Timmy, 225–26
Mid-Ohio, 194, 285, 298, 322, 353, 356–58
Miles, Ken, 175, 177, 179
Miller, Al, 145
Minter, Milt, 311, 357, 359, 364, 365, 369, 371
Molina, Debbie, 266, 271
Monaco Grand Prix
 1960 race, 51, 59, 61
 1961 race, 88, 90
 1962 race, 100, 101, 102
 1963 race, 127
Montlhéry, 72
Monza, 90, 93, 106, 134–35

Mosley, Max, 234
Mosport Park, 140–41, 186, 264, 266–71, 267, 270, 347–48
Moss, Stirling
 Belgian Grand Prix, Spa, 61
 British Grand Prix, 98
 Edmonton, 329
 Glover Trophy, 98
 Goodwood, 22, 24, 25, 46, 50, 87, 98
 Lady Wigram Trophy race, 81
 Lavant Cup, 87
 Los Angeles Times Grand Prix, 236
 Monaco Grand Prix, 90
 Mosport Park Can-Am race, 266
 Nassau Speed Week, 43
 New Zealand races, 80–81, 111
 Nürburgring, 53, 56, 59
 Riverside, 236
 San Francisco International Auto Show, 372
 trust of mechanics, 349
Motorsport Design Corporation (MDC), 178, 180
Motschenbacher, Lothar
 Bridgehampton, 186
 Donnybrooke, 326
 Edmonton, 327–28
 Elkhart Lake, 184, 186
 engine mechanic, 314
 Laguna Seca, 285
 Mid-Ohio, 194
 Mosport Park, 268–70, 271
 Mount Fuji Nippon Grand Prix, 252, 254
 Peyton Cramer's team, 183
 Riverside, 187, 188
 Road Atlanta, 315–16
 St. Jovite, 276, 277, 311
 Texas Speedway Can-Am race, 246
Mount Fuji Nippon Grand Prix, 248, 249–54
Muir, Lee, 339, 350–52, 355–56, 358, 366, 369–70
Munaron, Gino, 56
Mundy, Harry, 137
Munz, Gil, 190, 192
Murdock Inc., 213–14

N
Nagel, Bob, 194
Nairobi game reserve, Kenya, 111–12
Napier, Claude-Louis, 344
Nassau Speed Week, 42
Natal Grand Prix, 108
Nething, Fred, 190
New Zealand Grand Prix, 80–81, 110, 111, 117–19
Newman, Paul, 17, 238, 265
Nichols, Don
 agreement with Peter Bryant, 297, 305
 background, 299–300

Edmonton, 328
 meeting Peter Bryant, 197
 Mid-Ohio, 356
 Phoenix Racing Organizations, 299
 Rattlesnake Raceway, 18, 307–9
 St. Jovite, 309–10
 Shadow Mk2, 301
 Shadow Mk2 publicity, 304, 305
 Shadow Mk2 sponsorship, 297, 302–4
 Shadow Mk2 testing, 307–9
 Shadow Mk3 parts, 348
 Shadow team management, 299, 315, 337–39, 343, 349, 351, 353, 355, 358, 360–61, 365, 367, 370, 373
 Watkins Glen, 318
Nicolini, Paul, 145, 147, 152, 161, 162, 168
Niemcek, Brad, 342
Norris, Ken, 284, 286, 290, 293, 295
Norris Industries, 284, 290
North American Racing Team (NART), 140–41, 359
Nürburgring
 1960 season, 51, 52, 53–59, 57, 65–66, 67, 68–71
 1962 season, 104–5
 1963 season, 133–34
 pit pass, 53
 track conditions, 59
 track configuration, 55–56

O
Oliver, Jackie
 BRM team, 209, 222
 Can-Am points standings, 372
 Donnybrooke, 325–26, 360, 363–65
 driving style, 215
 Ecurie Vickie sponsorship, 294
 Edmonton, 327–28, 365–66
 Elkhart Lake, 322–24, 358–59
 Formula One race, Mexico, 234
 Laguna Seca (1969), 223–26, 228–30, 229
 Laguna Seca (1970), 280, 281, 284–86, 288, 289–90
 Laguna Seca (1971), 332, 334
 Laguna Seca (1972), 340, 341–42, 343, 361, 368–69
 Los Angeles Times Grand Prix, 235–40, 239, 291–93
 Lotus team, 13
 Mid-Ohio, 356–58
 Mosport Park, 264, 266, 267, 268–71, 270, 347–48
 Mount Fuji Nippon Grand Prix, 248, 251–54
 Rattlesnake Raceway, 18, 307–9
 Riverside (1969), 233, 234–40, 239
 Riverside (1971), 335, 336–37
 Riverside (1972), 362, 370, 371
 Road America, 307, 322–24, 358–59
 Road Atlanta, 315, 349–51
 St. Jovite, 272, 275–79, 308–9, 311–12
 Sebring, 209

Shadow Formula One racing, 360–61
 in Shadow Mk 2, 18
 Shadow Mk2 parts, 324
 Shadow Mk2 testing, 307–9, 320
 with Shadow Mk3, 340
 Shadow Mk3 testing, 341–42, 360, 369–70
 Shadow team, 343, 367, 372–73
 Texas Speedway, 242, 243, 245
 Ti22 introduction, 222
 Ti22 testing, 12, 218, 223
 U.S. Grand Prix, 222
 Watkins Glen, 316, 317, 318, 352–53
Oliver, Lynn
 friendship with Bryant family, 294
 Laguna Seca, 230
 Los Angeles Times dinner, 234
 Mount Fuji Nippon Grand Prix, 251, 252
 Texas Speedway, 242, 243
 travel with Jackie to Monterey, 223
Olson, John, 174, 176
O'Neil, Laurie, 120, 122
Ongais, Danny, 314
Ontario Motor Speedway, 369–70
Orange County Raceway, 210, 221, 256, 274, 341
Owen, Sir Alfred, 114, 130
Oxton, David, 79, 79, 110
Oxton, Steve, 79

P
Pabst, Augie, 142
Pace, Carlos, 358–60, 364–66
Pacific Raceway, Kent, Washington, 191
Palmer, Jim, 118, 119, 120, 122, 123
Paris Salon race, 72
Parnell, Reg
 See also Reg Parnell Racing
 Belgian Grand Prix, 103, 128
 Bowmaker Finance team, 93, 95, 96, 102
 BRDC International Trophy race, 126
 death, 143
 drivers, 184
 Dutch Grand Prix, 99
 French Grand Prix, 131
 Glover Trophy race, 126
 Goodwood, 22, 84, 124, 126
 Lakeside circuit, 122
 Lombank Trophy, 86–87
 management skills, 87, 135, 143
 mechanics, 360
 Monaco Grand Prix, 100, 102, 127, 128
 New Zealand races, 79, 110, 114, 115, 118, 119
 Nürburgring, 133
 piloting boat, 122
 publicity photos, 86
 Reims, 104, 131

Rouen, 104
Sandown Park, 123
Silverstone, 22, 126, 132–33
Snetterton, 86–87
South African races, 106, 109
South Pacific Trophy, 122
Spa-Francorchamps, 128
workshop, 81, 85, 184
Yeoman Credit Team, 46, 74–75, 77, 84, 90
Zandvoort, 99, 129
Zeltweg, 134
Parnell, Tim, 88, 126–27, 131, 134, 135
Parsons, Chuck
　Bridgehampton, 191
　Can-Am team, 195
　Elkhart Lake, 192
　Laguna Seca, 19, 285, 289
　Las Vegas, 194
　Los Angeles Times Grand Prix, 235, 238–40
　mechanic, 130
　Mid-Ohio, 194
　Mount Fuji Nippon Grand Prix, 249–54
　Pacific Raceway, 189, 191
　praise for Ti22, 236–37
　Riverside, 235, 238–40
　Road America, 193
　Simoniz team, 189–91
　Texas Speedway, 245–46
Parsons, Sherrie, 19, 189, 250, 254
Pau, 65, 69
Penske, Roger
　Elkhart Lake, 186
　Los Angeles Times Grand Prix, 142–43, 292
　Mosport Park, 347
　Riverside, 142–43
　Road Atlanta, 350–51
　use of turbocharged engines, 339, 347, 352
Penske team, 191, 339, 353, 365, 369
Pepsi Cola Canadian Grand Prix, 140–41
Petrie, Bill, 355
Phoenix Racing Organizations, 299, 302, 305
Phoenix Speedway, 151
Pierce, Britt
　Brands Hatch, 44, 45
　Goodwood, 24
　Monaco, 59
　Nassau Speed Week, 42, 43
　Nürburgring, 52, 53, 56, 58
　relationship with Colin Chapman, 62
　Taylor & Crawley Racing Team, 41–42, 50
Pilette, André, 126
Pilette, Teddy, 126
Polish Racing Drivers Club of America (PRDA), 342
Porsche cars

Can-Am dominance, 372
　Donnybrooke, 363–64, 365
　Dutch Grand Prix, 99
　Edmonton, 328, 365
　Elkhart Lake, 324, 359
　German Grand Prix, 68–69, 105
　Laguna Seca, 226, 361, 368–69
　Los Angeles Times Grand Prix, 235, 238
　Mid-Ohio, 322, 356–57
　Mosport Park, 270, 347–48
　Nassau Speed Week, 43
　Nürburgring, 56, 59, 66, 67, 68–69, 71, 105
　Porsche 718, 59, 67, 68–69, 72
　Porsche 718 RSK, 43
　Porsche 804, 105
　Porsche 906, 180
　Porsche 908, 270, 285, 311
　Porsche 911, 284–85
　Porsche 917, 246, 311
　Porsche 917/10, 18, 357, 364
　Porsche 917/10 Spyder, 316, 319
　Porsche 917/10K, 347–48, 359, 371
　Porsche 917/10K turbo, 356, 359
　Porsche 917PA, 226, 235
　power-to-weight ratio, 371
　Riverside, 235, 238, 362, 371
　Road America, 285, 324, 359
　Road Atlanta, 350–51
　St. Jovite, 311
　Solitude, 71–72, 72
　Texas Speedway, 246
　turbocharged engines, 339, 347–48, 363, 369
　Watkins Glen, 316, 319
　wings, 202
　Zandvoort, 99
　Zeltweg, 134
Posey, Sam, 193
Potton, Jimmy
　Bowmaker publicity photo, 94
　British Racing Mechanics Club, 137
　friendship with Peter Bryant, 121
　Karlskoga, 106
　Lady Wigram Trophy race, 120
　Lola F1 car, 94
　New Zealand trip, 76, 77–82, 110, 116, 117, 120
　Reg Parnell Racing, 125
　Roskilde, 106
　Sandown Park, 123
　South Pacific Trophy, 122
　Yeoman Credit team, 74, 76, 77–82, 79
Pro-Fab, 305, 349–52, 356
Profit, Hayden, 181
Pukekohe race track, New Zealand, 117–19

Q

Queener, Chuck, 143
Qvale, Kjell, 168

R

Rand Grand Prix, 107–8

Rattlesnake Raceway, 18, 307–8
Redman, Brian, 334, 336
Rees, Alan, 45
Reg Parnell Racing, 125, 130
Reims, 103–4, 125, 130–32
Remington, Phil, 176
Revcon Motor Homes, 375
Reventlow, Lance, 31, 233
Revson, Doug, 180
Revson, Peter
　Donnybrooke, 326, 363–64
　Edmonton, 327–28, 365
　Elkhart Lake, 185–86, 322, 324, 359
　Formula Junior racing, 125, 178
　Formula One racing, 339
　hiring Peter Bryant, 181
　Laguna Seca, 226, 285–86, 289, 336, 368–69
　Las Vegas, 186–87
　Los Angeles Times Grand Prix, 235, 236, 240, 291
　McLaren team, 18
　Mid-Ohio, 322, 357
　Mosport Park, 186, 267, 268, 270, 348
　Mount Fuji Nippon Grand Prix, 252, 254
　Peyton Cramer's team, 183–84
　Riverside (1967), 182, 186, 187
　Riverside (1968), 188
　Riverside (1969), 235, 236, 240
　Riverside (1971), 336–37
　Riverside (1972), 371
　Road America, 180, 322, 324
　Road Atlanta, 315, 350–51
　St. Jovite, 311–12
　Texas Speedway, 245
　Watkins Glen, 316, 319, 352–53
Reynolds, Mamie, 140
Richter, Les, 314
Riley, Colin, 19, 130, 189, 189–90
Rindt, Jochen, 134, 224
Riverside Raceway
　1963 season, 141–43, 233
　1964 season, 175, 177
　1967 season, 182, 186, 187
　1968 season, 188
　1969 season, 15, 221–22, 232, 233, 233–40, 239
　1970 season, 290–93
　1971 season, 335, 336–37
　1972 season, 362, 369, 370–72
　car testing, 177, 260, 314, 318, 320–21
　track configuration, 233–34, 291
Road America, 180, 193–94, 285, 307, 321–24, 358–59
Road Atlanta, 2, 315–16, 349–51
Robson, Neil, 4–5
Roche, Toto, 132
Rodriguez, Pedro

Laguna Seca, 285, 289
Los Angeles Times Grand Prix, Riverside, 141–43, 291–93
Mosport Park, 141
Nürburgring, 56, 58
Rodriguez, Ricardo, 56, 58, 103
Rolt, Tony, 24
Rosokovsky, Bill, 157
Rouen, 104
Ruby, Lloyd, 142
Rutherford, Johnny, 167

S

Sachs, Eddie, 167, 169–70
St. Jovite, 272, 275–79, 308–12
Salvadori, Roy
　Aintree, 87, 98, 104
　British Empire Trophy race, 85
　British Grand Prix, 104
　Dutch Grand Prix, 99
　German Grand Prix, 105
　Glover Trophy, 87, 98
　Goodwood, 22, 24, 25, 50, 87, 98
　Gran Premio de Napoli, 87–90
　Italian Grand Prix, 88, 90
　Karlskoga, 105–6
　Lady Wigram Trophy race, 81
　Lavant Cup, 87, 98
　Levin, New Zealand, 81
　Lombank Trophy, 87
　London Grand Prix at Crystal Palace, 102
　Los Angeles Times Grand Prix, Riverside, 142
　Monaco Grand Prix, 100
　Monza, 90
　New Zealand races, 77, 81
　Nürburgring, 56, 105
　Reims, 103
　Roskilde, 105–6
　Rouen, 104
　salary, 146
　Silverstone, 85, 99
　Snetterton, 87
　South African Grand Prix, 109
　Yeoman Credit team, 75, 77, 77, 79, 85, 86
　Zandvoort, 99
Samengo-Turner brothers, 87, 93, 96
Sandown Park, 123
Scarab cars, 31, 141, 142, 233
Scarfiotti, Ludovico, 56, 129
Scarlatti, Giorgio, 52, 56, 58
Schell, Harry, 50
Schlesser, Jo, 68, 72
Schmidt, Jerry, 276–77
Schroeder, Gordon, 235
Scirocco cars, 134
Scott, Skip
　Bridgehampton, 191
　Carl Haas's team, 19

Chevy, 195
contact in titanium business, 212
Elkhart Lake, 192
Formula 5000 series, 196, 197–98
Mid-Ohio, 194
Pacific Raceway, 189, 191
Riverside, 188
Road America, 193
Simoniz team, 189–91
Scuderia Filipinetti, 130
Sebring, 177, 207–9
Settember, Tony, 134
Shadow DN1, 367
Shadow Mk1 AVS, 197, 267, 268, 296, 297, 298, 300–301
Shadow Mk2
  aerodynamics, 315, 335
  brakes, 18, 314–15, 321
  cost-cutting, 299
  design, 301–3, 317
  Donnybrooke, 325–26
  Edmonton, 327–28
  Elkhart Lake, 322–24
  engine, 310, 313, 314
  fuel consumption, 337
  fuel-injection system, 311–12
  fuel mixture, 312–13, 322, 323, 329
  introductory press conference, 172
  Laguna Seca, 332, 333, 334
  Rattlesnake Raceway, 18, 307–9
  Riverside, 335, 336–37
  Road America, 322–24
  St. Jovite, 308–12
  specifications, 301
  sponsorship, 337
  springs, 324–25
  suspension, 324–25
  team, 315
  tires, 301, 314–16, 318, 320–26, 328, 336–37
  Watkins Glen, 316, 317, 318
Shadow Mk3
  aerodynamics, 338, 341, 344
  brakes, 348–49, 353, 358, 360, 366
  cooling problem, 351–52
  design, 337–39, 344, 348–49, 352
  Donnybrooke, 363–65
  downforce, 344
  Edmonton, 365–66
  engine, 351, 355, 356, 360, 366, 369–70
  fuel consumption, 337–38
  gearbox, 348, 350
  Laguna Seca, 340, 361, 368–69
  Mid-Ohio, 356–58
  Mosport Park, 348
  Orange County Raceway, 341
  publicity, 342
  radiator, 354
  rear bodywork, 346
  redesign, 354, 355, 355–56
  Riverside, 362, 371
  Road Atlanta, 2, 349–51
  San Francisco International Auto Show display, 372
  sponsorship, 339, 340, 370
  team, 339, 355, 356

testing, 341–42
tire problems, 360
transmission, 338, 348, 356
turbo engine, 355, 366, 369–70
in Vintage racing, 374
Watkins Glen, 351, 352–53, 355
Shadow team, 342, 343, 360–61
Shear, Burt, 258, 261–63
Shelby, Carroll
  car design, 142
  concept cars, 375, 375
  Los Angeles Times Grand Prix, Riverside, 142
  marriage, 81
Shelby American team, 173, 174, 175, 175–78, 314
Shelby Cobra factory, 173
Shelby Series One, 375, 375
Shelly, Tony, 81, 99, 120, 125
Sieff, Jonathan, 42, 43, 53
Siffert, Jo
  Edmonton, 328
  Elkhart Lake, 324
  Laguna Seca, 226, 336
  Los Angeles Times Grand Prix, Riverside, 235, 238
  Mid-Ohio, 322
  Road America, 324
  Texas Speedway, 246
  Watkins Glen, 316, 319
  Zeltweg, 134
Silverstone
  1958 season, 32
  1959 season, 35–39
  1960 season, 49, 50
  1961 season, 85, 91
  1962 season, 99
  1963 season, 126, 132–33
  car testing, 29
  pits, 40
Simoniz team, 189, 189–91, 193–95, 235
Simpson, O.J., 241
Sinclair, Fred, 147, 151, 152
Singer Le Mans car, 79–80
Smith, Carroll, 177–78
Smith, Dick, 243
Smith, Ike, 190
Smith, Stan, 37
Snetterton, 30, 32, 86–87, 98
Society of Automotive Engineers (SAC), 329–31
Solitude circuit, 71–72, 133
South Africa
  segregation, 108
South African Grand Prix, 106, 107, 108–9
Southgate, Tony, 95, 268, 360–61
Spa-Francorchamps, 61–63, 128–29
Spark plugs, 22, 243–44

Sparks, Art, 243
Spears, Harry, 42, 74, 106, 127
Spellman, Ronnie, 339
Spoilers, 202–3
Sports Car Club of America (SCCA)
  regulations, 290–91, 292, 293, 296, 305
Sports Headliners, 258, 282, 284
Springs
  progressive-rate, 324–25
Stacey, Alan, 32, 50, 63
Stafford, Arnold, 81, 125
Stanley, Jean, 130
Stanley, Louis, 130
Stewart, Jackie
  Donnybrooke, 326
  Edmonton, 327–28
  Elkhart Lake, 322–24
  Laguna Seca, 333–34, 336
  McLaren team, 339
  Mid-Ohio, 322
  Riverside, 336
  Road America, 322–24
  Road Atlanta, 315
  St. Jovite, 310–12
  Watkins Glen, 285, 316, 319
Stillwell, Bib, 122
Stokes, Sir Bernard, 344
Stroppe, Bill, 312
Stuart Lewis-Evans Trophy race, 74
Surtees, John
  Aintree, 87, 98–99, 104
  Australian Grand Prix, 121
  Belgian Grand Prix, 102–3
  Bowmaker Finance team, 95
  British Empire Trophy race, 91
  British Grand Prix, 104
  Brussels Grand Prix, 98
  Can-Am racing, 135, 183
  Dutch Grand Prix, 99
  Elkhart Lake, 185–86
  Ferrari team, 122, 130, 138, 139
  German Grand Prix, 105
  Glover Trophy, 87, 98
  Goodwood, 84, 87, 95, 98
  Gran Premio Siracusa, 92
  International 2000 Guineas at Mallory Park, 102
  Italian Grand Prix, Monza, 90
  Lady Wigram Trophy race, 120
  Laguna Seca, 226
  Lakeside circuit, 122
  Las Vegas, 187
  Lavant Cup, 87
  Levin, New Zealand, 119
  Lombank Trophy, 87, 98
  Los Angeles Times Grand Prix, 141–43, 233, 235, 238
  mechanics, 135
  Mexican Grand Prix, 142
  Monaco Grand Prix, 88, 90, 100
  Mosport Park, 140, 141
  Nairobi game reserve, Kenya, 111–12

  New Zealand races, 80, 110, 111, 112, 114, 117–20
  Nürburgring, 105, 134
  Pepsi Cola Canadian Grand Prix, 141
  Rand Grand Prix, 108
  Reims, 103
  Riverside, 136, 141–43, 187, 233, 235, 238
  Rouen, 104
  Scuderia Ferrari team, 125
  Silverstone, 91, 99, 132
  Snetterton, 87, 98
  Solitude, 72
  South African Grand Prix, 107, 108–9
  U.S. Grand Prix, 105
  USRRC racing, 184
  Watkins Glen, 105
  Yeoman Credit team, 75, 84, 85
  Zandvoort, 99
Sutton, Len, 169
Svenson, Gerry, 74, 96

T

T-G Racing, 333
Tadaki, Hidemasa, 250, 252
Tankum, Harley, 221–22
Tasman Series, 77, 79, 111
Taylor, Henry, 68, 87
Taylor, Michael
  Belgian Grand Prix, 61–62
  end of career, 63
  Goodwood, 42, 50
  hiring Bryant, Peter, 41
  Lotus 15, 41, 42
  Lotus 16, 47–48
  Lotus 18, 49, 50
  Monaco Grand Prix, 53, 61
  Nassau Speed Week, 42, 43
  Nürburgring, 55, 59
  Silverstone, 49, 50
  Spa, 61–62
  Taylor & Crawley Racing Team, 24, 44
Taylor, Trevor, 108, 126, 133
Taylor & Crawley Racing Team, 41–42, 52, 53–56, 63
Team Lotus
  Aintree 200, 126
  Belgian Grand Prix, Spa, 63, 128
  drivers, 13
  German Grand Prix, Nürburgring, 68
  Indianapolis 500, 157
  Italian Grand Prix, Monza, 90
  mechanics, 98
  New Zealand Grand Prix, 81
  salaries, 146
  tires, 157
Team McLaren
  Can-Am dominance, 18, 194, 225
  drivers, 18
  Edmonton, 329
  Goodyear sponsorship, 241

mechanics, 225–26
Mid-Ohio, 357
Mosport Park, 268–71
Riverside, 187
St. Jovite, 311
withdrawal from Can-Am racing, 372
Teretonga International race, 81, 120
Terry, Len, 26, 27, 29
Texaco
Ti22 sponsorship, 274
Texas Speedway, 242–46
Thiery, Jean-Claude, 73–74
Thomas, Bill, 181, 217, 218, 221, 225, 234, 242
Thompson, Danny, 149
Thompson, Dick, 142
Thompson, Mickey
Bonneville Salt Flats, 149, 153
business manager, 157
car design, 148, 148–49, 151, 154, 159, 160, 163
Dave MacDonald's funeral, 172
drag racing, 151
family, 149
French Grand Prix, Reims, 131
hiring Peter Bryant, 142, 145–46
Indianapolis 500, 144, 145, 145, 153, 154, 155, 155, 158–60, 162–65, 167, 169, 170
murder, 173
team, 147, 172
tires, 157
use of titanium, 211
Thompson, Trudy, 149, 173
Thompson cars, 159, 167
Threlfall, Tom, 45
Ti22 Mk1
aerodynamics, 203–4, 206, 214, 215, 234, 296
assembly, 207, 214
Autocoast sponsorship, 201
Can-Am series points, 374
chassis, 201, 204–6, 206, 212–13, 215–16
design, 234, 237, 260, 281, 317
drivers, 207, 215
engine, 206, 217–18, 228, 240, 242–43, 245, 258–59
fuel system, 216, 223, 228, 234
imitation, 359
isometric drawing of chassis, 16, 200
Laguna Seca, 223–25, 227, 228–30, 229, 332
Los Angeles Times Grand Prix, 221–22, 237–40
Mosport Park, 264, 267, 268–71, 270
Mount Fuji Nippon Grand Prix, 248, 251–54
naming, 201
publicity, 236, 258, 266, 269, 274
remains, 283–84
Riverside, 15, 232, 233, 234–35, 237–40

St. Jovite, 272, 275–79, 278
spoiler, 261
sponsors, 258, 261, 265–66, 268, 273–75, 282, 294
suspension, 206, 215, 239, 244–45
team, 206–7, 244, 257–59
testing, 210, 223, 258, 260, 261
Texaco commercial, 256, 274
Texas Speedway, 244–45
tires, 203
titanium, 151, 227
traction, 203, 215, 218
unveiling, 219
use of engine as stress member, 16
Vintage racing scene, 374
wings, 214, 232, 234, 235
Ti22 Mk2
aerodynamics, 287, 296
assembly, 274
braking system, 289
contingency sponsorships, 286
design, 281–82
engine, 281, 291
Laguna Seca, 280, 281, 284–91, 287, 288, 333
ownership, 295
publicity, 284
Riverside, 372
sponsorship, 290
staff, 283
Tilton, Mac, 178
Timanus, John, 323
Titanium
fabrication, 151–52, 212, 213, 329–30
properties, 201, 211–12
Titanium Metal Corporation of America (Timet), 212–13, 214, 237, 239, 297
Titanium Racing Components (TRC), 283
Titus, Jerry, 176, 333
Tomaso, Allesandro de, 139
Toomey, Dennis, 206, 207, 223
Toyota cars, 252, 254
Toyota team, 250, 252, 253, 254
Trintignant, Maurice
French Grand Prix, Reims, 131–32
German Grand Prix, 68
Monaco Grand Prix, 127, 128
Nürburgring, 59, 68
Pau, 69
Silverstone, 99
Trips, Wolfgang von, 56, 66, 68, 71, 90, 93
Truesdale, Larry, 203, 237–38, 240, 241, 261, 262, 282, 294, 304
Tulp, John, 140
Tyrrell, Ken, 327

U
UDT-Laystall team, 98
Ulichny, Bob, 329–31
United States Road Racing Championship (USRRC), 178, 180, 190
Universal Oil Products (UOP)
Donnybrooke, 326, 365
Edmonton, 328, 365
Elkhart Lake, 322, 324, 359
Flexonics division, 324–25, 351, 355, 359
Formula One sponsorship, 360–61
fuel mixture, 312–13, 329
Mid-Ohio, 357
Mine Well Screen Division, 326–27
Road America, 322, 324
Shadow Mk2 sponsorship, 304, 312–14, 316, 318, 322, 324, 326, 328, 329, 337
Shadow Mk3 sponsorship, 339, 340, 353, 357, 359, 367, 370, 372
unleaded gasoline, 304, 312–13, 322, 329
Watkins Glen, 316, 318
Unser, Bobby, 163
U.S. Grand Prix, 105, 222, 224

V
Vallelunga cars, 139
Valvoline
contingency sponsorship, 286
Van Valkenburg, Paul, 220
Vandervell, Tony, 22
Voight, Fritz
Indianapolis 500, 147, 152–53, 155–56, 162, 163, 172
Mickey Thompson's team, 147, 151, 172
sale of DeSoto to Peter Bryant, 175
Von Hanstein, Huschke, 56
Vyver, Syd van der, 106, 108

W
Walker, Ian, 141
Walker, Rob, 24, 80, 90, 108
Wall, Tim, 68, 111–12
Ward, John, 183, 184–85
Ward, Rodger, 142, 153, 167
Warner, Bill, 143
Warwick Farm, 121
Watkins Glen
1962 season, 105
1963 season, 141
1969 season, 224
1970 season, 285
1971 season, 316, 317, 318
1972 season, 351, 352–53
Watson, A.J., 167
Watson cars, 153, 159–60, 167

Weismann, Pete, 218, 300, 301, 338, 339, 348, 350, 356
Wharton, Ken, 24, 25
Whitehead, Gordon, 24, 25
Wilkins, Pete, 305
Willard, Al
family, 207
Laguna Seca, 220, 280
Mosport Park, 264
St. Jovite, 275, 278
Texas Speedway, 244
Ti22 team, 205, 206, 206, 207, 207, 214, 257, 271
Willets, Jerry, 178, 282
Williams, Ben
Donnybrooke, 365
Edmonton, 328, 329
Elkhart Lake, 322, 359
Mid-Ohio, 357
recruiting Peter Bryant to speak at SAE meeting, 329
St. Jovite, 311
UOP sponsorship of Shadow cars, 304, 337, 342, 353, 358, 359, 372
Watkins Glen, 316
Williams, Frank, 238
Willow Springs, 177, 223
Wilmot, Wally, 120
Wilson, Gary, 252
Wilson, John, 4–5
Wilson, Tug, 4–5, 96–98, 104–5
Wing, George, 214
Winning (film), 17
Woo, Danny, 169
Woods, Roy, 334, 336
Wyer, John, 209

Y
Yarbrough, Lee Roy, 240
Yates, Brock, 274, 342
Yeoman Credit Team, 46, 74–75, 77–82, 85–93
Yorke, David, 130, 135, 139, 140, 142, 209
Young, Eoin, 116, 120, 329
Young, Greg, 364
Yunick, Henry "Smokey," 164–65

Z
Zandvoort, 99–100, 129
Zeltweg, 134
Zerex Special cars, 142
Zimmerman, Don, 214, 216–17, 237, 257
Zipper, Otto, 142
Zolder, 180